SPAIN

The
$\int$piritual Traveler

SPAIN

A GUIDE TO SACRED SITES AND PILGRIM ROUTES

BEEBE BAHRAMI

HiddenSpring

To my parents,
who gave me a passion for travel,
and for the spiritual

*The cover image and all interior photos courtesy of Beebe Bahrami, except for the photo
on page 281, courtesy of Nahid Bahrami. All photos used with permission.*

Cover design by Alexandra Lord Gatje
Maps courtesy of author and Paulist Press, Inc.
Book design by Saija Autrand, Faces Type & Design

Library of Congress Cataloging-in-Publication Data

Bahrami, Beebe.
    The spiritual traveler : Spain : a guide to sacred sites and pilgrim routes / Beebe
Bahrami.
        p. cm.
    Includes bibliographical references (p.   ) and index.
    ISBN 978-1-58768-047-2 (alk. paper)
    1. Sacred space—Spain—Guidebooks. 2. Pilgrims and pilgrimages—Spain—
Guidebooks. 3. Spain—Guidebooks. I. Title.
    BL980.S7B35 2009
    203'.50946—dc22

                                                                          2008044969

Published by
HiddenSpring
An imprint of Paulist Press
997 Macarthur Boulevard
Mahwah, New Jersey 07430

www.hiddenspringbooks.com

Printed and bound in the
United States of America

Contents

ABOUT THE AUTHOR

Beebe Bahrami is a cultural anthropologist and writer who well over twenty years ago fell in love with the rich cultural and natural diversity of Spain. Since then she has lived and traveled extensively throughout Iberia, south, north, east, and west. Her specialty in anthropology is in myth, ritual, and religion. As a writer, she is known for her cross-cultural, travel, and food writing. Spain long has intrigued her as one of those areas in the world that possesses infinite manifestations of the spiritual, as if it is deeply present in the core of the land.

Prior to becoming an independent scholar and freelance writer, Beebe was the editor of *Expedition* magazine at the University of Pennsylvania Museum of Archaeology and Anthropology. She taught at the University of Notre Dame, the University of Pennsylvania, and at Philadelphia University. She was also a Fulbright scholar to Morocco, where she gathered the stories of Jews and Muslims whose ancestors were exiled from Spain during and after 1492. More recently she has been researching the folklore, history, and culture of fishing villages in Spain's northwest.

Beebe writes extensively on the western Mediterranean world and especially on Spain. Her writing appears in many publications, including *Michelin Green Guides*, *National Geographic* books, TransitionsAbroad.com, the *Pennsylvania Gazette*, *Expedition*, *Archaeology*, and *Bark* magazines. She annually divides her time between New Jersey and northwestern Spain.

Introduction

People think that Spain is the least developed nation in Europe but this is far from the truth; Spain is Europe's most ancient nation.
—from a conversation with a businessman
from Venezuela living in Madrid

CERTAIN PLACES POSSESS the ability to suspend time, where the visitor leaves the profane world and enters the eternal through the portal to the sacred. Some of these places are natural sites long noticed by passing or settling human groups as possessing this arresting, pulled-out-of-time quality. Other places married natural assets with human-made sanctity and over time were carved and re-carved by different peoples. A sacred Celtic spring became a Roman shrine and then became a Christian chapel. Over the centuries it was simply known as a sacred spot.

And some sacred experiences are not just about the place but more about the journey to get there. By its very nature, a pilgrimage is something that takes people out of their ordinary life and cares—removes the known scaffolding of their life—and that sends them on a walking meditation into the unknown with a singular purpose: deepening their connection to their spirit by arriving in many sacred places.

Spain is a European nation unusual for its geography and history. It juts out into the Atlantic Ocean and the Mediterranean and is as close to Africa as to the rest of Europe. Spain possesses more coastline and mountain ranges, and more land, than most other European nations. It is today, and has been for millennia, a crossroads of myriad cultures from Africa, the Middle East, Europe, the Americas, and Asia. Its paradox as a nation is that such a great crossroads has also endured pulses of time in isolation from the rest of Europe or from its own many regions, each encapsulated by mountains, coastal stretches, forests, and harsh plateaus and lowlands. This isolation has taken each indigenous and foreign influence alike and perfected it into a regional specialty. This paradoxical mix makes the sacred in Spain particularly original and moving. To many visitors, this explains why it is both familiar and exotic. Most poignantly, this paradox elevates the movement out of time into the sacred that defines spiritual experience at its most authentic.

As a peninsula jutting out into the Atlantic Ocean as much as into the Mediterranean Sea, as a land connected to Europe via a narrow mountainous strip shared with France, and as a place coming a mere nine miles near to North Africa, Spain is influenced by all these geographical realities, and their spiritual counterparts are palpable. For instance, in the north where mountain ranges and year-round rain have created an isolated, green, and intimate landscape, one finds the highest concentration of little remote hermitages, chapels, sacred oak groves, and sacred springs. The remoteness of the north preserved aspects of the ancient peoples who settled in these green hills, from the original Iberians to the Celtic speakers who came over the Pyrenees in pulsing migrations and mixed, creating tribes such as the Cantabri, the Astures, and the Gallaeci. Then there are the Basques who claim the most ancient and original ancestry in Iberia, who also live in the north. Homesteads and farming practices reflect the small, intimate landscapes. Places are separated by mountains and forests and people create more immediate worlds in their valley. It is such a hard area to conquer that there is rarely the presence of a hilltop fortress as one finds in hundreds of villages and towns further south. In contrast, the south is a vast open, arid place. Instead of small homesteads and farm plots, there are large estates with hired hands. Ancient Iberian culture here was less isolated and each incursion—be it for trade, as with the Greeks and Phoenicians, or under conquest, as with the Romans, Arabs, and Visigoths— added a new alteration to the older culture. The monasteries, mosques, and monuments here are grand, vast, defensive, and look out over the open plain, waiting for that rise of dust in the distance to announce the next visitor, friend or foe.

The east likewise is a deeply trodden place, receiving many trade-minded peoples of the ancient world. Its appeal reaches modern people today who flock to these ancient Mediterranean shores for the sun and the sea and a thick human presence. The west is like the north in its greater remoteness but of a different nature. There are gentle rolling hills, cork trees, wild foraging pigs, and a sense of independence. There monastic life is a little more austere than in the north but equally intimate, holding to its own valley or riverside.

While aspects of an ancient matriarchy exist in all parts of Spain today, as reflected in the infinite shrines and festivals dedicated to the Virgin Mary, the south also possesses greater expressions of an ancient patriarchy, one especially brought by the Romans and reinforced by the Arabs and Berbers. In the north this patriarchy is less influential and so some of those ancient matriarchal expressions are more pronounced. There are many shrines to Mary along the northern coast, especially the northwest, where Mary holds sway over the ocean waves. Often she is standing in a boat on the altar. Signs of her Son must be sought out. There may be a crucifix somewhere on the wall. Here is a land that still harbors ancient goddesses. Diana, Artemis, is known as the *xana* in Asturian folklore and she is, like the energies of her shared name, a fierce protector of pristine nature and of the innocent. She is an equalizer, insisting that men and women stand on equal footing, that humans live in harmony with nature, and that her waterways and forests remain whole and undisturbed.

Spain contains one of the world's great pilgrimage roads, the Camino de Santiago, which began in the ninth century with devout pilgrims arriving by many roads and seaways from all across Europe. Spain also possesses smaller and more local pilgrimages and sacred sites that reflect the vast richness of all its inhabitants, from the original Paleolithic inhabitants, to the original Iberians, most likely arriving from North Africa, to Celts, Phoenicians, Carthaginians, Romans, Visigoths, Arabs, and Berbers, and later, the emerging Castilians. More recently, especially after the end of the isolationist Franco period, since the 1980s there has been a new diversity arriving on Spanish shores. Born of the radical cultural and economic renaissance of recent years, Spaniards and diverse foreigners in Iberia are seeking new and old spiritualities, some native and others imported, but all sacred.

The spiritual traveler today will find the sacred strong in Spain, whether it is old or new. It is preserved in living histories and practices, timeless sacred routes, and subtle but still vibrant folkloric traditions and mythologies. While Spain has leaped at light speed into the twenty-first century after long decades under Franco, it is still a place that honors its sacred spots even if it is a nation that proclaims to be more secular than religious in its practices. People still flock to shrines and chapels, little pilgrim routes known to villages and towns, to festivals and rites that all possess the sacred's transformative powers at their heart, lifting people out of their time-based existence long enough to refresh their spirit in the energy of the ephemeral. Spain's dedication to the sacred and spiritual is attested by the many Spaniards who are actively seeking diverse spiritual paths—in Christianity, Islam, Judaism, paganism, Hinduism, Buddhism, Baha'ism, and the like—while still holding true to the festivals and seasonal rites of Advent, Holy Week, Lent, and the many saints' days and Marian days of each village, town, and city. Moreover, the practice of spirituality is more in the popular sphere, where people seek a direct link to the sacred, such as in the saying of the rosary at a little shrine dedicated to the Virgin Mary, in annually walking the *Via Crucis*—stations of the cross—during village saint days, or in visiting daily a church outside of Mass times in order to sit in meditation.

During one visit to Spain, I came across a book in Madrid, *España Magica y Misteriosa*, by Sebastian d'Arbo. D'Arbo draws on esoteric lore, folklore, anthropology, religion, and history to consider Spain from a sacred geographical perspective. In one fascinating chapter, he uses astrology to identify the character of the country and its regions in much the same way others use it to discern their own personality. He says that overall Spain is a Sagittarius, a fact established by the thirteenth-century king Alfonso X, the Learned, who was the first to systematically conduct an astrological investigation on the Iberian Peninsula and its regions. Sagittarius is "the sign of adventurers, conquistadors, and spiritual guides…it is the sign associated with Zeus…the guardian of law and religion" (1994: 32). D'Arbo says that each region of Spain has its own sign, too: Extremadura is an Aries; part of Andalusia is a Taurus (and curiously, the bullfighting capital of Spain) and another part a Leo; La Mancha and Murcia fall under Virgo; the Levant and Valencia are Libras; Catalonia is a Scorpio; Aragón and Navarre, like Spain, are Sagittarius; both Castile and Basque Country fall under Capricorn (is this why they lock horns all the time?); Galicia is a Pisces, the most watery of all signs for a region that is the main fishery for Europe; and Leon, Cantabria, and Asturias are all Aquarius, governed by the element of air.

Exploring spiritual Spain is like reading d'Arbo's book. There is as much a foothold in history as there is in well-founded legend and truth-seeded mythology. There is as much in the manuscripts of ancient libraries as there is in the folk wisdom and mind of villagers. A harmonious balance between rational empiricism and timeless esotericism is easy in this land of explorers, adventurers, mystics, and poets.

This book is an exploration and offering of Spain's many sacreds, from the land's deepest past to its most immediate present. It draws on prehistory and archaeology, history, anthropology, folklore, people's local wisdom in the form of oral histories, firsthand experience, a lot of walking around in remote wild vistas and congested cities, and always, always, talking to people in each place about their experiences.

While a rich and vast undertaking, the routes and sites selected here are those that represent the timeless and the sacred as they are manifested most authentically in Spain.

PART ONE

The Epic
of Sacred Spain

······················ ✿ ··

CHAPTER ONE

The Prehistory and History of the Land

IN SPAIN, layers of human presence from prehistory through to the present time exemplify many kinds of sacred sites and pilgrimages. From painted Paleolithic caves to the great Camino, the pilgrimage route across the north to Santiago de Compostela, to the smaller pilgrimages to a spring, a coast, a mountain, a chapel, a dolmen, or a vast plain, Spain is a rich mosaic of sacred sites. Spain is a land occupied by so many ancient peoples, and in ways more diverse than most of the rest of Europe, that it emits a feeling of many sacreds. Some sacreds are familiar, some are exotic. Together they infuse and flavor the whole like saffron in a pan of paella.

Consistent themes emerge in exploring the sacred in Spain. One is the prevalence of the Virgin Mary everywhere. She is the patron saint of every place, the protector and mother of all, and shows up much more than her Son. Small fishing villages and major cities all have a Mary who is the center of their ritual and sacred year. In many of these places, Mary can be linked to more ancient goddesses with similar traits. Throughout the Peninsula, she demonstrates a harmony and balance that exists between genders in the living society. Spain is a place where women are afforded more respect than I have witnessed in many other societies. And men are afforded the right to be feeling human beings with a full range of emotions and behaviors allowed them, much more than in other Western cultures. This gender balance alone makes the spiritual experience in Spain refreshing.

Another pattern is the prevalence of hybrid styles unique to European architecture, art, philosophy, and spirituality, because of the eight hundred plus years of contact with North Africans and Middle Easterners, who created an original multiethnic and multifaith civilization in much of Spain. This influence resulted in architectural styles in sacred and everyday buildings that are a blending of Christian, Jewish, and Muslim aesthetics, such as Mudéjar and Mozarabic. (Architectural styles are defined in part 3.) Many buildings may have a Romanesque base but a Mudéjar ceiling and columns, reflecting the mixed influence of these three communities.

A third prominent theme is that many churches and cathedrals were built over mosques that stood on the same ground. It was as much a part of the political competition between faiths as a practical matter of materials and location. And location was, after all, at the heart of the matter. Those same mosques might have been built over a Roman site and that Roman site over a sacred pre-Roman shrine and that shrine near a sacred stream, cave, mountain, or forest grove. Sacred spots tend to hold even as the faith around them changes. There is something to be said for the energy of a place that attracts this form of building, reverence, rebuilding, and more reverence while some places are left untouched and ignored and yet other places are used only for profane activities. The energy of such sacred places is a part of the great experience that helps a person transcend time and space and enter the present and Presence.

Early Cave Dwellers and Dolmen Builders

Throughout the Peninsula, there is evidence of Paleolithic peoples who occupied the diverse geography of Iberia some twenty thousand or more years ago, a time when much of northern Europe was under ice and snow and when southern Europe was the primary inhabitable area. Parts of southern France and across Spain appear to have been especially appealing, rich in microclimates that offered a diversity of edible flora and fauna and networks of caves that offered natural shelters. Mountains, rivers, streams, and coastline added to this rich offering. Today it is in the Paleolithic caves, such as Altamira, and along rock faces, such as Peña Tu, where remnants of the sacred life of Paleolithic to early Bronze Age peoples are found in Spain.

The Neolithic period, around six thousand years ago, is the time when dolmen builders lived in Iberia. They were the first farmers, bringing early agricultural techniques into the Peninsula. They lived in villages, were set-

View of the Atlantic Ocean from the Iron Age castro site of Santa Tecla in southwestern Galicia, near the Portuguese border

tled (unlike nomadic herders), and built holy sites in key spots near their settlements. Some of these sites were tombs only and others were both tombs and places for rituals, though we know very little about what these might have been: agrarian fertility rituals in the depths of the earth or perhaps coming of age rites or both? Dolmens exist all across Spain, from Andalusia to Galicia to Catalonia.

Iberians and Celts

The most common speculation about who the natives we call Iberians were is that they arrived around five thousand years ago from North Africa. But other theories consider that indigenous Iberians, the inhabitants of the Peninsula prior to Phoenician, Greek, Celtic, Viking, Roman, Arab, and Berber contact, were descendents of the prehistoric populations that settled there from the Paleolithic onward. This is also a theory concerning the Basque people's origins.

While origins are still debated, what are certain are the distinctive tribal social organization and unique art styles that flourished among the Iberians. Their ceramic paintings on clay vessels are especially gripping, showing elegant and dynamic line drawings of people with spiky hair and huge dilated eyes. There are scenes of hunting and fighting on foot and on horseback, of "duded up" women with armbands and breastplates, of people approaching a bull with vases or gourds at the ends of sticks, of hunters with their bows in a canoe, of deer, wolves, boars, and bulls.

The ancient Iberians occupied most of the Peninsula, concentrating predominantly in the center and all along the eastern coastline. They came into contact with seafaring Mediterranean traders and overland migrants from central Europe and together they forged hybrid cultures. Today the traveler will still feel this. Spanish culture has qualities not present elsewhere in Europe because of the mixing of these diverse ancient peoples.

During their expansion from somewhere to the east, Celtic-speaking people arrived in Spain around twenty-five hundred years ago. How and why these people arrived is still open to debate. The most likely scenario is one of a mobile people crossing the Pyrenees and fanning out into the Peninsula in several migratory waves, not so much of invasion and conquest, but of culture contact and *tessorae*, hospitality agreements. It appears that a well-organized, warrior-based social organization came with the Celts, and through such *tessorae*, Celts and indigenous Iberians influenced each other's cultures, mixed, and created a unique Celtiberian culture. The Celtiberians were especially concentrated around the mountainous territories in the northeast, around today's Navarre and Aragón.

Celtic-influenced tribes also spread to Portugal and from there northward to today's Galicia, Asturias, and Cantabria. In such northern reaches, these peoples founded small settlements in isolated mountain and coastal environments. They developed what is called the *castreña* culture, a culture based around the round stone huts that are still encountered in northwestern Spain, called *castros*.

Tartessans, Phoenicians, Greeks, and Carthaginians

Around twenty-six hundred to twenty-eight hundred years ago, the Tartessan culture flourished in southwestern Spain around Cádiz. Some believe this might be the land referred to as Tarshish in the Old Testament, a place from which the eastern Mediterranean procured its tin. Tin is not a widely occurring metal in the circum-Mediterranean, and Spain was known for its natural wealth in tin, as well as silver, iron, and gold. This among other clues may point to western Andalusia as the ancient land of Tartessos. Others say it sat at the classical world's gates of Hercules. The peoples of Tartessos were influenced by Phoenicians and Greeks.

Phoenician traders from Tyre in the eastern Mediterranean sailed across the Mediterranean to Iberia largely as merchants and traders, perhaps motivated by the precious metals that came from the Peninsula's mountains. Cádiz and Málaga are two of their original settlements in southern Spain. Málaga's origins may be as ancient as thirty-one hundred years old.

Greeks arrived in Spain around 600 BCE, setting up trading posts along the Mediterranean and parts of the Atlantic. Like the Phoenicians, their art and music mingled with indigenous forms, creating hybrid forms.

Carthaginians, people from the Phoenician city of Carthage, in today's Tunisia, invaded Iberia in the third century as a part of their wider power struggles against the Romans in the Mediterranean. They first arrived around 300 BCE. Defeated by Rome in the First Punic War, the Carthaginians turned their attention to southern and eastern Spain. The military leader Hamilcar Barca successfully took parts of Spain's Mediterranean coast, from Barcelona to Valencia to Andalusia, and founded the city of Cartagena, near Murcia, naming it after Carthage in Tunisia. His son Hannibal carried on his father's expansionist dreams of taking the Mediterranean world under his control, and although he had many successful conquests, he could not hold Rome back. His influence, and that of the Carthaginians in Spain, was short-lived. By 203 BCE, Hannibal was limited to North Africa, and Iberia fell more under the influence of Rome.

Romans in Spain

Romans began to invade and settle Spain in the third century BCE, overlaying and mingling their customs, laws, and sacred beliefs with more indigenous ones, but still not supplanting them, and in some areas, especially the far northwest, barely touching what came before. Complete Roman rule in Spain took two centuries to secure, a feat achieved under Augustus in 19 BCE. For four centuries after that, Spain was under the certain and unbroken Roman sphere of control and influence. One of the greatest surviving examples of this struggle for Spain between the natives and the Romans is found at Numantia, seven kilometers north of Soria in north central Spain (chapter 13).

Hispania, as it was known, became one of the Roman Empire's wealthiest territories, supplying precious metals as well as products from herding and agricultural activities. Throughout Spain, Roman towns and cities grew up over older settlements and new settlements were established. Many roads were constructed that connected cities and towns to one another in an efficient network.

Today some of the most prominent surviving remains of Roman Spain are at Mérida, Tarragona, Empúries, Sagunto, and Itálica. In the major Roman sites you will visit, there are temples dedicated to major Roman deities, but none as prominent as the temples to Diana. Spain seems to be the realm of this goddess of the wilds and of the hunt. It is possible that in Diana we see one of the best examples of cultural continuity and cross-cultural hybridization. Before the Romans, Diana may have been the prominent divine feminine presence that shaped Iberian cosmology and that has left us such folkloric holdovers as the *xana*, and the *mari*. These are two fiercely independent and capable female entities in northern Spain, who protect the wild world and uphold a morality to which humans must adhere or reap the consequences.

It was also during Roman Spain that Christianity made its first inroads into the Peninsula with wandering missionaries, including possibly St. James the Greater and Paul and missionaries sent by Peter. It was a rocky beginning that started the history of Christian martyrdom in Spain, from St. Eulalia of Mérida to St. Vincent in Saguntum, today's Sagunto, among

The mosaic geometric and floral-motif dome of Córdoba's mosque, Andalusia

others. But slowly, churches were built and Christianity became firmly established in Spain.

Today the most pronounced influences of Roman rule are less in monuments and more in the culture itself, in the form of religion, law, and language, all of which likewise would be altered and added to by Visigoths, Arabs, and North Africans and ultimately by the emerging Castilian society in the late Middle Ages.

Jewish Iberians: The Sephardim

It is possible that Jews arrived in Iberia before Roman rule, perhaps around twenty-five hundred years ago, but their numbers increased with the ease of movement and travel under Roman rule with the expanding Roman Empire. As with any successful minority peoples (consider Armenians and Zoroastrians, for example), they valued learning and skills highly, as such things were transportable and always in need. As a consequence, throughout Spain's long history its Jewish citizens have contributed to the body of knowledge in the sciences and the arts as well as to skilled crafts such as silverwork and weaving. In Roman Spain, in Muslim Spain centuries later, and in medieval Christian Spain (prior to 1480), Jews lived in a relative state of productivity and freedom as a people interwoven with other peoples of the Peninsula. This tide turned for a while with the arrival of the Visigoths, who, in their recent conversion to Christianity and in their desire to emulate and outdo the Romans before them, had the zeal of the new convert, which made it hard for anyone not willing to go along with the new Visigothic religion and rule. Jews fared poorly. When the Muslim conquerors invaded in the early eighth century, with the Qur'anic injunction to respect Peoples of the Book (i.e., Abrahamic peoples—Jews, Christians, and Muslims), Jews flourished in the newer more open society. Together with the new conquerors, along with the Christian communities, which also enjoyed new freedoms and an upswing in the economy, they shaped a new society.

The years of Muslim presence in Spain, from 711 to 1492, are long, complicated years, and they are hard to generalize. More often than not, however, Jews fared well during these eight hundred years. They were valued by both the Muslim south and the Christian north, not only for their skill as physicians and people of letters and learning, not only for their capable and beautiful crafts, but also for their neutral role as intermediaries between the two ruling halves of Spain. Jews were trusted as diplomats and messengers between Christian and Muslim kings. And while there were times of strife when the Jewish community suffered as a scapegoat—the sad reality of a minority, especially a successful one, anywhere in the world—for the most part, Jewish life in Spain was good in both Muslim and Christian realms during the Middle Ages. The Golden Age was truly in the tenth and eleventh centuries, when the Caliphate of Córdoba and then the *taifa*-state kings of Muslim Spain patronized the arts and learning and recruited talent from all areas. In both the Talmud and the Hadith (the sayings and deeds of the prophet Muhammed), pilgrimage and travel were praised for the knowledge one could gain in such endeavors. Iberian Jews and Muslims participated in a good deal of movement around the Muslim world and thus engendered an atmosphere of sharing, discovering, knowledge for knowledge's sake, and the exchange of ideas.

Likewise, around the same time, the Christian north was patronizing its own arts and learning and was not yet polarized into thinking in Christian versus Muslim terms. Moreover, the Christian north was not yet unified enough to be a serious threat or to turn its attention to persecution of its own minorities. As the Christian Reconquest gained steam, however, in the late eleventh century and into the twelfth and thirteenth centuries, the unifying north's Christian banner fueled a polarized response from the south, calling in reinforcements from a more zealous Islamic sect from northwest Africa to help stave off the Christian expansion. North and south grew more polarized in their religious identity; the Jewish minority suffered as a result. At the same time, in the late thirteenth century, as the Jewish communities of the south dispersed, some heading into Christian Spain and others into other Mediterranean reaches, mystical trends in the form of the Zohar and kabbalistic thinking emerged as a key trend.

The fourteenth and fifteenth centuries saw a further narrowing for Muslims and Jews, as Christian unity neared completion. In the late fifteenth century, the Spanish crown, desirous of unifying Spain into one Christian nation, finally had all the means to do so. In 1480 the Inquisition was set up to test the faith of all Christians, old and recently converted. By 1492, the Kingdom of Granada, the last Muslim kingdom remaining in Spain, was taken and absorbed. It was also the year Jews were forced to convert or leave. If they left, they lost everything. If they converted, they were now Christian and vulnerable to being taken before the Inquisition. By 1502, the same fate faced the Muslims of Spain. They too lost all by leaving, unless they submitted to baptism and the threat of the Inquisition.

Germanic Tribes and Visigothic Spain

As Roman rule weakened throughout Europe and the Mediterranean in the early fifth century, several Germanic tribes invaded Spain, from the Suevi, Vandals, and Alani, to the Visigoths, who came to stay. Visigoths sought to emulate the Romans, whom they admired for their prowess, and also sought to supersede them as the next great power. They did not consolidate their power in Spain until around AD 600; and even then, they were hard pressed to hold their power due to internal rivalry and violence toward each successor, coupled with shabby treatment of their subjects, who were likewise a fiercely independent people. They did infuse Spanish Roman Christianity with Visigothic elements. The Visigoths were Arian Christians not Trinitarian Christians and held Jesus as a man and a great prophet, but not as one with God. Likewise, they did not embrace the Trinity of Father, Son, and Holy Spirit and, unfortunately, they persecuted those who did, the Spanish Roman Catholics. This difference in outlook helps interpret some differences you will observe in the surviving Visigothic churches in Spain.

It was the Visigothic royal, Hermenegild, who through his own martyrdom shifted the Visigothic church from Arianism to Trinitarian Roman Catholicism. Hermenegild's own father was one of the greatest persecutors of Roman Catholics; a civil war erupted between the two men, ending in Hermenegild's death. His death was not in vain for his brother, Recared, established a policy of tolerance and converted to Roman Catholicism, encouraging others to do so as well. He is considered the first Catholic king of Spain. His long dead brother was sainted in 1586 to become Spain's St. Hermenegild.

As with the Romans, the Visigoths had a hard time containing the fiercely independent tribes in the north of Spain. The Visigoths never fully attained unity in Spain and in AD 711 they were ripe for invasion.

Medieval Spain

In the early eighth century, at the same time that an Arab military minority had conquered the territory known today as Morocco and gained the marginal allegiance of the Berber tribes, Visigothic rule in the Iberian Peninsula was in the midst of a succession battle. King Roderic won and took the throne in 711, though his rule was weak. Inflamed with a new, but also Abrahamic faith, the Berbers and Arabs swiftly invaded the Iberian Peninsula. Until AD 732, they held territory as far as southern France. These new Muslims held on in Iberia in varying degrees, creating a great mixing of civilizations and peoples, until the close of the fifteenth century.

A romantic historiographical image from Christian medieval Spain emerged of Don Pelayo, who in AD 718 fought back the attacking Muslim army. According to legend, Pelayo and his men were cornered in the cave of Covadonga in the Picos de Europa mountains of northern Spain when the Virgin Mary arrived in the nick of time to rain stones down onto the invaders' heads. Today, a shrine is set in the fabled cave and it has become a major pilgrimage site.

That victory, though not noted in the chronicles of the time and surviving through oral tales, set the tone for the north. In the latter half of the eighth century, small, poorly organized Christian kingdoms slowly emerged, pushing the invaders south of the mountains. Until AD 1086, nearly all of Iberia, except for this narrow northern strip between the Cantabrian mountains and the Atlantic, was under Muslim rule.

In AD 756, the Muslim Umayyad prince Abd al-Rahman I established himself as ruler in Córdoba. This he did after surviving both the Abbasid slaughter of his family in Damascus and after unsuccessfully seeking refuge with his Berber mother's tribe in Morocco.

During the medieval period, especially tenth-century Córdoba, Spain was in a Golden Age of arts and sciences, literature and medicine, poetry and music, spirituality and philosophy. Diverse religious and cultural groups from Europe, North Africa, and the Middle East sought one another out and cross-fertilized ideas both secular and sacred. At the same time, the non-Muslim north of Spain gathered its forces and began to forge its own sacred experience born of a Christianity mixed with Roman, Visigothic, and indigenous ideas as well as influences coming in from Jewish and Muslim Iberians. There were times of strife and times of coexistence, times when the Christian north paid tribute to the south for peaceful existence and then later when the Muslim south paid tribute to the north for the same. Throughout, peoples moved all across the Peninsula. Jews were essential to all because they were viewed as neutral—they were neither Christian nor Muslim, held no kingdom, but were trusted.

During the Cordoban period, begun by Abd al-Rahman I in 756, the cultural zenith of Islamic Spain occurred during the Cordoban Caliphate of Abd al-Rahman III (AD 912–961), his son al-Hakim II (961–976), the vizier al-Mansur (976–1002), and al-Mansur's son, Abd al-Malik (1002–1008). It is during this time under the Cordoban rulers' patronage that the three religious communities of Jews, Christians, and Muslims first came together to translate and interpret ancient Greek scientific texts and to develop and innovate new forms of literary, visual, and musical arts. It is this Golden Age from which the ideal notion of *convivencia*, interreligious coexistence, comes, though examples of *convivencia* exist during other periods of Islamic Spain.

The Cordoban period came to an end with Abd al-Malik's death, the last ruler to whom the Berber army remained loyal. From 1008 to 1031 began what is called the period of *fitnah*, or civil strife. After over two decades of struggle, precariously balanced *taifa* states, essentially city-states, emerged. Each *taifa* was ruled by its own king. Seville was a city-state ruled by the Abbadids of Seville, a Muslim ruling family of mixed Arab and Iberian ancestry. When a Berber general took over the rule of the province of Granada, he founded the city of Granada as a strategic defense in the mountains. Similar political structures arose in other regions, such as Murcia, Valencia, Toledo, Badajoz, and Zaragoza, to mention some of the largest and best known.

During these city-state kingdoms, the innovative arts and sciences of al-Andalus continued to flourish because each ruler was competing with the others to attract the best poets, musicians, doctors, and philosophers. The majority of Iberian territory was still under Muslim rule.

While political stability within the Muslim Iberian states was precarious during the *taifa* period, so too was the case in the Christian Iberian north, where petty squabbles over land and power kept the Christian city-states from organizing against their common conqueror. It was not until 1085, when Alfonso VI of Castile and León took Toledo, that the notion of the *reconquista*, Reconquest, by the Christian powers of Iberia became popular. By 1248, under King Fernando III's rule, all but the Kingdom of Granada came under Christian power.

Convivencia always existed side by side with conflict. When in one region the religious communities of Jews, Christians, and Muslims may have experienced *convivencia*, in another region, during the same period, one or two of the religious communities were in conflict and were perhaps even persecuted. This is the general case whether one looks at Christian rule or at Muslim rule, though the consensus is that Muslim rulers' treatment of their Jewish and Christian subjects was by far the fairer compared to Christian rulers' treatment of their Jewish and Muslim subjects. Moreover, each of the several Christian Spanish kingdoms treated its Muslim and Jewish communities differently. The best example of continued harmony and coexistence comes from the Kingdom of Valencia whose rulers (most of the time), especially James I (1213–1276), recognized the necessary symbiosis of the three religious communities in order to maintain economic strength.

The *taifa* period of multiple Muslim city-states ended with the increasing strength of the Christian-ruled north and was followed by two waves of Berber fundamentalist invasions: first the Almoravids (1085–1150), and then their conquerors, the Almohads (1150–1248). The Almoravid and Almohad conquests both mark periods of unified rule between the Peninsula and northwestern Africa. These conquests also represent a time of lessened *convivencia* because of the fundamentalist nature of the conquerors; both Almoravids and Almohads viewed Iberian Islam as corrupt. Ironically, after their conquest, they too succumbed to the softer, more lush life of Muslim Spain. Especially after the Almohads took over, another golden age emerged and this is when Europe received ideas from the likes of Averroës (whose translation and commentary of Aristotle fueled debates on reason and faith in Europe), and Maimonides, the great Jewish philosopher and rationalist. The new wave of Muslim invaders also polarized the divide between Christian and Muslim Spain, rallying the Christians to take up a fervent banner under one faith just as they had witnessed with the North African fundamentalists. The Muslims of al-Andalus deeply regretted the arrival of the Almohads and Almoravids even though they had called for help against an encroaching north.

As Christian Iberian kingdoms in the north began to successfully unite their powers, they rapidly gained Muslim-held territories. From 1212 to 1248, all previously Muslim-held territory except Granada was taken by the northern Christian kingdoms and divided among their heirs.

The medieval Iberian world of Jews, Christians, and Muslims was more mixed and blurred and interwoven and interdependent than it ever was clear and distinct. For instance, it is from medieval Spain that we get the terms *mozarabe* and *mudéjar*, which truly are witness to a real coexistence. Mozarabes were Christians who were living in the Muslim kingdoms of Iberia. Mudéjars were Muslims who were living in the Christian kingdoms of Iberia. Their presence in the different kingdoms led to a cross-fertilization of ideas and outlooks, the most pronounced today being in the sacred buildings in many parts of Spain. A church might be described as having Mudéjar ceilings, indicating that Muslim craftsmen or their style of work went into the church's construction. Likewise, a church might have Mozarabic styles, implying that the craftsmen had lived, or were living in a Muslim society (church building was permitted and protected in Muslim Spain during most periods). It all depended on what period we are speaking of, and the movement of people, which was constant. This mixing and blurring of lines is why that period had such a profound influence on Spanish culture, an influence that is still found today. You will see it and feel it in the unique sacred and secular arts and architecture, scholarship and music, spirituality and worship, intellectual and creative thought, as well as in the everyday way people interact, value friends and family, and enjoy food and drink.

It is in medieval Spain that aspects of Jewish, Christian, and Islamic mysticism mixed, and all three Abrahamic faiths developed some of the world's most moving mystical traditions. (St. Teresa of Ávila and St. John of the Cross were inheritors of these strains of the mystical.) These three faiths coexisted for some eight centuries, in uneven dynamics of strife and harmony (more of the latter than the former) and forged multiple sacreds in Spain.

The Nasrid Kingdom of Granada, which lasted from 1248 to 1492, was the final period of Iberian Islamic history. Though diminished in size and paying tribute to Christian kings, the Kingdom of Granada saw a final flourishing of the Muslim Iberian civilization. This was when the Alhambra in its final form was built.

In the late fifteenth century, Christian Spain unified fully in the union between Fernando of Aragón and Isabel of Castile.

For more than eight hundred years, both Iberian Muslims and Christians learned from each other that the one force that seemed to unify otherwise fiercely independent and regionally oriented Iberians was religion. Perhaps Fernando and Isabel felt that the way to prevent their own kingdoms from falling apart due to infighting was to unify against an outside force and use the idea of a unified Christian Spain as motivation (not to mention all the booty and land they gained). For this and many other complex reasons, on January 2, 1492, Isabel and Fernando rode into Granada and ousted Ben Abdallah, popularly known as Boabdil. Immediately they set about converting or expelling the Jews of Spain and in the next few years they turned the same practices on the Muslims.

Iberian Jews and Muslims scattered across the Mediterranean, east and south or onward to the New World as that frontier opened. Those Muslims who converted became known as *Moriscos* and converted Jews became known as *Conversos*. And while conversion allowed them to stay, they continued to be a minority in Spain and referred to as "new Christians." Both converted Muslims and converted Jews, even though many among them may have wanted to fully assimilate, were held as a distinct minority up until they were finally expelled in the early seventeenth century by Phillip III. Between 1609 and 1614, the Moriscos and Conversos were expelled from Spain.

Unified Catholic Spain

The time called the Renaissance was, in Spain, one of narrowed thought and possibilities. Ironically, medieval Spain stimulated the Renaissance in other places, such as Italy, through the translation school in Toledo. But Isabel and Fernando's policies of Catholic and territorial unification led to what I would consider the darker ages of Spain. Though Spain expanded into the New World, it pushed its ideas on it more than it absorbed the new worlds it encountered. But this was initial. I would wager that today, Spain has been absorbing those new ideas of the New World, both in its more honest revisionist thinking about itself and in the fact that immigrants from Latin America are arriving in Spain in high numbers.

After Spain was unified in the fifteenth century under the Catholic Kings, as Isabel and Fernando are called, the spiritual elements of faith and belief in Spain held on, but underground. Pagans, Jews, and Muslims were all baptized and, above ground, behaved as Christians. But some continued their older practices in hiding. And many assimilated and fully assumed a Christian life but had prior influences that they unconsciously replicated in their everyday life. As such, in spite of the controlling religious rule to homogenize the sacred, many sacreds continued, including a resplendent mystical Catholicism that emerged in the sixteenth century from St. Teresa of Ávila and St. John of the Cross. Unlike the church and state's party line, this Christianity was an intimate faith, one lush with a love for God, something it holds in common with Jewish and Muslim mysticism as much as with the pagan veneration of nature. This dynamic of one official faith above ground and many spiritual experiences beneath persisted by and large until the death of Spain's conservative and isolationist dictator, Francisco Franco, in 1975.

Queen Isabel and King Fernando lost their son and heir at an early age. Their daughter, Juana, married into the Austrian Hapsburg dynasty through alliance with Prince Philip—also called Philip the Handsome, given his appeal to women. Apparently Juana was perennially jealous and the two had many quarrels and some speculate that this constant interpersonal warfare contributed to Juana's mental instability. Juana La Loca, Juana the Mad, as she was called, had a son with Philip, who would become Spain's king Carlos I as well as the Holy Roman Emperor, called Charles V, which occurred around the same time he took the Spanish throne (1517–1556).

When Queen Isabel died in 1504, Philip took control of Castile until he died two years later, at which time King Fernando stepped in until his grand-

The Roman theater in Mérida, Extremadura

son, Carlos I, could take the throne. Carlos's reign was one of a Flanders-educated, non-Spanish-speaking king, but also one of Spain's largest reaches as an empire. Carlos inherited from his grandparents and his mother most all of Spain (Castile, Aragón, Navarra), as well as Sardinia, Sicily, Naples, Roussillon, and the vast colonies in both Africa and the New World. Spain in all this was a backwater as regards his rule; he gave the Flemish more consideration and roles in governance. As his parents before him, when the Spanish revolted, he put them down strongly. And this is a part of why, literature aside, I consider the Renaissance in Spain its darker centuries. Let us not forget, the Inquisition, formed in 1480 (and not abolished until 1820) under Isabel and Fernando, was an instrument of the modern state, a creation of early modern Spain, not medieval Spain, whose outlooks were more tolerant and willing to live with diversity.

It was under Carlos I/Charles V's rule that Cortés took Mexico, Mendoza took Argentina, Pizarro took Peru, Quesada took Colombia, Valdivia took Chile, Alvarada took Guatemala, and De Soto took parts of the United States. Huge wealth poured into the Spanish Hapsburg Empire but it was poorly spent, mostly on wars.

Philip II, Carlos I's son, born in 1527, held a reign of furthering policies of one-state, one-religion, and fought against incursions of Protestantism in Spain. In 1556, the year Phillip II took the throne, Carlos I retired to the monastery in Yuste, near Plasencia in Extremadura, where he died two years later. Phillip II commenced his rule with burning heretics at the stake in Valladolid under the offices of the Inquisition. He had inherited the absolutist attitudes of father and great grandparents. His rule was one of the bleakest after Isabel and Fernando's. His combination of religious confidence, absolute piety, and absolute control made for a dangerous ruler. No one was safe, not even church officials. It was Phillip II more than any other ruler who solidified one-way dogmatism in Spain, a legacy that would not fully unravel until the death of Franco.

When Phillip II died in 1598 and left this failing empire to his son, Philip III, he had as good as sealed the deal for the Moriscos, who would be expelled from 1609 to 1614, the same time that Cervantes was writing *Don Quixote*, which is filled with wonderful cryptic observations of mixed Jewish-Muslim-Christian Spain.

Along with Cervantes, the seventeenth century was a golden age of literature and art—perhaps because the creative, bold, and sensitive had a lot of meat to work with from the follies of their leaders—including playwright Lope de Vega, painters El Greco, Velázquez, Murillo, and Zurbarán.

Neither Philip III nor his son Philip IV, who ruled from 1621 to 1665, were strong leaders, leaving affairs of state to the Duke of Lerma for the former, and the Count-Duke of Olivares for the latter. Olivares was a man of integrity but, try as he did, he could not pull Spain out of the decline it had already begun to fall into decades, if not centuries, before. Under Philip IV, Spain lost Catalonia, Sicily, and Naples. The defining legacy of the next king, Carlos II (1665–1700), was that he did not produce an heir, thus leading to a struggle for succession to the throne. The victor was his relative, Philip V (1701–1746), a Bourbon and Louis XIV's grandson. Through the Bourbon dynasty, French ideas and customs mixed with aspects of Spanish culture.

In 1808 Spain was occupied by Napoleon Bonaparte and Spain's king Carlos IV was forced to step down, leaving Bonaparte's brother, Joseph (José I), on the throne. The French were finally pushed out in 1813.

In 1835 the Spanish liberal government under Juan Alvarez Mendizábal ordered the dismantling of religious orders and their property as a way of remedying the country's dire economic state. Religious orders left and monasteries' goods were sold off. Some monasteries were abandoned, sacked, and never rebuilt. Others were abandoned, possibly sacked, and then a few decades later rebuilt and repopulated by a religious order, usually a different one than the previous inhabitants but sometimes by the same order. This is why a medieval Benedictine monastery might today be occupied by Augustinian monks, for example.

In the eighteenth and nineteenth centuries, and really three-quarters into the twentieth century, Spain was in a state of decline both economically and politically, but artistically its peoples' genius continued to work, whether fully appreciated or not in the artists' lifetimes. This was a period that produced profound works of spiritual art, pieces that may not look "religious" but that communicate a deep transcendence of spirit or a great Presence. From Francisco de Goya's folk paintings of the countryside to Joaquín Sorolla's depictions of people, sea, and land, these works are infused with a light and energy that communicate across time what it is to be human and what it is to long for connection and meaning.

Modern Multifaith Spain

Since Franco's death, a rich tapestry of faith and spirituality has burst to the surface, coming out of its sacred hiding places: New Iberian spiritualities build upon old, from Hindu and Buddhist traditions to contemporary Jewish and Muslim presences. Some of the oldest pre-Christian and pre-Roman gods and goddesses are also returning or asserting that they never left. A new age has come, one that has authentic lineages that speak of an undying sacred that has always been present but emerges and retreats in a sine wave of dormancy and engagement. Around 77 percent of Spaniards describe themselves as Roman Catholic, but of that number 46 percent claim to never attend Mass. At the same time, Christian devotional practices flourish with other spiritualities in Spain. This can be witnessed by a visit to any neighborhood church in a high-density urban neighborhood and during pilgrimage cycles to saints' shrines across the rural landscape. Ironically, some formerly Catholic Latin Americans are now coming to Spain and evangelizing variations of Protestantism, something Isabel, Fernando, and their progeny tried so hard to prevent in the fifteenth and sixteenth centuries.

Some Spaniards are looking back at their family histories, their names, and their places of birth and pondering if they might not have been among the Moriscos and Conversos who assimilated enough to go unnoticed during the seventeenth-century expulsions. Some of these people are converting to what they believe is their ancestral religion. There is especially a significant movement among people converting to Islam for this reason, and creating Muslim communities of many colors and interpretations, but all claiming their Islam to be of the special Andalusian variety, born on the soil of Iberia. New mosques are being built, both by converts and by immigrant Muslims from North Africa, the Middle East, and South and Southeast Asia.

Simultaneously, old synagogues are active again and new ones are being built. Some Sephardic Jews are returning to Spain from other parts of the Mediterranean, Europe, and the New World, reclaiming their ancestral birthright and setting up communities and temples throughout Spain.

Benalmádena (chapter 16), eleven kilometers west of Málaga, claims Europe's biggest Buddhist stupa, or temple, and Buddhist communities are numerous across Spain. Valencia just finished building the country's largest Hindu temple, both for immigrant populations and for Spaniards dedicated to a Hindu path.

And perhaps Spain is truly returning to its most ancient roots in the pagan and nature-based movements that are emerging everywhere, where there is a reverence for nature and a world where everything is infused with spirit and worthy of mindful engagement and awareness. These practices never went away fully. Every village, town, and city has a person at the weekly market selling medicinal herbs. This knowledge of the healing power of plants is not just a physical, medical knowledge, but one that dates back to a time and practice when people understood that plants had spirits and offered their special energies to cure human maladies.

PART TWO

The Sacred Landscape

CHAPTER TWO

❁

$\mathscr{D}$olmens and Castros

THE EARLY FARMING AND HERDING PEOPLES, during Spain's Bronze Age, are as yet little understood, though excavations of their sites are ongoing and revealing interesting details. Though not covered in this book, the Balearic Islands of Mallorca, Minorca, and Ibiza possess a heavy list of Bronze Age megalithic structures, such as t-shaped limestone formations (*taulus*), upside-down boat-shaped stone tombs (*navetas*), and towering stone mounds (*talaiots*). As of yet, no one understands what these were for, though burials have been found near some. They date to around four thousand years ago.

Similarly, on the Peninsula, megalithic dolmens, upright huge stones that form chambers thought mostly to be tombs, cover the entire Iberian territory: for example, Galicia's Dolmen de Axeitos (chapter 10); the Asturian dolmen beneath the eighth-century Chapel of Santa Cruz (chapter 9); the three magnificent dolmen tombs in Antequera (chapter 15); a huge

The Iron Age Castro de Baroña along the western Atlantic coast in Galicia

The Neolithic Dolmen de Axeitos in Galicia

concentration of dolmens, perhaps Spain's largest, scattered near the site of San Miguel de Excelsis in Navarra; the dolmen Valencia de Alcántara near Cáceres in Extremadura; and dozens of dolmens in wine country around Laguardia (chapter 13).

The people who built these were Iberia's early farmers, who also likely had herds and still hunted and gathered wild foods as well. Their stone monuments were in some cases tombs and in other cases sites of rituals and possibly defense or a combination of these. A recent find a few kilometers north of Antequera's three dolmens in Andalusia reveals a Bronze Age farming settlement called Los Silillos. It possibly was the residence of the people who built Antequera's dolmens. So far only a small stretch of the settlement has been excavated, but it already reveals farming and stone-working tools, some made of copper. Their homes are circular, a shape popular with later Iron Age peoples as well. The site dates from around 2500 to 1900 BCE.

Sites called *castros* were built by the next Iberian inhabitants of the Iron Age. These peoples coincide with migrating waves of Celtic-speaking tribes into the Peninsula. Castro sites exist in all the areas where Celtic-speakers and the cultural hybrids of Celtiberians lived, largely across the north and northwest and in parts of central Iberia. Castro settlements are mostly made up of clustered round buildings comprising homes, work-shops, and storage areas. Around the entire cluster a fortified stone wall was built for added protection. The majority of castros were built on hill-tops for this reason—defense. Some of the best preserved and most famous castros in Spain are Castros de Baroña, Santa Tecla, and Coaña (all covered in chapter 10) and the Celtiberian site of Numantia (chapter 13). The area around Ávila also has significant Iron Age sites under excavation, most associated with the Vettones who built hilltop castros, offering altars, and huge boulders carved into the shapes of bulls and pigs (chapter 14).

Castro sites reflect the sacred woven into everything of everyday awareness. Iron Age peoples, and most probably the Bronze Age and Neolithic peoples before them, saw the divine in everything, an animistic take on creation. On Iron Age castro sites, this is best seen in the stone-carved symbols found as part of old doorways and windows or foundation stones. The museum for the castro site of Santa Tecla (chapter 10) best shows these symbols with their collection of suns, moons, stars, spirals, and elemental symbols in carved stones found on the site.

The Neolithic Dolmen de Menga in Antequera, Andalusia

$\int$acred Springs, Mountains, and Caves

Springs

CELTIC SPEAKERS MADE OFFERINGS to gods and goddesses in springs and waterways. These same places then became sites of powerful healing waters at a Roman or a Christian shrine, usually associated with a deity or nymph, or a local vision of the Virgin Mary in the Christian case. Water is the ancient element for the sacred feminine, a symbol of the otherworld, of the unconscious. Watery places were on the edge of this world, a border crossing, a thin-veiled portal where the visible world met the invisible. That healing grace still pours forth from them in modern times, speaks of their power and of the persistent yearning of the human soul for expression no matter how secular a culture grows.

Pagan sites of veneration were often connected to springs, and as new inhabitants and conquerors arrived in Iberia with their respective faiths, they appropriated the sacred spring as a part of their shrine or temple space. Romans and the copycat Visigoths after them were especially in sync with this way of selecting sacred sites. Examples of Visigoth churches built near sacred springs are Santa Comba de Bande around fifty kilometers south of Ourense in Galicia; San Juan de Baños, ten kilometers south of Palencia in León; San Antolín's crypt in Palencia; Santa Eulalia de Bóveda, four kilometers south of Lugo in Galicia; and the Monasterio de

Valvanera in Rioja with its nearby fountain, Fuensanta, fabled to possess healing waters (chapter 13).

When Muslims conquered Visigothic territory, they built their holy places over Visigothic ones. Later Christians did the same to Islamic shrines. As such, all persist in being near claimed and reclaimed holy springs, wells, and fountains. As you travel to the various sacred sites across Spain, you will find the healing fountain or spring to be almost omnipresent.

Mountains and Caves

Our English word *transhumance* comes from the Spanish *transhumancia,* meaning pastoral nomadism, the taking of sheep, goats, and cows from summer to winter pastures and back again in an annual cycle. We get our word from Spanish because it is a much more ancient art in Spain, one harkening back to the earliest of herders in Europe. Spain is the rare modern nation that still has pastoral nomads, especially along the Sierra de Gredos Mountains in western Spain (chapter 14).

For people who have spent millennia crossing Spain's numerous mountain passes with their herds, making their living in this raw and romantic

A local holy cave of prayer, meditation, and visions discovered in one of many aromatic footpaths in the Sierra de Mariola, Bocairent, Valencia

manner, mountains must be the ultimate god, even if they have channeled that energy into a monotheistic One with a strong mother.

Mountains and caves often go hand in hand, one residing in the other, one masculine, reaching to the Sky God, and the other feminine and going deep into the earth toward the Mother Goddess. Frequently in the Middle Ages an image of the Virgin Mary was miraculously found in a cave and her shrine was then built on that cave's mountain.

Montserrat is a great example of this (chapter 12). Prior to being the home of the Black Madonna of Montserrat, a temple to Venus stood on these haunting and odd limestone mountains in Catalonia. The surrounding sweep of hill and plain is a strange contrast to the rising white, foamy vertical towers of Montserrat. It is likely that prior to Venus, this mountain was sacred to indigenous Iberians, perhaps a throne to one of their nature gods.

Though the Virgin of Montserrat now stands in a basilica built in her honor, the site of her discovery by shepherds was in a cave, called the Santa Cova, where a chapel now stands built right into the wall of the vertical mountain. Not far away is a hermit's cave, a place where hermits have come for centuries for silent meditation and total retreat from the world's distractions.

Mountains are where heaven and Earth make their first contact and as such are the locale of many pilgrimage shrines, emulating literally a person's ascent to heaven like the prophets before them. Nearly every village, town, and city in Spain has a pilgrimage road, leading to a shrine to either the Virgin Mary, Jesus, a favorite local saint, or all three. Usually these pilgrimages ascend a hill or a mountain.

Symbolism linking heaven and Earth beyond high altitude shrines is also everywhere. The Star of David is such with its descending male triangle from heaven joining the ascending female triangle from Earth. In church altars across Spain, the usual placement of Mary and Jesus puts Mary in the altar center with Jesus above her. Or, when Jesus is not on the altar, we have a depiction of God above Mary, either as an abstract triangle surrounded by a wreath of roses or clouds or as a bearded male Creator.

Caves are often a gateway to another world, accessed through a mountain. From the Paleolithic to the present, mountainous caverns and mountaintops have been places where humans seek contact with the divine. In Spain shrines exist in both places, the majority today dedicated to a local manifestation of the Virgin Mary and the others to local occurrences and legends surrounding certain saints that have a unique history with that village, town, or city. These same places were likely veneration points for pre-

Christian gods, a power spot taken over by the next spirituality that was to sweep across the Peninsula.

The mountain cave of Covadonga in Asturias (chapter 9) is perhaps one of Spain's most famous sacred mountain spots after Montserrat. It is the resting place of a powerful, action-oriented Mary, one who helped the warrior Pelayo defeat the invading North Africans at one of the northernmost reaches of Spain. One legend says that she was there all along, prior to Christianity, waiting in the womb of stone for her power to be utilized and pulled forth (see chapter 8 for the legend). In neighboring Cantabria, a similar shrine to Mary, that of Lebeña, bears a similar story (chapter 8).

The Monastery of Montserrat, Catalonia

In southern Spain, throughout the Alpujarra mountains, the mountain of Mulhacén holds sacred sway, once for Muslims and now for Christians, with myriad little pilgrim roads to hilltop hermitages (see Our Lady of the Snows in chapter 16). Several Buddhist retreats are camouflaged in the Alpujarras as well and visiting them feels like being on a sacred mountain in Tibet or Nepal.

Many other mountains have Virgin Mary shrines at their top. There is Nuestra Señora de la Peña de Francia, a mountain range in western Spain whose highest peak is the Peña de Francia (chapter 14). And the famous Lady of Puig came to King Jaime I in the thirteenth century, on the eve of battle before he was to take Valencia; she appeared on Mount Puig, north of Valencia (chapter 11). Now there is a monastery in the town of Puig dedicated to this Virgin.

In the interior of eastern Spain, an ancient ancestry unfolds in the Sierra Mariola (chapter 15). This mountain range is venerated for the diverse plant and animal life and medicinal and aromatic herbs that grow throughout its hills. Locals have harvested these herbs for centuries, perhaps millennia. The Sierra Mariola has been occupied for millennia by humans attracted to its rich ecosystem, its herbs, and its vast cave system. The power of this place is so profound that visitors feel an invisible energy, like a special charge in the air, as rich as the aromatic spells given off under the midday sun.

The oldest caves in Iberia go back to the Paleolithic, when early humans occupied stretches of southern France and into Iberia. Their cave etchings and paintings were executed with a style and vision that left even great modern painters like Picasso in awe. Some caves show evidence of residence; others are filled with exquisite paintings, seeming to be used only for special times and rituals.

It is clear these Paleolithic caves were intentional places, with animated and carefully created images of animals whose placement in the caves has a ritualistic mood. In a world when humans lived much more in contact with the natural world than we do today, it is hard not to imagine that these paintings had deep symbolic significance, some even depicting or facilitating transcendent experiences.

Among the many caves, some of the best to visit are in the north of Spain. These are Tito Bustillo and Cueva El Pindal in Asturias, Altamira and Cueva del Castillo in Cantabria, and Cueva de Santimamiñe in Pais Vasco (all in chapter 8). Altamira is closed to visits but has a reproduction of its most spectacular chamber right next door, along with an excellent museum. Paleolithic caves also exist, though in less concentration, in central and southern Spain, such as around Málaga and Almería.

Many millennia later, numerous Christian monasteries and hermitages were built right into cave openings. One wonders if this was not a harkening back to an earlier connection through these earthly veins into a deep ancestral spirituality. Such monasteries are San Juan de la Peña in Navarra and the Monasterio de Suso in Rioja (chapter 13), the Monasterio de Santa María La Real in Nájera (chapter 7), and the Santuario de San Saturio in Soria (chapter 13).

San Saturio is an astounding cave dwelling. The entire hermitage and chapel have been built onto a cave system so that from the outside you see a monastic building standing midway along the mountain slope dipping down to the Duero River. But upon reaching it you must enter a cave entrance via a deep shelf in the rock. Approximately one hundred feet under the shelf is a small cave opening that takes you to a half nature-made, half human-made interior. San Saturio's human-made part is very masculine as is the shrine to this male saint set at the very top, nearest the sky. But within the belly is an ethereal shrine to the Virgin, a very feminine shrine within a very feminine natural place of cave and river. Could this hermitage's appeal be in its balance of male and female, heaven and Earth?

The cave niche where the Virgin Mary appeared to the king Don Garcia in the tenth century, now set at the back of the church of the Monasterio de Santa Maria la Real in Nájera, on the Camino to Santiago, La Rioja

CHAPTER FOUR

✻

$\mathcal{S}$acred Cities

NOTIONS HERE OF WHAT MAKES a city sacred come from what the Spanish have shown and told me defines a sacred city for them.

One sort of sacred city in Spain comes about as a sacred spot that through a vision or revelation became an epicenter of miracles and devotion that grew into a city. Another type of sacred city already existed but came to take on a particularly charged spiritual significance for the people through certain events or through an overarching symbolic charge that place had and still has for certain large groups of people. Santiago de Compostela is a good example of the first sort of sacred city. It began as a burial site wherein miraculous things happened and a pilgrimage to it made it into a city. The other sort of sacred city is nicely represented by Toledo, Córdoba, Granada (chapter 15), and Ávila (chapter 14). These cities possess a history that is sacred to certain religious groups as well as possess a seductive aura for visitors of any lean.

But even more widely, there is a sacred element inherently built in to nearly all villages, towns, and cities in Spain. Every settlement however big or small has annual pilgrimages, or *romerias*, to a hermitage or shrine. Most places have several of these throughout the year, not just one. Spanish cities are connected to their hinterland. The land is sacred and the city a part of it. In some ways modern Spaniards have lost none of the omnipresent sacredness that their Iberian and Celtiberian ancestors had, where everything potentially emanated from the gods. This might seem contradicted by the decidedly secular post-Franco modern society, but little shrines on corners and over doorways or wall niches indicate that the gods still live among the people.

Pilgrim paths go from the city to peripheral hermitages in the countryside. They speak of a radiating sacredness, of a connection of city folk with the wilder countryside, and of a cyclical going out into the wild world to seek one's spirit when spring arrives and turns to summer or when winter is on its way and the world is readying for inward reflection and slumber. The hermitages, *ermitas*, are everywhere. Though they will be closed all year expect for the day of their sacred pilgrimage or saint's feast day, they are built in some of the most breathtaking spots around cities, towns, and villages. Their spirit is strong any time of year. But if you visit during a local hermitage's romeria, you will be in for a treat of sacred walking, sacred and profane song, food, drink, and lively cheer.

Finally, the old Spanish cities and towns have a sun pattern design. The heart center is the Plaza Mayor and streets, like the sun's rays, radiate out from there. Such organic urban planning gives a place heart and soul. People have a rich social life because of this plan, indicating on a fundamental level that each of society's members is held as important, as sacred. It is very hard to be alone in a place whose citizens revolve around a heart center. These heart centers possess covered markets, several churches and chapels, and myriad food, clothing, and services shops, all interspersed with packed cafés and pubs. Everyone comes and goes along the rays of the sun, to the center and out again and back the next day, recharging their batteries each time. Daily life in Spanish villages, towns, and cities pos-

View of the Alhambra from Granada's Albaicin neighborhood, Andalusia

sesses a spirit of community that is uplifting and transcendent. It is so nurturing spiritually to be in such a place that lives thus that I wish we could emulate this dedication to one another through our built environment, bringing warming sun patterns to our all too commonly soulless and centerless suburbs of North America.

Power Spots: Sacred Cities That Arise from Vision or Revelation

Santiago de Compostela is the sacred city par excellence. The city's entire existence came into being over a vision given to a hermit who followed a field of stars in the ninth century. In that field, he discovered what the bishop Theodomir confirmed was the tomb of Saint James the Greater. This spot of discovery is where the medieval cathedral of Santiago now stands in the heart of the city.

The tomb indeed contained a body without a head; St. James had been decapitated in AD 44 and legend weaves a tale of a stone boat bearing him and his two most dedicated disciples away from the Holy Land to Galicia. Buried on a sacred mountain, Pico Sacro, within a pre-Christian burial space, St. James would lie dormant until needed. With the North African conquest, Christian identity in Spain had a mirror against which to formulate its shape. A hermit, a field of stars, and one of the great apostles were just the ticket.

But there is another headless contender, a more local Galician saint, Priscillian, who could be buried there instead of St. James. Priscillian was a charismatic ascetic accused of sorcery by the Catholic bishops under Emperor Maximus. His movement espoused a number of things in conflict with official practices, such as the belief that Jesus did not exist prior to his birth via the Blessed Virgin Mary. This belief led his followers to fast on Christmas Day and on Sundays. They also believed in the transmigration of souls. Priscillian was tried for heresy and found guilty of practicing magic. He was martyred by beheading in AD 386. Some believe that he was buried on Pico Sacro.

Whoever's headless body that tomb contained, St. James was a much better candidate to rally the spirit and mood to win the conquest of the to-and-fro chess game instigated by the Muslims.

Since the ninth century, St. James's tomb and shrine became one of the most important pilgrimage sites across Europe and remarkably it continues to be so today. People who walk to this sacred city come for all manner of reasons, just like their medieval counterparts. Called the *Camino* (chapter 7), this is a pilgrim's road whose diverse European paths converge in the north of Spain at the Pyrenees and then proceed as one across the entire north until it reaches Santiago de Compostela and St. James's tomb near the Atlantic coast.

From the time when St. James's interred bones were discovered, in AD 813 or 814, the site was named the *field of stars*, possibly giving this name to the city, St. James *(Sant Iago)* of the field of stars *(campus stellae)*. After World War II, however, excavations took place underneath the cathedral in Santiago and archaeologists discovered that there indeed was an ancient

View of Toledo and the city's cathedral from the outer banks of the Tajo River, Castilla La Mancha

burial site there. It included the tomb of Bishop Theodomir, the man who verified the hermit's vision and broadcast the news of St. James's tomb. The ancient burial mound was known as a *compostum*.

Whether the city's name is derived from "field of stars" or from "burial heap" its ancient lineage is authentic and gave rise to the city as a sacred site from its beginning. Moreover, long before the arrival of Christianity to this remote region of the Peninsula, Galicia was largely under Celtic influence. Today the Celtic tradition is deemed by many as important as is the Christian.

It is very probable that Santiago lies on a more ancient ritual road that goes all the way to the Atlantic coast. There is a good deal of pagan overlay to the story of St. James and of the *Camino*. Scholars, regional folklorists, and local storytellers consider the probability of an ancient initiatory path that pre-Christian Iberians took, east to west across northern Spain. It could have been a road in honor of the great power of the sun

and its east-west path of death and rebirth, culminating in the final destination on the Galician coast, the village of Finisterre, where the Atlantic
dramatically swallowed up the sun. This indigenous road might likewise
have then been reinforced by the Romans and their sun worship; they did
build an altar to the sun in Finisterre. Jutting out into what the Galicians
call the Costa da Muerte, "Coast of Death," Finisterre might have been
considered a gateway to the world of the dead; some believe the physical
gateway stands at the spot of the city of Santiago de Compostela.

To the ancients, this gateway was most likely a door not only to the
world of the dead but to resurrection. Herein is another curious connection they had with the Christians to come. Not only does Jesus represent
passing through the gateway of death to resurrection but so too does St.
James's return, as it were, again and again, in battle against the Iberian
Muslims.

Even in the legends of St. James's dead body's arrival in Galicia, we
have interesting pagan clues. When his stone boat arrived from Jerusalem,
it came to shore along the Coast of Death. Here we get another resurrection about to happen. On the shore, a matriarchal and pagan queen,
Queen Lupa, was overseeing the wedding of her daughter to a local prince.
The latter sat on horseback. When St. James's boat ran aground, the horse
was spooked and ran with the groom into the dark mysterious waters of the
Atlantic. They did not emerge for a long time and were thought lost but
through the sacred intervention of St. James, the groom and horse
emerged from the water covered head to hoof and foot with scallop shells.

Scallop shells are taken as the natural symbol of the goddess and the
ancient initiatory symbol of the pre-Christian pilgrimage to Finisterre. Initiates took this pilgrimage by following the stars as well as by a belief that
the earth beneath them had a certain energy—ley lines if you will—that
guided them to the final land of the setting sun.

Scallop shells as a sacred feminine symbol also point to the fact that
Galicia was matriarchal. This was the case prior to Roman contact. Even
after Roman culture, and then the later Christian patriarchy, seeped into
the area, matriarchal practices persisted, some right up to the present day
in the remotest of areas. This legend seems to suggest that the indigenous
matriarchy was finding a way to balance the new patriarchy that had just
arrived and was not about to go away. There are other tales regarding St.
James's arrival in Galicia, which pick up the trail in chapter 7.

Among other sacred cities born of power spots in Spain, another good
example is A Coruña, also in Galicia. This place goes back to the Gallaeci,
the indigenous Celtic-speaking inhabitants who are the legendary builders

of Breogan's tower. Historically, it was the Romans who first built this old lighthouse watchtower overlooking the Atlantic. But among certain Galicians, legend tells that the tower predates Romans and was the spot from which Breogan and his sons set sail to Ireland and took Celtic customs to the northern island. As such, A Coruña is a holy place for Galicians who cherish their Celtic ancestry and its associated nature-based spirituality. Breogan is so important in Galicia that he is mentioned in Galicia's national anthem and is considered the founding father of Galicia (see chapter 10).

Guadalupe is another city founded on vision and legend (chapter 14). These visions concern the Virgen de Guadalupe, who was found buried on a hill by a shepherd who had been divinely guided there by her. Some esoteric legends say that contact with the iconic image of the Blessed Virgin resulted in amazing things. Once it brought a local farmer's dead cow back to life. Another says she raised a bereft rancher's son from the dead. Soon thereafter, Guadalupe's shrine was built on the spot where the icon was found, which is the current monastery of Guadalupe. The town grew up around its miraculous resident.

Zaragoza is in a sense another one of these cities of visions except that it already existed when its vision arrived. St. James is fabled to have evangelized in Spain. In AD 40 it is said that he visited Zaragoza where he saw a vision of the Virgin Mary. In his vision she swept down from heaven astride the top of a jasper pillar carved and carried by two angels (chapter 13). The spot on which this happened was already a sacred spot to Celtiberians and to Romans after them and the pillar might have been a sacred marker in this field. The sacred spot sits in the heart of Zaragoza, on the bank of the Rio Ebro. Today, a basilica dedicated to the Virgin stands on the spot the pillar came down to St. James. St. James's vision came as encouragement to him not to give up his work. That vision really put Zaragoza on the sacred map. The Virgen del Pilar is the patroness of all Spain.

Historically and Symbolically Charged Cities That Become Sacred

Many of Spain's town and city origins go back into the far reaches of time as hilltop defensive villages. Such settlements of the Iron Age Iberians and Celtic speakers persisted as Romans, Visigoths, and North

*Urban vista of Santiago de Compostela with the towers of the
city's famous pilgrim's cathedral, Galicia*

Africans arrived and built over them. Segovia, Ávila, and Zaragoza are
good examples of these.

Other cities were founded by seafarers from the classical world: Greeks,
Phoenicians, Carthaginians, and Romans and over time grew into significant sacred cities, such as Empúries, Barcelona, Sagunto, and Valencia. The
latter is one of the homes to one of the potentially authentic Holy Grails in
the world, not to mention one of the most compassionate of Virgins, the
Virgen de los Desamparados, the Virgin of the Helpless, or Abandoned.

Other cities came into being in the Middle Ages as hamlets huddled
around a great fortified castle. Under times of duress, people left their little
homes below the castle-fortress hill and went behind the castle walls until
the danger had passed. Little by little these clusters emerged into towns
and cities radiating out from that original center. Burgos is a good example
of this. Originally a castle and huddled villages, literally called *burgos,* the
city became Castile's capital and has taken on sacred significance with its
cathedral and other sacred buildings and monasteries. Burgos also sits next
door to the region that claims Europe's oldest hominid remains, giving this
region an ancestral significance that is profound for the continent and that
also delineates just how very ancient Iberia is from the human perspective.

So many people have occupied the Iberian Peninsula that many places
have layers over layers of significance and sacredness. Some cities are espe-

cially charged with historical and symbolic meaning. Cities such as Toledo, Seville, Córdoba, and Granada receive annual visitors drawn to them for their mixed Jewish, Islamic, and Christian history (chapter 15). Among these visitors are *returnees,* Jews and Muslims who claim Iberian origins and whose ancestors were expelled centuries ago. They come to these cities to reclaim their sacred past.

Finally, there are those who in the cities are reviving ancient spiritualities, reclaiming all of Iberia's sacred birth rite, not just the most recent overlay of Catholicism, though even that is experiencing a mystical revival in small pockets. Modern-day Spanish seekers are enjoying the religious freedom of their modern society and many authentic spiritualities are coming back. Nature-revering animistic pagan spiritualities of the earliest Europeans and of the Celts and Celtiberians are back. Weekend tours of otherwise secular urbanites are going to monasteries, shrines, and hermitages in the countryside to take the fresh air and to learn about one's heritage. Some Sephardic Jews are returning and establishing homes and synagogues in a place that for millennia was home to their ancestors. North Africans on their way to France for work make detours to Andalusia's Islamic cities to pay their respects. Some Catholic Spaniards claiming they are descended from Moriscos, Iberian Muslims who were forced to convert five hundred years ago, are converting to Islam and altering their lifestyle. Others are taking up yoga and meditation and seeking an ancient spirituality that has no track record on the Peninsula—a clean slate if you will—and are exploring Hinduism and Buddhism, which are also arriving with immigrants from Asia. Ironically, I have also met missionaries from Latin America, former Catholics who have become Protestants, who are coming to Spain to evangelize a new Christianity. In all, while Spain is a secular nation, as you travel to city and through countryside, you will find that it is humming with vibrant spiritual energy.

$\int$ acred Animals and Plants

Sacred Animals

MUCH LIKE IBERIA'S PALEOLITHIC occupation by early humans, animals also found the Peninsula a more hospitable place when vast stretches of Europe lay under cold and ice. Human existence and animal existence in Iberia are intertwined from very early times. A particular number of animal species were crucial to Iberian peoples' physical and spiritual existence, such as horses, deer, bison and bulls, boars, and wolves. This holds true today even with rapid developments and many decades of industrialization. Spain is still at its heart an agrarian and herding society, one whose psyche is entwined with that of the animals and plants with which they have shared existence for millennia.

A great example of this is the annual demonstrations of shepherds and their animals in Madrid when the streets fill with sheep, donkeys, and men and women with long sticks. They come to demand continued protection of ancient migratory routes through Spain. Moving animals from summer to winter pastures and back, transhumance, is such an ancient skill in Iberia that we get our English word from the Spanish, *transhumancia*.

Cave paintings, pottery vessels, ancient designs forged in copper, bronze, and iron, and stone carvings from all ages—including more recently the capitals of Romanesque churches with their mythic-moral teachings using animal and plant symbols—all depict certain animals again and again, holding sacred sway with human beings and their spirituality. The ancient animals who appear over and over are first and foremost horses, deer and elk, wolves, bears, bulls, and wild boar. Two other ancient animals appear frequently, the rabbit and the Iberian lynx. There are many other critical beings, such as eagles, falcons, storks, goats, foxes, weasels, badgers, and minks, but these are the primary players in the mytho-sacred world of Spain.

A Bronze Age Vetton bull from the region on display in a public building in Ávila, Castilla y León

In a shamanic sense, places can have power animals just like people. Power animals are the sacred spirit of an animal that joins with a person as something of a spiritual guardian and companion. The horse must be Spain's primary power animal. The horse makes a very early appearance and it has persisted. Wild horses roam still in remote parts of Galicia. From the time of the Paleolithic cave paintings right up to the present, each people who occupied Iberia depicted horses as central creatures in their sacred art. When Greeks invaded parts of Iberia, they noted the prowess of the horse-riding Iberians and their great skill in defense and warfare. Amid the mystical animal populations painted at Altamira and other cave sites across Spain, the horse is a frequent resident. Early Iberian and Celtiberian pottery vessels, with their distinctive animated black illustration designs, show the horse with people most prevalently.

Among Iberians and Celtiberians, beautiful fibulae, sturdy broaches or clasps, of horses or horse and rider can be seen in the Numantine museum in Soria (chapter 13). In this same museum are exquisite vessel paintings of the Iberians and Celtiberians with their animated characters of hunters and warriors on horseback.

Other ancient and holy creatures who also still make Spain home are the bear, the wolf, the Iberian lynx, the wild boar, and the bull. Bears, wolves, and lynx have been severely endangered, and although the wolf and the bear are making a comeback, the Iberian lynx is frighteningly on the verge of disappearing.

Evidence of bears was uncovered at Atapuerca near Burgos (chapter 7) where railroad workers uncovered two caves that revealed hominid presence in Europe as far back as 800,000 years ago. This is still the oldest hominid site in Europe. In one of the cave pits archaeologists found the bones of cave bears, implying a connection between early humans and bears.

Bears still roam parts of northern Spain though they were once more prevalent in other parts of the Peninsula. Stories of Asturia's king Favila being mauled by a bear are told with as much admiration for the bear as for the strong king who succumbed to this early but noble death. He only ruled for two years, AD 737–739, before a fatal day of bear hunting brought his term to an early end.

The bear also is a miracle creature in modern conservation efforts, and Spain is one of the last European strongholds for the brown bear. Bears have long been admired for their great strength and for their regenerative abilities, sleeping a near-death hibernation to emerge vital and reborn in the spring. Like the deer, the bear in Old European mythic thinking is associated with Artemis, the goddess of birth and innocence. Deer and bears are held as ideals of birthing and motherhood in how they regenerate themselves (horns with the deer and hibernation with the bears) and how they care for their young.

The bear is also the symbol of Madrid. There in the center of the city near the Puerta del Sol stands a sculpture of a bear nibbling at what is called a *madroño* tree, a Mediterranean tree that produces red berries that bears like to eat. Here the bear has come to represent the inhabitants' resilience and strength in the face of adversity as well as their general joy for life.

Wolves are making a comeback through better understanding and conservation efforts, and roam large parts of the northern and central Peninsula, though they are still an endangered creature. In the recent past, wolves were almost eliminated by a program under Franco that encouraged farmers and ranchers to kill them. Thankfully, that has been countered with better knowledge and conservation efforts. Spain today is one of the last refuges for the European wolf.

*Romanesque horses carved on the entrace portal of Girona's Monestir
de Sant Pere de Galligants, Catalonia*

In the medieval period, there was a strong association of the wolf with
nature's more sinister occult side, most likely those aspects of being human
that people pushed down and concealed. In a less sinister manner, in pre-
Roman Spain wolves were associated with the afterlife. With the Romans,
the wolf was the symbol of their people's birth in the form of the twins
Romulus and Remus who were suckled by a mother wolf. Though wolves
compete with humans for similar food sources—wolves are even known to
gulp down grape clusters hanging in vineyards when in need of a quick
energy boost—they also hold us in awe of their intelligence, their social
organization, and their almost telepathic cunning.

As evidence of the wolf's reverence by the Iron Age peoples, we have a
clay trumpet from Numantia (chapter 13) whose bell is shaped in the head
of a wolf with its mouth open. Ceramic vessel paintings of the Iberians and
Celtiberians also show hunting wolves chasing a deer or elk. Given their
social nature and strength, it is easy to see them as nearly human but with
traits we would like to emulate.

In parts of northern Spain, wolves' teeth were believed to possess
healing powers and were worn by the sick person until they got better. For
Iberian Celtic speakers, the wolf's prowess went with them into battle, in
the shape of war horns and with their pelts on warriors' backs. To these
same peoples the wolf was seen as the animal associated with the Other
World and in possession of certain mystical powers that come from that
realm.

The Iberian lynx was admired by Romans for its stealth and speed, so much so that the Roman legions in Iberia used it to represent them on their armor and banners. For indigenous Iberians, the lynx was equated with underworld divinity: its prowess reflected a connection to a divine source. The lynx arrived in Iberia with the Ice Age migrations from Eurasia and stayed long enough to become its own species. After millennia of solid existence, the Iberian lynx are treacherously close to extinction in spite of conservation efforts. This is due to an epidemic decline in the rabbit population, their main source of food. They are also gravely threatened by car collisions, falling into fox traps, poisoning, and poaching. Once living all across Iberia, they now live in only two small protected reserves in Andalusia. Recent in-captivity births have encouraged some to hope for a possible comeback if the young lynx can successfully be introduced into the wild.

Rabbits, the lynx's most important food, also date back to the ancient Iberians. The European rabbit most likely originated in the Iberian Peninsula. When Phoenicians arrived here over three thousand years ago from other parts of the Mediterranean they were taken by the strange creatures and their curious nature. Thinking they were similar to the hyrax, a small mammal with a blunt tail from the Middle East and North Africa, they called the rabbits *shafan*, "hyrax" in Phoenician, a language most closely related to Hebrew and Aramaic. They labeled Iberia, *i-shfanim*, the island of the "rabbits." With the arrival of the Romans, *i-shfanim* morphed into Hispania, which eventually developed into España. This is one theory about the etymology of Spain's name, but it more importantly points to the deep roots between rabbits and Iberians. Rabbits also proved a prolific food source until recent times, when diseases have treacherously decimated their populations. Admired for their abundance, speed, and strength, rabbits were portrayed on some Iberian Roman coins during the rule of Hadrian (AD 117–138) at the feet of a reclining, olive branch–holding personification of Iberia. Another coin shows Hispania with her olive branch kneeling before the emperor Hadrian with a rabbit sitting between them. Hadrian was from Hispania. That he chose the rabbit to represent his birthplace is significant.

Deer and elk are among the most ancient creatures in Spain connected to humans. Cave art and even remains of deer and elk, as in a ritual burial pit in Tito Bustillo cave in Asturias (chapter 8), reflect a long fascination with these animals. They have long been both a source of food as well as potent symbols of strength, regenerative powers, and nobility, and are often considered the mystics of the animal world in ancient European mythology. In some places in northern Spain, people used to pass a deer's antler through spring water in order to remove the effects of the evil eye.

The bull and the boar are memorialized in the great stone carved boulders around Ávila, either as funerary markers, territorial markers, sacred ritual sites, or all of the above. Both animals continue to this day to feed the soul and belly of the Spanish. The Iberian pig might be one of the most important animals to the Spanish economy, with its unique acorn-eating habits (the oak likewise being highly sacred here). This is especially true in Castilla y León and Extremadura, where acorns, pigs, and the Virgin Mary are intimately intertwined (chapter 14).

The boar was sacred to the Celtic speakers of Iberia. It was seen as a supernatural creature, a symbol of the druids as well as of a Celtic warrior, given their fierce and aggressive nature when under attack. A terrific funerary altar with great stone boars and lions and a needlelike obelisk was found near the village of Chinchilla in La Mancha, close to Albacete. It is now on exhibit in Madrid's archaeology museum. Dating to the sixth century BCE, it makes a strong statement, towering overhead with its powerful, masculine beasts guarding it.

The boar and bull are also carved in Romanesque church capitals. A particularly Celtic-looking boar can be seen at the Romanesque church of La Oliva near Villaviciosa, Asturias.

Bulls clearly are associated with Spain, though their sacredness does not come through in the modern bullfight. Bulls are, however, among the animals depicted in cave paintings, indicating their importance as an animal ally, as food, and as spiritual force for early Iberians. Across the Mediterranean the bull has also been associated with the goddess, its crescent moon–shaped horns being her symbol. This is the very symbol on which the Virgin Mary stands, as she is also associated with the crescent moon. In this case, it represents her immortality, that she is beyond time and the temporal phases of the moon. This is a direct carry-over from several pagan goddesses, including Isis.

The bull has also been an animal many ancient cultures sacrificed, such as within the Roman cult of Mithra. A Mithraeum of this nature has been uncovered in Mérida in southwestern Spain (chapter 14). Prior to the Roman cult, ancient Iberians venerated the bull. They likely sacrificed it to a higher power as well as ate it for food. The best examples of this veneration are seen in the land of the Vettones around Ávila where great stone bulls and boars have been found across the landscape. The most famous are the Toros de Guisando dating to around the fourth to third centuries BCE. The Vettones were herders and hunters whose life likely was seminomadic, moving from summer to winter pastures and settlements. Their survival depended on several animals, among the most important being the bull and the wild boar. Horses were also important, so much so that a person was buried with his horse's spurs and bridle.

A few other animals important to mention are snakes, bees, storks, eagles, falcons, frogs, lizards, scallops, dogs, and cats.

The serpent in ancient European mythology was the symbol of the goddess and the cyclical nature of life, but has since come to represent the ego and all other things human beings needed to overcome to transcend the pain and suffering of the world. One of the most exquisite representations of serpents in Spanish sacred art is in the church of San Pedro de la Rua in Estella, where on the altar near the Virgin Mary are three serpents braided into one pillar to the Virgin's right (chapter 7). Because these enigmatic serpents are not under Mary's feet, as they are traditionally placed, perhaps they partake of the ancient symbol of the goddess as well. And as three, not one, perhaps they also represent the non-dualistic realm, having moved beyond light and dark by weaving these polarities into a timeless whole.

Bees figure in several legends, especially in Rioja and Castilla y León, in one case associated with the miracles of San Juan de Ortega on the pilgrim's road near Burgos (chapter 7), and in another with the discovery of Rioja's patroness, the Virgin Mary of Valvanera (chapter 13).

Storks are revered everywhere they decide to perch, and some towns encourage their nesting on the building tops by placing posts and supports to hold the nesting materials. Storks return year after year. For humans down below, this faithfulness has become a comfort that is given sacred reign; in revering the storks, people hope to receive some sympathetic magic, transference of steadiness, faithfulness, and solidity that the storks possess. Among birds, eagles and falcons are royal animals and figure in sacred stories concerning kings and holy spots, such as the founding of the monastery in Nájera (chapter 7).

Frogs and lizards are potentially returning souls of the departed who did not make the pilgrimage while alive to San Andrés de Teixido on the north coast of Galicia (chapter 10). This belief is so widespread that locals traditionally have been careful not to harm these creatures, just in case they are a human soul making their sacred journey.

The scallop shell originated as a symbol of the goddess and was appropriated by the Christian pilgrimage to Santiago de Compostela around the time the matriarchal ways of the north were being overcome by a patriarchal faith (chapters 4 and 7). But the importance of the goddess has remained, in the form of Mary as well as in how easy it is to be female in

Spain compared to other Mediterranean nations. Mary's prevalence, so often overshadowing her Son, actually makes one wonder if the goddess cult and matriarchy still aren't the norm here (chapter 6).

Sacred Plants

In the realm of the sacred plant kingdom across Spain we find sacred forests and trees, healing and magical herbs, sacred flowers, and mushrooms. Spain has some of Europe's largest protected natural parks, among them diverse and enchanted forests. The most stunning, and heavily protected, is Muniellos in Asturias, where a primordial European beech forest stands, descendents of the original beech forests that once stretched across Iberia and other parts of Europe. It is such a treasure that only twenty people are allowed in the forest a day and the waiting list can be long, weeks and months long.

Among the holiest of trees in Spain are oak, beech, yew, cypress, chestnut, holly, and olive. One or several varieties of these trees are often found intentionally planted or selected around sacred sites. Oak is perhaps the most common of shrine trees. Often a single tree is deemed holy, such as the cypress at the entrance to Santo Domingo de Silos's monastery.

Certain fruit trees are also sacred, especially the pomegranate, the fig, and the apple. Each has either mythological or Biblical references. The apple in particular is prevalent as the fruit held in the Virgin Mary's hand when she is seated on her throne with Jesus on her lap on myriad altars across Spain. The apple represents humanity's redemption and salvation. Though not

A venerated fig tree on Málaga's Plaza de San Agustín, Andalusia

The symbol of the city of Granada, the pomegranate, from which the name "Granada" is derived, Andalusia

named in Genesis, the apple is frequently associated with the fruit eaten in Eden. As such, the apple tree is sometimes shown as the wood of the cross, that is, of sin and redemption.

The pomegranate, the symbol of the city of Granada, is associated with fertility and eternity. A fruit of Persephone, who exists half the year in the Underworld and half above ground, reflects the association between fertility and eternity in the overall cycle of life. In Christianity, the pomegranate with its seeds exposed—as it often is depicted in church art—represents the resurrection: an image of hope and plenty, an opening of the tomb to find something great waiting within. The fig tree, though some associate it with Adam and Eve and their demise, is really a tree of knowledge and a tree of plenty. And they grow abundantly throughout Spain, showering the earth with plentiful dark, sweet fruit.

Trees are important spiritual entities in Spain. I often see a great old tree being venerated in a city—a stone protective wall built around it and it being lovingly cared for by someone. Surrounding churches and shrines in the city and the country, certain native trees are intentionally selected or planted. For example, the Marian church in Cantabria, Santa Maria de Lebeña, has a yew and an olive tree standing next to it that were planted when this tenth-century church was built. They are as important to the place as the Celtic sun stone found at the altar and the Virgin of the shrine to whom it was built.

Trees are held so dear in Asturias that several have been declared natural monuments by the Asturian agency for natural spaces. The trees were selected as monuments either for their immense age or for sentimental, communal reasons. Curiously, nearly all of these Ent-like beings grow next to a chapel or country church. For instance, in front of the parochial church of San Julián in the village of Tueya, Lavandera, in the Gijón area, the natural monument, a truffle oak, *Quercus robur*, lives at 21 meters height, a trunk circumference of 6.7 meters, and a canopy diameter of 25 meters. Likewise, other monumental oaks grow near the chapel of San Pedro, in Valentín, in the Tineo area (believed to be over five hundred years old), another near the chapel of San Antonio in Bermeigo (Quirós district), and another revered oak grows near the church of Santa Coloma in the Allande area. Likewise, sacred *Taxus baccata*, English yew, grow near chapels, such as near the Santa Maria church in Bermeigo (Quirós). There is another sacred yew in Lago (Allande area) by its chapel of Santa Maria, and another in the mountain town of Salas next to the parochial church of San Martín. San Martín's yew is believed to be over eight hundred years old.

It is no accident that oak groves ring around little churches and chapels. Oak has been held sacred for millennia in Spain as well as in many other European areas. Chapels likely were built in sites held sacred by prior faith inhabitants and so also mark possible continuity there as well. A sacred spring may not be far away.

Among the most sacred of trees is the great oak of Guernica, symbol of the ancient, enduring, and lyrical culture of the Basque people. Since Franco encouraged German planes to bomb the city in 1937, this oak has become a more potent symbol of the Basque people's endurance. The great old tree, now dead, has been resurrected by a young, resilient replacement tree that is growing its roots in an already deep vein (chapter 8). It was under the branches of its predecessor that the Basque parliament met from the Middle Ages until 1876.

One of the most spirited forests I've been in is in the valley of San Millán de la Cogolla in Rioja. There the forest can be experienced on a path to the hermit's cave of the fifth-century San Millán in a forest of beech and pine—the earth covered in rich soil, rocks, and mosses, and everywhere is a mushroom lovers' paradise. Here the trees talk a little more loudly than in other forests, as if the modern world hasn't discouraged them yet. It is easy to see why the fifth-century hermit turned miracle worker picked this place (see chapter 13).

In addition to trees, other plants are deemed sacred. The lily certainly is the universal symbol for the Virgin Mary and, on entering a church where a wedding has just taken place, this is the most common aroma emanating from the altar, near the Virgin. Roses serve the same symbolism. The lily explicitly aligned itself with the Virgin in Nájera as one of three symbols the King of Navarra found with her in a cave one day while out hunting (chapter 7).

Healing medicinal herbs have a long tradition of magical veneration and cultivation and are still widely used to treat all manner of maladies. The people of the Sierra Mariola around Bocairent (chapter 15) in southeastern Spain have for millennia gathered wild herbs, such as rosemary, lavender, thyme, and sage, to use for healing as well as culinary applications. Every day along the side of the cathedral in Granada, herbalists have traditionally sold medicinal herbs and teas as well as cooking spices. They are as much a part of the experience of visiting the cathedral as the building itself. For St. John's Night celebrations on June 24, in honor of St. John the Baptist, people build bonfires and jump over them for good luck and to chase away bad luck; at midnight they gather herbs and place them in spring water. As the sun rises on the next morning, they take this herb water and wash themselves with it as a final purifying act. Collectively, fire, water, and herbs work to cleanse a person of all the dark energy of the prior year, readying them for the next.

The continued practice of healing plant lore and of traditional healers who work with plants, *curanderos*, are still present in every region of Spain. Many weekly markets have an herb seller, someone who harvests, dries, and sells herbs for both culinary and medicinal purposes.

In the mountains of Andalusia's Sierra de Aracena, as well as in the forests and mountains of the north, grows the fabled mushroom fly agaric (*Armanita muscaria*), the very mushroom of fairy tales on which little elves perch, all red with white spots. In fact this hallucinogenic mushroom was used by the shamans of old Europe and of Asia in aiding a shift of consciousness and shamanic visions. Though not recommended for the uninitiated clumsy modern who only seeks escape, not wisdom, this mushroom's presence here is still a nice link to sacred European ancestry from a time when altered states were in better, more capable hands. The fly agaric is in fact deadly if ingested, though ancient Iberians found a way to process it for optimal use without mortality as a side effect. The Sierra de Aracena is mostly rugged scrub hills with isolated, half-abandoned villages and their citrus orchards. It also has stretches of untouched oak forest, and it is among these hallowed trees where the fly agaric likes to grow.

Plants, animals, and humans are intertwined with one another, whether we recognize this in our daily lives or not. In a place like Spain, with its ancient Paleolithic foundation where survival and veneration are interwoven with plants and animals, this connection has held on in spite of centuries of human alteration. Even today in the postmodern era with rapid changes underway, Spain's roots to its herding, planting, gathering, and hunting past are still deep. The garden of Europe, Spain produces the greatest exports of fruits and vegetables for the rest of Europe. Its herders and ranchers are still engaged in full livelihoods and shepherds are quite visible throughout the country. And yuppie urbanites literally flee to the countryside each festival and weekend to reconnect with the wild world of their ancestry.

CHAPTER SIX

The Importance of Mary

SPAIN IS A PART OF EUROPE WHERE matriarchy was
well documented and strong and held on in certain pockets long after the
Romans and Christianity took root. Queen Isabel la Católica of the fifteenth century is said to have enjoyed easy movement and power because
of holdovers of the matriarchal culture. And the prominence of the Virgin
Mary as the main focus of Christian veneration above and beyond her Son
also speaks of this culture's persistence.

The first time I really got an inside glimpse of the eternal depth of the
importance of Mary was at the end of the long holy week, Semana Santa.
Commencing with Palm Sunday and wrapping up with Easter, I was condi-
tioned like most Americans to believe that the culmination of holy week
was the great resurrection of Jesus and his message to mankind of our eternal nature. So it was that I arose early Easter morning in Seville, donned
my formal attire, and readied to go to the neighborhood church for an
inspirational message and celebration. It had already been a long week, all
of the streets of Seville caught up in processions of floats of Mary and of
scenes of the last days of Jesus passing through town. During that week,
many times were profoundly transcendent due to the shift of focus from
everyday activities to holy processions. Floats left different churches for
their circuits at different times of night and day. The week had climaxed
on Friday night with a display of macabre floats depicting Jesus' crucifixion. Saturday was deeply emotional as people displayed Mary's loss and her

grief over her Son's death. By Saturday evening, we were spent, but I was certain that Sunday would rejuvenate us.

Well, my adopted Spanish family slept in and when I went out to join the celebration, the streets were dead. It was as if the entire town had evacuated overnight and I hadn't gotten the word. When I asked my adopted Spanish sister about this, when she finally woke up at 1 p.m., she explained, "We value Jesus, it's just that we identify with Mary. We feel her loss, to us that is real. We feel her love for her Son. She is like our mother. We can talk to her. She can intercede for us on any matter with God. She's one of us. She's like our own mothers."

Some people I spoke to felt they could approach her before they could approach Jesus because she was so human. She then could put in a good word with Jesus and requests in this manner could get to God's ears more swiftly. Others also explained that they identify with Mary as human, especially her loss of her Son. The experience of such great loss and deep sadness creates someone who understands, who is compassionate and empathetic to human suffering. As such, especially in Andalusia, people identify more with the grieving Mary than with the rising Son. In the south, many statues of Mary show her as the Mater Dolorosa, with crystal tears running down her cheek.

While this experience of the Virgin is especially pronounced in the south of Spain, it seems less fatalistic in other regions without losing a sense of the Passion of Mary as the one mortals can turn to more immediately for help and intervention. She is present in every village, town, and city—north, south, east, and west—holding sacred ground for humans in a nurturing and gentle manner. For instance, she is *the* patron saint of fishermen as they venture out into the dangers of the sea, as much as she is

Mary and Jesus on the altar of Eunate's octagonal chapel on the Camino de Santiago, Navarra

A granite Galician crucero *in Santiago de Compostela showing Mary standing on the cross, a common depiction in northern Spain, especially in the northwest*

the patroness of inland sheepherders, farmers, and city folk. Even among the secular, Mary is special and her saint's day is celebrated everywhere with reverence and a temporary suspension of mundane concerns.

The writer Jason Webster, who has spent time in both Spain and in the Middle East, finds another interesting aspect of Mary. He has noticed veneration of Mary in the countries in Europe where Muslims historically invaded and lived with Christians, noting Spain, southern France, and southern Italy. This is likely because Mary, revered as the Mother of God by Catholics, is also the most revered woman in the Muslim holy book, the Qur'an. Not only is there an entire *sura*, "chapter," entitled "Mary" that is dedicated to her, but she is the most referred to woman and the *only* woman referred to by name in the Qur'an.

Mary might have been a point of agreement and reverence between the two competing religions, so much so that practitioners from both found their common ground through Mary. If this is so, then the appearance of Mary takes on new significance, as when she appeared to Pelayo at Covadonga or the many times her image was found by Christian kings on the eve of a battle against Iberian Muslims. Were they competing for her grace? And what about Our Lady of Fatima—a Mary with the prophet

Muhammad's daughter's name—in Portugal, a country that shares much of the same Muslim history with Spain?

I think the power of Mary stems more fundamentally from the human need for both a Father God and a Mother Goddess. This longing predates all the patriarchal Abrahamic religions; this dualistic balance pervades all that we do, whether we are conscious of it or not. I think Mary's importance stems most greatly from the need to have the sacred feminine as much as the sacred masculine. In places where patriarchal faiths took over, she is the avenue for reinventing the goddess and for holding this important sacred energy.

There are other symbolic manifestations of this important balance. Joseph Campbell pointed out that in many depictions of Mother and Child, Jesus sits on his mother's lap as if it is a throne, harkening back to a more ancient image of the king sitting on the throne of mother earth from whom he derives his earthly power.

Another prominent Marian theme in Spain is the discovery stories of ancient and miraculous carvings of her image. There are many of these all over Spain that local legends say went underground on the eve of the Muslim invasion in AD 711. Many stories say these icons mysteriously disappeared as if possessing a will of their own, while others simply say the monks responsible for the icons hid them but then forgot where. Curiously, all were hidden in deep places in the earth, caves and grottos, the primary home of the Mother Goddess.

One by one, these images returned above ground and always at key moments, such as when the Christian conquest of Muslim lands was gaining force and success, or when a Christian king needed to rally his troops. Such was the case of Our Lady of Puig who revealed herself on the eve of the battle for Valencia to King Jaime I on Mount Puig, north of Valencia. Our Ladies of Guadalupe and of Montserrat appeared to shepherds, powerful symbols also in Christianity, during key moments in the Middle Ages when each Christian territory was conquering territories under Muslim rule. The most famous Mary-revealed story might be Pelayo's battle in the early eighth century at Covadonga where Mary came out of hiding and defeated the larger Muslim army.

An aspect of Spain, one that might surprise people, is that it is not as much the macho, patriarchal culture many people think it is. There is a strong, ancient current of a matriarchal spirit that infuses the whole country. While this infusion, in my experience, feels strongest in the north of the country today, it exists everywhere: When La Dama de Elche, the Iberian statue of a strong woman dug up just north of Murcia in southern

Spain, was discovered over a hundred years ago, she quickly became the symbol of Spain. She is a strong, feminine presence. Some speculate an ancient goddess. Today she is a symbol of the prominent female side of Spain. Then there is the passionate, personal, and seductive competition between the two famous Marys of Seville, La Macarena and La Esperanza, during holy week when the town rises into a competition over whose Mary is more beautiful and more powerful. And there is the fact that Spanish romantic relationships are some of the most balanced and graceful I have witnessed in any country.

It is no accident that it was in Spain that a regional government legislated regulations that fashion models needed to pass a healthy weight standard, set by the World Health Organization, to be allowed on the runway of Madrid's annual Cibeles fashion show. (Cibeles, incidentally, is an ancient Mediterranean Mother Goddess.) Madrid was boldly defying a globally accepted industry of underweight, unhealthy, objectified women as fashionable. In 2006, the year of the ruling, 30 percent of models were turned away because they were considered too thin. One wonders, why had no other "developed" nation done that before?

Spain has also been among the most vocal nations in Europe and around the world about domestic violence as well as about human rights. And, Spanish women enjoy better wages for their professional work than other European, or American, women; although there still is a wage gap between women and men, it is nevertheless narrower. Lastly, Spain legalized gay marriage, one of the few European nations to do so. The Spanish are more open-minded about alternative sexuality, another indication that machismo is not so very strong in Spain.

Of sacred expressions, every village, hill, stream, and mountain has a Mary that is its patron. She is the messenger, the therapist, the one people turn to in need and in joy. She is also the manifestation of the older sacred feminine that holds sway in Spain. Mary is the most recent expression of the goddess in a land that has a deep connection to this ancient European manifestation of matriarchy. Mary, as the goddess, has a long Mediterranean lineage that connects to fertility and abundance, such as with the ancient goddesses Isis, Demeter, Cibeles, Ceres, Ashtarte, and Thanit, as well as Artemis and the Celtic goddess Ana. Spain once had numerous temples to Diana, a goddess whose cult was strong here. Of all the goddesses of the ancient world, Diana/Artemis is the most feminist and fiercest protector of pristine nature and innocence. She is independent and strong. Her veneration sites were natural areas, especially springs. The Celtic goddess Ana seems to have fused with Diana in the north, and then with feminine and feminist beings known as *xanas*, also in the north, in Asturias. Parallels exist in Galicia and Basque Country. Similar to these goddesses, Marian shrines are placed near springs, in groves, caves, and mountaintops. Mary's profound Earth-connectedness can be seen expressed in some sweet unexpected ways, too, such as acorn or scallop-shaped key chains for sale that when opened—or un-screwed from their cap as is the case of the acorn key chain—reveal a little statue of Mary in their center.

Seville's La Esperanza Virgin Mary during the Holy Week processions of Semana Santa leading up to Easter, Andalusia

While there are almost infinite Marys across Spain, some of the most powerful that you will encounter in your peregrinations in this book are: La Virgen de Covadonga (Asturias); Nuestra Señora de Lebeña (Cantabria); the Black Madonna of Montserrat (Catalonia); La Macarena and La Esperanza of Seville (Andalusia); Nuestra Señora de Guadalupe (Extremadura); La Virgen de Unbe near Bilbao (Pais Vasco); El Pilar de Zaragoza (Aragón); and La Virgen de los Desamparados (Valencia).

As you seek out one of the better known shrines and hermitages, be sure to look in serene, quiet spots for the unmarked but dearly beloved chapel or shrine to Mary out in the middle of the woods, in a cave, along a mountainside, by a stream, or at the entrance of a village. Mary, and her other manifestations as nurturing, loving goddess, is everywhere in Spain.

PART THREE

Pilgrim Routes Through Sacred Spain

$\mathscr{I}$ntroduction to Part Three

As with sacred sites, it is likely that pilgrim routes, in part or in whole, were preceded by pre-Christian sacred rites and roads that punctuated the year or that brought people together from further afield than the usual settlement cluster of day-to-day existence. Sacred landscapes and sites are a part of the human experience, whether called a special energy field, ley lines, or power areas; it seems every land on Earth has areas where the population agrees there is a strong, otherworldly feeling. In Spain almost every village, town, and city will have some form of annual pilgrimage to a local shrine, either on the feast day of that particular saint or as a part of the Easter observances. You will notice shrines and hermitages everywhere you go. All of them have a following and a sacred route during the year. Each has been shaped by the local idiosyncrasies and relationships with the sacred.

Pilgrim routes and sacred sites have a tremendous capacity to transform a person as no other place or experience can. In anthropology, this transformation is recognized as directly related to the act of a sacred place or pilgrimage removing the person from their ordinary, everyday surroundings and throwing them into unknown encounters with unfamiliar landscapes and characters, which very well might change lives. In other words, it's the old-fashioned way of breaking out of the box. Pilgrimage takes us outside ourselves.

Scallop shell marker in León for the Camino de Santiago, Castilla y León

A sacred site can do the same. The labyrinth at Chartres Cathedral was built for the purpose of giving those who could not go on the great pilgrimage to Santiago de Compostela—or to Rome or to Jerusalem—a way to partake of the same pilgrim's contemplative walking: going deeper within so as to expand more outwardly.

People were as aware of the transforming power of pilgrimage in the past as in the present—in some cases even more so. The Camino to Santiago de Compostela was considered one of the great adventures a person could take in medieval Europe. It had as many worldly adventures attached to it as spiritual ones. And today, many seekers on the Camino

The current and universal scallop shell way marker is used for all the routes to Santiago. This one was encountered on the Northern Route in Asturias.

make the trek for both spiritual and secular reasons. Many enjoy the challenge of relying on themselves, being in the great outdoors, and meeting people from far-flung corners of the world. Even the more secular seekers often find themselves unexpectedly having profound sacred experiences. And while each person has a unique experience on a pilgrimage, a unifying thread is that it possesses inner challenges and insights that mirror the outer adventure.

So as you commence these routes, look for the falling aside of old boundaries and for an expansion within and without. Be prepared for returning home a different person from before you left, filled with new ideas and connections with the world and with the sacred.

SACRED ARCHITECTURAL STYLES IN SPAIN

Eighteen thousand years ago, people inhabited cave sites in northern Spain; artists, who were likely also shamans, selected certain cave walls and roofs for their shape and potential for etching and painting the remarkable Paleolithic images of bison, deer, bulls, boar, horses, and the like. The Paleolithic caves are the beginning point of spiritual architecture in Spain. Next are the altars built by Celtic speakers, Romans, and Visigoths. Much of the sacred architecture after the Celtic and the Roman periods is Romanesque, Gothic, Islamic, Mozarabic, Mudéjar, and Baroque. There are also areas with pre-Romanesque structures, such as in north-central and northwestern Spain. Another hybrid style, infusing Judaic concepts with architectural styles from both Christian and Muslim Spain can be identified, which I would call Sephardic. The best examples of this are in Toledo and Córdoba. Likewise, Visigothic structures, which show elements of pre-Romanesque, Roman, and Byzantine influences, are found in spots in central, eastern, and northern Spain. The most unique Spanish architecture are those hybrid styles that resulted from the unique mixing of peoples in the Peninsula: pre-Romanesque, Mozarabic, and Mudéjar. But even the Romanesque, Gothic, Baroque, and Islamic styles have purely Spanish twists in their interpretation.

Here are some architectural definitions to sort out all these styles:

Visigothic style is a Germanic influence in Iberian art and architecture. Like the pre-Romanesque, it is simple and small and used mostly for intimate spaces. Designs are drawn from nature and plant and animal motifs dominate. These structures were built in the fifth to seventh centuries.

Pre-Romanesque style is a type that developed in northwestern Spain that blended Visigothic styles with indigenous aesthetics to conceive a native expression of early Christianity in Iberia. Its distinguishing features are its warm, intimate spaces, its golden stone, and its carvings and fresco paintings that depict naturalistic and mythic images. Such moods and imagery have parallels in the later Romanesque style even though they developed independently. These edifices were built in the eighth and ninth centuries.

Romanesque style is warm, intimate, and built of local stone that is carved into the signature scenes of mythic beings, of people carrying out everyday tasks as well as sacred acts, of plants, and of woven swirling designs that are like ornamental vines. Romanesque is one of the dominant styles in Iberia and comes directly from French influences, largely from the Cluny order in France and from later Cistercians, both of whose reach in Iberia came through the Camino, the pilgrimage road to Santiago de Compostela. Profane Romanesque images can be so honest that some might even make a modern visitor blush. Romanesque architecture flourished especially in the eleventh and twelfth centuries at the time when the medieval pilgrimage to Santiago was at its peak.

Gothic style, first introduced into Spain from France by the Cistercians, is in some ways a purist's response to the ornate and organic nature of Romanesque buildings, which admittedly bear many representations of the profane as well as of the sacred. The main spirit behind Gothic architecture and art is to create elegant, clean lines that show the grandeur of God but that do not distract from this message. Gothic churches are taller and bigger and usually possess a signature mandalalike rose window at one or both ends of the nave. On Gothic exteriors, especially the portals, you might see many human figures—mostly biblical and extra-biblical religious characters but also local patrons, nobles, and merchants whose commissions of religious sites earned them a stone portrait on the building. Gothic styles dominated from the thirteenth to the fifteenth century. Gothic churches and cathedrals are refreshing to wander into, with their clean, towering lines.

Islamic styles, such as what you will see in Córdoba, Seville, and Granada, are a result of many influences. Iberian Islamic styles are a fruitful marriage of influences coming from Umayyad Syria, Arabia, Egypt, and Berber aesthetics from North Africa, as well as Byzantine influences from today's Turkey, and further east from Persia. These fused and innovated into styles distinct to Iberia, the finest example being the Cordoban mosque, from its forest of pillars to its inlaid prayer niche.

Sephardic styles largely look like the styles of the dominant culture. In Barcelona the synagogue was first built during the Roman period and looks Roman in its foundation. It survived into the Middle Ages and so also has Catalonian elements of this time. Likewise, the synagogue in Córdoba, built during the Cordoban Caliphate, looks like a brother temple to the mosque, though much smaller. Its similarities are in the inlaid work, carved plaster, and scalloped archways. The synagogue of Santa María la Blanca in Toledo looks very much like a northern Moroccan mosque, influenced heavily by the Andalusian style of Muslim Iberians who traversed North Africa and Spain.

Mozarabic refers to Christian styles that developed and found expression under Muslim rule and patronage. It refers both to Christians who lived under Muslim rule and to Christians who lived under Muslim rule and then immigrated with their unique aesthetic to Christian-dominated parts of Spain.

Mudéjar is a broad term referring to the work of Muslim artists, artisans, and craftsmen living under Christian patronage. Usually this took place as Christian forces took over previously held Muslim territories and commissioned Muslims to create or modify structures. The most prominent Mudéjar style can be seen in the towers and outer walls of buildings where brick and tile are used as if weaving a carpet, interspersed in a beautiful and colorful woven mosaic design. Mudéjar design is also present in carved and painted wooden ceiling beams in many churches and palaces and in wooden or inlaid doors.

Plateresque is a uniquely Spanish expression born out of the ornamental late-Gothic style and executed through a new worldview of great wealth coming from the Americas. Its name is derived from silversmithing (*platería*) given the ornamental bauble style of the stone carving designs. It really only lasted during the sixteenth century.

Baroque. The best example of seventeenth- and eighteenth-century Baroque architecture in Spain, possibly in Europe, is in Santiago de Compostela. Most Baroque structures in Spain are larger than their forebears in order to offer a large enough canvas for the extremely ornate facades, which were more about showing off a patron's wealth than any spiritual act of glory. **Churrigueresque** is a style of Baroque on steroids, instigated by the Churriguera brothers. It is extreme Baroque, with designs that come across most of the time as though the artist ate too much sugar. Unlike Romanesque and Gothic, where the use of ornament is limited either to stone and fresco (in the case of Romanesque) or to a single-focus carved altar panel painted with gold in a sea of somber stone pillars and arches, Baroque and its hyper cousin Churrigueresque seem to feel that any clean space is a waste and so cover all stone surfaces with ornamentation; this overdecoration feels like an antiquarian's overcrowded shop or a great aunt's overstuffed parlor.

Neoclassical styles returned to simplicity, most likely in response to the chaotic decor of Baroque. Here clean lines and semicircular arches return, in stone or in stucco. This is the dominant style of the nineteenth century.

Today, modern sacred styles are as diverse as the religions, ancient and new, that exist in Spain. New mosques reflect modern Spanish, North African, and Levantine influences. Synagogues are in modern buildings and re-create Sephardic rites. Buddhist temples rise on mountaintops and in cityscapes, reflecting modern Spanish styles as well as their stream of origin—be it Tibetan, Thai, Japanese, or Chinese. Old Christian churches show the designs of several eras added on to them and many structures carry the influences of several architectural styles. New churches look more like North American Catholic churches, with abstract stained glass windows set in a simple rectangular building. And Antoni Gaudí's work-in-progress, the modernist Sagrada Familia Cathedral in Barcelona, continues to be built; each year new additions reveal more of the artist's original vision from the early 1900s. Here it is remarkable to see great cathedral-building in practice and it gives a good idea of what it took to build the older relatives.

Note to the Reader

I am biased toward the sacred structures of all Iberian inhabitants that preceded and overlapped to a degree the era of Gothic architecture. This includes early Christian, Visigothic, pre-Romanesque, Mozarabic, Romanesque, Mudéjar, and early Gothic churches of the Christians, the synagogues and mosques of the Jews and Muslims, the dolmens of the Bronze Age, the castros of the Iron Age Celtic speakers, and the caves, springs, and mountains of the prehistoric to modern peoples.

I find that a significant spiritual death took place as Spain and all of Europe entered a greater materialistic age of expansion and power mongering—after people gained confidence in their faith but refused to use it for the betterment of humanity, using it instead for greater power and subjugation. I have checked this out with other spiritual travelers and find they largely agree. As such, in general but not absolutely, late-Gothic, Baroque, and some Neoclassical structures hit me as soulless or as so concerned with mortal power that they forget God and spirit along the way.

I also have found that after long centuries of totalitarian restraints on faith, from the Inquisition to Franco, the Spanish relish in their freedom

Stone way marker kindly placed by earlier pilgrims to clear up some ambiguity on the road, Galicia

and have learned a good deal about humanity. Current Spanish trends in spirituality speak of a people who know their shadow, are not going to forget it, but who are enjoying the light and are returning to a deeper, more authentic spirituality—one akin to their prehistoric cave-painting ancestors, their dolmen builders, and their Romanesque church builders.

In spite of my stated biases, I have strived painstakingly to give an accurate portrait of the country and the people.

CHAPTER SEVEN

The Pilgrimage to Santiago de Compostela

The Camino is like a river: all these people coming from everywhere like tributary streams. They enter a finite river, one that empties ultimately in the Atlantic Ocean at Finisterre. Then the river becomes infinite, as limitless as the ocean: we are transformed from limited to limitless by walking it.

—From a German pilgrim on his way home

LEGENDS ABOUND ABOUT THE CAMINO, from both pre-Christian and Christian times. Nearly all of the stories of the Camino, including those of St. James, are unsubstantiated, impossible to prove or disprove. That is one of the great beauties of this pilgrimage: it is totally in a realm beyond time, a realm of legend and myth. This does not mean it is false; it means it is experiential, transcendent, and infused with magical spirit. It is the task of each pilgrim to find his or her own truth by walking and trusting the road. This is where its power lies.

Some of the most intriguing stories—the ones that seem plausible given patterns in human history and geographical phenomenon—are of an ancient road, one that far predated the Christian one, that was sacred and a path for spiritual initiates. Whether they were druids, priests, holy people, mystery school students, or all of the above, we cannot know. But that this road existed as a spiritual path, much like it became for early medieval Christians, is very likely. The road also might have been known by these early Christians and appropriated for their new faith, which had

The cloisters of the Monasterio de Santa Maria la Real in Nájera, La Rioja

no less a spiritual impulse and desire for direct experience with the Divine as those cosmic systems before it.

Some speculate that this was a fertility route to honor the creator goddess or that it was a death road following the dying sun, or an initiatory road for shamans and druids. Well why not? Prior to and after Indo-European expansion into Europe, the north of Spain, from Basque Country to Galicia, remained a stronghold of the old European goddess culture, a pre-Indo-European culture that is one of the more indigenous expressions of early European peoples. Today vestiges of this past persist in northern Spain, as in the Basque goddess *Mari*, the Asturian *xana*, and the matriarchal inheritance practices still found in remote parts of Galicia, practices that before Roman contact were regional norms. That the Camino, which passes through these rich matriarchal lands, might have once been a road dedicated to the divine feminine, dedicated to the goddess of fertility, is a possibility.

This area was also the recipient of waves of migrating and settling Celtic speakers, who brought their beliefs—something of a mix between the pre- and post-Indo-European, a mélange of both the matriarchal and the patriarchal societies through which they traveled—with them. And pre-Christian Romans, who named *Finisterre* ("end of the earth"), the outcrop of land at the far west of Galicia, also added their sun cult with its cosmology of the sun's dying in the west (and resurrecting in the east).

Perhaps all these influences affected one another as well. What all hold in common with the current Christian Camino is a sense that the area transforms you, that it is neither pagan nor Christian, that no one can claim it with their dogma or ideology, but rather that it will write itself on the traveler and reveal mysteries of life, or challenges, to those who traverse it, each with his or her own issues and agendas.

There are also many physical roads to Santiago de Compostela. This chapter focuses on the *Camino Frances*, the French Route, the most traveled road to Santiago in Spain. There is also the northern coastal route from San Sebastian along the coast and then cutting inland at Galicia. There is the English Route where ships arrived in A Coruña's harbor and pilgrims took to the road in northern Galicia toward Santiago de Compostela. There is the Portuguese Route coming in from O Porto and Vigo. There is the Via de Plata, Silver Route, originating in the south in Seville. There is the Aragonese Route, a road that crosses the Pyrenees from France further east than the French Route and enters Spain at the province of Aragón rather than Navarra, and then joins up with the French Route in Puente la Reina, just southwest of Pamplona. There are also roads from Madrid, from the Mediterranean starting at Valencia or Alicante, and one from Montserrat to Zaragoza, which intersects with the French Route in Logroño. Beyond Spain, four main roads stem from France as well, which converge with the French Route in Puente la Reina. Prior to planes, buses, and trains, European travelers from across the Continent also had known roads from their own cities and towns that often connected with the four French roads and onward into Spain.

Given all this, what about some sacred seekers' enthusiasm over the possible ley lines on the Camino, those great sacred Earth power points that are said to open the spirit? If they exist, which I think they do, they are living energies, not fixed and static on a particular line. I think there is a relationship between the Earth and all life on Earth and this dynamic of energy and matter manifests in ley lines. With all the prayer and intention and directed consciousness coming from all the people walking the Camino over all the centuries, this energy dance can be quite palpable. The diverse natural world the pilgrim passes through is rich and inspiring.

Among the human-made delights on the Camino is the vast collection of Romanesque architecture that dominates the road, so much so that it has also been called the Romanesque Road. Romanesque architecture and art, as well as monastic life, religious ideas and reform, and worship, entered Spain from France through the Benedictine order of Cluny. Medieval Spanish culture in the north was heavily influenced by this connection with France. But what drove it? Ironically, gold from al-Andalus.

The Romanesque movement, the power of the Cluny order, and the peak of the medieval pilgrimage to Santiago all took place in the eleventh century, a direct result of the turning of the tide in the Muslim-Christian hegemonic struggle for the Peninsula. (The climax of this struggle might have been when al-Mansur and his Cordoban forces reached Santiago in AD 997, sacked the city, and took away its bells to Córdoba.) Many Islamic Iberian *taifa* kingdoms paid tributes to King Fernando I of Castile and León (1037–1065) and later to his son, Alfonso VI (1065–1109). In turn, these two kings gave an annual payment of al-Andalus gold to Cluny, who in return developed the Camino with building campaigns and French settlers, who helped repopulate frontier lands taken from the Muslims. This all in turn stabilized not only the Camino but the Christian kingdoms of Spain, giving them more steam to plow ahead, which they did.

It was so much gold that the Cluny order not only rebuilt their own church but also fueled the expansion and power of the order beyond Cluny's borders. Cluny depended on the continued flow of gold from Muslim Spain. When the Almoravids flooded into the Peninsula from Morocco at the end of the eleventh century, this flow was halted and it had such a profound effect that it took the Cluny order half a century to regain stable footing.

Through Navarra and Rioja, the French and Basque influences are strong given the cultural lineage to both places. The French influence was strong not only because of proximity to the French border at the Pyrenees but also because of the encouragement of the monarchs Alfonso VI of Castile and León (1030–1109) and Sancho Ramírez, who ruled over Aragón (1063–1094) and Navarra (1076–1094), to invite French settlers to inhabit places along the Camino in order to build up its population and defend against the frontier with the Muslim south. Before these two monarchs, the major pioneer king who promoted development along the Camino was Sancho III, "the Great," of Navarra (1000–1035).

The Muslim invasion of AD 711 guaranteed the further diversity of Iberia and was a main causal factor in the development of the Camino. But do not believe that these worlds were entirely separate just because kings and bishops made it so. Muslim craftsmen (Mudéjars) and Islamicized Christian craftsmen (Mozarabes) were employed as builders of many Christian buildings along the Camino.

As the Camino grew in popularity, many settlements grew up around it, explaining the many interesting detours you can make from the main stopping places. Villages surrounding stops on the Camino also built sacred churches, hermitages, hospitals, hostels, and shops. Some pilgrims never returned home but instead settled somewhere along the road, adding to it their unique background, ideas, and experiences.

Pilgrimage is about each person's individual journey on a sacred path, one that is simultaneously inner and outer. There is no right or wrong way to take a pilgrimage; each person must determine the best way for herself or himself. There are many who are adamant that you must walk the entire pilgrimage, that you must get your pilgrim's passport in Roncesvalles, and that you must stay in the *refugios* or you have not done the pilgrimage properly. That is only one way and I would advise against spending too much time listening to anyone who espouses only one way to God and self.

There are many others, legitimate pilgrims, who take years to walk the Camino, doing it in parts. Others have cycled it. In the Middle Ages, it was not uncommon to walk and to ride donkey and horseback parts of the way. Today some drive it and find their own bliss, though this is a different experience from that of relying on one's footfall all the way. But all ways are legitimate. Find yours and relish in the discoveries, inner and outer, that it reveals. And do consider lingering where your spirit calls you to do so and taking detours at the same urging.

For the most part, the current pilgrimage roads are well marked, whether you walk, cycle, or drive, though some signs can get washed out during a rainstorm or the like. While walking, I discovered numerous detours along the walking path that were not otherwise noted in any of the published guides. Be prepared for this. Be sure to get good maps from the tourist offices along the way and keep your eyes open for the signs, the eternal task of the pilgrim. If you drive, the roads have signs stating you

A distance marker in the mountains of Galicia on the Camino de Santiago

are on the Camino de Santiago. The walking paths are marked with a series of diverse signs, from yellow arrows painted on rocks and pillars and trees, to different styles of scallop shells and distance markers on concrete or wooden posts. In the end, others will help you and the Camino itself will guide you. This, after all, is a big part of a pilgrimage: look for signs, be prepared for anything, and trust the road.

Main Route (522.5 miles/845.5 km):
Roncesvalles—Pamplona—Eunate—Puente la Reina—Cirauqui—Estella —Irache—Torres del Rio—Logroño—Nájera—Santo Domingo de la Calzada—Redecilla del Camino—Tosantos—San Juan de Ortega— Atapuerca—Burgos—Frómista—Carrión de los Condes—Sahagún —San Miguel de la Escalada—León—Astorga—Rabanal del Camino— Molinaseca—Ponferrada—Villafranca del Bierzo—O Cebreiro—Samos —Sarria—Portomarín—Santiago de Compostela

RONCESVALLES (ORREAGA)—Navarra

This is the most common entry point into Spain from the French border. There are several other roads that come over the Pyrenees from France, entering Spain either here or from the more difficult pass further east at Jaca. Many modern-day pilgrims either start walking the Camino from Roncesvalles or from just over the Pyrenees in St.-Jean-Pied-de-Port. If you begin in St. Jean, it is a good, long, and challenging day of climbing the mountain pass to Roncesvalles, a first step that leaves walking pilgrims both deeply foot weary and also exhilarated at their first accomplishment. There are no right or wrong ways to start or carry out the Camino—start where it works for you.

Roncesvalles was famous as a threshold place before the pilgrimage to St. James's tomb in Santiago. It was the site of the decisive eighth-century battle between Charlemagne's nephew, Roland, and the Basques. Roland lost his life and inspired the later twelfth-century *Chanson de Roland*, "Song of Roland," which was really medieval Christian propaganda in light of the frontier battles with Muslim Spain. In truth, the eighth-century occurrences that involved Roland had to do with his defeat at the hands of local Basques, who were defending the control of their own land. In legend, though, it was easier to fold the event into the already existing polarity between Islam and Christianity than to muss it up with the truth of locals defending their own. (Of course, the battles between Muslims and

Christians in Spain influenced the alliances and political interests of other battles, including the one at Roncesvalles.)

Still, Roland's defeat near Roncesvalles put the town on the map for posterity; later it became a destination for pilgrims, both as a convenient stopping place upon crossing the Pyrenees at Valcarlos Pass, as well as a place to pay homage to one of Europe's legendary events and people. As such, today in Roncesvalles you will find as much on Roland and Charlemagne as on the sacred Camino, including what is claimed to be Charlemagne's chess-set on display in the museum of Roncesvalles' monastery.

Roncesvalles is interesting for its historical significance more than for any remaining sacred monuments. It is a sacred mountain passage, and some go as far as to consider it to be a threshold or power spot of a mystical nature in addition to its physical role as passageway—a place of cultural magic. The main sacred site is the monastery founded in the mid-twelfth century, modified many times since, and that now is still managed and occupied by a small group of Augustinian monks. The Collegiate Church here, likewise rebuilt and renovated many times so as to nearly mask its medieval origins, is built on a higher spot over the cloister and preserves a medieval statue of Nuestra Señora de Roncesvalles. She appeared to a child on this spot in some remote memory of the Middle Ages. Though her revelation is wrapped in mist, her veneration is very strong to this day, as with Mary all across Spain.

The Camino trail from Roncesvalles is through forest and valley, passing through villages and towns of Burguete and Zubiri, onward toward Pamplona, the capital of the medieval Kingdom of Navarra.

Roncesvalles to Pamplona (29 miles/47 km):
Take N-135 to Pamplona.

PAMPLONA (IRUÑA)—Navarra

Pamplona is at the heart of many struggles given its position at several crossroads: Basque, French, and Castilian. Moreover, Pamplona sits in a strategic place on the frontier between medieval Muslim and Christian Spain. Pamplona was founded around 77 BCE by Pompey the Great, who gave his name to the city: either Pompelo or Pompeiopolis. And prior to Muslim occupation in the eighth century, Visigoths also inhabited the city.

Pamplona was conquered by Muslims in AD 732 and then lost to Charlemagne. When the Frankish leader destroyed the city's walls, the locals rose up and defeated his nephew, Roland, who was leading a retreat-

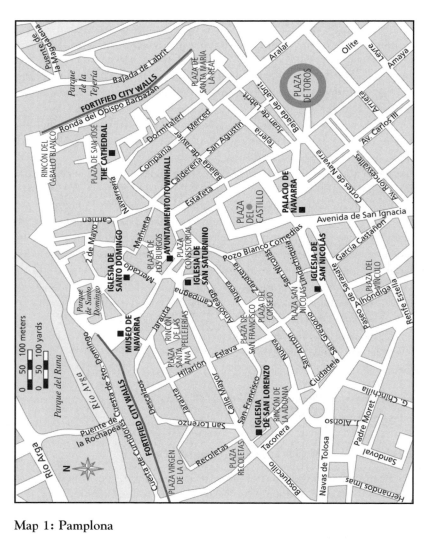

Map 1: Pamplona

ing army over the Pyrenees at Roncesvalles in 778, thus ending Charlemagne's rule in the area.

In 913 Pamplona was destroyed by Muslim incursions. It was under the Navarrese king Sancho III, "the Great," in the eleventh century that Pamplona experienced a major rebuilding. He encouraged French Navarrese to settle in the city. They came and built up two neighborhoods, San Nicolás and San Cernín, and brought their crafts and trades. The medieval city flourished and was also often the center of tensions between allegiances to Castile and those to France.

In 1423 Carlos III, king of Navarra, unified the city and Pamplona became even more powerful, though the tensions were still there. A century later Castilians and Navarrese French vied for the city in the battle of 1521, the very battle where a young Ignatius Loyola, a Basque mercenary fighting for Castile, was so severely injured that he rethought his ways as he later spent months in bed, unable to walk. (See chapter 8 under Azpeitia on Loyola and his founding of the Jesuit order.) Pamplona then became connected to Castile. Today it is the capital of the autonomous province of Navarra. It is a delightfully green city surrounded by green hills and agricultural land. Approaching it and departing from it on the Camino are a pleasure.

Pamplona is the first major city pilgrims encounter and has a wonderfully welcoming spirit. It is a delightfully traditional Iberian city with its labyrinthine streets still well preserved, several medieval monuments, and many traditional craft and food shops vibrantly thriving in the medieval city core—salted cod shops, fruit and vegetable sellers, tailors, hat makers, lace sellers, hand-crafted toys, bakers, chocolatiers, and the like.

Pamplona's Gothic cathedral has a beautiful interior hidden by a hideous Baroque facade. Get past this decoy and go inside to enjoy the delicate archways and the peaceful lacelike cloisters.

San Fermin

The Iglesia de San Lorenzo houses a little chapel to San Fermin, one of Pamplona's important patron saints and the one who takes on special significance during the famous week-long running of the bulls in mid-July in Pamplona. These summer festivals are called *Los Sanfermines* and include bullfights and a good deal of eating and drinking. You will find replicas of San Fermin throughout town. My favorite sighting of him is along the row of bottles in some bars, usually above the espresso machine.

Two churches of particular interest in Pamplona are the Iglesia de San Saturnino, also known as San Cernín, and the Iglesia de San Nicolás.

Iglesia de San Saturnino

San Saturnino is considered another of Pamplona's patron saints, and this church, along with San Nicolás, forms the spiritual centers of the ancient Navarrese who inhabited this region. San Saturnino is believed to have baptized Pamplona's first Christians on the site of the current church. The church is a mix of Romanesque and Gothic styles and dates from the twelfth to the fifteenth century. There are wonderful Romanesque characters inhabiting the entrance portal.

Iglesia de San Nicolás

A beautiful twelfth-century Romanesque-transition-to-Gothic structure with sweeping high spaces that are nonetheless intimate and enveloping, this church gets used well on a daily basis by locals. Like so many churches in Navarra and neighboring Rioja, San Nicolás (as well as San Saturnino) was built for defensive purposes as much as for spiritual reasons and so is thick walled and protective.

Pamplona to Eunate (15 miles/24 km):
Take N-111, which becomes A-12, exit to Obanos and take NA-601 to Eunate.

EUNATE—Navarra

This eight-sided Romanesque church, the Iglesia de Santa María de Eunate, exists in a shroud of mystery as to its purpose and its creators. Many posit that it was built by Templar knights; it seems more likely that it was not, but was influenced by Templar architecture. It was constructed in the twelfth century. Eunate is a unique structure and offers a deep connection with the surrounding countryside, as if the spirits of the land are woven into its walls.

Eunate's octagonal structure is surrounded by an open-air octagonal cloister with thirty-three arches, a style and number that distinguish the place as architecturally unique. The area around the arches may have been a funerary space.

The cloister makes me think of Islamic prayer beads, which can number thirty-three: a Muslim in meditation on the ninety-nine names of God will circulate the beads three times in his hands. Could some curious

The enigmatic and octagonal chapel of Eunate on the
Camino de Santiago in Navarra

Christian-Islamic crossover have occurred at Eunate where people circled the cloister three times in deep prayer?

The name *Eunate* in Basque apparently means "one hundred doors" or "house of one hundred doors." Could the hundredth door, after three rotations about the cloister, be the entrance portal into the church? The resemblance to medieval walking meditations on labyrinths, such as the one at Chartres cathedral in France, as well as to the Islamic prayer bead meditation is intriguing. It would not be the first time both sides borrowed sacred architectural forms from each other across the Peninsula. Prayer beads and cloisters both serve the purpose of circular contemplation—one with fingers and the other with feet. As farfetched as this might sound, we need to bear in mind that Islam and Christianity lived side by side for over eight hundred years in Iberia, a length of history that would seep into many unnoticed aspects of life, and no less in the way people approached their spirituality.

Eunate to Puente la Reina (4 miles/6 km):
Backtrack on NA-601 to Puente la Reina.

PUENTE LA REINA—Navarra

This village preserves the medieval atmosphere of the old pilgrimage. It was the meeting point of the two roads that came over the Somport and the Valcarlos passes from France. These two roads joined here into the one main road that continued to Santiago across the north of Spain.

Puente la Reina is delightfully set in a wine- and produce-growing area and the walk here through vineyards and vegetable gardens is well rewarded with delicious local fair for dinner. The most prominent features in town are the Iglesia de Crucifijo at the east end, with its grounds dedicated to vegetable gardens, the Romanesque Iglesia de Santiago on the Rua Mayor, and the stone bridge leading across the river Arga and out of town.

The Iglesia de Crucifijo, "Church of the Cross," gets its name from a y-shaped, ornately carved wooden cross presumably brought here by a German pilgrim. The church first started as a smaller Romanesque chapel, likely built by Muslim craftsmen. As this building was also a medieval pilgrim's hostel and soon outgrew its size, in the fourteenth century it was extended, adding Gothic elements as well as the famous wooden cross.

The Iglesia de Santiago was once a Romanesque church but only its main door retains this era in a Mudéjar style with its scalloped archway, reminding the visitor of the mixing of worlds. Here, as with the Iglesia de Crucifijo, we have Muslim craftsmen working on an important Christian sacred site. It is a good lesson for our times to think not that the worlds were, or are, all that separate, but that we share much, in economics and arts as well as in spiritual ancestry and outlook.

The town derives its name from the bridge (*puente*) that the queen (*reina*) Doña Mayor built for pilgrims in the eleventh century. She was married to King Sancho the Great who was one of the important patrons of the Camino. Bridges were among the best things monarchs and nobles could build to enhance the Camino because water crossings proved to be pilgrims' greatest challenges. And because bridges made the road more comfortable and accessible, more people with varied handicaps could take up the pilgrimage. That this bridge is around a thousand years old also speaks of the power of good public works to preserve one's name.

Puente la Reina to Cirauqui (4.5 miles/7 km):
Take N-111 to A-12 to Cirauqui.

CIRAUQUI—Navarra

Part of the Camino here connects to an older Roman road, a little under two thousand years old and still trod upon by passing pilgrims. This well-preserved medieval hilltop village is home also to the Iglesia de San Román, dating to the thirteenth century and possessing a Mudéjar multi-lobed portal, reflecting a related ancestry to the main door of Iglesia de Santiago in Puente la Reina. The surrounding vistas are enchanting rolling hills—green in spring and summer and harvested and brown in the autumn and winter—through vineyards and almond groves.

Cirauqui to Estella (10.5 miles/17 km):
Take A-12; exit onto N-111A to Estella.

ESTELLA (LIZARRA)—Navarra

The twelfth-century seat of Navarrese kings, Estella goes back to ancient times with references from Ptolemy and from Strabo, indicating a likely more ancient ancestry than even these Greek and Roman observers. Before King Sancho Ramírez built the medieval city of Estella, where many French settlers came to live in the late eleventh century, it was a small settlement occupied by Basque-speaking natives and called Lizarra. The town today is referred to by both names.

As a major pilgrim town from the end of the eleventh century on, Estella possesses many beautiful Navarrese Romanesque buildings. The town is built within folds of hill and valley and straddles the river Ega. This gives it an animated, reveal-and-conceal plan. It has also preserved much of its twelfth-century style, which adds greatly to Estella's appeal. Estella has many historical churches given its prosperity as a major pilgrimage town in a rich agricultural area also active in printing and crafts.

The name *Estella* derives from the Marian legend where shepherds in 1085 saw a showering of stars and ran to the spot where they fell to find a cave with an image of the Virgin Mary within it. That cave is now the spot on which the Basilica de Nuestra Señora del Puy stands.

The Basilica del Puy

Some speculate that the current site of the Basilica de Nuestra Señora del Puy was possibly a pre-Christian sacred site. Being at the high point of the settlement, it could well have been an offering altar for certain nature divinities. Curiously, though the current Basilica housing Estella's patroness, Mary of Puy, only dates to the 1950s, it feels as if an ancient energy still resides in the stones on which it is built. There is an unmistakable vibrancy here. Also curious, the new shrine is built in a neo-Mudéjar style, one well disposed to create geometric patterns of the star that made Estella so famous—an eight-pointed Islamic-styled star in this case—and that gave the city her name. (Estella is derived from the Latin *stella*, which gives us the Castilian *estrella*, both meaning "star.") Prior to the current church, others existed on the same spot but were destroyed. Until the first half of the twentieth century, a Baroque chapel held the honor of housing La Señora del Puy's image.

Iglesia de San Pedro de la Rua

This is easily one of the earthiest and most inviting churches in Spain. Climb the many stairs up to the entrance where the church and its cloisters have been built into the wall of stone of the hill you've just ascended. The interior is symmetrical and rounded and embraces the visitor. Among some of the unique inhabitants are the characters engraved all around the Mudéjar multilobed Romanesque entrance portal, with a mix of equally Islamic-influenced fantastical creatures, Celtic-style knots, and biblical stories. The two winged-bird-animals on the left capital nearest the door are believed to come from Persian influence.

Inside, three apses define the front altar space, the central one with a Gothic polychrome Virgin Mary from the thirteenth or fourteenth century. The left column of this Marian chapel has a curious pillar carved into three serpents braided like a woman's hair. The cloister, in its delightful natural context of the mountainside's rock wall, is an open-air place conducive to meditation and walking. In the center quadrants are tombstones of the ancient style, hybrids of earlier pre-Christian funerary symbols, usually the sun; this image easily morphed into an equal-armed cross, which, like the more ancient sun symbols, fit within rounded disks of stone. The western side of the cloister also possesses Mudéjar elements in the animals and plants depicted and confirms the great likelihood that Muslim craftsmen from Islamic Spain were employed in the construction of this late-twelfth- to thirteenth-century church.

Below San Pedro de la Rua is the medieval palace of the kings of Navarra, with its carved capitals. The most interesting carving is on the westernmost corner and depicts Charlemagne's nephew Roland fighting a giant known as Ferragut, described in the chronicle of Bishop Turpin as the ruler of Nájera, west of Logroño. Ferragut was of Syrian origin and was so large and strong that fighting him was like fighting forty men. We can assume Roland was successful here, only to survive long enough to meet his end at Roncesvalles.

Other Sacred Spaces in Estella

The **Iglesia de Santa María Jus del Castillo** was the synagogue until AD 1145 when it was transformed into a church. It stands in the area where one of Navarra's major Jewish populations lived—testimony to the large Jewish community whom, along with French settlers, Sancho Ramirez encouraged to come and populate his lands to establish greater security against Muslim incursions into the north once they had been pushed south. Currently it is a heavily fortified Romanesque and Gothic structure that at the time of writing was closed for restoration.

The **Convento de Santo Domingo** is today a private senior residence with a cheerful air. This convent housed Dominican nuns until 1839. It is a dignified and well-maintained building. The church, with its Gothic windows, still survives and stands on a high hill over the town. Because it is a senior residence the interior is not open to the public, but a walk about the outside is worth it. Just below the monastery is the **Iglesia de Santo Sepulcro** with dynamic characters carved in its Romanesque arches and columns. It is the first church pilgrims encounter when they enter Estella.

The late Romanesque **Iglesia de San Miguel** stands on one of the higher spots in Estella and, though largely destroyed in 1512, it still preserves its interesting north portal. The tympanum possesses a mandorla with Christ surrounded by the words, "The vision you contemplate here is neither God nor man, but it is God and man that are represented by this sacred image."

Estella to Monasterio de Irache (2 miles/3 km):
Take NA-122 to Irache.

MONASTERIO DE IRACHE—Navarra

Just outside of Estella on the way to Torres del Rio is the Monasterio de Irache, originally a Benedictine monastery that was founded around the middle of the tenth century. It later became a Cistercian monastery and then a Benedictine university until it shut down in 1833. The monastery church retains its twelfth-century origins while the rest of the monastery derives from later sixteenth-century construction. At some future point this monastery will be converted into a Parador, one of the historic buildings managed by the government and converted into luxury hotels. As you approach Irache, the monastery stands monumentally amid its vineyards, which produce excellent wines with the Monasterio de Irache label, a survivor of the monastery's heritage on the Camino. More specifically for pilgrims, the Bodegas Irache maintains a fountain next to its winery that has two spouts, one for water and the other flowing with wine.

Irache to Torres del Rio (16 miles/26 km):
Take A-12; exit onto N-111 for Los Arcos and Torres del Rio.

TORRES DEL RIO—Navarra

Torres del Rio is most famous for its Holy Sepulchral church, reflective of the Church of the Holy Sepulcher in Jerusalem. Like Eunate, this is a twelfth-century Romanesque and eight-sided church. Its round tower (*torre*) is what gives the town its name. The cross-ribbed vaulting of the ceiling is another technique from Muslim Spain incorporated into Christian sacred architecture. The cross-ribbing meets at the center peak of the rounded ceiling to form an eight-pointed Islamic-inspired star. It is also a pretty, steep, hill-settlement town surrounded by vineyards.

Torres del Rio to Logroño (13.5 miles/22 km):
Take N-111, which becomes A-13, to Logroño.

LOGROÑO—La Rioja

The Camino in the Middle Ages turned Logroño from a small farming community into an expanding town and a major pilgrim stop.

If you are walking the Camino, shortly after you cross into Rioja, near Logroño, the paved part of the walking path turns from asphalt gray to wine-colored pavement. It remains this way into Logroño as you continue to pass vineyards, homes, and, eventually, the great cemetery on the eastern edge of town, which is so large there is a map at its entrance gate to help visitors navigate to their beloved's tomb. (Cemetery passageways have street names.)

Next is the lush expanse of the Rio Ebro, which cuts through a wonderful park in the city. This river is the path to follow for any wine lover in Rioja as it snakes through the prime wine-growing areas so famous in the world.

The pilgrim's path then leads into the old medieval quarter of the city, which is small and well maintained. The rest of the city is freely modern but is wide, open, clean, and airy. All in all, Logroño is an easy city to inhabit.

Its main sacred centers are four: the cathedral, the Iglesia de Santa María de Palacio, the Iglesia de San Bartolomé, and the Iglesia de Santiago. The latter has a gruesome animated relief carving of St. James in his manifestation as the Moor Slayer, a fairly unattractive facade but still one of a historical reminder that people used their saints for peace as well as for war-making. It was made in the seventeenth century and depicts the battle at Clavijo, just eighteen kilometers south of Logroño, in AD 845 between Ramiro I and the Muslim ruler, Abd al-Rahman II. The battle at Clavijo was the first place where St. James in his more violent propagandist form as *Matamoros* ("Moor Slayer") appeared in the battle between the brethren Abrahamic faiths of Christianity and Islam.

The sacred gems of Logroño are San Bartolomé and Santa María de Palacio.

San Bartolomé

This twelfth-century church is well used by locals as a place for prayer and respite from the profane world beyond its walls. It is a solid and lyrical Romanesque stone structure. Inside, in the back on the choir balcony is a powerful depiction in the form of a mandorla of Christ on his throne. At night when the church is lit by indirect lamp and candlelight, this mandorla is the only part of the back wall that is lit, creating an ethereal heaven-calling-Earth effect that is natural not hokey.

This is a delightful medieval church spared the excessive ornamentation of later Baroque altars. It retains simple stone sculptures and has shallow stone niches for sacred persona rather than those gold embossed overly ornate side chapels of other places, which can often distract from a more directed spiritual focus of meditation. San Bartolomé is, in other words, a rare medieval church that feels as if you have stepped into the earlier Middle Ages when churches were more places of worship and less canvases on which royalty could show how powerful they were.

The scenes on the external western facade depict St. Bartholomew's life. One of the twelve apostles, Bartholomew is also called Nathaniel. The left panel shows his martyrdom in Armenia, where he was flayed alive and then beheaded. This manner of execution has made him the patron saint of tanners and leatherworkers.

Santa María de Palacio

The charm of this place is not its building. Once this church was a more charming and intimate Romanesque church that was connected to Alfonso VII's palace, hence the name *de Palacio*. What you encounter now is mostly the result of the more rational and soulless sixteenth to eighteenth century. But still, there is magic in these walls. The charm of this place is twofold: First, it is actively used by locals as a daily haunt. During the *paseo*, just before Mass in the early evening, gaggles of family and friends take a turn around the aisles, visiting favorite chapels, sharing heavy concerns with saints and friends, asking Mary and Jesus for intercession. Second, it houses Nuestra Señora del Ebro, a mysterious Gothic wood-carved polychrome statue of Mother and Child that was found floating down the Rio Ebro toward the end of the nineteenth century. No one knows from where she came but the style dates the work to the thirteenth century. Given the lack of provenance, the Virgin was given the name of the river in which she was found.

Logroño to Nájera (17 miles/27 km):
Leave Logroño on LO-20; take A-12, which becomes N-120 to Nájera.

NÁJERA—La Rioja

Nájera is tucked in between and against red sandstone cliffs that distinguish this Riojan town from others. The town straddles the lovely Navarrete river, with its appealing medieval town on the north bank and its comfortable and more modern new town on the south bank. The most important sacred monument here is the Monasterio de Santa María la Real. It is an especially moving place because it is built into the red sandstone cliff, its back wall formed naturally by the mountain. You really get to enjoy this nature-meets-human effort when you visit the church. In the back are the tombs of Navarrese royalty from the tenth century, a time when Nájera was a kingdom all its own, separate from Navarra and Castile. (As such, it was the site of battles not only between Christian and Muslim but between Christian kings of Navarra and Castile.)

Between this illustrious row of tombs that have as their backdrop the natural cave wall is a cavernous passageway into the mountain that leads to the cave of Santa María la Real, patroness of Nájera, a lovely Gothic Lady surrounded by lilies and the glow of candlelight. The experience it affords is of connecting us with our ancestry of early humans going deep into the caves for ritual transformation.

Legend recounts that one day the king, Don Garcia, was out hunting partridge with his falcon. When he released the raptor in pursuit of its prey both birds disappeared into a thicket of trees. The king dismounted and walked into the trees to look for them and encountered a cave from which a resplendent light poured forth. When he went in he saw a lamp-lit altar on which sat the Virgin and Child with a cluster of white lilies and a bell. On either side of this celestial pair sat the falcon and the partridge. He had a church built around this cave and consecrated it in 1056. Much of what you see, church and monastery, was rebuilt during the fifteenth and sixteenth centuries. But the Lady in her cave retains that ancient timeless feel. There you will find Santa María la Real holding a bell, her Child on her lap, and before her a vase of fragrant fresh-cut white lilies, all illuminated by candle and lamplight. It is likely that this cave is like many others found in the area and was carved out of the soft sandstone by early inhabitants of the area, around the third century AD, and used for living spaces and for defense.

The cloisters are perfectly balanced and invite walking meditations, though most of the sculpted figures are beheaded and can be a bit disturbing. This was the work of Napoleon's troops in 1809 during the War of Independence. In the cloisters, you will also encounter the juxtaposed tombs of Doña Toda and her beloved husband, Diego López de Haro, a local nobleman who was distinguished in his skill in the Battle of Las Navas de Tolosa in 1212, which was the decisive battle that turned the tide of Muslim dominion in Iberia and gave the Christian kingdoms the upper hand. He died in 1216. Doña Toda was his second wife and their love was of such profound and epic proportions that they desired to be next to each other for eternity. As such, their tombs lay side by side and are of two distinct and equally interesting Romanesque styles.

Nájera to Santo Domingo de la Calzada (12 miles/19 km):
Take N-120 to Santo Domingo de la Calzada.

SANTO DOMINGO DE LA CALZADA—La Rioja

King Alfonso VI of Castile, one of the main commissioners of works to develop the Camino and make it more accommodating to pilgrims, hired two engineers, also to become saints, whose names you will encounter along the road: St. Dominic (Santo Domingo) and St. John of Ortega (San

Juan de Ortega, and originally, Juan de Quintanaortuño). Though responsible for many works—bridges, roads, hospitals, churches, hostels—along the pilgrim's road, this town gets its name from Santo Domingo because he lived here and founded the settlement in the eleventh century. Prior to founding Santo Domingo de la Calzada, he lived the hermetic ideal in isolated woodland nearby along the river Oja, which flows just to the west of Santo Domingo de la Calzada. (Incidentally, Rio Oja becomes *Rioja*, which is how this region received its name.) Santo Domingo's background was not deemed distinctive enough for a nearby monastery to allow him membership and so he turned his vision and skill to creating a better infrastructure for pilgrims along the Camino. Many stone bridges in the area can be traced back to him and San Juan. Only when you realize just how many rivers flow across the mountains, valleys, and plains of northern Spain, and how many stone bridges you use to cross them, does this saintly pair's work, as well as that of other bridge builders, become truly significant.

In a few more kilometers you will encounter Santo Domingo's disciple's namesake settlement, San Juan de Ortega.

Santo Domingo had several important structures built here, the most important might be the bridge that allowed easy passage across the river Oja. He also had built a church, a hostel for pilgrims, and a hospital. A few decades after Santo Domingo's death (1109) the church was rebuilt into a larger Collegiate church. In 1232 the church was elevated to the status of a cathedral when Nájera's bishop shifted his residence here. Santo Domingo's tomb rests in the cathedral.

Although the thirteenth-century Romanesque and Gothic cathedral justifiably gets most of the attention from pilgrims and other visitors, I have to say it is a bit dark inside and, moreover, possesses a strange air, one I think brought on by the presence of a rooster and a hen living in the confines of a cage built overhead near the southern transept, across from Santo Domingo's tomb. The two birds represent a medieval miracle that took place here: A pilgrim was wrongly accused of stealing and was hanged. When his hanging body remained alive for three days, his parents begged the local authorities to let him down, never ceasing to proclaim their son's innocence. The local judge was just sitting down to a meal of roasted birds—rooster and hen—and said sarcastically, "I'll release your son when these two stand up and sing." At that moment the two cooked fowl came back to life and stood up and would not halt their singing until the pilgrim was brought down from the gallows.

This one miracle has distinguished Santo Domingo de la Calzada from other places on the Camino. Adding to the magic of the tale, the current hen and rooster held in the cathedral are reputed to be descendents of the two birds of miraculous fame: not only did the two revive their lives but also regained their ability to reproduce. Thankfully, the pair is one of several who rotate throughout the month. Otherwise it would be a dismal and dark existence for light-loving birds.

Santo Domingo de la Calzada, not an unpleasant town but not as easy to inhabit as neighboring Nájera, possesses what I would consider a more spiritual space than the cathedral. A small hermitage chapel stands nearby, on the same plaza where you will also find the cathedral's bell tower, which is curiously separated from its church. Within the little single-nave Gothic hermitage chapel there is warmth, light, and quiet for contemplation and prayer. On the altar stands the Virgen de la Plaza. She is a harvest divinity and is processed around town two times a year, once on August 15 to honor Mary's ascension to heaven, and the other during the harvest season on September 18 for the Fiestas de Gracias, thanksgiving festivals. She is Santo Domingo de la Calzada's patroness.

Santo Domingo de la Calzada to Redecilla del Camino (6.5 miles/10.5 km):
Take N-120 to Redecilla del Camino.

REDECILLA DEL CAMINO—Castilla y León

This is the first stop in a Castilian town after leaving Rioja and is among the pretty villages along this stretch toward Burgos. Its main sacred site is the Iglesia de la Virgen de la Calle, a simple Baroque church with an earlier (twelfth century) Romanesque baptismal font that is carved from top to bottom with an idealized celestial city. The base forms eight tightly carved columns made from what appears to be one piece of stone.

Redecilla del Camino to Tosantos (9.5 miles/15 km):
Take N-120 to Tosantos.

TOSANTOS—Castilla y León

Just before you reach the village of Tosantos is a dramatic church built up into a cliff-side cave where the miraculous Romanesque image of Nuestra Señora de la Peña was found and currently resides.

Shortly, the trail to San Juan de Ortega will pass through the Montes de Oca, once a place that was dangerous for pilgrims due to the bandits who hid in the twists and turns of the hills and mountains. Santo Domingo and San Juan de Ortega did much to tame these hills for pilgrims. Today it is a peaceful and beautiful hiking area in a spirited natural setting, a last mountainous passage before arriving at the great Spanish tableland, the *meseta,* whose big sky and broad horizon passage will be your constant companion for the rest of your journey across Castilla y León. The village of San Juan de Ortega marks this transition, appearing suddenly on the open plain to the pilgrim after a day of walking through the Montes de Oca.

Tosantos to San Juan de Ortega (16 miles/26 km):
Take N-120; turn right onto BU-V-7012; take BU-V-7017.

SAN JUAN DE ORTEGA—Castilla y León

This village has but a few inhabitants, yet it is a main stop on the Camino given an important sacred monument here: the monastery church of San Nicolás founded, designed, and partly built by San Juan de Ortega in AD 1142. From 1431 until the monastery was disbanded in 1835, it was occupied by Jeronymite monks.

San Juan's church is called San Nicolás based on a miraculous intercession from this saint (San Nicolás de Bari) that saved his life at sea when he was returning from his travels to the Holy Land, a journey he took shortly after his teacher Santo Domingo's death. When San Juan de Ortega returned to Spain, he settled in the Montes de Oca and he built a chapel in honor of San Nicolás, a location that was to become his namesake village. *Ortega* is derived from *ortiga,* meaning "nettles," which were plentiful in the wild spot on the Camino that he chose for his chapel and abode. He was buried in the chapel when he died in 1163.

Started in the twelfth century and completed by the fifteenth century, the monastery church of San Nicolás, with its light-colored stone and sweeping Gothic arches, is a sweet place to be. The Gothic aspects were the addition of Queen Isabel la Católica, who, in the late fifteenth century, visited San Juan de Ortega because he was the saint reputed to help with infertility as well as to help women conceive male children. Earlier, in the mid-fifteenth century, an Augustinian prior had opened San Juan's tomb and the smell of roses spilled forth, as did a swarm of white bees. It was fabled that the bees represented yet-to-be-born souls who awaited women praying for a child; they gathered around the saint, a legendary protector of children, and waited for their chance to incarnate. The bee is an ancient symbol in many cultures for the soul, fertility, prosperity, and plenty.

Beyond these unique stories, one wonderfully unusual aspect distinguishes the monastery church's design: Twice a year people gather here during the equinox, on March 21 and September 22, to witness sunlight entering the church at 5 p.m. and shedding a precise ray of light on the Romanesque carved capital of the Annunciation in the church's crossing, which pinpoints the Virgin Mary's belly. This too must be a part of the powerful fertility rites sought here over the centuries.

San Juan de Ortega to Atapuerca (5 miles/8 km):
Take BU-V-7017; turn right onto BU-V-7012 and continue to Atapuerca.

ATAPUERCA—Castilla y León

The landscape you pass through between San Juan de Ortega and Burgos takes you through the Sierra de Atapuerca, an important region where the oldest hominid remains on the European continent have been found, some dating to approximately eight hundred thousand years ago.

Ongoing excavations continue to reveal new evidence for ancient occupancy. This presence reinforces a feeling that this is a very ancient land, one found appealing as far back as our pre–Homo sapien ancestors, not just among the bipedal moderns walking the Camino for the past thousand years. Visits can be arranged by calling ☎ 902-024-246 or e-mailing info@visitasatapuerca.com (🖳 www.visitasatapuerca.com). The archaeological site is accessed via either the village of Ibeas de Juarros or further north at the village of Atapuerca.

Atapuerca to Burgos (15 miles/24 km):
Leave Atapuerca S toward Santovenia and continue to N-120; turn right onto N-120 to Burgos.

BURGOS—Castilla y León

The city was founded as a frontier settlement in the ninth century, first a castle surrounded by humbler settlements collectively called *burgos*, "villages," which expanded and fused more or less into one entity. In the tenth century, Fernán González, the first count of the newly independent Castile (and rival to King Sancho I of Navarra), made Burgos his capital. The city reached its political height in the eleventh century when it was made the capital for the united kingdoms of León and Castile. This status was contested when Christians took Toledo in 1085 and moved the court there two years later. But Burgos's political influence lasted until 1492 when the capital was shifted to Valladolid. But even after this, Burgos remained a powerful economic center.

This entire legacy bears witness in the feel and the cosmopolitan mood of the current city. Burgos is also the home of the famous El Cid, born Rodrigo Díaz, whose mercenary and knightly exploits make for the most romantic storytelling from eleventh-century Spain. There is a plaza dedicated to him, showing him astride his steed (Babieca) with his famous sword (Tizona) pointed forward, ever ready to take on a cause. Indeed, recently when six suspected Islamic terrorists were detained in Burgos, a newspaper's op-ed page had a cartoon of El Cid on his horse with sword pointed out, looking a bit world weary. Extending from El Cid's plaza is the bridge, Puente de San Pablo, whose two sides are heralded with statues of famous personalities of Burgos. The stone statues have a neo-medieval style that feels a bit like wandering into Middle Earth.

There are many sacred monuments to see here. Among them are the Monasterio de San Juan, the Iglesia de San Gil, the Iglesia de San Esteban, the Iglesia de San Nicolás (closed for renovation at the time of writing), the Iglesia de San Lesmes, the cathedral, and the two monasteries that act like parentheses to the city, the Cartuja de Miraflores, a Carthusian monastery on the eastern outskirts, and the Monasterio de las Huelgas, a Cistercian convent on the western edge. Both monasteries can be reached by a delightful river walk that stretches across Burgos on the south bank of the Arlanzón river. Here I dwell on the church of San Lesmes, the cathedral, and the two monasteries, plus a little tour to a sweet church founded by the Clarist nuns that has historical significance but is off the usual tourist path. It has an enchanting spiritual nature and is used by locals as a place for daily meditation.

Iglesia de San Lesmes

This is a nice medium-sized church on the Plaza de San Juan and passed by pilgrims shortly after entering in Burgos. It is dedicated to Burgos's patron saint, whose tomb lies on the front of the nave's central aisle. The church was connected with the hospital of San Juan and was dedicated to helping the sick and poor on the Camino. It became a particularly important place at the end of the eleventh century, when it was headed by the French Benedictine monk Adelelmo, whose name in Castilian became

Lesmes. He was particularly dedicated to helping those in greatest need. After his death in 1097, he was declared Burgos's patron saint.

Burgos's Cathedral

This is Spain's third largest cathedral, after those in Seville and Toledo. It was built between the thirteenth and the eighteenth centuries and is like a spiritual open-book journal with all its sacred symbols and powerful or allegorical people carved about its outside and inside walls; each era of religious and political elite has engraved its mark on these stones. The cathedral moves many visitors for its incorporation of symbols

Interior view of the rose window in Burgos's Gothic cathedral, Castilla y León

from many faiths, most notably the Star of David rose window facing the Plaza de Santa María, the transept's lantern in the Islamic eight-pointed star motif marking not only the heart center of the cathedral but also the spot under which lays El Cid's and his beloved Doña Jimena's tombs, and the prevalent sun and wheel of fortune symbols—inside and out—harkening to a pre-Christian and pagan mystical past.

El Cid himself was a mixing of worlds, in spite of his later romantic status as Catholic hero; he was a mercenary who fought for both Muslim and Christian kings, depending on who was being nicer and who had bigger purse strings. His nickname is telling in that it is Arabic, *al-sid*, meaning "Lord" or "Sir."

Cartuja de Miraflores

Still owned and occupied by the Carthusians, this territory at the eastern outskirts of Burgos was once the Castilian king Juan II's hunting grounds. He gave the land to the order in 1442. It is a delightfully secluded fifteenth-century monastery separated from the rest of Burgos by a tranquil pine forest. Twenty monks make the Cartuja de Miraflores their home and dedication. Their order is secluded from the public but they welcome visitors to enjoy their church, where the tombs of Juan II and his wife, Queen Isabel of Portugal, hold the central space before the altar. Stand and look at their star-shaped tomb, and dedicate equal patience to the carvings on the choir seats that line the pathway toward the altar. All possess intricate layers of carvings, symbols, and stories. The Lady of this place is Nuestra Señora de la Leche, Our Lady of the Milk. She is also called Nuestra Señora de Miraflores. You can see her on the king and queen's eight-pointed star-shaped tomb, on one of the alabaster side panels underneath the side of the tomb where Juan II lays.

Monasterio de las Huelgas

Beyond the pilgrim's *albergue* on the very western edge of Burgos stands the Monasterio de las Huelgas, a simple Gothic Cistercian convent with many Mudéjar elements, which houses several royal tombs. It was a convent for women with royal and aristocratic backgrounds, as well as a holy setting in which to knight Spanish kings at the beginning of their reign. There are two cloisters, one a large Gothic cloister whose ceiling was uncovered some years ago to expose Mudéjar stuccowork beneath. The smaller convent cloister has wonderful Romanesque double columns with intimate proportions and simplicity. It is connected to a Mudéjar chapel from the late twelfth or early thirteenth century.

Next, in a nearby garden is the Mudéjar Chapel of Santiago. Approaching its entrance feels as if you are suddenly transported to the entrance of Málaga's Islamic fortress, the Alcazaba, with the signature horseshoe arch brickwork doorway. Inside the chapel is a statue of St. James holding a sword and with movable arms. It is said that this statue of St. James was outfitted as such so that King Fernando III (1201–1252) could be knighted by someone not beneath his status. His epithet is "el Santo." He was the king of Castile who took Córdoba, Seville, Murcia, and Jaen from Muslim rule and reduced the Nasrid king of Granada to a vassal who had to pay tribute to Castile. His policies with the Muslims and Jews in his newly gained territories were pretty brutal and segregationist. Finally, it was Fernando III who declared Castilian the official language of the growing Christian kingdom that over two centuries later would become modern Spain.

Iglesia de Santa Clara

Attached to the still occupied and active Clarist convent, which is connected to the church, you will find the Iglesia de Santa Clara on the south side of the river at the intersection of the streets Calle Santa Clara and Calle Ramón y Cajal, very close to where the museum of human evolution and its associated conference and research center are going up. This church is very much a part of the neighborhood. Its likely fourteenth-century foundation stones are below the modern street level and so when you enter you must step down and off the modern street and into the earlier street level. Inside is a rounded stone candlelit space—rustic Gothic might be the best way to describe it—that immediately embraces and invites the visitor. In back, behind a closed grilled iron gate sit the nuns in their own prayer niche. Several aisles, radiating like sun rays from the center of the church toward the altar, offer different places for peaceful meditation. The overall effect is like a vase full of flowers with the nuns in the base of the vase, the grilled gate at the vase mouth, and the aisles and altar spreading beyond as the radiating flowers.

Burgos to Frómista (50 miles/80.5 km):
Leave Burgos on N-120 to A-231; exit right onto N-611 to Frómista.

FRÓMISTA—Castilla y León

Frómista possesses one of the most typically Romanesque and French-style churches of the Camino, the Iglesia de San Martín. If one wanted to find out what unmixed Romanesque looked like, unlike many structures that later received Gothic overlays, this would be the place to come, though you will have to use some imagination—later restorations, in the eighteenth and nineteenth centuries, plus the conversion of the church into a museum, have added different sorts of overlays. But its proportions reflect the ideal harmony striven for in Romanesque spaces. Founded in 1066, its original Romanesque carvings are still preserved. In these are many beautifully rendered themes such as biblical references, historical tales, and moral and exemplary stories, including ones depicting certain dynamics within marriage: marriage itself, marital strife and arguing and, ultimately, its resolution and reconciliation. This seems to be a reminder to all who attended church here that we are not islands when we wed but still need to rely on others in the community to assist us in our status as a married couple.

Frómista to Carrión de los Condes (12 miles/19 km):
Take P-980 W to Carrión de los Condes.

CARRIÓN DE LOS CONDES—Castilla y León

Carrión de los Condes's sacred sites of particular interest are its two pilgrims' churches. The Iglesia de Santa María del Camino is a huge twelfth-century church. Inside stands its crown jewel, the polychrome statue of Nuestra Señora del Camino, also from the twelfth century. The Iglesia de Santiago is best known for its Romanesque sculptures that are especially expressive, from the intricately carved folds of fabric in clothing to detailed and animated facial gestures.

Carrión de los Condes to Sahagún (24.5 miles/39.5 km):
Take P-980 W to N-120; follow signs to A-231; exit at Sahagún.

SAHAGÚN—Castilla y León

In Sahagún's town heart stands Fray Bernardino de Sahagún (AD 1499–1590), a missionary and historian to the New World from Sahagún, who is considered Spain's first anthropologist because of his sixteenth-century study of the Aztecs. Before the New World journeys, the town of Sahagún made its name as one of the main towns on the Camino. And before that, it was the legendary site where Romans martyred the saints Facundus and his brother Primitivus by tossing them into the river Cea in AD 303. Sahagún will always bear their memory as the town's very name is a condensed variation on "Sanctus Facundus." There were several small Roman settlements in the area. One likely one is near the Virgen del Puente hermitage.

In the Middle Ages, Sahagún was a major religious, commercial, and craft center that once housed four substantial medieval communities: Jews, Christians, Muslims, and Franks—a mix of French and northern and central European settlers helping repopulate lands of the frontier between Christian and Muslim Iberia. These four communities were both distinct and integrated, living together in a state of symbiosis and mutual reliance. A small town today, Sahagún's history can still be felt in its many medieval buildings of burned ochre stone and brick. It is a vibrant place surrounded by verdant vegetable gardens and well-tended sheep. Vineyards can be seen further afield and speak of this region's decent wines.

All that remains of one of the most important Benedictine monasteries in Spain is an arch, a tower, and the ruins of a chapel on the western edge of town. The original monastery was founded in the ninth century, destroyed twice by Muslims, and then refounded and rebuilt in the eleventh century by Alfonso VI. During this time, it came under Cluniac influence and its abbot was Bernard of Aquitaine. Bernard of Aquitaine was Alfonso VI's confessor and later became the Archbishop of Toledo and Primate of Spain. As such, Sahagún became an important religious center. The Benedictine monastery underwent many alterations and ultimately was destroyed by fire in the eighteenth century.

Sahagún's most interesting legacy is the persisting influence of the Muslim craftsmen who moved and settled here from the south. Their signature style is in the Mudéjar brickwork around town. Their settlement along the Camino speaks of a more pluralistic worldview than the north-south frontier often embodies.

Four churches in particular bear the Mudéjar style: the Ermita del Puente near the pilgrim's path entering the east side of Sahagún, the Iglesia de San Tirso, the Iglesia de San Lorenzo, in Sahagún's town center, and the Iglesia de la Peregrina on the south edge of town. The latter revealed a surprise during renovations a few years ago that uncovered colorful carved plaster of geometric and fanciful plant designs by prior Muslim craftsmen under a solid layer of stucco. The church of La Peregrina dates to the fourteenth century.

San Tirso is the oldest Mudéjar-Romanesque fusion church in Sahagún, dating to the early twelfth century. It possesses a square lace-brick bell tower and a triple apse. It is beautifully proportioned inside. Located near the altar on the nave floor is a stone inlaid mystical Seal of Solomon/Star of David with the eye of God in its center.

The thirteenth-century San Lorenzo likewise has a wonderful square Mudéjar brickwork bell tower and a welcoming arched porch.

The Ermita del Puente is outside of town, surrounded by wheat and alfalfa fields and native inhabitants of frogs, salamanders, groundhogs, and birds. The building's strong Islamic influence is best witnessed in its half-sunken horseshoe arches and woven three-dimensional brickwork. It once served as a hospital for pilgrims.

Sahagún to San Miguel de Escalada (34 miles/55 km):
Take A-231 W toward León; exit N onto N-601; turn right toward Villafalé and Villiguer and continue to San Miguel de Escalada.

SAN MIGUEL DE ESCALADA—Castilla y León

San Miguel de Escalada was a common detour in the Middle Ages, though today most pilgrims skip it. It is worth taking. Go off the main road to the north, after passing through Mansilla de las Mulas. San Miguel de Escalada is one of the loveliest examples of medieval Mozarabic-style architecture on the Camino and also a simple building with beautiful symmetry and styling, from its horseshoe arch patio to it square stone chapel. It is also the largest Mozarabic church in Spain. Set in a green rolling landscape, San Miguel de Escalada was built by Cordoban Christians coming north in the tenth century. With them they brought Islamic architectural styles that predate the Romanesque.

San Miguel de Escalada has within it many elements from many of Spain's peoples: The interior is replete with columns from older Roman and Visigothic sites (the church is built on an old Roman site). The nave is structured to reflect Visigothic worship rites, not Roman. There you will see naturalistic images, plants and animals, very similar to Islamic art. Later, Mudéjar styles influenced the church's ceiling. The interior columns reflect the same peaceful forest concept that you experience on a grander scale in the mosque of Córdoba, a doubtless immediate influence in this church's construction.

San Miguel de Escalada to León (17.5 miles/28 km):
Backtrack to N-601 and take it NW (right) to León.

LEÓN—Castilla y León

I am biased toward color and light; so this cathedral in my opinion is the most beautiful and moving cathedral in Spain. This thirteenth-century Gothic cathedral is rife with beautifully wrought stained-glass windows bearing many sacred stories in such saturated and illuminated colors that entering here slices away the mortal profane world outside and transports a person into a celestial sphere. The baptismal font in Redecilla del Camino might depict an idea of a heavenly city; the cathedral in León gives the visitor a firsthand feel for what it might feel like to enter one. Even those without my bias are likely to agree that compared to the many grayer and darker cathedrals—more monuments to kings and queens than to the Divine—this cathedral feels as if the power issues more from God's direction.

Moreover, the cathedral vehemently guards its position as a sacred place and people are not allowed to take pictures, with or without flash, and are encouraged to visit the cathedral for spiritual upliftment and not touristy gawking. As such, they do not charge an admissions fee the way so many other churches and cathedrals across Spain do, but in return they ask that people do not come here and act like tourists.

León was founded by Romans. In AD 913, it became an early capital, after it was moved from Oviedo, of the expanding Asturian kingdom. But León's spiritual history took off in the eleventh century, when the remains of San Isidoro and San Vicente came here to rest. San Isidoro (AD 560–636) had been the Archbishop of Seville during Visigothic rule. During the Middle Ages, San Isidoro at times appeared in battle in similar manners as St. James. Among his more peaceful miracles were curing the deaf, mute, and paralyzed. His reliquary now rests in the Basilica de San Isidoro a few streets northwest from the cathedral.

Prior to becoming the Basilica de San Isidoro, this spot held a Roman temple over which a ninth-century monastery was built. First dedicated to St. John the Baptist and later to St. Pelayus, the monastery was destroyed by al-Mansur. It was rebuilt in the early eleventh century. The present survivor from the eleventh-century church is the most interesting part, the royal pantheon with the best-preserved Romanesque frescoes still in their original placement and form. It is like walking into a medieval Altamira. It is a small space, so the arched overhead frescoes are very near the eye, giving a greater cavernous feel. The colors are so vivid and the people and animals are dynamic and full of character, with strong Byzantine aesthetics. In addition to representing religious parables, a part of the ceiling shows the Annunciation to the Shepherds, and some panels along the arches depict the agricultural rhythms of the twelve months of the year. March is depicted as someone pruning a grapevine, April shows someone planting seedlings, September is the *vendimia* (wine harvest), October is for gathering chestnuts and fattening the pigs, November is the *matanza* (pig slaughter), and so on. Other scenes depicted here are the Last Supper, Herod's slaughter of the innocents, and Christ Ruler of All (Pantocrator).

León to Astorga (32 miles/51.5 km):
Take N-120 W of León and follow signs to Astorga.

ASTORGA—Castilla y León

Astorga's cathedral is the main focus for the pilgrim, but long before the Camino, in Roman times this town was on the Via de Plata, the mining ore route that delivered minerals to the south. As trade in metals declined, the pilgrimage road became Astorga's economic life. By the fifteenth century, it was a wealthy center leading the townspeople to rebuild their Roman town walls, which you will find still standing and surrounding the town. At the same time they built the current cathedral. Moreover, this area has connections to the matriarchal traditions also found in Asturias and Galicia. Here the pilgrim passes through intercrossing local areas within the northwest of Spain—León, Asturias, and Galicia—that speak of different cultural systems reinforced by the remoteness of this part of Spain. The Camino passes through a vein of it but much lies beyond the Camino. The district of which Astorga is the capital is called Maragatería. This regional name comes from the native inhabitants of the area, known as *maragatos*. People have speculated that the maragatos are descendents of either Berbers from the original Islamic invasion in the eighth century, Phoenicians, or the Celtic speakers who settled in this region. That there is such a debate speaks to the town's interest in its diverse past.

Astorga's cathedral commands attention as you enter the heart of town. It was built in the spot where a Romanesque church once stood. It is Gothic with a southern facade of heavily sculpted Plateresque sandstone.

Astorga to Rabanal del Camino (13 miles/21 km):
Take LE-142 W to Rabanal del Camino.

RABANAL DEL CAMINO—Castilla y León

Outdoorsy and natural with beautiful views, this pretty stone town is an appealing stop on the Camino. It was once overseen by Templars, like nearby Ponferrada. Near the pilgrim's *albergue* (Refugio Gaucelmo) is a restored Benedictine monastery where chant is a part of the evening Mass. Across the way is the Romanesque Iglesia de Santa María de la Asunción. On the edge of the village is the hermitage Ermita del Bendite Cristo de la Vera Cruz.

Rabanal del Camino to Molinaseca (17 miles/27.5 km):
Take LE-142 W to Molinaseca.

MOLINASECA—Castilla y León

A pretty town on the banks of the Rio Meruelo, this was the purported home of Queen Urraca (1033–1101), something of a fierce warrior queen who fought against her second husband, Alfonso I (king of Aragón), and against her son, Alfonso VII. She was the queen of Castile and León and a Castilian princess before that. Her first husband was Raimundo de Borgoña, whom the Castilians recognized as their king. In Zamora she defended the city against attacks from her brother Sancho II (king of Castile and León from AD 1065–1072). That's a lot of action for a woman engaged in a man's world at the time; and given that we are in a fabled land of traditional matriarchs, this might have been well-supported by the locals.

Molinaseca to Ponferrada (5 miles/8 km):
Take LE-142 to Ponferrada.

PONFERRADA—Castilla y León

The Virgen de la Encina holds court here as does the towering Templar castle (Castillo de los Templarios) built in 1282. For pilgrims past it was a custom to pass through the castle on their way to visit Santa María de la Encina. *Encina* is the Holm oak that bears a special nut, called a *bellota*. This is the favorite food of the Iberian black-hoofed pig, which makes their flesh very tasty to humans. Cured hams from *bellota*-eating pigs taste nutty and succulent and are widely sought after throughout the world. Nuts, pigs, and Virgins go hand in hand in Spain (see chapter 14). But here, the Virgin bears the name of the *encina* because, in 1200, Templar knights discovered her image hidden inside a Holm oak.

Before crossing the Río Sil heading toward Villafranca del Bierzo, you will find a gem of a church on the outskirts of Ponferrada: Santo Tomás de las Ollas, an eleventh-century Mozarabic church. It is a warm golden-stone place with a human-scale rounded apse and horseshoe arches and with a wonderful pre-Romanesque fusion of designs of native Iberians, Visigoths, and Arabized Christians.

Ponferrada to Villafranca del Bierzo (16 miles/26 km):
Take CL-631 to A-6; take exit 407 to Villafranca del Bierzo.

VILLAFRANCA DEL BIERZO—Castilla y León

Settled between two rivers and amid a landscape of vineyards and green hills, this is one of the loveliest towns along the western stretch of the Camino. Of greatest significance here is Villafranca's Romanesque church, the Iglesia de Santiago. This is where those pilgrims too weak to carry on could earn full credit for walking the Camino. They would arrive at the church's Puerta del Perdón, "Door of Pardon," and receive their absolution and blessings.

Villafranca del Bierzo to O Cebreiro (19 miles/31 km):
Return to A-6 and head NW to O Cebreiro; exit S on LU-633; follow signs to O Cebreiro.

O CEBREIRO—Galicia

This village's only reason for existing today is to receive pilgrims who have just made the difficult climb up from Villafranca del Bierzo into Galicia's infinite green mountains. It bears signs of its more ancestral village in the round-shaped, thatch-roofed homes called *palozzas*. These resemble the *castros*, Iron Age Celtic-speaking Galaeci homes, of the people to whom Galicians trace their deeper ancestry. As such it is a powerful introduction to Galicia and signals to the pilgrim that she or he has entered a different realm.

O Cebreiro possesses a lovely stone church and nearby monastery, whose foundations and plans date to the ninth century but that have since been renovated due to centuries of neglect as well as wear and tear. The site offers spiritually inspiring mountain vistas, sunsets, and sunrises on all sides, proving that the greatest architect of all is nature and divinity.

O Cebreiro, moreover, possesses one of the great miracles of the Camino. In O Cebreiro's church, in the late thirteenth or early fourteenth century, a priest was enacting the Eucharist with the mood of a skeptic. As he perfunctorily performed Mass, the only person in attendance was a poor man, a peasant who had braved a fierce snowstorm to arrive at church and receive communion. At the moment of the priest's greatest doubt, the communion wafer and the wine turned into real flesh and blood. It is said that so much blood poured forth that they filled several wine jars with it and kept these as proof of the miracle.

It is a strong consensus with many pilgrims that this area marks the beginning of some of the prettiest vistas on the Camino. While every region has its stunning landscapes, what is special about Galicia's is that the stunning landscapes do not take a break. It is a heady last stretch to the holy city of Santiago. It also has a trickster quality—villages appear to be nearby and then the pilgrim walks around a bend, where the destination village disappears from sight, only to reappear later, seemingly further away.

A local Gallego, what Galicians call themselves, confirmed that this happens to everyone, especially after walking the vast plain of Castilla y León's wheat fields where it's just you, and the horizon and the meseta villages hold their position like firm anchors for the walker.

O Cebreiro to Samos (24.5 miles/39.5 km):
Take LU-633 to Samos.

SAMOS—Galicia

The monastery of Samos is a huge Benedictine monastery that is still active, with seventeen monks living there, from ages twenty to ninety-six. Its founding dates back to the sixth century but vestiges of neither this early

A painting at the entrance to Padrón's Iglesia de Santiago that depicts the story of St. James's body being transported by stone boat to Galicia by his two most devout disciples. They moored, according to legend, on the very spot of this church's altar, Galicia

Visigothic period nor the later Romanesque remain. It was temporarily abandoned and destroyed during the eighth-century Muslim invasion. Much of what you see today was built in the sixteenth to eighteenth centuries, plus further reconstruction when the monastery was destroyed by a fire in 1951. In spite of the more modern structures, that this is one of the earliest Benedictine monasteries in Spain, established during the Visigoths, gives it an ancient feel. Indeed, it was not originally on the pilgrimage road but its early existence and the promise of a certain place to sleep led pilgrims to detour here. By and by, it became a part of the road.

What is most enchanting about this monastery is its setting in the valley and within the small town of Samos. The abbot, who greets pilgrims and visitors and organizes visits to the monastery, is cheerful and welcoming. The monastery grounds are well used. In the autumn corn stalks in the monastic fields make for a nice foreground to the rich walls of Galician granite behind them.

The second floor of the monastery cloister possesses a series of wraparound frescoes depicting the life of St. Benedict, founder of the Benedictine order, done by the modern artist Enrique Navarro in 1963. While some critics feel these frescoes are too modern for this older structure, they are both in keeping with the monastery's continual alterations over the centuries and also dramatic and original in their visual and expressive scale, offering another unique feature to this sacred site.

Samos to Sarria (7.5 miles/12 km):
Take LU-633 NW to Sarria.

SARRIA—Galicia

Originating under Romans as Flavia Lambris, medieval Sarria was founded by the king of León and Galicia, Alfonso IX, in 1230. There is a statue of him near the Iglesia del Salvador as pilgrims leave Sarria, right before the castle ruins. There is a marvelous carving of Jesus in majesty in a Gallego-Romanesque style that looks like folk art and Celtic art mixed. The other interesting sacred site is the Iglesia de Santa Marina, downhill from Salvador and in the heart of medieval Sarria.

As pilgrims pass the El Salvador church and the hilltop castle, to the right is a wonderful *crucero*, Galician-style cross, with warmly carved characters of Jesus on one side, Mary on the other, and two other women standing on either side of the cross. (They could be other women at the cross or they could be local women, patronesses perhaps?) In Galicia these cruceros can be seen nearly everywhere and each place inhabits them with as many beings as they like, given local interests, though Jesus and Mary are universally present. Jesus is rarely alone on the cross in Galicia. These cruceros are also seen on other parts of the Camino, though not as prevalently as here in Galicia.

Sarria to Portomarín (14 miles/22.5 km):
Take LU-633 W to Portomarín.

PORTOMARÍN—Galicia

Had a new reservoir not been built in the 1950s, you would have found Portomarín on lower ground, near the river Miño's bank. Portomarín gets its name literally as the mouth to the sea, a place that once had a rich life on the water. Today it is a warm small town almost entirely dedicated to receiving pilgrims. When the reservoir was built, the town was abandoned and rebuilt higher up where it now stands. Everything but the historical

Romanesque buildings were destroyed. These stone buildings were dismantled stone by stone and rebuilt where you now can visit them. At the heart of Portomarín is the most important sacred site, the Iglesia de San Nicolás, also called by some the Iglesia de San Juan, but they are one and the same. It is a late-Romanesque church and very solid, square, and heavily fortified. Its position in the heart of town grounds the entire settlement. It has especially delightful bull heads carved in the upper frame of the western portal. Around Christ Pantocrator in the center of the tympanum here are the twenty-seven Elders of the Apocalypse joyously holding their musical instruments. On the north side, the tympanum depicts the Annunciation and on the south side St. Nicolás. When you stand on the bridge that leads to the new Portomarín, look north along the Miño—there you can see the ruins of the old town on the right bank. The other Romanesque church moved to higher ground is the twelfth-century Iglesia de San Pedro.

Portomarín to Santiago de Compostela (65 miles/105 km):
Take LU-633 to N-540 N; go W (left) at N-547 and continue to Santiago.

SANTIAGO DE COMPOSTELA—Galicia

Before Santiago became the holy city for St. James and his miracle, it was a Roman burial mound, and before that, most likely a Celtic burial site. There are many mysterious layers over this earth and justifiably so. There is a magical quality here, in part given by nature and attracting humans to it and in part created by those settlers as they layered their mystical beliefs and experiences over those of the prior generations to create an enduring pull to the place.

This sacred destination is a beautiful city made of naturally polychrome granite that is further enhanced by the constant rainfall that wets and illuminates the stones. It also helps lyrical moss and little plants grow out of nooks and crannies in the buildings' stones. Carved into the stone walls throughout the medieval city are myriad mystical reminders of the city's holiness: a door lintel with Adam and Eve, a window with a carved scallop or two scallops with St. James's sword in between, or a personal tympanum to a nonreligious building with Mary in heaven rejoicing with all gathered around her. The entire medieval old city center of Santiago is imbued with a mystical energy: this is where millions of pilgrims over a thousand years have arrived and rejoiced. There are many parochial churches throughout the city as well as monumental buildings associated with the pilgrimage and the pilgrim economy. But at the heart of all the

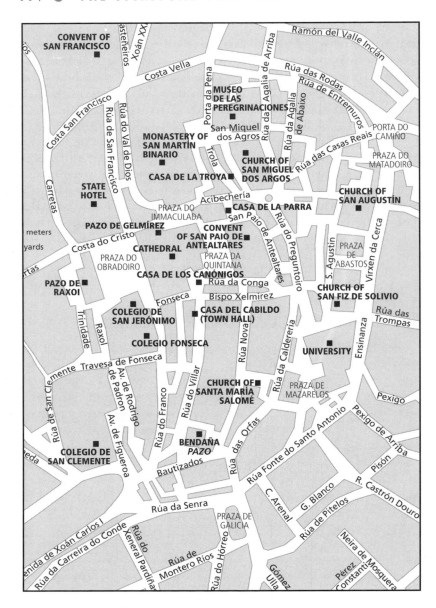

Map 2: Santiago de Compostela

stone medieval streets, their very trajectory, like rays from the sun returning to their source, is the cathedral wherein lies St. James (or Priscillian).

Santiago's Cathedral

The final goal of the pilgrimage experience is to arrive at Santiago's
Cathedral. This is not simply the cathedral that has received thousands of
pilgrims at the end of their journey. It is also a treasure of religion, of spirituality, of art, and of mystery. The mystery is that each time one visits this
site, it is different—there is more to explore.

The cathedral was built in the twelfth century, replacing a church that
was constructed in the ninth century over St. James's tomb. While the
main external facade to the cathedral is now an eighteenth-century
Baroque construction, make sure to go through it and immediately stop at
the twelfth-century facade now protected right inside the main entrance.
Called the Pórtico de la Gloria, it is a far more compelling and beautiful
facade built by Master Mateo, who incorporated exquisite imagery of hell,
purgatory, and heaven from the bottom of the facade to the top. Everyone
is here. To the left are the prophets and to the right are the apostles. Jesus
sits in the center of the tympanum and beneath him on the central pillar
stands St. James. Right beneath him is a piece of granite with the deep
impression of the human right hand, worn into the stone after eight hundred years of pilgrims touching that stone upon arriving in the cathedral. I
used to see people of all stripes still reverently touching that stone for good
luck and blessings, a ritual among millions of pilgrims past. Today this is
not possible; to preserve the medieval work, a railing has been placed to
discourage touching the stones. On the opposite side of the stone hand
impression is a possible carving of the artist himself. People who believe
this is Master Mateo, especially people who make their living from the
arts, used to go and touch their brow to his, hoping to transfer creative
mana or *baraka* to themselves. This too is now out of the question because
of the railing.

An emotional experience, even for the nonpilgrim, is to be near a pilgrim who has just arrived in the cathedral after weeks of challenging experiences on the road. When I experienced this, I had just emerged from the
central passage in the cathedral, which takes you behind a large gold and
bejeweled statue of St. James sitting right in the center of the main altar (a
Baroque statue made in 1665). The custom here is for pilgrims and visitors
alike to touch the image and ask for blessings from the saint. The woman
behind me was a pilgrim. She had walked the Camino for six weeks, solo,

beginning her journey in southern France. After I touched the statue and moved on, I turned around and saw this woman follow me out of the passage with heavy tears and an expression of sadness mixed with euphoria spread across her face. I then felt tears run down my face. I was feeling not only the strong emotion coming from her but an uncanny sense of letting go of past regrets that overtook me as I stood behind St. James and asked for clarity and strength. The cathedral's atmosphere contains a palpable charge, a transformative energy from the continuous flow of pilgrims, which is immediate and ever-present. Because of this unexpected power to facilitate positive change, it is an extraordinary place.

Beneath its medieval structure lies a more ancient burial mound, one confirmed by archaeological excavations in 1946. They confirmed the presence of a tomb that could have belonged to St. James or, as likely or more, to Priscillian, and they definitively found the tomb of Bishop Theodomir, dating his death at AD 847. Within this expanse was a first-century AD necropolis belonging to people who once worshiped the Roman gods Jupiter and Mercury as well as many obscure local deities.

Speculation that this had been a Celtic speakers' burial place as well as a Roman burial site is now more substantiated. It speaks of an old place that drew many people to it, layering their spiritualities and beliefs, their energies and outlooks into this one spot. It is an outpouring of energy and intention that has been unbroken and does not look like it will wane in the near future. This too could be how some power spots come about—first as a pull to some feature in the natural world, and then, in a dance between mortals and the site, a focusing of more and more energy that is palpable.

The twelfth-century, protected west portal of the cathedral in Santiago de Compostela, known as the Pórtico de la Gloria, Galicia

Although the pilgrimage officially ends here in Santiago, where people receive their pilgrim's credential, the Compostela, for some pilgrims there is a little farther to go to complete their Camino. For them, Finisterre still lies ahead and connects them to what might have been the more ancient, pre-Christian end point of the Camino—the end of the known world, the water's edge, and the land of the dying sun. If you have the time, this is a worthwhile trip to make and in my estimation completes the journey. There is nothing more final and transformative than arriving at a nature-made end point of striking raw danger and beauty, a dropping-off point where land ends and vast, limitless water begins. Some claim that truly completing the mystical pilgrimage to Santiago, especially the possible pre-Christian road, means going all the way to the ancient end of the Earth. Chapter 10 takes the journey there, along with a stop at Padrón, where St. James's stone boat came to rest after its long journey from Palestine.

·· ❋ ····································

CHAPTER EIGHT

Cueva de Tito Bustillo to Azpeitia

The usual residence of Mari was the Earth's interior, in those places situated near the center of the Earth, whose core communicated with the surface through diverse channels, such as caverns, grottos, or natural caves.

—Basque anthropologist Joxe Mari Barandiarán in d'Arbo's
España Mágica y Misteriosa (my translation)

THIS IS AN AREA OF HIGH CONCENTRATION for early human cave dwellings from the Upper Paleolithic era and for the magnificent flowering of cave art depicting a mystical relationship with the environment and with animals in particular, one that is still open to great speculation but is unmistakably spiritual, that is, representing transcendent experience.

Spanning from the eastern end of Asturias, across Cantabria and into Basque Country, this route takes in not only ancient caves and spirit dwelling places but also remarkable newer spirit dwelling places expressed through the Christian faith, one with a modern visitation from the Virgin Mary and the other with the birthplace of Ignacio Loyola, founder of the Jesuit order. This is also an ancient land of sun worshipers and of the Great Mother Goddess, called in Basque, *Mari. Mari* easily transforms into *María*, offering an unbroken pathway to feminine divinity.

Pais Vasco, Basque Country, or Euskadi in Basque, is an ancient land, perhaps the most ancient of all European peoples and places, as far as a single unbroken continuity to people, place, and language is factored. Perhaps this happened due to the region's intense geography, which can isolate people in mountain valleys and remote coastal points. Some of it must be attributed to the Basque ability to absorb new influences without losing the old.

Paleoarchaeologists inform us that the northern coast of Spain was a biologically diverse area for early humans seeking stable food sources. The mountains, valleys, and coastline provided a richness of foodstuffs year round when other parts of Europe were climatically more extreme. From Cantabria through Basque Country, in Spain and France, and into southern and central France, there is what is considered an arch of these caves occupied and modified by early humans. Some caves were used purely for ritual purposes and show no sign of everyday settlement, while other caves have given forth remains, indicating that people also lived in them.

This route ambles between valley, coast, and mountain, areas in such remarkable proximity that they give a direct sense of why early humans came here and why the Basque people have persisted for so long in this unique geography.

Main Route (280 miles/450 km):
Cueva de Tito Bustillo—Peña Tu—Colombres—Santo Toribio de Liébana—Santa María de Lebeña—Santillana del Mar—Altamira—Puente Viesgo—Santander—Bilbao—Unbe—San Juan de Gaztelugatxe—Cueva de Santimamiñe—Azpeitia

CUEVA DE TITO BUSTILLO—Asturias

This cave system is just behind the coastal fishing town of Ribadesella and connects to the southern reach of the town on the west bank of the Sella river.

This is the best Paleolithic cave in Asturias to view prehistoric cave paintings. It is a system of adjoining grottos beyond the cave mouth. It is especially famous for the depiction of horses and has a special cavern called *Galería de los Caballos*, the gallery of horses. Human presence here dates to earlier than twelve thousand years ago. Speleologist Tito Bustillo discovered the caves in 1968 but then died a few weeks after making his remarkable find.

On approach, the cave wall still looks ancient in spite of its proximity to Ribadesella; the area has been well maintained. Tours and visits are limited to control the cave's atmosphere and protect the art. It is hard to imagine not living here as early humans, for several microclimates greet the resident at the cave opening: the ocean, the river-estuary, the green valleys, and

The mountain and road leading to Tito Bustillo's Paleolithic cave system just outside of Ribadesella, Asturias

rolling hills and mountains. It had to have been one of the first gourmet capitals among humans, like Lascaux, Altamira, and Santimamiñe.

A DETOUR TO COVADONGA IN REMOTE VILLAGE FOLKTALES

Inland from Ribadesella and Tito Bustillo, toward Cangas de Onís, is the cavern mountain shrine of Covadonga, explored in chapter 9. This is another manifestation of the ancient Goddess appearing in new clothes. From Mari to María, her home is in the deep places in the Earth.

A few years ago, I came across an Asturian cyber storyteller. He posted a story on the Internet that he claimed was passed on by elders of remote villages in Asturias:

Long, long ago an air goddess, who had dropped herself into the ocean, was floating in the Atlantic near northern Spain. While in the water, she conceived a child. As the child gestated, the goddess continued to float.

As she neared the northern coast of Spain, she gave birth and a short time after she landed in Asturias. By this time, she was tired of the water and she wanted to get far away from it. A passing farmer and his donkey stopped and offered her a ride. "Lady, where are you going?" (This was long, long ago; long before this air goddess manifested as Mary, or her child as Jesus, so the farmer did not know who she was.) She answered, "Take me away from the water, far enough so that I do not hear the waves crashing on the rocks." So the farmer helped the goddess and her child onto his donkey and they went inland, toward the mountains. Each time he stopped to ask if it was far enough, Mary consulted her infant, who miraculously spoke to her. He said, "No, this is not far enough. The sound of the water is still too near." He had a halo of stars and light surrounding his crown. The farmer realized that these were not ordinary travelers but that he was in the presence of divinity.

Finally, deep in the mountains, near Cangas de Onís, mother and child told the farmer they would remain in the towering caverns that they could see from the foot of the mountain where the donkey had stopped. There they remained quietly for centuries. People who passed by occasionally glimpsed that there was an ephemeral presence in the mountain. Perhaps a water deity of the spring? Perhaps an earth deity of the peaks? And a child. It was not until the eighth century that Mary and Jesus announced themselves at Covadonga, the very same mountain the air goddess and child had settled into, and helped Don Pelayo and his men beat back the invading army of North Africans and Arabs who had already taken most of Iberia.

The cyber storyteller says the tale is about the goddess-based origins of his stretch of northern Spain, and that the Atlantic waters are as important a domain of the goddess as are the caves.

Cueva de Tito Bustillo to Peña Tu (14 miles/23 km):
Take N-632 E to A-8 E-70, which flows into N-634; exit right for Peña Tu just before reaching the village of Vidiago.

PEÑA TU—Asturias

This early Bronze Age rock carving dates to around 1500 BCE. Some believe it depicts an aspect of a sun-worshiping cosmology, and others, not necessarily in contradiction, think it may have been a funerary rock dedicated to a fallen warrior. The vertical stone outcropping on which Peña Tu is carved and painted stands over an area believed to have once been an ancient burial ground with mounds containing cremated ancestors. Its central position in this landscape has led some to describe the possible sun god as a sacred idol to the ancient people who created it.

The image depicts a being—the sun god?—to the right and next to it is the shape of a person. Below and to the left of this person are smaller people, like stick figures. Beyond them there are many little red dots in clusters and patterns as yet indiscernible. I took the trail to this site on an unrelentingly rainy day and the muddy, narrow, and steep path made for a challenging, though exhilarating, ascent. I confess, I was a dedicated sun worshiper by the time I located the rock art. Such early rock art is often called *arte rupestre*.

Peña Tu to Colombres (7 miles/11 km):
Take N-634 E to Colombres.

COLOMBRES—Asturias

Modern Colombres is famous for its Indiano homes, those of well-to-do return immigrants, especially in the nineteenth century. This has traditionally been an area of heavy immigration, from Galicia and Asturias, because these regions did not industrialize but rather held on to agrarian and fishing economies, which are subsistence based and vulnerable. (But nevertheless profoundly romantic, unlike industrial economies, which offer stability by comparison but lack any romance whatsoever.) For those poor immigrants who actually made it in their life abroad, some strove to return and show their success in their houses. And some among the returnees went beyond flamboyant houses and initiated public development projects to give back to their communities of birth.

Ironically, near this new wealth are some of the oldest remains of modern humans in northern Spain. *Backtrack on N-634 to signs for the village of Pimiango. Turn right off of N-634, pass through Pimiango and go toward the ocean and Cueva del Pindal:* the ancestors knew how to pick the pretty places. This is in a forested spot very near the water's edge.

Cueva del Pindal

Within this approximately three-hundred-meter-long cave are three different areas with some forty images of bison, deer, horses, an elephant, and a fish, as well as more abstract symbols. The paintings are done primarily in red paint, but black is also used, and like the other caves, the artists used shapes of the rocks, like natural sculpture, to enliven the image that they drew into three dimensions. These Paleolithic caves date to the Magdalenian period, like Tito Bustillo.

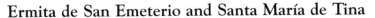

Ermita de San Emeterio and Santa María de Tina

Nearby the caves is a little coastal hermitage to San Emeterio dating to the sixteenth century (see Santander for more on him). A little further along the same path to the hermitage will take you to the tenth-century ruins of the monastery of Santa María de Tina.

Many of these little chapels and sites are used by local people for the season cycle of feast days, or for specific pilgrimages. They also are reminders that during the swelling medieval popularity of the pilgrimage to Santiago, not all pilgrims went the way of the most popular road, the Camino Frances (chapter 7), but also took other roads, such as the northern coastal road, which you are on. Many ruins go back to a time when they offered physical and spiritual shelter to such pilgrims.

All around you will not see beaches but great cliff drops into the ocean. The wild setting alone is imbued with sacredness.

Colombres to Santo Toribio de Liébana (28 miles/45 km):
Take AS-344 E to N-621 S, snaking along the Deva River to Potes; in Potes follow signs SW to the Monasterio de Santo Toribio de Liébana.

SANTO TORIBIO DE LIÉBANA—Cantabria

Like Caravaca de la Cruz in Murcia in southern Spain, the monastery here, **Monasterio de Santo Toribio de Liébana,** possesses a *lignum crucis,* this one said to come from the left-hand arm of Christ's cross. It was fabled to have been discovered and taken by the Emperor Constantine's mother, St. Elena, on the heights of Calvary Hill in Jerusalem in the fourth century. Saint Toribio carried Elena's discovery to Spain a century later and it found its home here in the Cantabrian mountains. Toribio (Turibius) was most likely the fifth-century bishop of Astorga near the border with León and Galicia. He had encountered this treasure on his pilgrimage to the Holy Land. It is said to be the largest piece of the True Cross, so large that the nail hole that pinned though Jesus' left hand is within it.

In 1958 the *lignum crucis* was carbon-14 dated and does appear to be of Jesus' era. The wood was also discovered to belong to a tree indigenous to Palestine. Some have speculated that the piece of wood came from one of the other two crosses belonging to the two thieves who were crucified with Jesus. Whatever cross it came from, this powerful sliver of wood is said to have cured many epidemics and sick people in the area.

Pilgrims flock here regularly but more so on Jubilee Years, which are when St. Toribio's feast day of April 16 occurs on a Sunday. The monastery itself dates to around AD 828. Legend says that St. Toribio, with divine assistance, tamed vicious wild beasts who carried the stones to this site for its construction. Beautiful stones they are, especially against the lush green surrounding of the Liébana valley.

Santo Toribio de Liébana to Santa María de Lebeña (5 miles/8 km):
Return to Potes; take N-621 N toward the coastal highway; halfway before reaching the coast, detour right to Santa María de Lebeña.

SANTA MARÍA DE LEBEÑA—Cantabria

Santa María de Lebeña's stone step to the altar was in recent times discovered, upon being raised, to be covered with Celtic sun symbols as well as a human figure possibly drawn in blood. Some speculate that the stone is around two thousand years old and was used in the original building of the church. Could this indicate that this spot was a Celtic sacred site? It is likely; or the stone could have come from such a spot nearby and was appropriated, as is nearly always the case, by the next religion on the rise.

Santa María de Lebeña is a tenth-century Mozarabic church and the best example of this pre-Romanesque style in the province. It has Visigothic horseshoe arches of different sizes giving a warming human quality to the imperfect but inviting building. Outside, tree spirits hold court as an olive and a yew tree stand near the church. These two were planted here at the time of the church's construction, making them over a thousand years old. The church should be open regularly in the summer. During the other seasons, ask about town for the caretaker who can open the door for you.

Santa María de Lebeña to Santillana del Mar (46.5 miles/75 km):
Return to N-621 N and stay on it to the coast, heading toward San Vicente de la Barquera; connect to CA-131 and continue to Santillana del Mar.

SANTILLANA DEL MAR—Cantabria

Santillana del Mar has long been heralded as one of the prettiest medieval coastal villages, and, as such, it is quite firmly on a touristy track. But this does not take from its charm, as the town has preserved its legacy. It was once an important town to Castilian nobility and it sits on the pilgrimage road to Santiago for pilgrims who took the northern coastal road. Finally, the town is the destination of its own pilgrimage site, the twelfth-century Romanesque Collegiate Church of Santa Juliana and its cloisters.

Santa Juliana was martyred in the early fourth century AD in southern Italy (in Cumae or in Naples). By the eighth century, her remains arrived here in the hands of pilgrim monks. The monastery was built as a resting place for her relics and became a place of pilgrimage. By the eleventh century, its influence led it to become a collegiate church.

Over the rustic Romanesque portal of the monastery church, above Christ Pantocrator, stands a later Baroque depiction of Santa Juliana standing on a winged demon. She is often represented this way, because in the best-known story of her life she engaged in a sparring contest with the devil, who was trying to overcome her dedication to God by trying to convince her to marry, a wish also strong on her father's and her suitor's minds. Martyred a virgin, we can ascertain that she won this contest and remained unmarried. Santillana the town is named after this saint, a condensing of *Santa Juliana*.

Santillana del Mar again came onto the map and became well trafficked in the early twentieth century when the Paleolithic cave of Altamira was discovered nearby. This town is the gateway to the cave.

Santillana del Mar to Altamira (2.5 miles/4 km):
Follow signs to Altamira from Santillana del Mar.

ALTAMIRA—Cantabria

This "Paleolithic Sistine Chapel" (or, more accurately, the Sistine Chapel is a Renaissance Altamira or Lascaux) is no longer open to the public but a reproduction called the Neocueva, "New Cave," is open next door along with an excellent adjoining museum and interactive didactic center on the Paleolithic. The museum covers everything from facts and speculations about early humans, from tool-making and fishing and hunting techniques to sacred beliefs and outlooks. Although the Neocueva cannot be the same experience as walking into the real cave, it exists to protect the original cave from further degradation, after so many unchecked decades of humid hordes threatening the cave art's luster with their body heat and breath.

The original cave has several galleries with paintings that were rendered with natural colored pigments of ochre, brown, and red, and outlined in black charcoal. The ancient artists sometimes also engraved their images. They likewise studied the contours of the cave wall and ceiling, picking places in the natural bulge or dip of the wall that looked like a part of the animal they were painting, making it a part of the painting and giving it a more dynamic, three-dimensional quality.

The Neocueva is a skillful copy of the original cave's entrance and its most impressive chamber gallery, the Sala de los Polícromos. It is a vast roofed area with numerous bison, horses, and deer, as well as negative hand prints and mysterious symbols. And while, again, you cannot see the original cave, it lies quietly next door, thus giving the visitor the feel of the very place that human ancestors some eighteen thousand to fifteen thousand years ago considered a part of their intimate world. While the climate and plant cover is no longer that of the Paleolithic, the contours of the land more or less are the same; they reflect a delightful feng shui of moving, curved landscapes that have both an appeal to the human eye and a great physicality.

While the debate about the sacred content of these paintings—Were they done by a shaman? Did they have magical properties? Were they a part of an initiation rite? Were they about communing with the spirit of the animals to ensure good hunting?—will likely never have a definite answer to satisfy all investigators, I think it is safe to speculate that our Paleolithic ancestors lived more fully in their environment than we do. They relied more heavily on the natural world to sustain them and very likely assigned more personal qualities to it because of that, meaning more sacred qualities as well. As such, the relationship between the sacred and the everyday world was more immediate and interconnected. We moderns forget how many artificial barriers we have placed between ourselves and the natural world, not only through technological adaptations, but through philosophical alterations as well. A part of the pleasure in coming here is that between visiting the landscape and the museum, which does a good job of laying before the visitor all these ideas and the findings, one contemplates this reality, our very place in the larger scheme of things and who we might have once been and who we still are.

Altamira's cave paintings were discovered in 1879 by Marcelino Sanz de Sautuola and his daughter, Maria. It was actually Maria who saw them first because her height gave her an advantage of seeing the low roof more readily. Sautuola published their findings the next year, but skeptics maligned the work saying Altamira's paintings were a hoax. It was not until the early twentieth century that people began to realize that at Altamira they were witnessing truly ancient, first paintings. Sautuola died before he could see this shifting of public opinion.

The fluid and dynamic bodies of the animals, which make you feel they are running, looking at you, communicating something to you, have captivated many, including modern artists. On a visit to the caves, Pablo Picasso came away saying, "Después de Altamira, todo es decadencia [After Altamira, it's all downhill]." Even this great twentieth-century master, well known for his prodigious ego, recognized and deferred to the mastery and unique vision of these earliest artists.

Altamira to Puente Viesgo (16 miles/ 26 km):
Backtrack to Santillana del Mar; take CA-131 E to Torrelavega and pass through following signs to Vargas; take N-623 S and follow signs to Puente Viesgo where you will find signs to Cueva del Castillo.

PUENTE VIESGO—Cantabria

Altamira is a great introduction to Paleolithic caves with its excellent museum. Here you are now ready to enter the real thing. This area was occupied by Neanderthals as well as by early Homo sapiens. If you only have time to see one of the two caves, which are only five hundred meters from each other on the same hill, I recommend El Castillo, given its greater time depth. Visits are scheduled and are always with a guide, with limited numbers of people allowed in at a time.

Cueva de las Monedas and Cueva del Castillo

Just 1.5 kilometers above the village of Puente Viesgo are two caves that were occupied by early humans, Cueva de las Monedas and Cueva del Castillo.

The Cueva de las Monedas contains Magdalenian-period paintings dating to around twelve thousand years ago, making it contemporary with Altamira. This cave has abundant black charcoal drawings of many animals, the most numerous being horses. Other animals are rhinoceroses, goats, bison, a bear, a stag, and an animal as yet undetermined. Together they represent fauna found in a cold climate like that of the late Paleolithic in this part of Iberia.

The Cueva del Castillo has evidence of human presence from 150,000 years ago to approximately five thousand years ago. Its cave art may date from twenty thousand to thirteen thousand years ago (also contemporary with Altamira) and employs similar techniques of engraving and pigment use as well as the seeking out of contours in the cave wall and overhang for the placement of the depicted animals. In all there are around 180 animal paintings, forty-five handprints (the majority being the left hand), and fifty signs including stylistic groupings of dots. A stunning aspect of the handprints is that some of these hands, more than to be accidental, are missing fingers, implying a ritual disfiguration in practice.

The animals' images are diverse: horses, bison, stags, bears, goats, wild bulls, and two mammoths. El Castillo shows no signs of occupation indicating that this place was used only for ritual purposes. In one place, there are two hands outlined that look like they belong to the same person and were painted at the same time (blowing the pigment over the hands through a hollow stem, bone, or in one's mouth). Was this just from two artists messing around, one helping the other, or was there some significance to this two-handed print? Was one, the hand presser or the hand painter, a shaman? Could there have been a sense of pressing against the threshold of another world? Caves are like springs, mountaintops, and coastlines, offering a threshold between worlds, this one deep in the life-giving Earth. It is not hard to ponder these possibilities when in such a deep and ancient place.

Puente Viesgo to Santander (18 miles/29 km):
Backtrack to Torrelavega; take N-623 NE to Santander.

SANTANDER—Cantabria

Santander is a great seafaring and port city whose most important century was the nineteenth, when it grew dramatically and also became a resort destination for the fashionable and wealthy. Romans built here, calling the settlement Portus Victoriae. They built fortifying walls around the settlement in the fourth century AD but abandoned it by the early fifth.

In the eleventh century, a community grew up around the monastery holding relics of San Emeterio and San Celedonio. These remains were brought by monks fleeing a Muslim attack in Calahorra (today in southeastern Rioja) and the monastery and chapel of Santo Emeterio was built on the spot of the old Roman settlement. The cathedral was then built over the old chapel and dates from the thirteenth to the seventeenth century, though it was heavily damaged by a fire in 1941. Not restored to its original luster, the cathedral's greatest interest is its location as an old sacred site—especially the crypt. In the south portal is a vaulted passageway that leads to the crypt, now called the Iglesia del Cristo. The relics of the two aforementioned saints survive here and can be viewed on the apse's left side. Moreover, the Roman ruins beneath the cathedral can be glimpsed through a glass covering in a portion of the crypt's floor.

Another curious feature of the cathedral is that its baptismal font was once a fountain from a Muslim home in Seville. It was carried to Santander by soldiers who fought under King Fernando III in the Christian conquest of Seville in 1248. Look closely and you can see the Kufic inscriptions (a style of Arabic script that is somewhat boxy) that form the fountain's decoration.

Santander likely gets its name from one of its two patron saints, San Emeterio. This was first the name of the port, Puerto de San Emeter. San Emeter to Santander finally became the name for the entire settlement.

San Emeterio and San Celedonio were brothers born in either León or Calahorra (there are different opinions on this) during Roman rule in the third century AD. As young men, they were a part of the Roman legions. When they were persecuted during the reign of the Roman emperor Dioclecian, the brothers went to the proconsul of Calahorra and proclaimed the Christian faith. They were imprisoned and tortured. Refusing to renounce their new religion, Emeterio and Celedonio were eventually decapitated on the banks of the river Arnedo in AD 300.

Legend says that just before their deaths Emeterio threw his ring into the air and Celedonio his scarf and that both went up into flames in the sky before the eyes of all present. Legend also recounts that their two decapitated heads arrived in Santander in a stone ship that pierced through a rock on the coast and embedded itself into the beach. The rock that the ship bore through is called the Piercing of the Martyrs.

Santander, as the capital of Cantabria, land of early prehistoric cave inhabitants and artists, possesses a regional archaeology museum, Museo Prehistoría y Arqueólogica where finds are exhibited from several caves in Cantabria.

Santander to Bilbao (64 miles/103 km):
Take A-8/E-70 E to Bilbao.

BILBAO—Pais Vasco

Though Bilbao is a more recent city compared to many in Spain, founded in the fourteenth century on the banks of the river Nervión, it possesses its own miraculous energies, the most important belonging to the Virgen de Begoña, whose sanctuary stands near the early medieval settlement of Bilbao.

The legend of this patroness of Bilbao comes from the end of the seventeenth century. The Virgen de Begoña was already being venerated on this spot before the seventeenth century. Near her image there grew a holy Holm oak, the *encina,* a tree that is frequently associated with the Virgin in Spain. Someone went to cut the tree down and at that moment the Lady was heard shouting, "Begoña!" They ceased their destructive activity and then returned the next day to discover that construction materials had been divinely delivered next to the tree in order to build a hermitage to the Lady.

The current shrine is Gothic and built over the site of the earlier chapel where the Lady of Begoña appeared. To get there, start from the medieval neighborhood, the Casco Viejo on the right bank of the river, and at around the lower midpoint of the street Sendeja Esperanza Askao, take the outdoor elevator (*ascensor a Begoña*) up to the sanctuary.

Bilbao's elegant and slender Gothic cathedral is also worth a visit, with its easy welcoming interior (unusual for grand Gothic cathedrals), and if you are a worshiper of modern art, the Guggenheim Museum.

Bilbao to Unbe (7.5 miles/12 km):
Leave Bilbao on BI-637 NE heading toward Getxo; exit to Leioa on BI-2731. Pass Leioa and continue on BI-2731 to Unbe. Signs on this narrow road and in this tiny place can be easily missed so do stop and ask if you cannot locate the shrine.

UNBE—Pais Vasco

Unbe is the location of a shrine dedicated to the Virgin Mary after she appeared many times in the middle of the twentieth century to a local woman who lived here. A small place of a few settlements, the shrine was once a farmhouse that has been maintained on its land and is surrounded by the ancient chestnut and cypress trees loved and nurtured by the prior residents. Nearby, before you reach the shrine, is a sacred spring, one graced by the Virgin, that has curing powers and has cured many people of varied ailments. As one dedicated local said, "This water can cure ailments of all types, those that are physical, and those that are invisible, of the mind and the spirit."

The farmhouse belonged to Felisa Sistiaga and her husband. Her story comes from two sources, the published pamphlet available at the farmhouse, with her daughter's recounting of the spiritual occurrences here, and from talking to the caretaker of the shrine.

The shrine in the old farmhouse sitting room where the Virgen de Unbe
appeared on several occasions to the matron of the house, Pais Vasco

On the night of March 25, 1941, Felisa was sitting in her kitchen waiting for her husband to return from work. She suddenly looked up at the
kitchen window and saw a resplendent light approaching. Shortly after
that, she heard a knock on the door and went to open it, thinking it was
her husband and also wondering why he would knock when he knew the
door was unlocked. But when she opened the door, there was no one there.

So Felisa went back to the kitchen and sat down. Again, there was a
knock at the door and again when she opened it, there was no one there.
She decided to leave the door open. When she was returning to the
kitchen to sit down, she suddenly saw the Virgin Mary in a corner of the
house kneeling on a chair and surrounded on both sides by lit candles.
Felisa began to cry and told the Virgin Mary that she would rise up with
her. The Virgin said nothing and shortly disappeared.

For the next twenty-eight years, Felisa did not see the Virgin again but
she had two other spiritual visitors. The first apparition took place a few
years after this initial visit from Mary and was from an angel, which Felisa
saw standing next to the house, dressed in a white tunic. The second
apparition occurred in 1968: San Pedro (Saint Peter) entered Felisa's bed-
room at two in the morning and said to her, while extending his hand
holding a key, "You have been at the door of my home twice but both
times without a key." She replied, "I've never been to your house." San

Pedro repeated that she had been and again offered the key. He disappeared. She had not taken the key.

Her daughter recounts that her mother did not know at the time that it was San Pedro. After this visit, she and Felisa went to many churches in the area, looking for whose "home" it was to which the apparition referred. In the church of San Pedro in Deusto, Felisa recognized her visitor. There she realized that twice she had been to the gate of San Pedro's "house": it was the two times when she almost died while undergoing an operation.

Shortly after this, Felisa was visited by the Virgin Mary many times, each time with messages for Felisa to note down. The first return visit took place on March 28, 1969, when Felisa saw Mary standing near the house and the Virgin said nothing. The second, also silent visit, took place three weeks later. Each time Felisa asked her what she desired and she got no reply. But on the third appearance, on May 23, 1969, the Virgin appeared near the farm's well, and when Felisa spoke, she asked her to dedicate her life and house to her. This is why the farmhouse remains as it was when Felisa lived in it.

Thereafter the family had many tribulations, including Felisa's husband's falling ill. Around that time, the Virgin appeared to her and told her that the waters of the nearby spring were holy and would cure any illness. Her husband was cured by the water, as was Felisa's son when he became ill. Multiple people since have claimed similar results.

Mary appeared many times, with many messages for Felisa to transmit to others, particularly urging people to turn their consciousness to a higher level to depart from the pain and suffering of the world. The last time Felisa saw the Virgin Mary was December 8, 1988. On this day she said to Felisa, "Today in your presence I will address humanity. The demons are running loose on Earth. With the rosary you can overcome them. I await you all here. I desire my chapel. Don't give up. You are all protected." Felisa died on February 10, 1990. Of all the messages she received from Mary, the main concern within them all was that we humans know we are protected and loved by her and that we have the ability to pull out of darkness and receive the light, that we are higher beings than we realize.

Since Felisa's death, the farmhouse has been a shrine dedicated to Mary and will remain so. When you visit, you can see the various places where the Virgin appeared to Felisa in and around the house. The kitchen is preserved as it was and the living room is a shrine. There is another shrine in the animal pen below the house as Mary appeared to Felisa there too while she attended to the farm animals. And you can visit the sacred spring with its curing waters. On her visitation in 1988, Mary appeared to

Felisa on the path between the house and the spring, walking between the beautiful towering chestnut trees. You will see a path here, suggesting that you say the rosary and do a walking meditation along this lane. The trees here, as well as throughout the surrounding land, are ancient spirits themselves and give a part of the powerful feel to this location.

There is a dedicated elderly woman who is the caretaker of the shrine, a true devotee to Mary. I met her as she stood in the farmhouse doorway turning her rosary beads in her hand. As volunteer caretaker of the shrine, she may offer to give you a tour of the place and tell you the stories. She might also ask if you would like to say a rosary and will join you, or, as in my case, will guide you through it. She mentioned that when Felisa received visitations from Mary, if others were with her, they could not see Mary but some smelled roses, others heard celestial voices or music, and others would see an orb of light but could not make out a being within it.

After this pilgrimage to the sacred feminine, next continue to San Juan de Gaztelugatxe for a pilgrimage to the sacred masculine, in honor of St. John the Baptist.

Unbe to San Juan de Gaztelugatxe (15 miles/24 km):
Leave Unbe N to Laukiz; in Laukiz take a right toward Gatika and continue E to Mungia; in Mungia head NE on BI-631; take BI-3101 N to Bakio; go E on BU-2101 to San Juan de Gaztelugatxe.

SAN JUAN DE GAZTELUGATXE—Pais Vasco

Gaztelugatxe is Basque for "castle rock" and this dramatic church is built out on a stone outcropping in the Atlantic Ocean. It can be reached only via a stone bridge, half made by nature and half by man. To truly make the pilgrimage down, allow the day for the meandering labyrinthine wild footpath that snakes its way down to the bridge and over to the island shrine. It is an enchanting walk, filled with fern undergrowth in a great old pine forest that seems to have been left untouched by the speeding world behind and above this coast. The only inhabitants on the little stone island, in addition to St. John's spirit, are a few types of maritime birds.

This solitary hermitage to St. John the Baptist reflects his wild and solitary life. It is the site of many miracles, the first being that he is fabled to have arrived at this spot in three gigantic steps from Bermeo, some ten kilometers away to the east. Other miracles concern the curative powers of this place. His feast day on the summer solstice (June 24) is a lovely pagan confluence with Christian rites, a perfect blending given St. John

*The pilgrimage shrine of San Juan de Gaztelugatxe on its rock island connected
by a stone footbridge from the mainland, País Vasco*

the Baptist's wild man qualities. This part of Spain is known for its ancient
sun veneration, a practice that held on long after the arrival of Christianity, a fact that makes a hermitage here to St. John even more powerful. For
the summer solstice all around Spain, and especially prevalent in the north
of the country, people light fires as both a purification ritual, to burn away
the bad luck of the year, also to keep the sun company and encourage its
regeneration and return for another year of life giving light. In Christian
terms, it reminds us of St. John as the precursor to Jesus, telling the world
of the light to come: Jesus' "feast day" occurs almost exactly six months
later on December 25, the Roman feast day of Sol Invictus, the uncon-
quered sun. This was a day celebrating the sun's return to light after the
longest days of darkness in the year had been conquered. After late
December, the days slowly get longer, banishing the dark.

The rock island of Gaztelugatxe is fabled to be one of the sites of pagan
sun rituals that have carried over to the festival of St. John. The pilgrimage to his hermitage here is said to cure all manner of ailments if the pilgrim follows the path of St. John's three giant footsteps. These three
footfalls are believed to have started at the wall of Bermeo and gone next
to the neighborhood of Arene, then to Mount Burgoa, and finished at the
spot where the steps leading up to the hermitage now lie. Once the pil-

grims arrive here and ascend the two hundred plus steps up to the chapel, they also must ring the bell there three times while making their wish or request. It is also a place of special significance to fishermen and other seafarers, such as sailors, who make the pilgrimage to ask for protection and intercession out at sea.

First mention of this site was in the tenth century, as a strategic lookout along the coast. In AD 1334 it was the site of Basque resistance against King Alfonso XI of Castile and León. The hermitage also came under pirate attacks, including from English navigator Sir Francis Drake in the late sixteenth century.

San Juan de Gaztelugatxe to Cueva de Santimamiñe (17 miles/27 km): Take the coastal road E to Bermeo and continue to Mundaka; take BI-2235 to Gernika-Lumo; head NE toward Gautegiz-Arteaga on the other side of the Mundaka-Gernika estuary and follow signs to Santimamiñe.

CUEVA DE SANTIMAMIÑE—Pais Vasco

Cueva de Santimamiñe, also spelled Santamamiñe, in the Mundaka-Gernika estuary dates to the Magdalenian of the Paleolithic, around thirteen thousand to nine thousand years ago. A rich environment with several varied biological zones nearby—mountain, estuary, valley, and coast—it is an ideal place for those of us, past and present, who desire a varied, delicious diet. But beyond that, the environment has a mythic quality, as if legends of timeless places could be set here. It is in the heart of this ancient Old European land of the Basques and that may be a part of the energy here. Basque Country is one of the ancient places of the Mother Goddess, called Mari. Caves and deep places in the earth were her residence and one wonders if this evolves out of the experience of the landscape, one of tall, dark, and green mountains, estuaries, outcrops of jagged land, and many cave formations. That manifestations of Mari occur in other parts of Green Spain (the term for this rainy northern Atlantic stretch from Basque Country to Galicia) under other names and guises speaks of a possible Paleolithic ancestry that has held on.

The Cave of Santimamiñe was discovered in 1916 by a group of girls who were playing around the cave, climbing about a cavity to it. They climbed around until they got to the space, now called the gallery, where the paintings of animals halted them. They went back and told their teacher at a school in Gernika, who then got word out to the officials.

Serious investigations into Santimamiñe occurred between 1918 and 1926 and then later in the 1960s.

Not closed off entirely from visits, like Altamira is, the concern is nevertheless similar for preserving these rare paintings. The chamber with the vibrant paintings of bison and horses is off limits to the public but other parts of the cave can be visited and have limited opening hours with tour guides and limited group numbers per tour. Moreover, perhaps to avoid the packed nature of weekend vacationers, it is only open during weekdays. This may entice the more serious student of the Paleolithic to make the effort to seek it out. Although you can't visit the magnificent ancient paintings, you can walk in the footsteps of the ancients who used this cave for innumerable generations.

Bosque Pintado de Oma

The vision of a modern, and still living, indigenous artist, this magical painted forest is filled with cave drawing–like images of animals, humans, eyes, abstract shapes, and vibrant colors on living pine trees. Taken together, some of the images on separate trees form one larger image. The artist, a modern artist-shaman perhaps inspired by the ancestral legacy next door at Santimamiñe, is Agustín Ibarrola. *The trail to the painted forest is near Santimamiñe cave.*

Cueva de Santimamiñe to Azpeitia (41.5 miles/67 km):
Head N to Gautegiz-Arteaga and take BI-2238 E to Lekeitio; take BI-3428 E to Ondarroa; take GI-638 E to Deba; take N-634 E toward Zumaia; exit onto GI-631 S to Zestoa and Azpeitia.

AZPEITIA—Pais Vasco

In Azpeitia itself is the church of San Sebastián, where Ignacio Loyola was baptized. His shrine is approximately two to three kilometers southwest of here, on twenty-five hectares of pasture, farmland, forest, and hills.

Santuario de Loiola (Loyola)

The treat of coming here, in addition to the sacredness this locale holds for many people, is the chance to be a part of a living tradition in a fully active order and sanctuary. This shrine or sanctuary has at its heart the birthplace of Ignatius Loyola and the basilica in his honor. The birthplace is his ancestral home, called the Tower House, and belonged to the Oñaz y Loiola family, Ignatius Loyola's ancestral family. His is a great story of a potentially bad apple turned good.

Loyola's family was a long line of soldiers of fortune, often fighting for Castile against Muslim Iberians, the French, and when called for, other Basques. The tower itself is built in the Muslim style of the fourteenth century because Loyola's grandfather was exiled to the Muslim south to fight in Andalusia after he had fought against Basque neighbors and lost. His home was also destroyed. When he returned a few years later, he rebuilt it, as you see it today in the Tower House, incorporating styles he saw in Andalusia.

The young Iñigo, Ignatius's name before he took on its Latin version, followed in the footsteps of his ancestors, grandfather, father, and brothers and sought fortune and a good time in the name of fighting for Castile. It was a battle against the French and French-allied Basques in 1521 in Pamplona, where he was severely injured, that Loyola began to alter life's priorities. As he lay unable to move for long months while his injured legs mended, he began to fall into meditative states, have visions, and gain a greater inner understanding of life. It was during this time that he decided to become a warrior for Jesus, though that road would take a few years to unfold. It included pilgrimage to Rome, as well as being taken by the Inquisition upon his return (because he reputedly took interest in many spiritual practices and traditions including Jewish kabbalah, Islam, and the pre-Christian ideas and practice of the Basques).

After being tried and eventually released by the Inquisitor, Loyola left for Paris where he stayed for several years, studying Latin and honing his ideas for a spiritual life dedicated to God. It was in Paris with a small group of seven followers that, in 1534, he founded the Society of Jesus, the Jesuits. His order was recognized by the pope, who was the only part of the church hierarchy to whom they offered loyalty. Their vows are chastity, poverty, and making the pilgrimage to Jerusalem. They do not wear habits. They are open to exploring occult and esoteric matters and thus garnered such a reputation. Therefore, it is no surprise that among Jesuits are revolutionaries and nonconformists. They are a group that is fluid and open to change so as not only to renew spiritual faith and keep it alive but to continually strive to do the right thing.

The symbol Loyola developed for the Jesuits, curiously, is an ancient Basque symbol for the sun, respecting an ancient spiritual heritage of sun worship and reverence for the natural world as also filled with Spirit. Sun symbols have marked Basque tombs for hundreds of years.

The Tower House, with its Oñaz y Loiola family crest, may have once been a titled family's dwelling but its significance today is as the birthplace of Ignatius Loyola in 1491 as well as the place where he healed his injured legs and had his visions for a different life. Loyola died in 1556, at a time when there were around one thousand Jesuits in the order. He was officially recognized as a saint in 1622. The Jesuits took up ownership of the Tower House in 1681 and developed it into a sanctuary. Around this old residence are sacred structures that later Jesuits built to honor Loyola's spiritual visions, to keep his work current, and to offer a spiritual retreat center for pilgrims.

The Jesuits today are the largest Catholic order in the world and have been responsible for innumerable good works, such as building schools and promoting education.

At the sanctuary compound is the shrine to Loyola with the Baroque and Churrigueresque basilica at its center. The eight arches that stand in a ring around the nave have messages embedded into them. Each of the keystones at the center of each of the four large arches carries a letter. The four together spell *AMDG*, the acronym for one of Loyola's main tenets of life: *Ad Maiorem Dei Gloriam*, "For the Greater Glory of God." The four smaller arches likewise have keystone messages *Vi Va Je Sus*, together spelling *Viva Jesus*, "Jesus Lives." Because Loyola's coming to God has to do with his crisis as a soldier, you will see images depicting him as both soldier and as the founder of the Jesuit order.

Most of the Masses and liturgies are delivered in Basque and some in Castilian as well as a few services in both.

Spirituality Center

The nearby Spirituality Center (💻 www.santuariodeloyola.org) on the grounds is an active place that is testimony to the Jesuits' ability to adapt to the times. In addition to standard programs for Jesuits and for people seeking traditional Jesuit sacred exercises, the center also offers workshops in yoga, Zen meditation, Enneagrams, contemplative dance, emotional education, and more. In a private park the extent of twenty-five hectares, people coming here for the scheduled workshops or retreats can stay on the grounds and enjoy walking throughout the wild green rolling, and rainy, hills and forests.

CHAPTER NINE

*S*an Vicente de la Barquera to Navia

In Asturias they say that they are Español *and that the rest of us are* conquistadores.
    —A friendly jest from a woman from Toledo living in Ribadesella

THROUGHOUT EUROPE one will find sacred landscapes from the pre-Christian past; fountains, streams, islands, rivers, inlets, caves, and grottos were often perceived as soft spots, places in the landscape where the connection between here and the transcendent was thinner, more accessible. They were places of movement and change or deep penetration into another reality, like curtains being pulled aside. The early Christians reinforced this awareness by taking over these spots. Often, they are where a saint or Mary revealed themselves. Covadonga is a great case in point. The surviving *xanas* are another. The Astures and the Celts I am sure reinforced these sacred places, which their Neolithic and Bronze Age ancestors must have located. And northern Spain is one of those very ancient places in Europe—with its mountain, cave, and coastal systems—that attracted humanity's ancestors some twenty to thirty thousand years ago. You can feel their presence if you are quiet and attuned on a walk in these realms.

This is an area where some of Spain's oldest Christian chapels and churches stand. This includes the unique style known as pre-Romanesque, for which the best examples lie in the provinces of Asturias and Cantabria and which incorporate naturalist, pre-Christian ideas with Visigothic aes-

The shrine to the Virgin of Covadonga in the cave at Covadonga where legend says Pelayo fought off Arab and Berber invaders in the eighth century, Asturias

thetics. The results are sweet, inviting, deeply moving, and intimate places of worship regardless of your spiritual lean. Another special aspect of this area is the Marian shrines, which though abundant everywhere in Spain, take on a special expression here with the coastal vista. Many of what I like to call *Marys of the Boat* dot the Cantabrian and Asturian coast where one will find altars with Mary either standing in a boat or overseeing boats placed on the altar or in the nave, the captain and protectress of fisherman and farmers alike. This unique manifestation of Mary (sometimes you have to look hard before you find signs of Jesus in these chapels) is why I have chosen this area for detailing some of the Marian shrines in Spain. And amid these is the famous mountain shrine of Covadonga, one of the most famous Marys of Spain.

Most of the Marys of the Boat are seen only on their special feast day, each town having a different one throughout the year. But you feel her presence in these towns in many forms, from little shrines tucked in a village corner at a footpath intersection, to images of her in inlaid tile on walls, to posters and little statues for sale in gift shops. Moreover, the gaze of the fishermen and their folk in these towns is on her all year long, asking for protection for one more night out at sea. Fishing is still a dangerous way of life, even with better modern craft.

Main Route (205.5 miles/331 km):

San Vicente de la Barquera—Cué—Llanes—San Antolín de Bedón—
Covadonga—Cangas de Onís—Ribadesella—Villaviciosa—
Oviedo—Cudillero—Luarca—Navia

SAN VICENTE DE LA BARQUERA—Cantabria

We start here in a town on the western side of Cantabria where it nears the Asturian border. These two provinces share in common, along with León, the Picos de Europa natural park where some of the finest wildlife, hiking, and skiing are to be had in Europe. Cantabria and Asturias also share the Marys of the Boat, given both regions' deep dependence on fishing. San Vicente was one of the important stops for pilgrims taking the northern coastal route to Santiago.

Nuestra Señora de la Barquera

San Vicente de la Barquera has one of the Marys of the Boat par excellence. It is a dramatic spot where snowcapped mountains of the Picos de Europa can be seen from the town's fortress-castle, which looks out over the harbor and two beaches formed on either side of the San Vicente de la Barquera river. Near the westernmost end of town, on a small ascent up, stands the hermitage of Nuestra Señora de la Barquera (Our Lady of the Boat), protectress and patron of seafarers and fishermen.

Long ago the Virgen de la Barquera arrived at this very spot aboard a small boat without any help: no crew, no lights, not even oars. Since then, she has accurately indicated the direction of future winds for fishermen.

Attached to her hermitage is a small simple hotel for the serious pilgrim. Inside the shrine, the altar is taken up by an image of the Lady of the Boat. From the ceiling overhead hangs a magnificent model sailing boat. This site has been a place of sea people's veneration since the fifteenth century. La Barquera's festival days take place in early September.

Also in town is a major castle-fortress and a thirteenth-century fortified church at the highest point of the settlement.

Iglesia de Santa María de Los Angeles

Founded in the thirteenth century, the majority of this church reflects a late-Gothic style though two Romanesque doorways remain. This church served as a stopping point for pilgrims to Santiago on the northern coastal route rather than the more common inland French Road, or *Camino Frances* (chapter 7).

San Vicente de la Barquera to Cué (23 miles/37 km):
Take N-634 W to Llanes; follow the signs to Cué.

CUÉ—Asturias

If you are near Cué on St. John's festival (June 24), or in the nearby village of Andrín, you will get to experience flower petal carpet paintings along the streets throughout the village. It is openly acknowledged as a pre-Christian rite of the summer equinox subsumed into the Christian cosmology. In honor of St. John the Baptist, something of a Wild Green Man whose element is water, this feast day in Asturias, as well as throughout parts of Spain, includes building bonfires around which people dance and sing, over which people jump, and in some particularly tradition-bound places, in which people burn old, defunct things. (Curiously, this is exactly what Iranians of all religious backgrounds do the Wednesday before the first day of spring—another pagan rite of purification wonderfully preserved.) After fire revelry, some places near beaches, where the fires are often built, witness the locals going into the ocean for a purifying dip. As an acquaintance from Málaga confirmed, "St. John's night is a pagan observance absorbed into Christianity; it's all about purification and clearing of energy using the elements of fire and water." This really sums it up and is the best example of how pagan customs throughout Spain have taken on Christian clothing and survive millennia later.

But the area of Cué and Andrín is unique in the creation of the floral designs on the streets. Weeks prior to the evening, villagers meet and design what that year's carpet themes will be. They are always of religious significance, reflecting local saints and Jesus and Mary, as well as natural designs and mandalas. Then about a week before St. John's night, you can see gatherings of people in someone's courtyard, separating thousands, if not millions, of flower petals from their stems and setting them aside in cool crates. The night of St. John's, after dinner, villagers begin to draw the designs in chalk on the village streets and then fill in the designs with their painting medium of flower petals, grass clippings, and topsoil. Crates strewn around the work area look like a great giant artist's palettes.

The next day, everyone waits for the communion rites of that year's youngsters to take place at Cué's main church on the highest hill. From there, the young people are the first allowed to march into town and, in a festive mood, walk on the flower carpets laid out the night before. Then everyone can walk on them and, like a Tibetan sand mandala, it is meant to be transient, used for its transformative power and then swept away. The crushed multicolor petals on the roads the day after are almost as beautiful as the carpet the day before. Eventually, local women get their house brooms out and sweep away the organic mélange for composting and use in the nearby vegetable fields.

During any other time of year, Cué and Andrín, with its Virgen de Andrín shrine on the edge of town, are lovely coastal Asturian villages through which to pass and take in the pound and flow of the ocean as well as the little churches, chapels, and graveyards, which whisper about a fishing and agrarian past not so long ago.

Capilla el Cristo

Nearby is a little forest walking trail and pilgrimage to Capilla el Cristo, a little chapel dedicated to Jesus in the woods. Signs to it, saying "La Cuesta Capilla el Cristo" can be located near the road, Avenida de la Conception, heading out of Llanes toward Cué. The path has stations of the cross marked with stone crosses on the roadside. Processions follow this road on Easter. The hermitage is surrounded by native oak trees in high concentration, speaking of a conscious planting some time ago or of the thinning of other native trees near the chapel.

Cué to Llanes (2 miles/3 km):
Take the main road leaving Cué, which leads to Llanes.

LLANES—Asturias

Prehistoric caves and Bronze Age rock art attest to the longtime attraction among humans to living along this coast. Today is no exception; and often people from Madrid as well as Cantabria and Basque Country flock to this coastal haven for sun, salt air, and good seafood. (Llanes has an active fishing fleet.) It has a long harbor and offers nice protection when salty wind and frequent rain beat the area. It should come as little surprise that sacred females in boats exist here—in this case, the most famous boat lady is Santa Ana, who stands in a boat with her daughter, the young Virgin Mary. They, along with another Mary, Mary of la Guia, are Llanes's patronesses and protectresses of fishermen.

Santa Ana and Young Mary

July 26 each year marks Santa Ana's procession, where people deck themselves and their boats and set sail within the harbor as Santa Ana and young Mary stand in their boat and are carried in procession throughout town and harbor. Some have commented that this is a blessing ceremony, making offerings to assure another year of calm and safety, as well as a clearing ceremony to dismantle old, stale energy and reinvigorate the town, people, and boats with good vibes. It is a festive, happy, flower-filled, and colorful festival.

La Virgen de la Guia

Folk knowledge says that because fishermen have been afraid of witches and the curses they could cast upon such a vulnerable profession they began making offerings to the Virgen de la Guia asking her to see that they return to port safely.

For feast days in Llanes there are three groups who have a healthy competition among one another: those dedicated to La Guia's, those to San Roque's, and those to La Magdalena's. La Guia is the most ancient veneration and the most profound as far as what it indicates about the life of the people. Her feast day is September 8 and she protects fisherman from the dangers of the seafaring life.

The Virgen de la Guia's hermitage stands at the highest hill in Llanes, is open on Tuesday afternoons, and is often a gathering place for women of all ages who maintain the shrine as well as enjoy one another's company.

Dances, processions, and offerings occur during the September festival to assure another good year without incidents. The Virgen de la Guia's symbol is a lily, which is also associated with the group, or club, who are dedicated to her.

Llanes to San Antolín de Bedón (7.5 miles/12km):
Take N-634 W; just after Posada and Niembro, follow signs to the Monasterio de San Antolín de Bedón.

SAN ANTOLÍN DE BEDÓN—Asturias

This Cistercian Romanesque church was built from the late twelfth to the early thirteenth century. Like so many structures by the Cistercians, who idealized buildings of simplicity and perfect balance, this one possesses acoustics to make any musician covetous. A whisper is delicately magnified in the most graceful ways, a chant haunting and deeply moving. At the time of writing, it was under renovation so access to the interior is uncertain, but the grounds are also enchanted. This church was built two centuries after a Benedictine monastery was founded here; today it is private property so pay attention to the signs and requests when visiting here.

San Antolín de Bedón sits tucked just to the east of the Bedón River, which opens into the Atlantic a few meters away, onto the beach called San Antolín. Outside of the too-close main road behind the beach, the area is wild, rife with nature spirits, and deeply magical. The church is tucked enough into the hillside and river valley as to block the view and sound of the road. Footpaths for the astute emerge and this is a lovely place for walking and feeling the spirit of the land.

San Antolín to Covadonga (25 miles/40 km):
Take N-634 E back to Posada; turn right on AS-115 and head S; take AS-114 W; take AS-262 S to Covadonga.

COVADONGA—Asturias

The legend goes that in AD 718 or AD 722 a fierce Asturian chief called Pelayo and a handful of local mountain rebels who followed his lead were holed up in the mountain of Covadonga, backed literally into a corner, with the advance of the vastly larger army of Berbers and Arabs camped below. Pelayo and his men were ridiculously outnumbered, and when Pelayo wondered what to do, Mary appeared to him and rained down stones upon the Muslim army and defeated them. Popular histories then go on to claim that this was the decisive battle that expelled Muslims from northern Spain once and for all.

In reality, it took more than Pelayo and victory at Covadonga to expel North Africans and Arabs from Asturias. That took another few decades. One document and some local folklore back this buried reality, one concealed beneath a popular history of a polemic between two competing faiths. In truth, the legendary tale of Pelayo at Covadonga would take a few more decades to emerge and be heralded or even to be made real.

The Folklore of Covadonga

The earliest account of the eighth-century Muslim conquest of Iberia, including the north, comes from a Christian cleric living in the same century and writing in or around AD 754, hence the name of the chronicle, *The Chronicle of 754*. In it there is no mention of Pelayo or of a battle at Covadonga. Both came into being through oral histories and likely a lot of legend.

But Pelayo existed, if anything, in the form of the first king of Asturias, and his descendents went on to forge the Asturian and Leonese kingdoms.

Today Pelayo is the patron of Asturias and represents many things Asturian, perhaps most resolutely the sense of independence of these seafaring and farming people.

The Virgin of Covadonga has become an even greater national icon, much like her sisters in other Spanish places, like Zaragoza's Virgen del Pilar and Catalonia's La Moreneta of Montserrat. She is the patroness of Asturias and year round there are many visitors to her cave shrine in the scared mountain where Pelayo was aided by the Lady in his darkest hour. As you approach the shrine you will pass by a spring that also has magical qualities.

Later in the middle of the medieval period, this divine intervention frame story would appear again and again with the Virgin appearing, or sometimes Saint James, on the eve of a frightful battle or at the very moment of greatest need. These visitations always alerted that the Christians would be victorious. (In later centuries, visitations from the Virgin took on more universal themes, such as world peace, much like the Virgin of Unbe in Basque Country.) One can imagine that on the Muslim side there were similar stories but in a Muslim mythic language. While these battles were really about land, power, and booty, they gained legitimacy through a language of faith.

Another story, one I read from a cyber storyteller from Asturias, who claimed it was told by old people of the villages around where he grew up, assigned a deeper ancestry to the Lady who resides here. It was a pre-Christian tale of a goddess who had taken up residence centuries before in Covadonga. By Pelayo's time, she had become firmly Christian, a universal manner through which ancient gods and goddesses persist in new clothing (see chapter 8 for the full story).

THE CONTEMPORARY ROMANCE OF PELAYO

I was with two Spanish friends on a drive to the mountains from coastal Asturias when I asked them about Pelayo.

"He's as Asturian as you'll get," began María, "and so he must be Spanish."

"But not Castilian."

"That's right. You're catching on." María paused and then said, "Pelayo was a Celt."

At this point, Carlos jumped in, "No, Celts don't have blond hair like he did. They were short, stocky, brown-haired people. Pelayo was tall, blond, muscular. He was a Visigoth."

"But I thought he was an Asture," I interrupted, "from the Asture tribe of Celtic speakers, not a Visigoth."

"Yes," Carlos patiently explained, "he was an Asture but not a Celt. They're short and brown-haired compared to him!" I was confused. Then I realized that Carlos was referring to the romantic portrait of Pelayo at the shrine of Covadonga. There he is portrayed as tall, handsome, strong, and blond. But nothing describes him as all Asturian, all Celtic, or all Visigothic.

I later looked more closely at that portrait and realized, like the shrine, elements of all three—the traditional Asturian designs, Celtic swirls, and Visigothic motifs—were incorporated into the portrait, allowing Pelayo to forge a relationship with each viewer's subjective mind and preferred allegiances. María made him a Celt. To her, Celts were tall, blond, and muscular. Carlos was unimpressed, seeing Celts as looking more like everyday Spaniards. He saw Pelayo as even more emblematic of a northern tribe and made him a Visigoth, and perhaps equally important, a Christian. María could not have cared less, it seemed, if he were a pagan or not.

I think Pelayo represents all Asturians, and so, he is an Asture for sure, and Celtic and Visigothic. Some might add a touch of Roman or Castilian in him; others might like to add the Viking element, which was also a part of these northern reaches. As no one really knows what Pelayo looked like—there is barely any information about him at all—he has become something of a group dream.

Covadonga to Cangas de Onís (7 miles/11 km):
Take AS-262 N; follow signs to Cangas de Onís.

CANGAS DE ONÍS—Asturias

Shortly after Pelayo's legendary victory, the new Asturian kingdom and its throne centered in Cangas de Onís, the mountain town nearest Covadonga. Favila became the second king of Asturias. He was one of two sons to the famous Pelayo. He inherited the small striving Asturian kingdom, which was well on its way to becoming Christian but which was still immersed in plenty of pagan elements and tendencies.

Favila's rule was short, from AD 737 to 739. The manner of his death actually added to his prowess and legend, and short rule: he was mauled by a bear while out hunting. The bear's descendents still roam the wilds of Asturias after many well-won modern conservation efforts, though we can't be entirely sure where Favila's descendents are. That his short rule came about from a lethal bear and not from citizens' unrest speaks of his popularity and why his name is everywhere in Asturias.

Because all of Favila's children were too young to take their father's throne, Favila's brother-in-law, Alfonso I, "The Catholic" (739–757), took the post. He was also a beloved king. Indeed, Asturian royal history is full of beloved kings. Several kings after him, King Alfonso II (791–842) moved the capital to Oviedo.

Today, Cangas de Onís is the frontier town of choice for trekkers entering the Picos de Europa natural park for hiking, camping, and skiing.

Dolmens and the Chapel of Santa Cruz

One of the most intriguing aspects of Cangas de Onís is the pre-Romanesque Capilla de Santa Cruz, a little chapel on the edge of town that was built in AD 737 by King Favila and his wife, Queen Froiliuba. The chapel had been modified over time and was later rebuilt after its destruction during Spain's civil war (1936–1939).

At the entrance are the strong and naturalistic depictions of the oak tree as Jesus and the crescent moon as Mary. Notice the column base to your left at the bottom of the steps. Here there is a stone carving of a cross with an oak leaf emerging from its trunk. Underneath the oak cross is the downward pointing new moon. Throughout sacred Christian sites in Spain, Mary anchors the Earth and Jesus above her, heaven. This at Santa Cruz is perhaps one of the most beautiful depictions of this meeting of Earth and heaven. Next, on the wood-carved tympanum over the chapel entrance, is the cross as the Tree of Life, and it is surrounded by branching oak and leaves. The tympanum itself looks curiously like a ship's wheel. All the surrounding trees in an area of mixed indigenous trees are exclusively oak. I have noticed this selective planting, or thinning of other trees, especially across the north where the oak thrives. It always occurs around sacred sites, giving a high density of oak in the vicinity and the resumption of the natural mixed forest just beyond the sacred oak groves. The oak was a sacred tree for many ancient Europeans and its importance persists here.

Inside, the chapel adds to the profound importance of this site. The chapel is built over a cluster of Neolithic dolmens, some with carvings or paintings on them, primarily of zigzag formations. It is very likely that this site was used consistently as a sacred spot even after the end of the Neolithic and that it was the natural building place for Favila's new church. The dolmens were probably erected here around four thousand years ago and belonged to the early farming and herding peoples who lived here then.

Cangas de Onís to Ribadesella (15 miles/24 km):
Take N-625 N to N-634 and turn right; continue on N-634 to Ribadesella.

RIBADESELLA—Asturias

Set on the Atlantic coast in eastern Asturias where the Sella River empties into the ocean, this town has two halves. The eastern half is where most of the old town stands, including the shrine to the fishermen's Mary. The western side has a long beach, the Playa Santa Maria, along which you can witness a promenade of what are called *Indiano* homes. These are houses built by return immigrants from the New World who made enough wealth to build these nineteenth-century mansions.

Ribadesella was founded in 1270 as a fishing town. It is still an active fishing town and you will see many boats, most of medium and small sizes, making their daily and weekly accounting with the ocean.

The Marian fisherman's chapel, the Virgen de la Guia, is at Ribadesella's highest point, overlooking the sea. Though you will likely find the chapel locked, you can peek through an opening in the door and see her standing in light blue attire on the altar, a boat upheld on her left arm as she leans on an anchor with her right hand. The side wall along the little nave is mounted with dozens of model boats, many with great sails. Her feast day is the first Sunday in June.

On your way up to visit Ribadesella's Mary of the Boat, you can pass along the river mouth promenade lined with depictions of mythic characters from pan-Asturian folklore; these are the pre-Christian manifestations of a sacred life way that have survived. Now considered folkloric, they once represented very real forces in nature as well as those energies within a person's psyche. Some of the most famous are:

- The *xana* is something of a water and earth goddess, possibly derived from the Celtic Ana or the Roman Diana but harkened to a more ancient sacred feminine than either of these two. Like Diana/Artemis she protects wild nature and defends the innocent. She looks harmless enough and is a bit of a moral trickster. If you fail the moral test, you will be publicly embarrassed or worse. If you pass, you will be rewarded with her vast treasure, which she guards at the entrances of waterways and natural springs. She is the force of pristine nature in balance.

- The *cuélebre* is the xana's consort. He is a gigantic dragonlike serpent who protects the xana's treasure. I see him as a part of the masculine sacred that balances the feminine.

- The *nuberu* is a wild-looking man with grayish skin and wild furs who is a force of nature and makes storms, lightning, and rain. He is unpredictable and wanders around the hills, mountains, and coast in an erratic manner and can erupt without warning.

- The *trasgu* is a delightful and mischievous house elf character. If you find a loaf of bread missing in the morning or your kitchen cupboards are completely reorganized with things in places other than where you left them, it is he. He can be an ally if you offer him food. If not, he will be worse than a team of mice let loose in your kitchen at night.

- The *serenas* are Asturian mermaids. Most are depicted with a twin tail, as in Romanesque churches throughout Spain and France. They are both temptresses of sailors and fishermen as well as idealized aspects of femininity. This dualistic nature makes them particularly complex creatures.

- The horned, Pan-like *busqosu* should not be erroneously equated with the devil, as some have done. Instead, see him in his more-ancient guise, as the protector of the forest, of the wild animals and of the herds. This was his original, and more authentic, meaning across the ancient north.

- The *diañu burlón,* another horned creature, this time a goat, is a trickster and also a shapeshifter. He especially likes to joke around and fool people.

The Paleolithic cave with wonderful paintings of ancient horses, Cueva de Tito Bustillo (chapter 8), is on the edge of town set into a mountainside near the water's edge and continues to give the place a prehistoric feel in spite of the more recent square, pyramid-roofed Asturian *hórreos* that stands near it.

Ribadesella to Villaviciosa (23 miles/37 km):
Take N-632 W to Villaviciosa.

VILLAVICIOSA—Asturias

Going inland from Ribadesella you will pass through Asturias's prime apple-growing and cider-making country. Called *sidra*, this golden elixir has complex characteristics a result of *terroir*, climate, and the fruit varietals. Villaviciosa is considered the cider capital.

In spite of Villaviciosa's name, "vicious town" (a name from might in battle or from a disgruntled one-time visitor?), it is a laid-back and sweet town. Villaviciosa's region is full of prehistoric, Roman, and early medieval remains. Much of the layout of the current old town was laid down during Alfonso X's reign, in the thirteenth century.

The best example of this time, and the most sacred spot, is a little gem, the Iglesia de Santa María de la Oliva. It was built in the thirteenth and fourteenth centuries and has several characters, animals and saints, carved in its capitals of the earthy Romanesque style. The porch is a little refuge within a refuge and the church stands on a little central plaza in the heart of town that sees, and likely for centuries has seen, the daily gathering of locals who stop to visit on their way to run errands. It is rare to see a sacred place woven so closely into the everyday life of the people.

Villaviciosa to Oviedo (26 miles/42 km):
Take A-8 SW, which becomes A-64, continue on A-64 as it goes W, to Oviedo.

OVIEDO—Asturias

The early Asturian kings desired a more central, arable, and accessible spot than Cangas de Onís, and by the rule of Alfonso II, in AD 808, Oviedo became the new northern capital. Between Alfonso II (791–842) and Ramiro I (842–850), Oviedo boasts of three of Asturia's finest pre-Romanesque buildings, built in the lyrical early Christian, northern, Visigothic style of the ninth century. Their stone walls are of warm ochre, so warm that it is as if sunlight was mixed into the mortar. The spaces are intimate and human-scale, bringing God to eye level. The images are everyday people and animals, reminding us of how close to the land our ancestors once lived, never taking for granted the fall harvest or the slaughter for winter. In the early tenth century, as the Kingdom of Asturias continued its territorial expansion southward, the capital was once more moved, from Oviedo to León.

Oviedo experienced industrial prosperity in the 1800s with the discovery of coal in the city's neighboring green rolling hills. A city with liberal

Oviedo's cathedral, Asturias

and socialist leanings, and strong-willed and idealistic humanitarian residents, the Oviedans did not fare well under Franco, who violently suppressed a revolt in 1934 and kept the city pressed low throughout his rule. It really was not until Franco's death that the city was able to revive its liberal and humanitarian outlook.

Pre-Romanesque Santa María del Naranco and San Miguel de Lillo

These two stand near each other at the northwest edge of the city, just beyond the last neighborhood here and into farmland and green rolling hills. If you have time and like walking, follow the road, Avenida de Canto los Monumentos. This is a wonderful way to approach these ancient buildings in their own time. Two roadside bars at the highest climb—strategically placed—are good places to stop for refreshments.

In his *Handbook for Travellers in Spain,* the nineteenth-century English traveler and writer Richard Ford described this same walk as forested and wild. Today, a neighborhood of walled-off luxury homes lines the two sides of the road for the first half of the ascent. After that, it is almost as in Ford's time: forest mingled with green pastures, farms, grazing cows and horses alongside Asturian square, pyramid-roofed granaries on stilts (*hórreos*). Just beyond the steep hill (after passing the two bars) emerge the two numinous amber yellow pre-Romanesque stone buildings.

Naranco and Lillo were both built under the Asturian king Ramiro I, who succeeded Alfonso II. Both buildings were constructed from a type of stone that appears to have absorbed the rays of the sun and to reflect light from within.

The first building nearest the road is the church of Santa María del Naranco, a very tall, narrow, and perfectly symmetrical structure, with engraved animals and symbolic carvings of kingship throughout its pillars and walls. It is an unusual shape for a church largely because it was originally intended to be the royal residence during the summer months.

The second pre-Romanesque building is set a little higher up the hill from Naranco and was a royal chapel. Called the Capilla de San Miguel de Lillo, it is in more disrepair, but teams of experts have discovered the chapel's original walls and have outlined them on the ground. The remaining parts are magical: walls had once been painted with rich, saturated colors in shapes depicting holy figures, animals, plants, and symbols. Pillars supporting the heavy vaulted ceiling have twining motifs making worshipers feel as if they are in a forest. As if to say sacred and profane were more comfortable in the past than they are today, acrobats and animal tamers join the carved animals and sacred personalities on the arches, columns, and walls.

Pre-Romanesque San Julian de los Prados

Situated on the eastern side of town and now surrounded by green that protects it from the encroaching road system on all sides, the pre-Romanesque church of San Julian de los Prados is a small, warm chapel. It was built by King Alfonso II and predates Lillo and Naranco; it is the oldest pre-Romanesque church in Spain. The interior is simple but there are Roman-inspired murals painted on the walls, preserving a common style of interior decoration from the eighth and ninth centuries.

All three pre-Romanesque sites in Oviedo offer an interesting comparison of early northern Spanish styles, before the strong influence of the Romanesque would arrive from France in the tenth to the twelfth century. What they all have in common, both the pre-Romanesque and the Romanesque, is an intimacy of space and a strong lean toward a great mix of symbolic, literal, and allegorical imagery that people would glance at or meditate on during prayer and liturgical services.

Medieval City and Cathedral

Oviedo's town center is the heart of the old medieval neighborhood and, as was the case in the Middle Ages, the church held the center of the center, in this instance, the cathedral. Dominantly Gothic, its older parts, seen if you walk around the right side of the outside and glance into the gates of this side churchyard, are Romanesque. The great stone plaza before the cathedral until 2007 staged the annual great bonfire of St. John's night on June 23, when people enacted a pagan rite of purification for their town and enjoyed the general revelry and singing. The decision to ban this bonfire came from the city government out of concern for preserving this historic district from potential fire damage. It is controversial, as many citizens claim the surrounding plaza is all of stone and over the decades past fires never endangered them. In 2007 they held a silent candlelight vigil on the spot, lamenting that their city had lost its annual purification rite. At the time of writing, this controversy is still being creatively solved and might result in a bonfire elsewhere in the city. Diehards claim that there can only be one place for it, in the city's heart. It's hard to argue with that—the city with the heart of fire.

Nearby the cathedral are other ancient buildings and the best way to see them is to wander around the pedestrian stone streets of the medieval neighborhood and let them reveal themselves to you. Most beyond the cathedral are not open to the public.

Oviedo to Cudillero (36.5 miles/59 km):

Get onto A-66 N, the Autovía Ruta de Plata, to Avilés and Gijón; keep left to take exit 12 to A-8 toward Avilés; take N-632 W to Cudillero.

CUDILLERO—Asturias

Like many other coastal Asturian towns and villages, Cudillero's medieval founding was as a fishing village and today it remains so. Fishing and commercial maritime work, from shipping to the merchant marine, are the lifeblood of Cudillero past and present. In the seventeenth century, the town saw its heyday as an important Spanish harbor. Three groups of people traditionally lived in this area: the *pixuetos* (fishermen), the *marinuetos* (farmers and commerce-focused people), and the *vaqueros de Alzada* (seminomadic transhumant herders). Cudillero proper is the traditional home of the *pixuetos*.

Some sources claim, from Richard Ford to the official publications of the Asturian municipalities, that elements of Gaelic, Breton, and Basque hold firm in the dialect of Asturias, known as Bable. This is especially true in the fishing town of Cudillero, famed for its own dialect of Bable called *pixueto*. Some believe that this rare language was preserved because it is the language of fisherman who would go off for weeks and months, having only one another to speak to and the sea. Everywhere I went in Cudillero, I heard *pixueto*; it appears to be firmly rooted, even in these times of rapid change. The *pixueto* words most likely related to Breton, Gaelic, and Basque are fishing terms. It is a legacy of a nonbounded nation of the sea where fisherman from different regions exchange ideas and words and create a floating community.

Cudillero is also a place with a magnificent annual ritual for the fishermen. Their water Mary is none other than the Virgen de Covadonga, also called La Santina. During the entire year, La Santina is actually submerged in the waters of the Atlantic ocean in the old port of Cudillero, giving direct contact and protection to the fishermen throughout the year. Once a year, in early September, she is brought above water by divers in wetsuits. Her image is set on a wooden pedestal where the male *pixuetos* adorn her with hand-embroidered tapestries. Accompanied by bagpipers and townspeople, the fishermen carry La Santina to the parochial church, where they gather to honor her as the protectress of seafaring folk. It is a dramatic moment when the scuba divers surface with the lady on their shoulders. At the end of a day of above-ground thanksgiving and festivities, La Santina is returned back underwater. There for another year, her grace will infuse the waters and the passing boats and men with protective powers and safe return from the sea.

Cudillero to Luarca (29.5 miles/47.5):
Take N-632 W.

LUARCA—Asturias

Luarca was an important medieval fishing town like Llanes and was especially known for whaling. Across town you will see remarkable tile painted images of men in small boats harpooning these great big mammals. Today it remains one of the main active fishing towns on the Asturian coast.

Another image you will see is of men gathered around a table on which stands a small model house and a small model boat. They are drawing lots: to go out to sea or to stay on land and farm. Going out to sea was so treacherous that they devised this democratic method of drawing names randomly out of each of the models to decide who would stay on land and who would go out into the great blue.

Both of these images—of whaling and of drawing lots—are rendered near the entrance to the fishermen's warehouse on the harbor. This is the place just feet from the main harbor where they quickly move their catch off the boats and onto ice on large palettes and where wholesale fish buyers haggle for a good deal. The restaurants along the harbor that overlook this scene are the best places to eat, given their immediate access to the freshest catch.

Nuestra Señora del Rosario

Luarca's patroness, La Señora del Rosario, emerges from her hermitage on August 15, the day of Mary's ascension to heaven. She is the patron of fishermen and this day also marks a day of festivities planned by the town's seafarers. Much of the festivities take place at the old wharf.

La Virgen de la Blanca

Another mariners' Mary, La Blanca, resides in the chapel near the cemetery and lighthouse at the outermost and highest reach of the town. Her procession takes place on September 8 and commences from the Capilla de la Virgen de la Blanca.

LUARCA'S MAGIC FOUNTAIN

The standard history of the conquest of Iberia by Arabs and Berbers in AD 711 says that these North African invaders crossed the Strait of Gibraltar and in very little time defeated the Visigoths, sweeping as far north as southern France before being turned back. In AD 718, we are told, one brave Christian soldier called Pelayo defeated the advancing North African army in Spain's northern Cantabrian Mountains, at the site called Covadonga. That date and geography popularly mark the limit of Muslim, North African expansion and conquest in Iberia. We are told that thereafter, all but this northern strip of Spain was occupied and ruled by Muslims.

The *Chronicle of 754*, written by a Christian cleric living in eighth-century Muslim Spain, recounts the history of the Arab and Berber conquest of Spain and makes absolutely no mention of Pelayo's battle in AD 718. Then what really happened in those first decades of the eighth century in northern Spain?

Not far from Luarca is the small village of Villademoro, whose name and claim to fame come from its sturdy, square, and defensive tower. In Villademoro, literally "town of the Moor," locals believe invading Muslims built the tower, though any original stones from that time are only in its foundation, because the tower had been demolished and then rebuilt centuries later.

In my research, I found a book on the municipality's history and culture, *Asturias, Concejo a Concejo: Valdes y Cudillero*. In it is a curious little folktale from the eighth century:

Luarca's lighthouse and chapel of La Virgen de la Blanca, one of many Marys on this coastline dedicated to protecting seafaring folk, Asturias

Once upon a time, the story begins, there was a famous Muslim governor of Luarca. He had a very beautiful daughter named Fatima. The governor was among those who had fought against Pelayo and his army in the mountains at Covadonga in AD 718. Apparently, Covadonga was not a great enough defeat to discourage the Muslims from staying, not if they had a governor appointed to this farthest north region in Spain.

In the story, the Muslim governor of Luarca has just captured a Christian by the name of Rodrigo whom he has condemned to death. The story doesn't tell us what the young man has done, but the governor gives Rodrigo one last request and the handsome young man asks that he be allowed to drink from *La Fuente del Bruxu,* the Magician's Fountain in the center of town. The governor laughs, "Fine! You'll have your drink and then we'll take your head!"

Of course, Fatima catches a glimpse of Rodrigo and falls wildly in love with him. Aware of her father's proclamation, she rushes to the Magician's Fountain, where *xanas* are known to live. (*Xanas* are feminist water deities, most likely holdovers from pre-Christian times and still a part of the Asturian folk landscape.) She explains the situation to the *xanas,* who like to help truehearted people. They assure Fatima that they will protect Rodrigo and help her.

The next day, Rodrigo is brought to the fountain. When he has drunk his fill of water, the *xanas* help Fatima in confusing the executioners, allowing the two lovers to escape and run away together. It is hoped that Rodrigo and Fatima lived happily ever after in a place where their Muslim-Christian union was celebrated. It is also told that the governor returned to the fountain for the rest of his days, lamenting the loss of his daughter and chiding the *xanas* for the part that they played.

This tale reminds me of the kernels of truth hidden in folktales, truths that official histories and accounts have tried to wipe away. I also feel that this story is relevant to our times. We spend a lot of energy defining others and ourselves with definite, bold lines. We invest a lot of intellect in and debate over official histories that sterilize the complexities of real people's experiences. We see those in power needing to create official histories in order to establish their hegemony, just as kings in both Christian and Muslim Spain did for over eight hundred years. But we also see little, innocent stories slipping unnoticed over the border, reminding us of a deeper, richer, messier reality.

HÓRREOS

Hórreos, granaries, are a common form of vernacular architecture in Galicia and Asturias, each with its own regional styles. They stand on granite or wooden posts above ground and large stone disks rest between the posts and the building. The steps leading up to the granary do not join with the structure. The granaries are raised above ground to protect the stored grain and other foods from both mold and vermin. The stone disks are an added measure to keep rats and mice from scurrying past the posts. Another deterrent to rodents are the cats who like to perch on those stone disks. Most hórreos are decorated with sacred symbols, from granite crosses to carved geometric designs, such as trisqueles, to protect against malignant spirits and the evil eye of an envious neighbor or stranger.

Luarca to Navia (11 km/18 km):
Take N-634 W.

NAVIA—Asturias

Unfortunately, because of a paper mill upriver from its beautiful river mouth port, the water quality, and sometimes the air, is questionable. But Navia has a spectacular tradition with a Mary of the Boat. Navia's port and fishing life are still quite active and one of Asturias's largest. Humans will nevertheless need to strike a better balance with and respect for Gaia here if they want their Marian festivals to continue generating grace and protection. How can one persist in the fishing life, or even in the tourism from beautiful beaches and footpaths, when a mill upriver pollutes the air and water? This has been an ancestral heartland and nearby are some remarkable Iron Age remains. Clearly people have been drawn to the magical alchemy of green mountains, blue fresh and salt water, and big open sky for a long time.

Nuestra Señora la Virgen de la Barca

Navia's Mary of the Boat leaves her chapel once a year on August 15 for a festival of boat sailing, street processions, and general fanfare to assure another year of protection and grace.

Having taken in haunting coastal waterways and goddess-turned-Marian shrines, this route ends near where another ancestral route begins. Navia is only a few kilometers away from the Celtic Castro of Coaña, the starting point for the route of myths and legends in chapter 10.

CHAPTER TEN

$\mathcal{C}$oaña to Santa Tecla

People ask why I live here, with all the rain and gray, but I love it here, it is so green and cool. I lived for a while in Tenerife, but it just wasn't my climate.

—A newspaper-stand owner in Santiago talking to three
other Spaniards and a man from Senegal

THIS IS THE CELTS' AND LEGENDS' ROUTE, for here in Galicia and western Asturias are some of the highest concentrations of Celtic-speaking peoples' Iron Age settlements, round stone enclaves known as *castros*. Less common, though ubiquitous enough, are carved stone tombs with sacred symbols familiar to the shaman's world, of Earth and heaven-spiraling pathways, labyrinths, and triskelions, and others.

It is the legends' route also because here we have a high concentration of pre- and post-Christian folktales that add color to the telling of why a place or person is sacred. Many of these tales are a mix of sacred pagan and Christian ideas, such as visions of Mary in ancestrally matriarchal areas, of a prince covered in scallop shells, or of a Roman tower believed to really be a legendary Celtic tower. We have nature spirits and mists, treacherous cliff drops and pirates, also the stuff of legends. Moreover, this is a traditional land of *brujas* and *meigas*, two types of witches, both considered masters of the natural world. *Meigas* also overlap with traditional herbal healers, *curanderas*, many of whom still practice today and often combine the physical and the spiritual through their use of herbs. This green, mountainous, coastal northwest reach of Spain has been so long isolated from other parts of the country that the experience of the spiritual here takes on a distinctive regional flair. The entire route passes through beautiful coastlines, fishing villages, estuaries, and vibrant green hills. Rain is always a possibility.

Main Route (418 miles/673 km):
Castro de Coaña—San Martín de Mondoñedo—Foz—San Andrés de Teixido—Cedeira—A Coruña—Muxía—Finisterre—Noia—Castro de Baroña—Dolmen de Axeito—Padrón—Armenteira—Poio—Pontevedra—Baiona—Santa Tecla

Navia to Castro de Coaña (3 miles/5 km):
Take AS-12 SW toward Boal, which snakes along the west bank of the river Navia; pass the village of Coaña; follow the signs to the *castro*.

CASTRO DE COAÑA—Asturias

Arriving at Coaña from Navia takes you through a winding narrow road that snakes between lush green hills worn from thousands of years of occupation and farming. Coaña, on its higher hill, overlooks the valley and river that flow to Navia and the Atlantic ocean. This is a Celtic Asturian settlement, a *castro* dating to around 200 BCE and then overtaken and occupied by Romans by the second century AD. You can see

The Castro de Coaña, Asturias

this transition as the older buildings are mostly round and clustered around the hill, whereas the Roman acropolis is walled off, taking a symbolic seat of power at the top of the hill. These peoples coexisted, the Celtic-speaking Astures living under Roman domination toward the end of the settlements' period.

Castros were nearly all built for protection from attack and tend to be found on hilltops that offered good visibility of any approach from the outside. Astures, like other Celtic speakers on the Peninsula, had a cosmology made up of many divinities that were present in the natural world. As such, their sacred places were woven into everything and were a part of their home's design and décor. The elements, plants, and animals also had their spiritual dimensions. Sacredness was woven into the fabric of everyday life, not just something set aside in a special temple, though altars of offering and sacrifice were also present.

In spite of Asturias's history of having been occupied by Romans in the second century AD, it seemed to have a peaceful air in its last days. Perhaps this sense is given by the still-existent building plans of both peoples. But it is equally likely, given the region's isolation from the core Roman world, that these Celtic speakers, though under Roman rule, also had an influence on their Roman rulers, softening the edges and coexisting in a cultural mélange. Evidence for this comes through the greater survival of old, pre-Roman and pre-Christian cultural forms that persisted in Galicia, and in some remote areas they still persist like bread crumbs on a path to the remote past.

Coaña to San Martín de Mondoñedo (37 miles/60 km):
Backtrack to Coaña village and continue N on the same road passing through Jarrio; take E-70/N-634 W; after Ribadeo, follow the signs to Foz; take the Foz exit, but instead of heading into the town (right), go left and follow the signs to San Martín de Mondoñedo.

SAN MARTÍN DE MONDOÑEDO—Galicia

In this quiet rural setting just inland from Foz, we are in the vicinity of what was once the action-packed seat of the bishop in northeastern Galicia. It was also a place of many miracles when under the care of one of its bishops, San Gonzalo.

San Martín de Mondoñedo—named in honor of two Saint Martins, one from Tours, France, and the other from Dumio, Portugal—is an early Romanesque building. Though heavily built on the outside, its interior is warm, simple carved stonework. It was founded in the ninth century, with additions and changes continuing until the fourteenth century.

The church has a fascinating granite cross, *crucero*, on its grounds, where on one side we have the crucified Christ and on the other we have Mary holding her son after he is taken down from the cross.

San Martín's west portal is made in part from some reused columns from a prior Visigothic structure and shows plant designs reflecting Visigothic influence. The tympanum has the *Agnus Dei*, "Lamb of God," with the sheep and the cross, as well as a chrismon—what looks like a six-armed star, the Greek letters chi-rho, which together form the graphic symbol for Christ. Inside, the transept capitals have allegorical carvings. One is of Lazarus lying under a rich man's table dying of hunger while the man eats an overflow of food. Only a dog shows compassion and licks Lazarus's feet. This is a poignant image in Galicia, a province that has had a tragic history of famine.

San Martín de Mondoñedo's history came about from events farther north in England. When England was under attack from Jutes, Angeles, and Saxons, and the Roman legions retreated from the island, many Celtic tribes fled, leaving for Brittany just over the English Channel in northwestern France. But a few made their way to Galicia and settled on the coast between Ferrol and Navia. There they founded a bishopric province. As the seat of their bishopric they chose Bretoña (the name reflecting the settlers' origins), a little town further inland and south of the town of Mondoñedo (whose history is also tied to San Martín de Mondoñedo's and also became the seat of the bishop and has an interesting cathedral as a result).

Bretoña today holds annual festivals in honor of the Celtic god Lugh, the god of the sun and of creation, in the beginning of August. This came about in recent times, a post-Franco manner of retrieving and celebrating their Celtic ancestry.

The new bishopric province from Bretoña established strong ties with the bishop in Dumia, the capital of the Suevi, who settled in northern Portugal, near Braga. The people of Dumia took refuge in Bretoña when their city was attacked by Vikings. Later, King Alfonso III of Asturias and León (c. 838–910) made San Martín de Mondoñedo the seat of the bishop after Bretoña was sacked by Vikings. This placed the new religious center nearer the coast.

Under Alfonso III, the bishop Sabarico headed San Martín de Mondoñedo. He was succeeded by several others, some of whom became renowned. One was San Rosendo (tenth century), who later went on to found a monastery in Celanova, where he died. It is in his honor that San Martín to this day holds Jubilee status, every seven years. The most recent Jubilee year was from November 26, 2006–November 26, 2007.

Another famous bishop was the aforementioned San Gonzalo (eleventh to twelfth century), who is buried here. Near the basilica, you will find a fountain known as the Fonte Obispo or Fuente de la Zapata. One day the bishop Gonzalo dropped his slipper here and from the spot where the slipper struck ground a spring gushed forth. No ordinary spring, its water was soon discovered to possess miraculous powers.

San Martín's days as bishopric ended in AD 1112 when the seat shifted inland again, this time to Mondoñedo.

San Martín de Mondoñedo to Foz (3.5 miles/5.5 km):
Backtrack to Foz.

FOZ—Galicia

Foz's ancestry is tied up with the Phoenicians, whose trade ships likely used this river-mouth entrance to transport goods, with the Celtic speakers who settled here in different waves, and with the Romans. As a major port on this stretch of coast, it had contacts with other Iberian Atlantic trade ports, such as with Gijón in Asturias. Like some Asturian coastal towns, such as nearby Luarca and Puerto de Vega, Foz was also a whaling town.

The two sacred highlights of Foz are a magical church, Iglesia de Santiago, in the old part of town near the port, and the Celtic Castro de Fazouro just west of town. The area around Foz, once you leave the constant resort construction of the soon-to-be-overdeveloped coastline, is untouched and holding on to the old ways. Because of this, just a few meters inland, you will find green forests and hills, much like what you encountered on the way to San Martín de Mondoñedo. I am afraid that Foz is going to be lost to the development madness, but try not to let its blight stop you from seeing the untouched beauty around it. Some of the names of stores in town—such as Libreria Breogán ("Breogán's Books"—Breogán refers to the mythic Celtic founding father of the Galicians; see A Coruña below for his story) and Fruteria Diva, "Diva Fruits"—reflect the locals' awareness that they live on an ancient sacred spot.

Iglesia Parroquial de Santiago

Also known as the Iglesia de Refugio, likely referring to the church's role in giving shelter to pilgrims on the coastal route to Santiago de Compostela, this little church is the parochial church and stands in the older part of Foz, facing toward the port. The church appears to be mostly of the sixteenth century, something of a neo-Romanesque or rural Gothic, or something in between. It is in a section of town that has thankfully been untouched by the resort-development craze beyond its confines. Here you will find lovely little homes with their glassed-in balconies and signs of the fishing life. Homes are mostly painted white, a stunning contrast against the smoky gray granite foundations and slate rooftops. Nuns might be saying their prayers in the morning, and if so, you may find the inner door locked. Hours for Mass—several on the weekend and two in the evening on weekdays—when the church will be open to the public, are posted on the door (and can change, so I am not noting them here).

Foz to Castro de Fazouro (7.5 miles/12 km):
Leave Foz W along the coastal road to the village of Fazouro; follow signs for Os Castros (the castro) and Praia Arealonga (Arealonga beach). Turn right and go over a very narrow stone and concrete bridge leading to the Castro de Fazouro.

Castro de Fazouro

This castro, though it doesn't look like much today, existed in three settlements. Its location is beautiful and doubtless one of the reasons the Iron Age peoples built here. Another was defense and yet another might have been a desire to be near the water's edge for sacred purposes: the coast, like springs, caves, and mountaintops, is a threshold place, a place of the thinner veil between this world and the next.

The first castro settlement here was built in the eighth century BCE, the second from the fifth to the seventh century BCE, and the third and final settlement was built from the second century BCE to the first century AD. After that, like Coaña in Asturias, Fazouro became a hybrid residence, shared with Romans and locals and called Romano-Gallego (Gallego is the word for the Galician people and for the Galician language, which is largely Portuguese with a good shot of Castilian). The Romano-Gallego settlement dates to the first through the third centuries AD.

Castro de Fazouro to San Andrés de Teixido (53.5 miles/86 km):
Take N-642 W to Viveiro and Ortigueira; after Ortigueira continue to Mera; at Mera turn right and go to Feas; in Feas turn left to Seixo; pass Seixo and continue to San Andrés de Teixido, which will be the road to your left when you come upon a T-intersection; shortly you will see a road open to your

right; take it, and go cautiously as this is a very narrow cliffside road with two-way traffic and dramatic views (and drops) overlooking the Atlantic.

SAN ANDRÉS DE TEIXIDO—Galicia

If you make it here in this lifetime, you can avoid a journey here in death. This is the import assigned a pilgrimage to San Andrés de Teixido—everyone has to come here one way or another ("A San Andrés de Teixido, que no vai vivo vai morto [To San Andrés de Teixido, if you don't go in life, you'll go in death]"). Some folks further add that if you missed making the pilgrimage while alive, your pilgrimage here in death may take you in the form of a reincarnated lizard or frog. Locals traditionally have taken care around such creatures so as not to harm a potential pilgrim coming here from the afterlife. San Andrés de Teixido couldn't be more off the beaten track, so when you do get here, it is a sacred sense of accomplishment.

San Andrés is St. Andrew, and the shrine is in honor of this apostle, martyr, and brother of Simon Peter. He was also a fisherman, something that more than anything connects him to this rugged coastline of fishermen. Before Jesus' arrival, St. Andrew was a disciple of St. John the Baptist. In his shrine in San Andrés de Teixido you will find him depicted with a saltire cross, which forms a large X, like the saltire animal barricade that prevents animals but not people from jumping over. Knights of Malta brought relics of St. Andrew from the Holy Land to this little hamlet where they built the shrine.

But before you think the story here is only about a male saint in a very masculine shrine in a very sky-oriented place, you should know that San Andrés also has an herb associated with him that is considered an aphrodisiac in Galician folklore. Apparently long ago, after Mass, people would consume this plant in large doses and let nature take its course. Folks looking for a partner have come on pilgrimage here for that purpose. The plant itself is colloquially called clavel marino, sea carnation, but is more likely plumbagináceae armeria maritima, sea pink or thrift, a member of the sea lavender family.

On September 8, people make a pilgrimage here, where they invite the dead to join them. Moreover, anyone who came close to dying the year before gets to be carried in a coffin to the shrine. All along the pathway to the shrine you will find merchants selling all sorts of religious and touristy wares, from amulets and wax offerings—some in the shape of body parts like arms, legs, hands, and feet—to baked goods that let the pilgrim carry away the blessing of the place to share with friends at home. The shrine is a small,

View of the dramatic coastline from the remote shrine of San Andrés de Teixido, Galicia

simple stone building with a dramatic view of the cliffs and crashing ocean below. Cows, sheep, goats, and horses graze on the steep green hillsides nearby (many of the horses you see here are wild—they have little need for the saltire). A walled-in cemetery stands a few meters below the shrine.

San Andrés de Teixido to Cedeira (9 miles/14 km):
Take the road out of San Andrés de Teixido; go right at the first intersection; go left at the next intersection and continue to Cedeira.

CEDEIRA—Galicia

From Cedeira's port you can climb through pine and eucalyptus forest to a cliff-top lookout over the Atlantic, a different view but equally dramatic from what you saw at San Andrés de Teixido. This takes you to Ermita de San Antonio de Corveiro, a seventeenth-century shrine with a rustic granite *crucero*, a double-sided cross, so emblematic of Galician crosses. This one shows Mary facing the hermitage and land, and Jesus the ocean, making me wonder if each watches over those who stay behind and those who go out to sea to make sure everyone is protected. This placement of *cruceros* is intentional. At convents where a crucero is present, Mary faces the convent, and at monasteries, Jesus faces the monastic buildings. The *crucero* here stands between the hermitage's entrance and the cliff drop to the ocean below.

Cedeira to A Coruña (45.5 miles/73 km):
Take AC-566 S to Ferrol; take AP-9 S then W to A Coruña.

A CORUÑA—Galicia

A Coruña is Celtic, Phoenician, Roman, Galician, and English, the latter having to do with both the sailors' connection and A Coruña's being the disembarking point for pilgrims from the British Isles going to Santiago de Compostela. Legend says that Hercules founded A Coruña. Celtic speakers lived here, Phoenicians traded here, and the Romans made this harbor a major port, called Ardobicum Coronium. The harbor is still a major shipping center as well as being home to one of Europe's major fishing fleets.

This is also the birthplace of Galician national identity, with its Tower of Hercules, more indigenously considered the Tower of Breogán, Galicia's mythic founding father, a legendary Celtic king, whose name is sung in the Galician national anthem. He had two sons, Ith and Bile. While historical data points to the tower's origins as Roman, built in the second century AD as a watchtower and a lighthouse, Galician folklore, infused with its grains of truth, says otherwise.

The Tower of Hercules

At the northern tip of the city overlooking a brooding ocean on a finger of land sits the Tower of Hercules, whose original Roman shape was altered to what you see today by Carlos III in 1790. The Roman outer ramp, exposed to the elements, was enclosed within the square walls of the tower, making them interior ramps.

Among the stories told by Galicians claiming that beneath or before this tower there was once an earlier Celtic one, one story I will share is the claim of a Galician man I met years ago in Santiago de Compostela. He was a self-proclaimed and widely respected Celtic-Viking druid, both possible ancestries for these northwestern reaches. His lineage he claimed came from a long line of Galician seers and he was recapturing this ancestry after the late twentieth-century liberation from Franco's oppressive years, when any expression of faith outside of a very conservative Catholicism was dangerous. He was well liked and sought out in Galicia for ceremonies and festivals. He worked with archival materials, esoteric materials and manners, as well as with a great knowledge of the region and its people, whose stories he gathered. This is his telling of Breogán and the tower:

> Celtic Galicia was founded by the *Saefes* Celts in the sixth century BC, who brought with them their magico-religious traditions, including the veneration of the Celtic god Dagda. Dagda could mend the dead and wounded from battle, as long as he had their head—the residence of the soul—and restore them to life and health with the exception of their voice. But if their heads were missing, the soldier was doomed to wander eternally without his soul (which is why the Celts cut and carried off the heads of their enemies). On the first day of the Celtic New Year, November 1, or *Samhain*, the skulls of the dead were illuminated and decorated as a part of the celebrations. Breogán's sons took this Samhain tradition to Ireland.
>
> Breogán founded, according to legend, the city of Brigantium, which today is known as La Coruña, where he built a tall tower called the Tower of Hercules. From this tower, on a very clear day, Breogán's son Ith saw a green land far, far away. He embarked for it and in turn found a green land full of honey, fruit, wheat, and fish. He enjoyed a little of these pleasures but was killed by the people of this land, the Tuatha De Danann. Ith's sons returned to the green land and avenged their father's death by defeating the Tuatha De Danann. They founded a Galician royal dynasty in Erin. Because they brought their customs with them, so it is that Samhain is celebrated in Ireland.

For those of you who are of Irish ancestry or have a very different reckoning about Ireland's ancestry, bear in mind that we are in a mythic world here, a local telling of their own ancestry. We need not to discount it but to listen to what it is telling us of a particular people's legends and experiences. This story curiously reflects a greater feeling of connection to Ireland than to the rest of Spain.

A recent genetics study, published in the *American Journal of Human Genetics*, found that the Irish and Scottish are closely related to northwestern Iberians. The same study found genetic kinship with the Basques as well, suggesting that the connection between northern Spain and the British Isles goes back before Iron Age Celts inhabited both areas. It indicates a possibility that some ancient Iberians may have migrated to Ireland between six thousand and three thousand years ago and that the link between the two regions comes from just after the last ice age and from retreating ice sheets rather than from Celtic invasions.

There may be more truth in the legend of Breogán than we realize. We might need to reconsider him as a pre-Indo-European, or pre-Celtic king.

Modern Menhirs

Near the tower, on the coastal cliff of land just south, you can see the menhir park, a modern park dedicated to Galician people's ancestral and historical legacies. The modern *menhirs,* or standing stones, are set in a mystical configuration, with geometric holes cut out of them to let you peer through the stone. Against the green of the field and the blue of ocean and sky, it is a sweeping place to stand, however modern the art.

Nearby is a Stonehenge-inspired memorial, as well as a Muslim cemetery, both honoring those who died during Franco's dictatorship. The view of the Tower of Hercules is best from here and it ties old and new together poignantly. This coastline has seen its share of warfare and attack as well as times of peace, which the city is now enjoying. It is a clean, open, and sea-loving city.

A Coruña to Muxía (60 miles/96 km):
Take AG-55 SW from Coruña to just past Carballo and exit onto AC-552 W to Berdoias; take AC-440 W to Muxía.

MUXÍA—Galicia

This is the home of the Santuario da Virxe da Barca, Sanctuary of the Virgin of the Boat, a solid twin-towered gray granite temple on the edge of the sea. The patroness of Muxía, the Lady of the Boat, is crucial to interceding in fishermen's well-being and keeping them safe while out at sea.

The pilgrimage, *romería,* in her honor is on September 8. As a part of it, people visit the sacred exotic stone formations, shaped by wind and sea, that are in front of the church and that are claimed as a part of the Virgin's boat when she visited this spot.

There is the narrow rock opening of a stone, called the Pedra dos Cadrís, that people climb beneath and that is said to be the keel. The fabled stone hull is the Pedra de Abalar, which rocks back and forth, though it is said only those who are free of sin can make it rock. Visiting these rocks and the church will bring about good luck and healing to the pilgrim.

The church to Mary stands over an older Celtic sacred temple, one that may have been in existence well into the medieval period as this part of Galicia took to Christianity later than other parts of Spain. Some of the stones near the church are said to come from the earlier Celtic site and to belong to Mary's boat that landed here. According to this legend, when St. James was evangelizing on this coastline, he was having little success in bringing the locals around to embracing Christ, at which point Mary appeared in a boat. That was the decisive turning point.

Muxía to Finisterre (21 miles/34 km):
Take AC-440 toward Molinos; turn right toward Villarmid; continue S; take AC-552 S just after you pass Bermún and proceed toward Cée; follow signs to Fisterra/Finisterre.

FINISTERRE—Galicia

If you are a pilgrim to Santiago and are making this last leg of the pilgrim's journey, called the *Camino de Finisterre*, you would likely come from Santiago via Negreira and Olveiroa. Some pilgrims also go north to Muxía first and then on to Finisterre (or vice versa).

Finisterre was a destination long before the Christian Camino, and its incorporation into the medieval Catholic road is likely due to this ancestry as a prior sacred site. Romans built an altar here, called the Ara Solis, to the setting—dying—sun, one that looked to be dying as its red sphere dramatically set below the distant unknown and mysterious waters. Before the Romans, Finisterre might also have been a threshold place, an initiatory road for indigenous peoples. Some of these theories are explored in the introduction to the Camino in chapter 7.

From Finisterre's village center walk toward the Cabo Fisterra/Cabo Finisterre, Finisterre's cape, south of town. This will take you up to the cliff-top of this westernmost finger of land toward the lighthouse, the location of the fabled Roman Ara Solis. Along the way, you will pass another important pilgrimage site, the church Igrexia de Santa María das Areas, a Romanesque church from the twelfth century. Its image of Jesus, Santo Cristo da Barba Dourada, a fifteenth-century Gothic work, is believed to have been thrown overboard from an English vessel that was lightening its loads during a bad storm. But the storm persisted until a Finisterran fisherman, also being tossed in the dangerous waters, encountered the image of Christ and pulled it aboard his fishing boat. At that moment, the storm ceased and the waters were still. Other legends attached to this image are that its beard and fingernails grow. But I have not heard of anyone who has trimmed either and Jesus looks decently groomed. Perhaps that is a part of the miracle as well—he takes care of his own hair and nails. Holy week, *semana santa*, the week leading up to Easter Sunday takes on a double complementary meaning in Finisterre where locals celebrate Christ's Resurrection with that of the reborn sun, showing beautifully how different cosmologies can actually tell us the same thing.

Pilgrims who come to Finisterre enact three rituals that reflect this hybrid pagan-Christian sun and water veneration: they walk to the lighthouse, site of the old Ara Solis, and bathe in the waters of Cabo Finisterre; they burn an old garment worn on the pilgrimage; and they watch the sun set into the ocean. Women having trouble conceiving used to head higher, to a dolmen on Mount Fache, where they believed rubbing the erect stone would help make them pregnant. This pagan ritual ended when an eighteenth-century bishop oversaw the ancient dolmen's destruction. This act is symbolic on so many levels. The road from the lighthouse continues up to this mountaintop. Though the dolmen is gone, the views are still stunning.

Today Cape Finisterre is still an awe-inspiring place, especially when the wind picks up and you are climbing to the lighthouse and hoping not to be blown off the mountainside into the jagged rocks and violent water below, along what is called the Costa da Morte, Coast of Death—named both for treacherous rocks and wind and for the loss of many a seaman's life over the centuries in the name of making a living.

Finisterre to Noia (56.5 miles/91 km):
Return to Cée; take the coastal road AC-550 S to Noia.

NOIA—Galicia

The town name Noia comes from Noah. Mythic local tellings assert that it was near here that Noah's ark first hit earth when the floodwaters began to recede and that it was from here that his dove found the olive branch to return to the ark with evidence of land. The ark is believed to have anchored on Mount Barbanza just south of Noia, a place revered by the Iron Age Celtic speakers who lived here, which is sprinkled with earlier Bronze Age dolmens.

In Noia are two interesting churches. The elaborately carved fifteenth-century Iglesia de San Martín has a wonderful portal with the Elders of the Apocalypse and their happy music making. Nearby is the older church of

Santa María a Nova (fourteenth century), with a cemetery that possesses more pagan than Christian carvings on its tombstones, some depicting the trades of the deceased and others whose symbolism is as yet mysterious.

Noia to Castro de Baroña (10.5 miles/17 km):

Take AC-550 S toward Porto do Son and stay on AC-550 and follow signs to the Castro de Baroña. The signs on this little coastal road can be easily missed, but there is a roadside bar on your right, Restaurante O Castro, that stands right above and in front of the trails to the castro below.

CASTRO DE BAROÑA—Galicia

Wear good shoes, such as cross-trainers, to hike down. It is not a difficult walk but a rocky one. You will go through a wonderful pine forest that, like the curtains of a stage, will open to reveal one of Spain's most dramatic Iron Age castro sites. The drama is greater if you can get there on a sunny day when the grandeur is not hidden in mist.

The Castro de Baroña is an Iron Age castro, fortress-village, that dates to some twenty-five hundred years ago. Rock outcroppings jut out, sweep above, and drop down into the Atlantic Ocean; on all sides are stunning vistas. It was a good strategic point in ancient times as well as an inspirational one when not under attack. The ancient builders used the natural stone shapes and outcroppings to construct their round homes. Some homes cluster in threes so that three concentric circles echo the triskelion, the Celtic trinity that represented many trios: god, goddess, and creator; maid, mother, and crone; earth, air, and water (and later, with the influence of Christianity, the Father, Son, and Holy Ghost). There is a palpable joy about the place, as if the ancient inhabitants knew they had a good thing and were a happy lot.

Of more modern making, some tours are having fun with neo-

The Castro de Baroña, Galicia

Celtic legend making, saying that if you can spot the natural lion-head–shaped rock formation that is a part of the castro settlement you will be granted honorary membership in the reborn "Celtic Clan of Baroña."

There has been a Celtic revival movement in Galicia—as well as neighboring Asturias, Cantabria, and northern León—that has been building over the past twenty years, a response to Franco's death and the opening of Spanish society to exploring its new identity. For many, this has meant excavating the distant, non-Christian past. In many ways this Celtic revival in Galicia mirrors the Islamic revival in Andalusia, where Catholic Spaniards are "re"-converting to Islam (see chapters 15 and 16, especially under Granada, for more on this).

Castro de Baroña to the Dolmen de Axeitos (12 miles/19 km):
Take AC-550 S toward Xuño and Oleiros; shortly after Oleiros, turn right onto AC-303 toward Olveira; the Dolmen de Axeitos is before you get to Olveira; follow the signs for the dolmen.

DOLMEN DE AXEITOS—Galicia

Set in a field of yellow flowers or grasses, depending on the time of year, the Dolmen de Axeitos is protected in its own stone-bordered space. A Neolithic collective tomb dating to around six thousand years ago, this dolmen is a sixteen-square-meter rock supported by eight smaller ones. It is in a grove of oak trees, reinforcing the ancient connection between oak and the sacred in many parts of Iberia. Beyond the oak are native pine trees.

I strongly recommend stopping in Campelos, a small town near the dolmen, and having lunch at the Restaurante Dolmen on the edge of the village.

Dolmen de Axeitos to Padrón (23 miles/37 km):
Take AC-303 E; cross over AC-550 and toward A Pobra; take AC-305 NE to Padrón.

PADRÓN—Galicia

In AD 44 Herod ordered the decapitation of St. James the Greater, whose headless body was taken from its tomb by two disciples and set on a stone boat in Jaffa, Palestine (the stone boat curiously made from Galician granite). Over six days and nights they sailed across the Mediterranean and up to the coast of Galicia where the boat came to a stop at the settlement of Padrón.

Padrón's holy center today is the Iglesia de Santiago de Padrón in the heart of town. It is under the church's altar where a door swings open to reveal St. James's boat's mooring post (mooring stone in Gallego is *pedrón*). Before this altar you are standing on the fabled spot where his granite boat stopped with his decapitated body and his two dedicated disciples at his side. On entering the church you will see illustrations of this sailing trio. You may also encounter the town beggar, who if present will show you the mooring post and inform you, correctly, that the mooring post has a more ancient sacredness than St. James.

This pillar was a part of an altar devoted to the sea god Neptune. Both during Neptune-venerating times and during St. James's boat's arrival, Padrón was on the coast. Silting over the centuries has made the town an inland one, but its seafaring past is well preserved in the church.

There are many variations of legends told about St. James's arrival and his strange stone boat and attendants. Most mention that they interrupted a wedding in progress, the wedding of Queen Lupa's daughter no less, the next in line for matriarchal rule in the region. The boat and its foreign visitors startled the bridegroom and his horse and the two plunged into the water to later emerge covered in scallop shells.

The story is not done yet, and already there are so many rich and suggestive symbolic messages here concerning the struggle between the established matriarchy and the new-coming patriarchy. On the matriarchal side is the scallop shell, the universal feminine symbol, not just of Venus, but of the womb. Scallop shells cover the groom, announcing that he is still under female rule. On the patriarchal side is a saint from a newly minted Abrahamic faith from the patriarchal Near East, arriving around AD 44 before even Romans had a chance to overtake this northwestern corner of Iberia with their brand of patriarchy. Does this Padrónian legend indeed point to the ancient road of the goddess, a story powerful enough to capture the attention of a young Christianity that would appropriate it with its Near Eastern god? And is the potency of the Virgin Mary a way the goddess held her authority in the inevitable power swing? I think so; and I am not alone or original in these thoughts. It is an old well-known story. But the clothes this story wears here are unique and interesting, covering the story with local nuances and dynamics at play.

So, after the startled bridegroom returns covered in scallop shells, the newcomers ask Queen Lupa if they may bury their beloved master in her realm. She wants the newcomers gone and suggests they go to Mount Ilicino where "cows" who can transport the body to the hill for burial live. But in truth, on Mount Ilicino live dangerous bulls, who she hopes will do away with the strangers. But instead, through saintly intercession, the bulls are tamed and the disciples bury St. James on the mount. The queen, according to Christian legend, is impressed enough to convert to Christianity and rename Mount Ilicino, Pico Sacro, Sacred Peak. She gives the disciples the settlement of Libredón, at the foot of a Celtic castro, as the burial site.

These are elements of popular and complementary tellings of St. James's postmortem arrival in Spain. If he really came here after life, it may be because he had traveled to and evangelized in Iberia before his martyrdom. But none of these ideas can be securely proven, and so we remain in the realm of mythic possibilities.

Libredón on the Pico Sacro was likely a burial site for the Gallaeci Celtic speakers of this region and then later became a necropolis during Roman times. Today it stands beneath the cathedral in Santiago de Compostela, so this gives you an idea of how far the two disciples traveled from Padrón to bury their master (about twenty kilometers).

There under Pico Sacro St. James bided his time, waiting for the right moment in human history to reveal his presence in northwestern Spain. The ideal time came, from the Christian perspective, in the early ninth century when the Christian territories of Spain had been squeezed into a narrow northern strip and the little kingdoms wanted to organize and reclaim territory from the Muslims south of them. As such, a Galician hermit followed a trail of stars to the burial site and came upon St. James, whose tomb was confirmed by the local bishop, Theodomir. (The rest of this story can be found in chapters 4 and 7.)

To complicate matters, in the fourth century, a Galician heretic-mystic-hermit-monk, Priscillian, was martyred by decapitation because his ideas of the early Christian way were at odds with the conventions of the early church (chapter 4). He was possibly buried at the same burial mound as the fabled St. James. Was it his tomb or that of St. James that was found under a bright star in the ninth century? I leave that for each seeker to work out.

Padrón is a nice town to visit, especially on Sundays when their weekly market takes up the center of town and overflows along all the streets and out beyond town. This is a perfect time to see the church, visit the sacred Neptunian stone, and then take in a market breakfast of either steamed octopus (*pulpo*) and red wine or a cone-full of Spanish donuts (*churros*) and coffee or hot chocolate.

In the church, along each side, you can locate St. James in his two popular forms from the Middle Ages, as pilgrim and as Moor Slayer. A small side altar to Santa Lucia is here too, a saint whom locals visit to cure problems. Our working beggar took off my glasses here and asked Santa Lucia to improve my eyesight. I imagine the "sight" she improves is more than physical.

Padrón to Poio (23 miles/37 km):
Follow signs to AP-9/E-1 and go S to Pontevedra; as you near Pontevedra, follow signs to Poio.

Detour to Santa María de Armenteira:
Before Poio, you can make a detour, at exit 119 off of AP-9/E-1 heading for Meis and San Salvador de Meis. At the latter you will turn left, S, on a little road leading to the twelfth-century Cistercian monastery, Santa María de Armenteira.

With hints of Mudéjar craftsmen, the monastery of Santa María de Armenteira is set in a green little valley at the heart of the finger of land demarcated to the north by the Ría de Arousa and to the south by the Ría de Pontevedra.

Return to AP-9/E-1 and proceed to Poio.

MONASTERIO DE POIO—Galicia

The monastery in Poio has a strong sixteenth- to eighteenth-century structure but its origins date back to the seventh century, when it was established by the Visigothic St. Fructuoso, a somewhat unorthodox saint. Granted, unorthodox saints abound in Galicia, probably given its remote, pre-Christian, and Celtic influences. Poio is among the remotest outreaches, along the Rias Baixas with its intertwining watery estuaries, fingers of land jutting into the Atlantic, and rolling green hills that hide the next village just beyond.

St. Fructuoso belonged to the royal family. He could walk across water, which he did to reach the little island of Tambo nearby. You can get a glimpse of St. Fructuoso here; he is depicted in the uppermost right-hand panel of the altar piece on the left side of the church's nave. His saint's day is celebrated on April 16.

Also buried at Poio's church is another Galician saint, St. Trahamunda. Her legend involves the recurring theme of a stone boat, carved of granite from Galicia much like the one that bore St. James to Padrón. St.

Trahamunda's boat carried her from Córdoba, probably along the Guadalquivir River and into the Atlantic and up to Galicia. Her corpse arrived in Galicia with her hands holding a palm tree from Spain's south.

Another legend says that she was a very pretty young woman from Galicia at the time that it was invaded by Muslims from the south. She along with several other young women were taken to Córdoba to become a part of the city's harems, but she refused to renounce her faith. Though this was a nonissue to a Muslim man to have a Christian concubine, the legend still tells us that in her refusal to become a Muslim, she was imprisoned. For many years she pined away for her homeland in her prison cell. One day two angels appeared to her in prayer and transported her back to her natal Poio where she spent the rest of her days. Among Santa Trahamunda's miracles, she was fabled to cure the deaf.

Poio's monastery dates to the Benedictines in the tenth century. Its time of greatest influence and activity was in the sixteenth and seventeenth centuries, when it received many land-based endowments and became a center of theological learning.

Like the monks of so many monasteries that were dismantled in the 1830s, Poio's monks abandoned their monastery, but some sixty years later the Orden de la Merced reinhabited it and their friars currently oversee the establishment. Under their efforts, today Poio is again a center for spiritual and religious study, including seminars during the summer.

If you want a mini-walk through the Camino, the Cloister of the Crucero, Claustro del Crucero, has a visual depiction of literal and allegorical imagery in mosaic inlay along its four inner walls. Included in the imagery are the zodiac signs, which have been paired with different stops on the Camino.

The ongoing exhibit space in the monastery holds paintings from the 1960s and 1970s by Pedro García Lema, whose art is some of the most mystical and transcendent Christian art I've witnessed in any century.

Lastly, to get an honest feel for how large this monastery's population once was, visit the storage granary, a Galician-style *hórreo*, outside on the grounds. It claims to be Galicia's largest, a claim no one refutes.

PONTEVEDRA—Galicia

Pontevedra was once a major port city, from the thirteenth to the sixteenth century, and its medieval old quarter reflects its beauty from this period. There are many stone passageways and little plazas that fill with outdoor café tables in good weather.

The patroness of Pontevedra is La Peregrina, a manifestation of the Virgin Mary dressed in green and white as a pilgrim, looking very much like a female St. James. A great appeal of her sanctuary church, El Santuario de la Peregrina, is that it is small and round and easy to inhabit. It is fairly modern, a Neoclassical building from the eighteenth century. It marks the presence of one of the roads that lead to Santiago de Compostela, the Portuguese Route, which passes through here from the south on its way north to St. James's shrine. On the walls of the round sanctuary are wooden carved plaques for the stations of the cross; beneath each is a stone-carved scallop shell candle holder, also symbolizing the pilgrim's road to Santiago.

The Basilica de Santa María la Mayor, on the other side of historic Pontevedra, west of La Peregrina, was built by the fishermen's guild in the fifteenth and sixteenth centuries. Its style is transition Gothic to Renaissance with a good dose of elaborately carved Plateresque. At the top of the west portal are carvings of fishermen and their nets. Near the Basilica de Santa María la Mayor, on the street called Sor Lucia, is the Capilla de las Apariciones. This is where the Virgin Mary appeared to Lucia of Fatima. Lucia was one of the three children who in 1917 received visits in Fatima, Portugal, from the Virgin Mary. Eight years later, in 1925, Lucia was living as a nun in a Dorothean convent here in Pontevedra when the Marian visits continued. These apparitions and messages from Mary to Lucia occurred at this site and have become a part of the whole story and legacy of Fatima.

Of interest at the southwest edge of historic Pontevedra is the ruined form of the fourteenth- and fifteenth-century Gothic church of Santo Domingo. Damaged in 1835 from the looting and sacking that took place when Spain disbanded its monasteries, the church's open-air arches and tombs are actually beautiful in their ruined state. Dappled sun streaks in and green moss and ivy grow over formerly interior spaces, making it feel as if you are walking in a mysterious sanctuary, like out of the movie *Pan's Labyrinth*. In fact, it is now an open-air museum offering Roman tombstones, medieval Galician tombs of locals, craftsmen's tombs carved with their tools of the trade, and tombs of clergy and nobility.

Pontevedra to Baiona (34 miles/55 km):

Take N-550 S toward Redondela; at Redondela go W toward Vigo; take PO-552, the coastal road leaving Vigo to Baiona.

Detour to Nigrán:
On the way to Baiona consider a detour to the modernist church Templo Votivo del Mar in Nigrán, 4.5 miles/7 km before reaching Baiona on PO-552.

The Templo Votivo was built by Antonio Palacios in the 1930s, the same architect who built the Virgen de la Roca in Baiona. It is a strange mix of what looks like Gothic, Byzantine, and Celtic motifs. Though modern, it was built over the ruins of a Visigothic temple and incorporates some of the ruin's designs. It honors all the prior and current spiritual traditions of Galicia, from dolmen and castros to churches and cathedrals.

BAIONA—Galicia

Baiona is the location of the outdoor Virgen de la Roca, Virgin of the Rock, a granite statue of Mary and the site of an annual fishermen's festival and pilgrimage (the last Sunday in August); the Lady is the protectress of the seafaring folk.

Standing on the water's edge, the statue also serves as a lookout point. The Virgin holds a boat in her right hand and this is the place you climb to and look out from to get a view of the inlet, the islands (Islas Cies), and the ocean beyond. Inaugurated in 1930, the outdoor Virgin stands fifteen meters high and the staircase to the lookout point is from the inside. It can be a mystical experience—you have to go through the Mother of God to go higher and get a better view.

Begun in 1910, this statue was designed by the engineer Laureano Salgado Rodríguex and built by the architect Antonio Palacios. It is entirely of granite except for her hands and face, which are of marble. Next to the statue are a Via Crucis and stone picnic tables that are a part of the ritual and celebration of the seafarers' pilgrimage to the Virgen de la Roca.

In Baiona there is also a twelfth- to fourteenth-century Romanesque-Gothic church whose most distinctive features are the symbolic carvings of the different craft guilds, such as axes, knives, and chisels.

Baiona to Santa Tecla (19 miles/30 km):
Take PO-552 S to A Guarda; follow the signs up the hill to Santa Tecla, also called Santa Tegra.

SANTA TECLA—Galicia

The Celtic castro city of Santa Tecla, or locally known as Santa Tegra, benefited from the rich fauna and flora of this area of ocean, river, mountain, and valley. The moderns of A Guarda benefit in much the same way. A stone's throw from the border of Portugal, which is formed by the Miño River, Santa Tecla had human occupants back to the Bronze Age, when inhabitants left stone engravings on rock faces around Santa Tecla thirty-six hundred years ago. Later Iron Age people inhabited the area around twenty-six hundred years ago. They constructed the extensive defensive mountaintop town called Santa Tecla from the sixth to the second century BCE.

As happened in Coaña and Fazouro, Romans ultimately took over this Celtic-speaking settlement, removing the need for living in defensive fortress towns. Slowly these people abandoned Santa Tecla for living lower along the coastline, as the inhabitants did in A Guarda down below the dramatic windswept hilltop.

For the Iron Age people who lived here, as the museum on site amply demonstrates, this castro settlement's sacred life was woven into the environment and the natural world and its forces were revered as holy. Round homes, door frames, window ledges, and roof lintels all had sacred symbols carved into them, work you can see in the museum on the higher hilltop. The symbols were placed in homesteads both for grace and for protection. Among them were triskelions, spirals, sun signs, moon signs, eternal knots, circles, and the like. (The museum is headed by a very informative man who speaks English and delights in sharing Santa Tecla's history.)

Compared to the other Celtic castros, Santa Tecla housed a much larger population. Stone decorations are not the only items found at the settlement. Gold, silver, and bronze items such as torques, fibulae, coins, and knives have also been found, as well as glass and ceramic vessels. Moreover, much of the site is still unexcavated as can be seen from the contours just beneath the surface on the southern end of the archaeological site.

Later, following the Celtic speakers and Romans, early Christians also saw the power of this place. The cult of Santa Tecla (who was a disciple of St. Paul's and was martyred in Iconio, Anatolia, in AD 46) is likely to have been established here by the Visigoths. The chapel to Santa Tecla, near the museum and uphill from the Iron Age castro town, was built in the twelfth century and added to until the sixteenth century. It is a sweet, small chapel whose sole intent is a place of pilgrimage, veneration, and prayer. The location, overlooking the Miño river valley and Portugal on one side and the Atlantic Ocean and A Guarda below on the other, makes for awe-inspired contemplation.

CHAPTER ELEVEN

La Alcudia to Empúries

*La Dama de Elche is the true icon of our city and is greatly loved by the
people. She might be the ancient goddess Tanit because the Phoenicians
and Carthaginians had a prominent presence along this coast.*

—A native of Elche

THIS ITINERARY COVERS a part of the ancient coastal route
Via Augustus, the Roman road that crossed into Spain and passed through
Barcelona, Tarragona, Valencia, and ended in Cádiz. It begins in southwestern Spain and travels north along the Mediterranean coastline. This ancient
road contains sacred sites belonging to indigenous Iberians, Phoenicians,
Carthaginians, Greeks, Romans, Jews, Muslims, and Christians.

One of the treats of traveling in the Valencia-Alicante area is unique
glazed ceramic domes of the churches throughout the region. These multicolored, often cobalt blue or in striated pattern, domes are unique to
sacred architecture in Murcia and Valencia-Alicante. These domes often
correspond to churches built in the Baroque and Neoclassical styles and
they add more color and light to an area already graced by the Mediterranean Sea's light-bending qualities.

This route also passes through what after AD 1238 was the land of
King Jaime I (James I) of Aragón, who took Valencia from the Muslims
but did not alter the livelihood of the region, recognizing the great spiritual as well economic value of a land of *convivencia*. In such a populace,
the economy worked seven days a week. When Muslims took Friday off,
Jews and Christians carried on commerce and agriculture, fishing and
crafts. On Saturday, Jews rested and Muslims and Christians labored. And

on Sundays, Christians took their day of rest while Muslims and Jews carried on the work.

Long before Jaime I, Mediterranean traders and seafaring people recognized the wealth of Iberia and set up temporary and permanent trading settlements along the coast, placing their gods and goddesses as protectors of their lives and interests. Idols and amulets found on such sites attest to this.

Much of the sacred imagery partakes of its environment and reflects this back. As a result, we have miraculous boats bearing holy people arriving on shore, we have the miracle of water and rain arriving via divine grace to dry desert climes, and we have a high value placed on the products of earth and sea, from fish to wine, olives, and rice.

The route starts at Iberia's symbolically most powerful ancient site, La Alcudia, northeast of Murcia where the Dama de Elche was found, and it ends at the best-preserved Greek settlement in Spain, Empúries, north of Barcelona. Throughout, you will be traveling in a region, from Valencia-Alicante to Catalonia, where Valenciano and Catalán are spoken. These are related languages whose antecedent was Old Provençal. This also reflects this coastal region's mix and mingle in the greater Mediterranean world.

Main Route (407 miles/655 km):
La Alcudia de Elche—Elche—Valencia—El Puig—Sagunto—Tarragona—Barcelona—Empúries

LA ALCUDIA DE ELCHE—Valencia

La Alcudia de Elche is an archaeological site two kilometers directly south of the city of Elche that has been under excavation since the nineteenth century. It lies on private land but since 1996 the family who owns it with the Municipality of Elche and the University of Alicante has created the University Foundation for Archaeological Investigation at La Alcudia. Thanks to this, you will see archaeologists at work and enjoy a well-presented visit to the different parts of the excavation site as well as to an insightful museum that houses many of the finds here, including a good deal of sacred works.

La Alcudia marks an ancient settlement site that was home to some nine different civilizations, each one either on top of or next to the other. Such long-term occupancy by many peoples signals a powerful place, whether it shows one people gaining power by dominating another or the place itself having a pull on people for some reason, be it strategic location, enchanted setting, or good resources. La Alcudia is certainly at the center of the

ancient western coastal Mediterranean world.

Elche, the town nearby, was
once called Ilici by Romans, who
likely derived the name from the
native Iberians who lived in the
area and who called their settlement Helike. *La Alcudia* means
"mound," and given that its history is intimately tied to Elche's,
it is considered the "mound of
Elche."

Reaching as far back as some
seven thousand years ago, La
Alcudia's ancient residents included Neolithic inhabitants,
Bronze Age and Iron Age
peoples, Iberians, Phoenicians,
Greeks, Carthaginians, Romans,
Visigoths, and a brief period of
control by Byzantines. It was
occupied through the Muslim

*A reproduction of La Dama de Elche on
the spot where she was unearthed at
La Alcudia de Elche, Valencia*

conquest until around the tenth century. When North African Berbers
and Arabs conquered this territory in the eighth century, they settled at
the lower end of the town, preserving the Roman foundations. Thereafter,
the area gradually fell out of popular use, and became private farmland in
this rich agricultural region, which today is considered the garden of not
only Spain but Europe—more produce is grown and exported from the
areas of Murcia and Valencia-Alicante than anywhere else in Europe.

All these layers of civilizations are remarkable in and of themselves,
but for many what really put La Alcudia on the map was an accidental
find on August 4, 1897. That day, farm workers were taking a break, eating their lunch on the mound that they were terracing, preparing it for
planting. While they rested, a boy named Manolico continued in the terracing work. He swung his pick into the earth and instead of a soft, giving
thud, he hit something hard. He called to the others and the group
worked to uncover a fifty-six-centimeter high bust of a regal and ancient
lady. Manolico gave her the nickname *Reina Mora*, "Moorish Queen," a
name that immediately stuck with the populace. The Reina Mora was the
talk of the town and ultimately caught the attention of French archaeolo-

The sixth century BCE Iberian temple at La Alcudia de Elche, Valencia

gist Pierre Paris who convinced the private owners of the bust to sell it to the Louvre.

On August 30, 1897, the Reina Mora went to the Louvre, where the French called her La Dame d'Elche and where she remained for over forty years until World War II. Fearing the destruction of their antiquities with the German invasion of France, in 1941 the Louvre sent La Dama de Elche to Madrid for protection. She was installed in the Prado Museum for the next thirty years and then moved to her current place, in the archaeology museum in Madrid. Whether you see the original in Madrid or the well-executed reproduction on the spot in La Alcudia, you will find that on La Dama's left hair disk there is a chunk missing. That is where Manolico's pick hit the sculpture as it lay under the earth.

La Dama de Elche dates to either the fourth or fifth century BCE. Some argue she is purely Iberian and others say she is a mix of either Greek and Iberian or Phoenician and Iberian elements. Given how much of the fourth- and fifth-century Mediterranean world was trading and invading one another's borders, any of these ideas are possible. Moreover, her clothing looks a lot like contemporary festive dress among Berbers in southern Morocco, so there could be an influence somewhere there, too. Indeed, the northern and southern rims of the Mediterranean were one big integrated world, not the north-south divide we psychologically impose on that geography today.

Who La Dama was is equally uncertain, though a very Iberian-styled crematory funerary or offering niche in her back indicates some form of veneration. She might have been a grande dame of Iberian society, a queen or princess or wise woman of some manner. Or she could have been a goddess. Among the possible goddesses, she might be a manifestation of the Egyptian Isis whose cult went around the Mediterranean and, during the Hellenic period, Isis became a Greek goddess of marriage and fertility. Or La Dama de Elche might represent Tanit, the Phoenician goddess of fertility and fidelity and of the hearth. Another contender for La Dama is Cybele, the Great Mother to peoples of ancient Anatolia and later to the Romans. And there is always the possibility that La Dama de Elche may be an Iberian divinity about whom we have yet to learn. Or she might be a hybrid divinity, such as Greco-Iberian or Phoenician-Iberian. She certainly seems to command the Mother Goddess status in all the traditions that might claim her.

On site is a reproduction of the Dama de Elche in a shelter on the spot where she was dug up. It is possible that the original sculpture was of a complete body and that at some time it was cut into the bust shape it now holds. If you visit the original in Madrid, look closely for where the ghost of old pigment still holds on. In her prime, La Dama de Elche was polychrome painted. Her lips still reveal the red pigment they once possessed. There are other Iberian sculptures like La Dama, the most closely related being La Dama de Baza, found in Baza, a town northeast of Granada, who is full-bodied, seated in a throne-like posture, and has similar attire and styling. (The Baza original is also in the archaeology museum in Madrid and you can visit the two in the same gallery.) Finally, you can also see a three-dimensional color hologram of La Dama de Elche in the Museu de Prehistòria in Valencia, which is farther along this route.

La Dama de Elche speaks of the diverse flow of traders and invaders to this part of Spain. One modern feminist forum takes her as the goddess returning to the surface, both literally and metaphorically, to the consciousness of humanity, after her long dormancy underground—again, a literal underground as well as metaphorical underground of the unconscious.

Everywhere you look in Elche and its surrounding towns and villages, you will find signs of La Dama de Elche; she is certainly in people's waking consciousness. Her image has been replicated in art in bars, restaurants, and other public buildings. She has made her way onto stamps and coins. The power of being an original, possibly divine, persona from ancient

Iberia is strong in the modern Spanish psyche, as strong as the national feeling evoked in representations of the Celtiberian defense of Numancia near Soria against the Romans (see chapter 13).

There are other sacred aspects of La Alcudia, in addition to La Dama de Elche. Just before you reach the spot where La Dama de Elche was found is an area of Iberian and Roman houses. One in particular is called the *casa del culto a la cabeza cortada,* "house of the cult of the cut head." It appears that a Roman home was built around the second half of the first century AD over an older Iberian cult center where a human cranium was found on what was an altar. Other ritual objects were found near the cranium. Some posit that this might have been a place for sacrifice or placement of cut heads (after battle?). After Romans took over La Alcudia, but before the Roman home was built here, the emperor Augustus prohibited blood sacrifice in cult rites. As a result, finds at this site, in the Iberian-Roman transitional strata, reflect this shift in sacrificial offering and take on a symbolic form, where older prior real heads were replaced by ceramic replicas of human heads. I confess that this is not my idea of the ideal place to build a home.

Near the onsite museum is the Roman forum, where many activities took place: commercial, administrative, as well as sacred. Temple activities that existed in other parts of La Alcudia shifted to the forum after Roman occupation and settlement of the town.

Next to the forum is a well, *aljibe,* that was a part of the water system of a residence in the ancient town. Inside the well archaeologists found a little statue of Venus, which is now on display in the archaeology museum in Elche. Why the statue was there—intentionally or accidentally through the flow of time and reoccupation—is uncertain.

At the far end, next to each other, are an Iberian temple and a paleo-Christian church. The actual Iberian temple was found underneath the paleo-Christian church and what you are looking at is a reconstruction of that subterranean find. The Iberian temple was made of adobe and had a central area for offerings. Objects from the same era as the temple, sixth century BCE, are on display in the first gallery in the onsite museum (with depictions of mythic creatures and warriors in action). The art on the ceramics is graphic and offers some good visual ideas as to what people's dress and focus might have been during the indigenous Iberian presence here. Within the temple itself, archaeologists found several icons with female faces, suggesting that this temple was associated with a female divinity, if not the Great Mother herself. The temple was very likely contemporary with La Dama de Elche.

The rectangular early paleo-Christian church with its polychrome mosaic floor was built during the time of Roman Emperor Constantine I, around AD 320. The apse was added in the fifth century and the altar enclosure during the seventh century. This basilica was the seat of the regional Visigothic bishop (beginning in the fifth century) and briefly fell under Byzantine rule during Emperor Justinian's reign (sixth century AD). Thereafter, Ilici returned to Visigothic hands until the arrival of the North Africans shortly after AD 711.

La Alcudia de Elche to Elche (1 mile/2 km):
Head N to Elche.

ELCHE/ELX—Valencia

Elche's Medieval Mystery Play

Every year, in mid-August, the *Misterio de Elche* is enacted, a preserved medieval theatrical rite that has been in place since the fifteenth century but with earlier roots. To this day, the mystery play preserves medieval songs and language spoken and sung in Elche in the thirteenth century.

Before Roman rites became the universal liturgical form of worship in Spain, in place were the Visigothic and Mozarabic rites, largely unique to Spain. Among these rites, a very popular annual celebration was Mary's ascension to heaven, placed on August 15 by the seventh and eighth centuries. After Roman Christian rites dominated Iberian rituals, this celebration remained popular and became a secure part of the annual festival cycle, especially during and after the twelfth century and in the Kingdom of Aragón, which after 1238 extended across today's Aragón, Catalonia, and Valencia-Alicante.

It is said that the text for this sacred liturgy arrived in Elche with the Virgin Mary, called La Virgen de la Asunción, who appeared over the sea arriving on an arch. The mystery play concerns the Virgin's death and her assumption to heaven and her crowning in these celestial heights. The beautiful blue-domed seventeenth- to eighteenth-century Baroque Basílica de la Asunción de Santa María, the basilica where her play is enacted, has a built-in elaborate trapdoor in its ceiling—the round dome where the sky is painted with clouds—that lifts singer-actors up and down the basilica height to literally show the descent of angels arriving at Mary's deathbed and her assumption with them up to the stars. There is also a trapdoor in the stage platform below to allow for the descending troupe to change and ascend at a later moment in the story. No detail is overlooked, and costuming and ambience are rich and elaborate, creating another-time feel.

This is an impressive effort, in that the climate in this part of Spain in August, even in great stone churches, can be steamy hot. As the audience sits fanning themselves, consider the sweat and effort of the men and women dressed in ancient Near Eastern gowns and robes as they sing Mary to heaven.

The sacred song is a beautiful preservation of medieval polyphonic chant and the Elche mystery play has been declared by UNESCO a Masterwork of Oral and Intangible Patrimony of Humanity. As the official patronage group of the Mystery of Elche says, "Each August in Elche the Virgin dies so that the pueblo can live."

Museu Municipal de la Festa

A stop at the museum dedicated to La Festa, which is what locals call the annual mystery play, gives the event greater context, especially if you are visiting any time of year other than August 14 and 15 and will not see the play performed. The museum's site sits within the medieval hermitage of San Sebastian and has been transformed into the headquarters for the *Misterio de Elche*. Here the town has created a multidimensional show on the Elchian mystery play set in the old chapel. After you take this in, you can visit the museum with mystery-play props on display and then go next door to visit, or revisit, the Basílica de Santa María.

Ancient Palm Grove, El Palmeral

El Palmeral, Elche's central park filled with palms, was originally planted during Phoenician times and since then has been maintained as a continuous palm grove. During the Muslim occupation in the Middle Ages, the palm grove was expanded and further enhanced with the irrigation system Muslims set in place here, as well as throughout Valencia, Alicante, and Andalusia and beyond in Iberia, making the Peninsula flourish more than it ever had before. These irrigation systems are repaired and maintained today because they are still so effective in making the arid parts of Spain bloom.

This grove of some two hundred thousand palm trees is Europe's largest palm forest. These are also working palms. The fruit-bearing trees give a good date harvest. The palm fronds are used throughout the region for

Palm Sunday. It is a profound pleasure to walk amid the shade of so many palms, with their otherworldly shape. When the wind blows it takes a good strong one to disturb the shaded green world below.

Convento de la Mercè: Arab Baths

Perhaps symbolic of one faith taking over another, this convent is built over Elche's twelfth-century Arab bathhouse. While bathing had its days of polemic—to bathe too much marked one as a Muslim or a Jew in a more and more self-conscious Catholic Spain—this current placement is more a matter of making good use of abandoned real estate after Elche was conquered by Christian rulers; they had less need for bathing than for repopulating the evacuated places. To Elche's citizens today, these baths represent not a world contesting whose Abrahamic faith is bigger and better but rather a pride in their Islamic heritage and a time when Muslim Iberians enjoyed economic and cultural affluence and prosperity. More significantly, physical cleanliness was, and is, paramount to Muslims before entering into their daily prayers.

Shortly after 1270 under the direction of the king of Castile, the Islamic baths were given to a monk's order, Our Lady of Mercy, which founded the current convent.

Elche to Valencia (119 miles/192 km):

Take CV-84 N, which becomes N-325 and then A-31; head toward Elda and Sax; at Sax, follow signs to CV-80 toward Alcoy; take N-340 N toward Xátiva; after Xátiva N-340 connects to A-7 N to Valencia.

VALENCIA—Valencia

Valencia is an ancient Mediterranean city and currently Spain's third largest, after Madrid and Barcelona. It reflects the influences of all the Mediterranean peoples and civilizations from prehistory, antiquity, and the medieval period to the modern times. Like many coastal cities, it is open to outsiders and quite diverse. Most of the sacred sites mentioned here occur in the ancient neighborhood, known as *Barrio del Carmen*, where Roman remains lie beneath Arab ones, which lie beneath Christian structures. This neighborhood is embraced on the north side by the important River Turia, which has provided defense and water to the city for centuries.

Valencia was first a Greek settlement. In 138 BCE it was resettled by retiring Roman soldiers with pensions. They settled along the Turia River's banks (and called their home *Valentia*.) After the Roman retreat, Visigoths ruled here until the arrival of invading North Africans under whom Valencia became a major center for agriculture, silk production, papermaking, ceramics, and leather making, among other trades.

From AD 714 to 1238, Valencia was an Islamic city with a thriving commerce sustained by the three religious communities of Jews, Muslims, and Christians, not just of Iberian descent but from all across the Mediterranean world. Only briefly was this Islamic period interrupted, in the 1090s, when El Cid took Valencia for his own, briefly ousting the Muslim *taifa* king. But upon his death in 1099, Valencia reverted back to Muslim hands, to remain there until Jaime I's decisive battle in 1238 that took the city thereafter for Christian rule. Jaime I knew he would destroy the economy of this prosperous commercial port city if he altered the well-oiled balance of *convivencia*. So he let it be. Though as the Middle Ages flowed into the Early Modern period, with its transitional darkness of the fourteenth and fifteenth centuries, this *convivencia* was destroyed in the name of a Catholic unified Spain. Valencia was one of the ports, along with Denia further south, where the great exodus of Muslims and Jews took place.

Valencia was Spain's financial center in the fifteenth century, and it continued to prosper into the early seventeenth century, when the expulsion of the Moriscos led to a loss of around one-third of the agricultural population. (Though most Moriscos weren't rabble-rousers and just wanted to keep their lives intact, going to work and raising their families, there was a wild bunch from Hornachos in Extremadura who made sure to be a thorn in the side of Phillip III, the king who decreed the solution to the "Morisco problem." They had reign over their village and would charge a toll to anyone who wanted to use the road passing through town. They were also more wealthy than most Moriscos and worked out a bargain with the king, when they saw the writing on the wall, to purchase their departure to Morocco before the expulsion, when all Moriscos would lose their property, and to leave with their gold and goods. This deal was done and in 1608 the Hornachero Moriscos left, but not before one last bang. Much of their wealth came through banditry and counterfeiting Spanish coin. A few months after their departure the Bank of Valencia had to contend with public riots because it had unknowingly circulated counterfeited money from the Hornachero group. Phillip III's "solution" backfired in many ways and the Spanish economy, some argue, never fully recovered.)

Throughout the city, you will find bats etched, carved, and painted on public places, most prevalently on the manhole covers on the streets and sidewalks. The bat was King Jaime I's symbol. As the legend goes, when he was launching an attack against Valencian Muslims for the prize of their city, in the heat of battle an arrow rushed through the air aimed right at his heart. It was too swift for him to move out of the way, but at that moment a bat flew out of nowhere and took the arrow instead, sacrificing his life to save the king. So today, the ever-present bat in Valencia honors this tale of victory. To me it also speaks of a more ancestral connection to animals as shamanic power animals, working with us, even saving our lives. This deeper sacred connection to other forms of life is an important one to remember today, as humans think they are the end all and be all, but are swiftly and mindlessly destroying life on Earth.

Basílica de Nuestra Señora de los Desamparados

Our Lady of the Helpless, or Abandoned, has been Valencia's patroness saint since 1407; her saint's day is May 12. This is where locals in need of real spiritual sustenance and psychological counsel come and you will find visitors to this shrine coming and going at all hours, as it is open throughout the day and night. It is a real source of comfort to people. The basilica sits on the Plaza de la Virgen, the plaza named after this important patroness. In the heart of this plaza is a mischievous-looking sculpture of a Pan-like character, a pagan male energy balancing a strong veneration of the feminine divine. Together they make for real harmony: outside, people gather around Pan at café tables and take in a refreshing drink, soothing the physical, while inside, people take a refreshing sacred drink and soothe the soul. Nearby is the cathedral, another inviting space but for different reasons and different legends. Go there if you are ready to seek the Holy Grail.

Valencia's Cathedral and El Miguelete Tower

Valencia's Gothic cathedral was built over the mosque that stood here when Jaime I took the city. Muslims before him built over a Roman temple to Diana that once stood here. Jaime I initially left the mosque as it was but had it sanctified as a Christian place of worship, dedicating it to Santa María, the Mother of Christ. It was not until several decades later, in the thirteenth century, that the current cathedral was built in the mosque's place.

While nothing of the old mosque remains physically, the Water Tribunal that meets every Thursday at noon is a holdover of a practice held just outside the mosque since the ninth century, when it was set up under the reign of Abd al-Rahman II. You will find this tribunal at the cathedral's north portal, called the Portada de los Apóstoles, Gate of the Apostles. This is on the same spot it was held in Muslim times. Thursday is the chosen day because it fell on the last day of the Muslim workweek. This tradition of over one thousand years was so effective, like the irrigation systems that Muslims built, that it has been continued since then. The tribunal serves to settle water disputes among farmers and to manage the irrigation canals. Every Thursday, legal councilors gather and sit in the leather chairs in the circular area at the cathedral entrance. A crier calls out different regions around Valencia that fall under the tribunal's jurisdiction. If a farmer has a gripe, he speaks up when his region is called and states his case. The circle of elders hears him or her as well as the neighbor the complaint is against, and then makes a decision. The guilty party must carry out and pay for stated reparations. Nothing gets written down, but the decisions are a binding oral contract.

The octagonal Gothic bell tower of the cathedral is endearingly called Little Michael, El Miguelete, as it was consecrated in honor of St. Michael in 1418.

Inside as well as outside is the lacelike Gothic style with one exception, the south portal, which is older and reflects Romanesque work, especially in the faces and figures carved over the portal and in the carving of a waterspout that shows an old woman holding up her breasts to the world below. The faces are animated and moody. In all it reflects a world not afraid of seeing all that is human, feeling it and contemplating what aspects of it to engage for oneself.

The interior is grand and towering, as cathedrals are apt to be, but the crossing has some exquisite cobalt-blue medieval paintings of angels around the core that are still vibrant and saturated and give the place the feel of a small shrine.

Among the many famous works held within this temple, there can be no more famous one than the claimed Holy Grail held behind thick glass protection in the Capilla de Santa Calíz, the Chapel of the Holy Grail. The golden-colored agate cup is indeed a first-century BCE vessel and its stone is believed to come from the east. It was carried by St. Peter from the Holy Land to Rome, where it fell under the care of the popes. When Emperor Valerian began persecuting Christians in the third century, the pope swiftly sent the cup for protection to Huesca, in Aragón, where it fell into the care of the monastery of San Juan de la Peña (see chapter 13). Later, being a part of the property of the Crown of Aragón, it was sent to the cathedral in Valencia for more central display.

There are, of course, other stories of how the grail got here. Some street-talk fables opine that the chalice was brought here under the protection of the Templar knights, to their castle in Valencia. Before that they kept it under their care for one hundred years, hidden in their castle on the coast north of here in Peñiscola.

In the medieval period, the stone cup was given a stem and handles, taking on its more ornate and current appearance. This is considered to be *the* chalice Jesus used at the Last Supper and some claim it contains drops of his blood. There are, of course, several other chalices in the world that claim the same.

Be sure to also visit the chapel dedicated to Our Lady of Puig, the Virgin who showed herself to Jaime I before he went into battle with Valencian Muslims on the mountain Puig north of Valencia. Her appearance assured Jaime I's victory. We will visit her again, on that very hilltop in Puig, now a seaside resort town.

Santa Catalina

Among the churches for daily worship, Santa Catalina is a sweet respite. It is used by locals for quiet prayer. Its tower is as enticing as El Miguelete is at the cathedral nearby. Within the church's side chapels is a simple statue of Nuestra Señora de la Vocación, who has a distinctive bronze-colored disk placed over her belly. She looks down peacefully at the visitors from her perch and her hands are open in trust and reception. Her disk represents someone who has voluntarily emptied herself of human time-space desires and has opened space within to bring through divine will and grace.

While there is a solitary crucified Christ on the altar, the church is very feminine, surrounded by myriad expressions of Mary, as well as other female saints including Santa Catalina, in its side chapels.

Santa Catalina, St. Catherine, was born in Alexandria and lived in the third and fourth centuries. She was so strong in her faith that she refused marriage to the emperor, claiming she was already a bride of Christ's. For her daring in standing against conventional culture, she was tortured on a wheel, which broke under her divine presence. She was killed by beheading, but you will see her, as here, with a wheel, the instrument of her torture as well as the symbol of her strength in her connection to the divine.

This church also stands over what was once a mosque.

Visigothic Chapel and Crypt of St. Vincent

This small space represents a spot where several peoples built their sacred sites. A piece of mural from the Roman period was found here that has a painting of the god Mercury on it. Under the Romans, St. Vincent, originally from Zaragoza, was incarcerated, starved, and further tortured here. He died from his traumas in AD 304. St. Vincent's cult has been very strong throughout the province of Valencia and it spread from here to other parts of the Mediterranean.

Found on this spot were also remains of an early pre-Visigothic Christian church. Next this site was a Visigothic chapel and funerary site. It still contains stone panels with carvings in floral, geometric, and whimsical natural designs associated with the Visigoths. In the center is a solitary stone altar and nearby are a number of crypts, including two Visigothic tombs. After the Visigoths, Arabs turned the site into a bathhouse (tenth and eleventh centuries) with hot, warm, and cool rooms. The hot room used heated stones and water to create a sauna. Among the remains found here are Islamic-period ceramics and jewelry. After King Jaime I of Aragón took Valencia from the Muslims, the Visigothic chapel was still visible at the north end and he had it resurrected and rededicated to St. Vincent.

There is a fun multimedia display in the chapel and crypt that capably brings these different layers of history to life. You can ask for the presentation to be given in English.

Holy Jamón

If anyone doubts that spirito-religious feeling is declining with the rise of the secular age in a post-Franco Spain, let me tell you about the mysterious occurrence of the holy ham. In September of 1993 in Valencia—and I cannot tell you who or where—someone witnessed an apparition in a leg of jamón Serrano, that delightful Iberian delicacy that is like Italian prosciutto but nuttier. There in the fat and meat marbling was the classical iconographic face of Jesus. It quickly became an object of veneration and was mummified to preserve it. But before the mummification, it is said that the meat was used as therapeutic food to heal sick children. The ham is still somewhere in the city, though where I could not locate.

Valencia to Puig (9.5 miles/15 km):
Take CV-300 N to Puig.

EL PUIG—Valencia

The shrine and convent of La Virgen del Puig holds the center and heart of this easy-to-inhabit seaside resort town. La Virgen del Puig is critical to Jaime I's conquest of Valencia. Legend tells of the appearance of a sixth-century Byzantine Virgin Mary on the two hills of Puig. She had been hidden centuries before by monks who placed her under a bell and buried her on the eve of the Muslim invasion of the region. There she lay quietly until the arrival of King Jaime I in 1237 or 1238. Here there are two accounts. One is that the king himself saw her in a vision and discovered her hiding place. Another speaks of a monk who followed a trail of stars that led to her hiding place. In either case, the Virgin was brought to Jaime I and, upon seeing her, he gained confidence in his mission and defeated the Muslims at Puig and continued southward to Valencia where success was also guaranteed. He took Valencia in 1238 and shortly thereafter the monastery of Puig was founded to house the miraculous Lady. This is where you stand, on the spot where the Virgin of Puig was discovered.

The monastery's earlier construction was Romanesque, with only a facade of this period remaining. This portal leads to the side chapel, which is open for public worship during Mass. Beyond the Romanesque facade, the rest of the convent and shrine is Gothic.

Because of her importance in Jaime I's conquest of Valencia and the miracle of stars, a theme that she has in common with that great pilgrimage road to Santiago de Compostela, the Lady of Puig is the patron saint of the whole region.

Over the centuries, the monastery has served as monastery, prison, and finally residence of the royal family when they are in the area. The town has a generally good vibe and it seems to be a healthy place to live, with kind people from all over Europe living in Mediterranean bungalows. There seems to be perennially a lovely sea breeze and magical light at sunset.

Puig to Sagunto (5 miles/8 km):
Continue N following signs to Sagunt/Sagunto.

SAGUNTO—Valencia

Sagunto is the site of the ancient Iberian settlement of Arse, an ally of Rome in the third century BCE that came under attack by the Carthaginians led by Hannibal in 219 BCE. The Iberian natives fought hard, but when they saw defeat as inevitable, many took their own lives by throwing themselves into fires rather than face the humiliation of becoming Hannibal's prisoners of war. This defeat brought on the Second Punic War between Carthage and Rome, wherein Carthage was finally defeated years later in 202 BCE. This victory made the western Mediterranean a Roman domain and Saguntum, as it was called then, was rebuilt and became an important crossroads—by land and by sea—for trade and commerce.

As important and developed by Romans as Sagunto was, today its Roman temples are lost to us. It is certain that once a temple to Diana, goddess of the hunt and the wild, stood right next to the entrance to today's Iglesia de Santa María, reinforcing the presence of a female divinity. In addition to the ancient Diana, Saguntians also venerated Mercury, also known as Hermes, the god of commerce as well as the divine messenger, and images of him have been found here; some you can glimpse in the local museum.

A striking feature of Sagunto is its massive hilltop castle, supposedly Europe's largest. It should be, as it was used by everyone in this strategic spot on the Mediterranean. It marks the original settlement of Sagunto and archaeological excavations have unearthed remains of Iberians, Carthaginians, Romans, and North Africans.

The Roman theater, now walled in on one side to preserve it for live performances (and ticket sales?), sits just below the castle in the heart of the old town. But what is really striking about Sagunto's living sacred tradition is that a stroll through the old streets of town brings up a chapel, a hermitage, and a shrine every few feet. Tucked amid all this is the old Jewish neighborhood, too, quietly being brought out into fuller relief. Indeed, Sagunto feels like a restoration project in progress, but don't be put off by the transitional phase. Stay long enough to explore the hidden nooks and crannies. The main church, the Gothic Iglesia de Santa María (next to Diana's once-upon-a-time temple), is dedicated to Mary, as are the majority of the smaller chapels, whether their names indicate it or not, throughout town; Mary tends to be the center of the altars with Jesus farther back or smaller and overhead. In the Ermita de Sant Roc, Mary stands *above* Sant Roc (who is dressed as a pilgrim to Santiago de Compostela no less), reversing the usual male-female orientation of heaven and Earth, making heaven feminine.

At the Ermita de la Sangre, "hermitage of the blood," you will find yourself where the old synagogue once stood (here Mary is foregrounded with her son holding the background).

I tried hiking around a part of the perimeter of the castle, and although I found my ambition of making the whole perimeter (it is very big) too great for the day allotted, I did come upon some sacred graffiti in the process. There on the southern hill under the castle, I came upon a great upright boulder onto which someone spray-painted *Dios es amor*, "God is love." It was a nice universal sentiment created by a local Saguntian who celebrates the spirit of his or her multifaith past.

Sagunto to Tarragona (152 miles/245 km):
Leave Sagunto N on A-7; continue on N-340 and take it to Tarragona.

TARRAGONA—Catalonia

Tarragona was one of the most important Roman centers, then known as Tarraco, in Iberia from the third century BCE. Three centuries later, in the first century AD, Tarragona became the capital city for Imperial Rome's province, Hispania Tarraconensis. The forum was the capital's administrative, political, and economic center and it also had its temples, such as the Capitoline Temple, which was dedicated to the gods Jupiter, Juno, and Minerva, respectively the supreme god and goddess and the goddess of wisdom. Though the temples in the forum do not stand today, their location is indicated.

Roman ruins here are among the best-surviving ruins in Spain. It is a delight to simply wander through the medieval and overlapping Roman spaces in the city.

A settlement in the ancient wine-loving world, Tarragona was and is a wine-producing city. During Roman times, Tarragonan wine was reputed as being delicious. It was also a strong and hearty wine that traveled well. As such, it was exported throughout the wine-imbibing Mediterranean. With the medieval Christian conquest of the city, wine production returned with monks skilled in the art of wine making. Some of their wine was for commercial purposes and some for the altar for Mass. Some of this sacred wine is still produced in certain regions in and around Tarragona, such as De Muller wines, who make *vinos de misa*, wines for Mass.

Tuesday morning is the weekly market in Tarragona and the entire Rambla is taken over by clothing, household goods, and craft vendors. It offers a nice chance to see the locals doing what they've been doing since Phoenician times, trading, rubbing shoulders, and exchanging ideas. Sunday morning is the flea market, which wraps around the cathedral and medieval neighborhood at the higher point in town. Commerce and worship have long gone hand in hand as markets opened on Sundays to catch the masses from Mass. Likewise, mosques were (and in the Muslim world still are) always next to markets. The sacred heart of a community is the heart of a community in all ways.

On the northwest edge of town is the paleo-Christian necropolis, with pagan and Christian tombs spanning the third to the sixth century AD. Here there are nice examples of Roman, early Christian, and Visigothic sacred art.

Tarragona's classical-world importance was only rivaled by Mérida (Augusta Emerita) in southwestern Spain. Both were Roman provincial capitals of their regions. Prior to Romans, Tarragona's founding stones were laid by indigenous Iberians. These were layered over as in so many eastern shore towns by Phoenician traders and settlers and then by Romans. Throughout town, in honor of an ancient deity, you will likely find replicas of the ancient Phoenician goddess Tanit in artsy gift shops. Her cult spread throughout the western Mediterranean when Carthage was a dominant power. Carthaginian soldiers in particular were the likely bearers of Tanit to coastal Spain.

The Phoenician Goddess Tanit

One of the most influential of Phoenician deities is the goddess of fertility, fidelity, and abundance, Tanit. She would have been known as well as Astarte in the pan-Phoenician world. Tanit was especially big with the Carthaginians who treated her as one of the great divine forces in their world, often partnering with the male divinity Ba'al-Hammon, her consort in the sky. To Carthaginians, Tanit was a sky goddess and ruled over celestial bodies—moon, stars, and sun. She was also treated as the Great Mother, the Mother Goddess, and was the source of fertility, protection, and childbearing.

Tanit had many symbols associated with her. One was the palm tree, something of a symbol of the tree of life. She was also depicted riding the back of a lion and bearing a lance. She might have had a crown of wheat with the crescent moon on her head.

Tanit's worship in the Mediterranean goes back to the fifth century BCE. Her cult in a sense continued with the Roman dominance, as Tanit was associated with the Roman Juno and even with Cybele, the Roman Great Mother. With Mary as Great Mother now reigning over the highest point in Tarragona, over Jupiter's temple, one wonders if there is not another sacred continuity at work there.

Medieval Tarragona

After the Romans, Tarragona became a Visigothic center and a seat of the bishop. It was here that Visigothic Prince Hermenegild led the people in revolt against his father, King Leovigild. The prince had recently converted to Catholicism and was challenging the official Visigothic form of Christianity, Arianism, which denied that Jesus was the same as God but an agent of prophetic change. Leovigild defeated his son and had him killed.

Muslim-ruled Tarragona followed, though it was largely a Jewish city. Muslim-Jewish Tarragona was conquered in the mid-twelfth century by Ramón Berenguer IV who commissioned a new cathedral to be built. Given the city's significant Jewish population, the cathedral's architects were primarily Jewish. Much of their designs were Judeo-Islamic, something you can especially see today in the cathedral's cloisters, where narrow and long double horseshoe windows and multilobed stone designs line the walls of the otherwise Gothic structure. At the cloister's west end you will see a tenth-century *mihrab*, prayer niche, from an earlier mosque, which has been incorporated into the cloister design.

Adding to this ancestral meshing, the site of the cathedral was built at the highest point in town where there once stood the main Temple of Jupiter. The walk up to the cathedral along Carrer Major is a delight today, as it must have been during Roman and medieval times. You pass through medieval streets and passageways with the cathedral towering above.

Twelfth-Century Gothic Cathedral

At the entrance, there is a statue of Mary as a young Roman-looking woman with a long braid draped over her shoulder. It is a style like no other I have ever seen except perhaps in the works of the Pre-Raphaelites. It is lyrical and musical and a lovely introduction to the peaceful interior.

Jupiter may be at the heart of this place, as current excavations have confirmed that there was a Roman temple beneath the cathedral, a temple likely devoted to none other than Jupiter or Zeus. At the spot where Jupiter's image may have stood in an open-air temple on Tarragona's highest hill (sky), now the Virgin Mary stands in her closed-in cavernous space (earth). It is a very appealing place, perhaps because of its location at the top of town and over an ancient Roman temple.

The cathedral at first comes across as dark and foreboding, a feeling not everyone shakes, but then it wraps its energy around the visitor and makes for a space ideal for serene meditation. It also has several side chapels that are worth dwelling over. In the second chapel to the left when you enter through the portal you will find the Black Madonna of Montserrat, Catalonia's patroness. In the main chapel stands the altar of one of Tarragona's two major patrons, Santa Tecla. The other patron is Sant Magí.

Sant Magí and Santa Tecla

In addition to the Phoenician Tanit and the Roman Jupiter, Juno, and Minerva, Tarragona has two Christian patron saints dearest to the city and her traditions, Sant Magí, or San Magín, and Santa Tecla. Their festival days occur August 15-19 and September 15-24, respectively.

Sant Magí, or San Magín, is something of a local superhero. He was born to a well-to-do family and when his parents died, he divided his wealth among the needy and left to live the life of a hermit in a cave in the mountains of Brufaganya near Pontils north of Tarragona near the banks of the river Gaià. He was taken by Roman soldiers who took him to Tarragona and imprisoned him. Miraculously, angels lifted him out of his jail cell and carried him back to the hills of Brufaganya. But again, Roman soldiers came to take him back to his prison cell in Tarragona. On the way, the Romans suffered from severe thirst and Sant Magí tapped the earth and a river sprang forth, bringing into being the river Gaià. The soldiers drank their fill, but still took him on to Tarragona where he was martyred in August of AD 306.

To this day, Sant Magí's cave near Pontils is a pilgrimage site, and he is said to have brought forth many freshwater sources, which are also highly venerated places in the region. Therefore, he is a saint of water. In Tarragona there is a sacred underwater cave, on the eastern end of Platja del Miracle, Miracle Beach, that holds his image in it year round. But in mid-August, Sant Magí's image is brought above water by scuba divers and processed about town for his feast day on August 19. He is then returned back to his underwater cave for the rest of the year. This calls to mind the Virgin of Cudillero in Asturias (chapter 9), who lives underwater all year but one day. So in Tarragona we have two subterranean masculine divinities, Jupiter and Sant Magí, who hold down the earth and water while Mary and Tanit concern themselves with heaven and the stars.

Tarragona's other patron saint, Santa Tecla (Thecla) of Iconium (today's Konya in eastern Turkey) lived in the first century AD. She was to be married to a local youth, Thamyris, but around the time of her engagement, St. Paul is said to have showed up in town and, upon meeting him, Tecla converted to Christianity and took a vow of virginity. Such flagrant disruption of social convention led to the town expelling Paul from Iconium and to Tecla's death sentence. Local authorities were unsuccessful in killing her. First they tried burning her to death, but a great storm arrived and soaked the fire. Next she was placed in a pit with wild animals, but after she baptized herself with water from a nearby ditch, the animals wouldn't touch a hair on her head. Finally, it is fabled that she fled, disguised in men's clothing, and met up with Paul in Myra. For the next seventy-two years or so she preached Christianity and lived in a cave in Seleucia. When she was approached by men who wanted to harm her, she was already an established miracle worker and, with her prayers, the stones around her opened up and she disappeared behind them as they closed again. There is actually little evidence of any of this, but the stories have been transformative tales to many, and so Santa Tecla's cult took in areas of the Mediterranean and Europe.

Santa Tecla became connected to Tarragona because some believe that she visited the city with St. Paul, though historians have no records indicating that Paul ever came here. In the third century, early Christians founded a convent in Santa Tecla's name next door to the city of Tarragona. In the twelfth century, with the newly conquered Tarragona under a Christian power and with the building of the cathedral, devotion to Santa Tecla rose in popularity among the locals.

Across the medieval town, which greatly overlaps with the more ancient Roman one, the stones from ancient times are underfoot, interwoven with modern buildings or lying dormant and as yet uncovered by modern hands.

Just north of the Roman amphitheater near the beach is the ancient Via Augusta, which runs parallel with the coast. It still goes by that name and is a heavily used road today, the one you will take out of Tarragona on your way to Barcelona.

Tarragona to Barcelona (56 miles/90 km):
Leave Tarragona on the Via Augusta connecting to N-340; follow signs to Barcelona.

BARCELONA—Catalonia

It is probable that Barcelona was founded by the Carthaginian Hamilcar Barca, Hannibal's father, who conquered the territory circa 230 BCE. When Romans defeated the Carthaginians and took over the western Mediterranean, they made Barcelona a Roman town and named it Barcino. Most of Roman Barcelona is in the same site as the medieval neighborhood, the Barri Gòtic.

Pinched between the Franks and the North African Muslim expansion, in AD 878 Barcelona managed to establish itself as an independent power, a house of the Counts of Barcelona under Guifré el Pelós (popularly called Wilfred the Hairy; see chapter 12 for more on him). In the twelfth century, Barcelona became the seat of rule over several formerly independent Catalán counties. Under Ramón de Berenguer III's rule (1082–1131), Catalonia with Barcelona at its heart became a major sea power. Through a marriage alliance in 1137 Catalonia was joined to the Kingdom of Aragón. When Jaime I took the throne (1213–1276), he expanded the two kingdoms further by adding Valencia and the Balearic Islands. Following centuries saw greater expansion and power, but, when in 1479 Ferdinand of Aragón took the throne and then married Isabel of Castile, Catalonia fell under Castile's control.

Barcelona is Spain's second-largest city and a place where a lot is happening on many levels, economically, gastronomically, culturally, politically, and socially. While it is filled with diverse sacred sites, here I illuminate what I think are the most stunning historical spiritual sites, places that have real spirit to them whether they are on the top ten list or not. But truly, the sacred in Barcelona is more outside, along the streets and promenades, gardens and waterways. The sacred here is a special dynamic between land and sea and humans and nature in this threshold place of coastline. To really soak in the spiritual in Barcelona, take some unscheduled time to just walk around the neighborhoods of the Barri Gòtic, La Ribera, Eixample, and El Raval. Notice the mythic and mystical beings that have been carved on the walls and rooftops of otherwise secular buildings. Some of these are medieval creations and others Renaissance and Art Nouveau. But all reflect an almost pagan veneration of the spirit and natural forces, which weaves the sacred into everyday buildings. We see this in Celtic castro sites where the gods and goddesses and the spirits of nature are carved in the household doors and windows.

The best orientation to the sacred in Barcelona begins by locating the main boulevard, Via Laietana. All but two of the sacred sites that I share

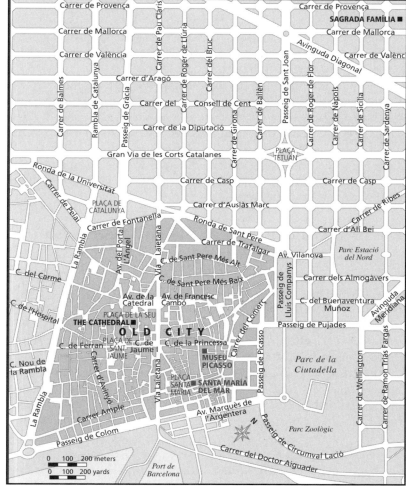

Map 3: Barcelona

here are centered around this marker. If you are on Laietana and facing the sea, the Barri Gòtic will be on the right and La Ribera on the left. The other two sites are farther afield. One is La Sagrada Familia Cathedral, farther north on the northern edge of Eixample. The other, Mount Tibidabo, is at the northwest edge of the city.

Laietana itself contains a mythic realm. Laietani is the Roman name of the people who originally lived here before the Phoenicians or Romans longed to possess this all-too-strategic spot on the Mediterranean. These Bronze Age inhabitants were farmers and left few remains, but this modern avenue was named after them. It runs perpendicular through the old city, connecting land and sea and crossing the heart of what was speculated to be the farmlands and oyster patches of the Laietani. The road itself is a modern monument to the ancestors.

The Barri Gòtic: Roman and Medieval Barcelona

Given that cathedrals are intended as places of political and religious power as well as sacred centers, for me they have to pass a few rigorous tests—my own experience joined with watching and talking to others who visit—to be considered truly spiritual places.

I have mixed feelings about Barcelona's fourteenth- and fifteenth-century Gothic cathedral, called **La Seu;** it feels dark and brooding at first. Others confirm this, but when we get to the cloisters the energy shifts into light and delight. I have further confirmed this by several return visits at different times and years. Passing through the grandeur and gold treasure, saintly relics and statues, at the cloisters a cloak is shed and authenticity of a spiritual nature shines in. Perhaps it is the living world there that keeps it clear and real; there is a wonderful garden in the heart of the cloisters, and at one corner there are feisty white geese, one with unusual blue eyes. Their pond-fountain is embellished with cast-bronze water-spouting frogs who, though made of metal, seem alive and might be mischievous companions to the geese.

Perhaps this animal and plant energy purifies an overly dense human space that has been blocked with crossed intentions. Whatever it is, in the cloisters the freeing Gothic arches, the plants, and the geese and their fountain form a sudden peaceful place apart from the rest. The cloister also reflects something of the people who really made things happen in Barcelona, the talented class of artisans and craftsmen. Surrounding the cloisters are saints' chapels that are dedicated to the medieval artists' guilds, which were a significant influence in the city.

Beyond the cloisters, the finest aspect of the cathedral is outside in my opinion. The cathedral offers a sturdy and beautiful public space on its plaza, where myriad performances and meetings between people take place every day and night. Also, if you look up on the western spire over the main facade you will see Mary standing up there shedding her grace over the city.

After taking in this realm of the late medieval, go outside and nearby, on Carrer Paradís, where you can experience remnants of a Roman temple. The Temple of Augustus still has four Corinthian columns standing. This spot marks the heart of Roman and of medieval Barcelona, and it is a sheer pleasure to wander in through its narrow stone labyrinthine streets. To explore the old Jewish section of the neighborhood walk toward the Plaça de Sant Jaume and take Carrer del Call at its northwest edge. Make a right onto Carrer de Sant Domènec del Call, and at the next crossing of streets— where you will really be in the heart of the narrow medieval passages— make a left onto Carrer de Marlet. Door number 5 on Carrer de Marlet is fairly unmarked, but this is the location of the Sinagoga Mayor, the main synagogue. The door will be open wide when it is open for visitors.

Around the time the cathedral was being built, Barcelona's vibrant and important Jewish community was beginning to feel squeezed. Their move-ments became more restricted, and as in other parts of Christian Spain, Jews began to live in designated neighborhoods, called *Calls* in Catalán. Before this, they could live wherever they pleased. Ironically, or perhaps because of the growing prejudices, the study of Kabbalah rose and Barcelona's Jewish community was one of the mystical heart centers for this tradition. (More on the Kabbalah in late-medieval Spain can be found in chapter 12.) In 1340 Hasday Crescas (also spelled Hasdai) was born in Barcelona. He was to become one of the most mystical, anti-rationalist thinkers of the fourteenth-century Jewish world, during a time when European intellectual trends were bent toward the rationalist treatises of Aristotle and Maimonides. Crescas wrote *Or Adonay* ("The Light of the Lord"), in which he argued that God's love and will superseded any intel-lectual orientation to the universe.

Barcelonan Shlomo ben Adret (1235–1310) was the Sinagoga Mayor's rabbi for over fifty years. He was a respected diplomat who put out many fires before there could be significant damage. He was also a Kabbalist and follower of Moshé ben Nahmán (see chapter 12). Reputed as a moderate who would bring disparate sides and views into harmony, he nevertheless was rigorous in his stance toward approaching the mystical. He published two pronouncements in 1305. One prohibited anyone younger than twenty-five years old to study either the Kabbalah or the natural sciences. The other was against people making allegorical interpretations of the Haggadah. The Haggadah is the ancient lore of the Jewish peoples, which complements the Talmud and contains materials outside of the Talmud. (Incidentally, the Barcelona Haggadah was produced between 1350 and 1360. It is now in London at the British Museum. It is among the most beautiful illuminated Hebrew manuscripts in the collection.)

As the rising power of Christian Spain grew more confident in itself, the experience of other religious groups was compromised. In Barcelona, the darkest day in this dynamic was August 5, 1391. August 5 is St. Dominic's feast day, and part of the festivities became overzealous and swelled into an uprising against the Jews of the city. After the uprising, the main street of the Call was shamefully renamed after St. Dominic. Other buildings were Christianized and dedicated to the same saint, and finally, the king took over the property of the neighborhood. After 1391 Barcelonan Jews left, dispersing to other cities and domains.

Surviving to this day in the city is one of the most important original and reconstructed Jewish synagogues in Spain. The **Sinagoga Mayor** is not only the city's oldest synagogue but perhaps Spain's oldest as well. Many of the synagogues across Iberia trace back to medieval roots. The synagogue space is two rooms. When you enter, you come into a room with multiple uses over the different centuries. It appears that the synagogue was built over a number of times. The Roman level is six feet lower than the modern level. There are stairs dating to this period leading into a room with Roman structures (it is uncertain what they were) overlaid with fifteenth-century dyeing vats. The vats belonged to a crypto-Jewish family, the d'Arguens. They were a Jewish family who converted to Christianity in order to avoid expulsion. But when they were either accused of or discovered to be still practicing Jewish rites in secret, they fled into France to avoid the Inquisition. Nasty business as it was, the Inquisition burned effigies of the family anyway to release its dark vileness upon the public.

Going into the second room, you will enter the true prayer space, the medieval synagogue. On its eastern wall is a plaque, reading "The Holy Jewish community of Barcelona has been praying in this direction for over a thousand years." The cast-iron menorah on the side wall was given to the synagogue in 1957 by Majorcan artist Ferrán Aguilo in honor of his own Jewish ancestors. There is indeed an interesting history of hidden Jews in Majorca, a legacy that holds to this day in a street in Las Palmas where converted Jews over the centuries forgot their Jewish background but unknowingly incorporated Jewish symbols and rites into their Catholic worship. If you want to read more about this fascinating history, see Kenneth Moore's *Those of the Street*.

The synagogue's foundation stones are deeper than street level. Its wall on Carrer Marlet is oriented toward Jerusalem, an orientation likely placed in Roman times. The evidence for this is that within the medieval synagogue are late-Roman remains of a wall also oriented toward Jerusalem.

Today in Barcelona there are three active and new synagogues, a Sephardic, an Orthodox, and a Reform synagogue. The ancient synagogue is also active but used only for special festivals. The people who work here are wonderfully informative and welcoming. I strongly recommend spending a relaxed amount of time exploring this little space.

On the northwest edge of the Barri Gòtic, in the **Plaça de Catalonia** stands a deeply symbolic cast-iron statue titled **Barcelona**. It is of a strong horse on whose back sits a sturdy and beautiful naked woman holding a ship over her head. On the other side of the horse, taking its reigns and leading it, is the Roman god Mercury, also known as Hermes, the messenger god. It is a perfect male-female balance, a ship of the feminine sea upheld by a horse of the masculine land, and above all, guided by Mercury's divine energy.

Iglesia de Santa María del Mar

The church is found on the other side of Via Laietana from the Barri Gòtic, going toward the sea.

This I find must be Barcelona's most beautiful church. The Iglesia de Santa María del Mar, Saint Mary of the Sea, is not only welcoming on the inside but also set in a welcoming neighborhood, one that is lived in and loved by its residents and that at the same time has the medieval feel of the Barri Gòtic. The approach to the church is fun, through a narrow weave of old streets, so that once you reach the church, rather than a grand plaza leading up to it, you simply stumble into its doorway to another world.

Built during the Gothic period, before the Gothic cathedral and after the nearby Gothic Santa María del Pi, Santa María del Mar seems to have the harmony and balance idealized by Gothic builders, one I don't feel in the other two Gothic structures. To be fair, Pi was beautiful until it was gutted during the Civil War.

When you enter Santa María del Mar, it is as if you suddenly breathe deeply and realize that you had been taking only shallow breaths before. Its proportions fit the body. Though grand, they are intimate and personal.

The rich, saturated stained glass fills the eyes and spirit with satiating color. And at the altar is the ultimate symbol, Mary holding her son, and before them stands a wood-carved boat.

Our Lady of the Sea, so close to the port, was not the first sacred temple built here. Before Santa María del Mar there stood a fourth-century church that had been built over the tomb of Santa Eulalia (see Mérida, in chapter 14 for more on her). Santa María del Mar was begun in 1329 and was built in fifty years, a rapid construction for a Gothic masterpiece. Santa Maria del Mar is the patroness of sailors, merchants, porters, and tradesmen; consequently, all these men gave their labor to build her church. This may explain why the church is unique—being built in a short span of time by the same set of people gives it a unity of style that shows off pure Gothic within one period in time.

A great part of this church's appeal is how uncluttered and serene the interior has remained. Stone, wood, colorful glass, and great airy space make the overall mood.

Two sites beyond these portside neighborhoods of La Ribera and Barri Gòtic that are critical to mention are Antoni Gaudí's cathedral, La Sagrada Familia, and the basilica on Mount Tibidabo.

La Sagrada Familia

La Sagrada Familia Cathedral, designed by Antoni Gaudí in the late 1800s, is a monument to modern faith that reflects a respect for tradition as well as a sense of playfulness and rejuvenation with the divine. Its naturalist foundation, a hallmark of Gaudí's vision of bringing nature's forms into the built environment, makes this grand structure reverent to all the spirit world—a world of nature as well as of humans and our divine conceptions. Everywhere you look is a plant or an animal, sometimes occurring in nature, sometimes mythic and fantastical, but always feeling real. There is also a lightness of being in this cathedral that escapes so many other sacred structures of its equivalent stature.

Antoni Gaudí is a famous Catalán architect, born in 1852 in Reus near Tarragona, whose avant-garde and naturalist works are all throughout Barcelona as well as in other parts of Spain. He dedicated over forty years of his life to this cathedral, designing and building it. From the beginning in 1883 until his death in 1926, he stayed with the project. The cathedral is still being built and each year shows progress. Funded by donations, the Sacred Family Cathedral is conceived as representing just that, the sacred family of Jesus. Gaudí designed twelve bell towers to represent twelve apostles. He also designed a central dome to represent Jesus, a tower to the Virgin Mary, and a tower for the four Evangelists. When you visit, you will see construction under way, which is another unique aspect of this holy site—it is still unfolding.

Tibidabo

Finally, no visit to sacred Barcelona is complete without an ascent to Mount Tibidabo in the forest and hills that make up the northwest edge of the city. In the Collserola hills, Mount Tibidabo is the highest point, and there stands the church Templo de Sagrat Cor, Temple of the Sacred Heart. It was built in a neo-Romanesque and neo-Gothic style in the early twentieth century. The monumental statue of Jesus there represents the story found in the Gospel of St. Matthew in which Jesus was tempted by the devil while fasting in the desert. The devil offered him all that he saw if he would worship the devil instead of God. Some Catalans will assure you that this view is far more enticing than that of the desert in which Jesus was fasting. Hence, this was more likely the place where he was tested. From this mountaintop you can see the plains of Barcelona and the Mediterranean sea.

To get there you will first take the blue streetcar, the Tramvia Blau, from Avinguda del Tibidabo to its end, and then get on the Tibidabo Funicular for the rest of the ascent.

St. George and the Dragon

St. George, known in Catalán as Sant Jordi and in Castilian as San Jorge, is the patron saint of both Aragón and Catalonia, a legacy that goes back to when the two kingdoms were united. St. George came to King Jaime I of Aragón's assistance in battle against Muslims, much like St. James was known to do across medieval polemical Spain.

But in Catalonia, Sant Jordi has more of a fairy-tale twist. It was he who rescued a Catalán princess in distress, who had been abducted by a menacing dragon. Sant Jordi slew the dragon, and as its spilled blood hit the ground, it transformed into a rose bush. Roses have become symbols of love, loyalty, and friendship.

Barcelona is the best place to see this metaphor played out annually. April 23 is Sant Jordi's Day, and it is also the day that two great writers died, both in 1616: Cervantes and Shakespeare. Every April 23, men traditionally give women roses and women give men books. The book tradition is actually a more recent add-on to the saint's day, dating to the clever commercial idea of a bookseller in 1923, but the rose tradition is said to go back centuries. In today's socially sophisticated Spain, the tradition is becoming one where men and women now exchange books, while men can and do still give women roses.

Barcelona to Empúries (64 miles/103 km):
Take N-11 to Girona; after Girona, take GI-623 E to L'Escala and follow signs to Empúries.

EMPÚRIES—Catalonia

Since the seventh century BCE people have lived along this shoreline. The first Iron Age natives were called Indiketes. They lived around the modern-day village of Sant Martí d'Empúries and they had trade contacts with Etruscans, Phoenicians, and Greeks. Greek traders in the sixth century settled nearby, establishing the earliest residence, called Emporion, meaning "market" in Greek. Caught between Carthaginian and Roman interests, ultimately Emporion was taken over by Romans, and in 195 BCE Romans set up a military settlement on the rise just above the Greek town. This settlement grew into a Roman town, which over the next two centuries became one town, fusing the Greek and the Roman settlements. Called Municipium Emporiae, the town thrived for another two and a half centuries. With the rise of the nearby Roman trade centers of Tarragona, Barcelona, and Girona, Emporiae, popularly called Empúries, or Ampurias today, declined and was abandoned. Many of the town's residents resettled at Sant Martí d'Empúries about one kilometer north on the coast. They continued to use Empúries as a burial ground, and some of the earliest Christian tombs in Spain are preserved here, dating from around the fourth to the seventh century AD.

Both Greek and Roman ancients really knew where to build—the view of the blue sea and the surrounding hills and forests is salve for the soul. Indeed, this appears to have been an important healing center in Greek times. At the entrance to the Greek city and the archaeological site, you will first encounter an Asklepieion, a second-century BCE sanctuary dedicated to Asclepius, the god of medicine. The sanctuary was a religious and healing center for the sick. Asclepius's statue, a replica of the original, which stands in the onsite museum, holds the sanctuary's center.

On your left upon entering is another sanctuary, this one from the first century BCE and dedicated to three gods, two originally Egyptian: Isis,

Serapis, and Zeus. Zeus is of course the supreme male deity, sky god, and father of the gods. Isis is the Great Mother brought in through the Egyptian pantheon and the goddess of fertility, childbirth, as well as the afterlife. And Serapis, who was a Hellenized version of Osiris, was Isis's consort. All three here were connected to health, healing, and medicine. The dedication to two Egyptian deities may come from the builder of the temple, a trader by the name of Noumas who hailed from the Egyptian coastal city of Alexandria.

At the far north end of the Greek town is the early Christian cemetery, where a narrow walled city of tombs is being uncovered as well as a paleo-Christian funerary church whose outline can be

A statue of the Greek god Asclepius, god of health and medicine, at the site of a religious and healing center dedicated to him at Empúries, Catalonia

discerned with its intact back wall. This stretch dates from the fourth to the seventh century AD.

Head up the rise to the Roman part of town. As you go, notice how the organic, nonlinear lines of the Greek town give way to more grandiose and straight lines of the Roman town.

Lining the north end of the forum are several temples, including one to the emperor Augustus (first century AD) and another, the Capitoline temple (first century BCE) dedicated to Jupiter, Juno, and Minerva, much like the one on the forum of Tarragona. In the same line of forum temples is another dedicated to Dionysus/Bacchus (first to second century AD), the god of wine. His bust can be seen in the onsite museum.

Only a quarter of the entire settlement has been excavated, giving you an idea of the scope of this ancient site. Moreover, the earlier Greek settlement is underneath the Greek town, which predates the Roman occupation.

CHAPTER TWELVE

·······················⚜·······················

$\mathcal{E}$scaladei to Girona

There are angels all around here. They're even in the fields.
— An American woman visiting Poblet

THIS MONASTERY AND WINE ROUTE explores medieval Catalonia, mostly Romanesque monasteries and churches along with the wine-making tradition that was revived along with the founding of these sacred houses.

Wine making in Catalonia may date as far back as the fourth century BCE but was interrupted with the Visigothic and the Muslim invasions of the early Middle Ages. It was through the monks of Cistercian and Carthusian monasteries, the earliest in Spain being here in Catalonia, that wine making returned. This is especially so in the famous Cistercian triangle of Poblet, Santes Creus, and Vallbono de les Monges, three monasteries that were directly instrumental in resurrecting wine making, adding to it vintner's knowledge from France.

Wine making may have been more ancient in other parts of Spain, perhaps dating to around 1000 BCE in Andalusia under Phoenician planters. The Muslim invasion did not curb wine making or drinking, which became an important daily aspect of Muslim Spain as well, despite wine drinking being forbidden in Islam. (The greatest example of this paradox comes from al-Mu'tamid of Seville's reign, a king who loved wine in all its manifestations and wrote prolific poetry about this and his other favorite indulgence, women.)

After the Muslim invasion in Catalonia the new conquerors did not remain long enough in the area to rebuild the wine-making tradition and were pushed south, where they did cultivate this old craft. But here in Catalonia it was up to the monks, many of whom arrived from France to help resettle the area. This is what makes the history of wine unique to this part of Spain.

The present route also passes through three important sacred Jewish centers—Barcelona, Girona, and Besalú—which together with Córdoba and Toledo are among the most important Jewish sites in Spain. In honor of these places, I also suggest a detour to a noted winemaker of excellent kosher wines that are exported to the United States, Israel, Mexico, and other parts of Europe.

Monasteries in Spain are famous for their history and their divinely inspired life as much for the patient, handcrafted culinary delights that they produce. In Spain several convents are known for famous cakes and biscuits, jams and sweet liqueurs, and several monasteries are known for their cheeses, honeys, and wines.

Wine holds a strong symbolic and metaphorical place in many of Spain's religions and spiritual outlooks. For Catholics, it is critical in the Mass. It becomes the blood of Christ through transubstantiation. Moreover, turning water into wine at the feast of Cana is the first known miracle performed by Jesus. For Jews, wine is a sanctified substance used in religious ceremonies. For Muslims, who are prohibited from drinking wine, it is nevertheless a metaphor for God's love among Muslim mystics, Sufis, including those of Spain.

Throughout Spain many monasteries have declined, but a good number remain active, with a small community of brothers or sisters. A few monasteries are open to the public at specific times of day. Some offer monastic hospitality; some, including those that may not be open to the public, still sell their artisanal culinary delights, including wines and liqueurs.

Monasteries were once central to medieval life, a place where produce was grown, where drink was made, and where the wealthy stored their treasures for safekeeping much like banks of today. Hardly at the fringe of community, despite their removed monastic life, monasteries were crucial in the activities of the society. Wine was among the central products monasteries made, both for themselves and for the masses (in both senses of the term). I like to think about someone long ago taking their donkey loaded with wineskins or jugs to Poblet, to purchase some of the strong and sacred drink from the brothers.

There are some ten different wine regions in this route and all of them have some association with a sacred story or a monastery. They are, from north to south in Catalonia: Ampurdán-Costa Brava, Pla de Bages, Alella, Penedès, Costers del Segre, Conca de Barberá, Tarragona, Montsant, Priorato, and Terra Alta.

Main Route (312 miles/ 502 km):
Escaladei—Santa Maria de Poblet—Montblanc—Vallbona de les Monges—Santes Creus—Villafranca de Penedès—Montserrat—San Fruitós de Bages—Ripoll—San Joan de les Abadesses—Besalú—Beuda—Vilabertran—Peralada—Monestir de Sant Pere de Rodes—Banyoles—Girona

ESCALADEI—Catalonia

This village is a wine center; the monastery is half a mile away and the vineyards surround both the monastery and the village. *Scala Dei* means "God's stairway." When the Carthusian monks came to settle the area, they met a shepherd who told them of a vision he had just seen: angels ascending a stairway into the clouds at the summit of nearby Montsant. The Carthusians built their monastery on the site of this sacred vision.

The location was perfect, with a good source of water and a rich array of Mediterranean medicinal and aromatic herbs throughout the hillsides. The soil also, centuries would bear out, was a unique one and perfect for wine. The *terroir* here is mainly arid schistose slate soil and an array of wonderful herbs. Nearby olive and hazelnut trees grow and not much else. Traditional grape varieties grown here are a variety of black Garnacha grape and the Cariñena grape. These wines tend to be strong, with a higher-than-normal alcohol content.

Locals also were engaged in wine making in the Middle Ages and were to give 10 percent of the grape harvest to the monastery, because the monks had originally planted the vines in the area. To guarantee proper harvest times, Scala Dei's patron saint became San Bruno, whose feast day perfectly falls in the first week of October and marks the beginning of grape-harvest season. As you explore you will notice the apropos village emblem: an *S* and a *D* to the left and right of a ladder at whose crest rests a cross.

Cartoixa de Scala Dei

This was the first Carthusian monastery founded in Spain. Like Poblet, Santes Creus, and Vallbona de les Monges, this monastery was founded in the twelfth century and resumed wine making that had been lost since the Visigothic and Muslim invasions of the area. Since then, the vine has been cultivated, first for Mass and for the monks' consumption and second for distribution and export, since Tarragona-region wine was known as a hearty and pleasurable wine throughout the Catholic world.

The monastery was abandoned in the nineteenth century and is now in ruins, but the families that own Cellers de Scala Dei, with winemaker Asunción Peyra at the heart of this effort, have strived to renovate and open the monastery to the public. She and the Cellers are your source for both wine and monastery in Scala Dei.

Cellers de Scala Dei

Established in 1973 by a cooperative of local families who are committed to maintaining their region's heritage, this winery revived and replanted the traditional monastic fields. Nearby you can visit the monastery ruins, an important part of the winery's vision in producing wine here. In addition to the traditional Garnacha grape, Cellers de Scala Dei has also planted an import, Cabernet Sauvignon. When blended together, these two varieties offer up one of the winery's most celebrated wines, Negre Scala Dei (Priorato wines are known for their dark color, deepest red that looks almost black, and hence this name). Another notable wine worth trying here is the most traditional one, honoring the monks who went before, the Cartoixa de Scala Dei Reserva. Visitors feel welcome at this winery: Rambla de la Cartoixa, s/n, 43379 Scala Dei, ☎ 977-82-70-27.

Kosher wine detour: Before proceeding northeast to Poblet, if you wish to seek out excellent kosher Montsant wines, visit the town of Capçanes and the winery by the same name. Though kosher wine is just a small fraction of the wine they produce, it is among its highly demanded wines, given its excellent quality. Capçanes is south of Scala Dei and the other wine towns of Gratallops and Falset (the latter being the hub of Montsant wineries). You may want to stop in these places, too. Falset's tourist office offers good guidance on local wineries: Carrer de Sant Marcel, 2; ☎ 977-83-10-23; 💻 www.priorat.org.

Escaladei to Santa Maria de Poblet (31 miles/50 km):
Take TV-7021 NE; go N onto C-242; take a right onto T-701; take T-700 N to Poblet.

SANTA MARIA DE POBLET—Catalonia

Once the forest around Poblet was the monastery's and today it is a protected natural park. But trees will forever be a part of this large Cistercian monastery, whose name means "white poplar grove," derived from the Latin *populetum*.

Poblet was begun in the twelfth century and was added to, altered, and renovated through to the eighteenth century. Like other monasteries of this epoch, Poblet was a part of the campaign to resettle territories in Spain that had been taken from Muslim control so as to secure the empty lands with enough settlements to discourage Muslim retaliation in taking back the lands. The twelfth century was also the period when several military church orders formed, such as the Knights Templar, the Order of Santiago, the Order of Calatrava, and the Hospitallers. Their main purpose was to defend the frontier and to protect pilgrims on their way to Santiago de Compostela (as well as Montserrat).

The monastery stands in its own little enclave of Poblet, a society in and of itself. It is surrounded by rolling green hills all of vineyards, one-lane two-way roads, and tiny hamlets. A three-quarter-hour hike from Esplugo de Francoli, just northeast of Poblet, is a tranquil manner in which to arrive at the monastery and is also a classic local pilgrimage.

In its heyday, Poblet was an important monastery for the Aragonese and Catalán nobles, and many are buried here, including Jaime I, who you will find in the church in a tomb embedded into an arched underpass near the apse. In his peaceful slumber, which you see in a beatific smile, he holds his sword hilt with his left hand and a vigilant lion lies beneath his resting feet. Other nobles lay in these curious in-the-air tombs, the purpose of which is to be perpetually in the path of prayers and benedictions so as to assure blessings in the afterlife. This was a common practice in many churches for anyone who could afford to acquire such an auspicious burial spot.

Poblet's Cistercian church possesses exquisite acoustics. The physical harmony that brings this about is equally delightful to experience. Throughout the monastery the stones glow with an ethereal pink-yellow hue. It is a truly magical place to be.

In 1835 across Spain monasteries were disbanded and Poblet emptied and was pillaged. The contents of the royal tombs were taken to Tarragona's cathedral for safekeeping but were restored to their original resting place in 1946 shortly after the Cistercian abbot general brought four monks from Italy to revivify the monastery. These refounding monks are

The cloister fountain in Santa Maria de Poblet's monastery, Catalonia

credited with making Poblet a vibrant spiritual center today. Indeed, walking among the green rolling hills, forest, and harmonious cloisters of Poblet—not to mention tasting the elegant and rare Pinot Noir produced by the brothers—is downright heavenly. The wines here are from the Conca de Barberà wine region.

Vins de Poblet Cellars

Within the monastery grounds you will see vineyards that are a part of the Cistercian wine-making revival, begun in 1989. The vines are a single grape variety, Pinot Noir, a difficult wine to produce but one that does well in this temperate climate with its cooling summers. The choice was also historical as the first Burgundian Cistercians grew this grape in the eleventh century, and Poblet wanted to maintain its spiritual heritage, also stemming back to the Burgundians.

The wine shop and cellars are immediately to your right when you enter the monastery through its outer gate. The Vins de Poblet cellars is housed in a nineteenth-century farm building.

Poblet to Montblanc (7 miles/11 km):
Take T-700 NE; take N-240 E and follow signs to Montblanc.

MONTBLANC—Catalonia

Montblanc was first inhabited by indigenous Iberians, but the current settlement's origins date to the twelfth century. Legend tells of a time in the Middle Ages when Montblanc was terrorized by a dragon that demanded a person a day. Lots were drawn and no one was excluded, not even the king's family. The day his daughter's lot came up, she went before the dragon as a sacrifice. But right at the moment she was to be consumed by the beast, St. George miraculously appeared on horseback and defeated the creature. On the spot where he spilled the dragon's blood, a rose bush emerged and bloomed. It is for this reason that each year on St. George's Day (St. George is Catalonia's patron saint) men throughout Spain give the women they love roses (more on this custom under Barcelona in chapter 11).

One of Montblanc's quirkiest histories is the story of Anselm Turmeda, a Franciscan monk who hailed from here. In the middle of his holy career he converted to Islam. Born in the fourteenth century, Turmeda studied theology in Paris and Bologna. In 1387 he went to Tunis, where he renounced Christianity and became a Muslim, changing his name to Abd Allah. He remained in Tunis and died in 1423. Before he died he wrote, in Arabic, his treatise on refuting Christian dogma. Today you will find him among the Sufi saints who are venerated in North Africa.

Iglesia de Santa María la Mayor

This fourteenth-century church replaces the earlier twelfth-century Romanesque church of Santa María. It stands on the highest point of the town.

Iglesia de Sant Fracesc

Only the church of the fourteenth-century Franciscan monastery survives, just outside the town's walls. After its deterioration and abandonment, the church became a wine warehouse in the nineteenth century. In the twentieth century, the church was restored as a church. It is nevertheless worth sampling Montblanc wines in honor of this building's prior sanctified quarry in the surrounding bodegas.

Montblanc's weekly markets take place on Tuesday and Friday. As the capital of the Conca de Barberà wine region, this is a good base for exploring the wine.

Montblanc to Vallbona de les Monges (14 miles/23 km):
Follow signs to C-14 N and continue until signs for Rocallaura and Vallbona; turn left and continue to Vallbona de les Monges.

VALLBONA DE LES MONGES

Founded in 1153 and incorporated into the Cistercian order in 1176, Vallbona de les Monges is a little less visited than the other two Cistercian monasteries of this famous triangle, Poblet and Santes Creus, largely because it is a little farther north and harder to reach without a car. It is unique in this trilogy in that it is a female monastery, run by Cistercian nuns. It is also unique in that it has remained an active convent without interruption over its eight hundred years of occupation. This bodes well for the crafts of the place (music, pottery, and paintings), including wine making.

Vallbona de les Monges received nuns from many of Catalonia's illustrious medieval families and its halls are filled with their legacy. While Jaime I is buried at Poblet, his wife and daughter, Doña Violante and Doña Sancha are buried here.

There are guest quarters for visitors who wish to stay and absorb the sacred rhythms over more than a day's time. The Virgin of the Cloister in the modern chapel is very likely the first image venerated at Vallbona.

Wines of Vallbona de les Monges: A local Conca de Barberà winery in Vallbona de les Monges is L'Olivera: La Plana, s/n, 25268 Vallbona de les Monges, ☎ 973-33-02-76.

Vallbona to Santes Creus (27 miles/43 km):
Return to C-14 and go briefly N to T-233; take a right and cross C-241 to TP-2311; take TP-2311 to C-37 and turn left; at El Pont d'Armentera turn right onto TP-2002 and continue to Monestir Santes Creus.

SANTES CREUS—Catalonia

A Cistercian monastery and a pretty village near Poblet and Vallbona de les Monges, Santes Creus is no longer inhabited by monks and so the entire ground is open to visitors. Like Poblet, this monastery was founded in 1150 and is considered the closest to the Benedictine ideal for monastic architecture. Smaller than Poblet, it is also more delicate in its cloisters and spaces, adding a sweetness that exudes from the stone walls. Several legends are attached to this monastery as is a rich wine-making tradition.

Santes Creus to Villafranca de Penedès (24 miles/38 km):
Take TP-2002 S; enter AP-2/E-90 E; take AP-7/E-15 toward Villafranca de Penedès.

VILLAFRANCA DE PENEDÈS—Catalonia

This is in the heart of Penedès wine country and has a Gothic church on the Plaça de Jaume I dedicated to none other than Mary, the Basílica de Santa María. Across the street from the basilica are two joined museums dedicated to the area's archaeology, history, and wine making. Around Poblet you likely saw some vineyards with the Torres name. Torres is Villafranca's main wine-making family and its winery can be visited just outside of Villafranca, a few kilometers northwest near Pacs del Penedès (🖥 www.torres.es).

From the Penedès vineyards you can see the serrated toothy mountain range of Montserrat. Penedès has been a wine region since at least the fourth century BCE, making it one of the most ancient wine areas in the western Mediterranean.

Villafranca de Penedès to Montserrat (30 miles/48 km):
Take AP-7/E-15 NE; take exit 25 N onto A-2; take exit 575 to Montserrat.

MONTSERRAT—Catalonia

As you approach this sacred site from the surrounding flat terrain, otherworldly vertical peaks appear, which have been shaped by time, wind, and rain into whimsical and mythic shapes effecting a shift of consciousness into the dreamtime.

The mountain of Montserrat has been sacred for a long time; in Roman times there stood on the same mountain an ancient temple to Venus. It is the perfect continuity to explain the fervor and passion that people have for the sacred feminine venerated here today. *La Moreneta,* the Virgin Mary of Montserrat, is a wood-carved polychrome Mary with a lovely black-skinned complexion, as is the Baby Jesus who sits upon her lap as if on a throne.

In AD 880 shepherds discovered La Moreneta when a light came down from heaven toward them and marked the spot. Later when holy men could not remove the statue from the spot, they realized its will was to remain on this sacred mountain. Barcelona's count at the time, Wilfred the Hairy, commissioned a chapel to be built around the statue. Later the

Benedictine monks of Ripoll acquired the site in 976 (curiously, the same year that Al-Mansur took power in Córdoba) and built the monastery. The Black Madonna of Montserrat took up residence in the basilica on the mountain, and the original cave and chapel where she was first seen and venerated is the Santa Cova, which remains an important pilgrimage within the pilgrimage to Montserrat.

Montserrat has unceasingly been the spiritual heart of Catalonia since La Moreneta's arrival. After Santiago de Compostela, Montserrat was the second most important pilgrimage site in Spain. Ignacio Loyola came here to pray before the Virgin of Montserrat before he went off to found the Jesuit order in 1522.

Montserrat Basilica's western portal meshes the natural and the built sacred worlds, Catalonia

Dedication to the Virgin did not wane as the world grew more secular. The site today receives fervent pilgrims from all across Europe, Asia, Africa, and the Americas. The sense of this being a power spot is clear when you arrive. For instance, once I saw a visiting group from Poland enact a ritual in the marble circle inlay in the atrium at Montserrat (designed by Father Benet Martinez around 1952). Each person took turns standing in the circle's center with their arms held out at shoulder level. "I *feel* something," one of them uttered. When I asked what they were doing, the group leader said, "This is a very powerful spot. Standing there one can receive blessings." Curiously, that marble inlay depicts sea animals surrounded by Latin writing referring to the rite of baptism and to Mary. For ancients, in the pre-Christian worldview, water was the element of the sacred feminine. This offers a curious and apt juxtaposition for the current devotion as well. When I returned to the atrium, about an hour and a half later, the Poles were gone but a group of people from England were copying the energy ritual, standing in the circle's center. One elderly man with fishing cap, shorts, and camera hanging about his neck suddenly said to his wife, "Yes. I think I feel something."

You can attend Mass any day of the week and at several times a day, as this is an active monastery. Mass is in the basilica, and there is a separate entrance and line for waiting to go up behind the high altar to have a personal audience with La Moreneta, who you can touch through a small opening in the protective glass. The line is often long, but fascinating, for in it you will see the diversity and international draw of this sacred site. There is a good chance you will hear the Escalonía boys choir while there as they perform almost every day in the basilica.

Outside, the sacredness extends to the inspiration of this site, the mountains. All around Montserrat below the monastery and basilica are pilgrimage paths to shrines, caves, and hermitages dedicated to the Virgin. The most important one marks the original place where La Moreneta was found and where the first chapel was built, the Santa Cova.

Surrounding the base of the mountain is a circumambulating path punctuated every fifteen to twenty feet with little shrines and plaques honoring the Virgins of different Catalán regions, cities, towns, and villages, as if they are attendants to the Great Mother above them in the basilica, receiving blessings for their respective places and people by being placed in this power spot. Indeed, there are so many shrines in so many directions that I would advise either a long stay to explore them all or to trust your instinct and explore one direction that calls to you without feeling rushed.

Wine and Elixirs: Aromas de Montserrat

Though Montserrat is not a wine-producing area, the monks at Montserrat distill a liquor known as Aromas de Montserrat that is infused with the mountain's herbs. This is yet another way to take in the spirit of this place.

From the Penedès wine region, the serrated Montserrat stands as a dramatic backdrop to this illustrious wine region's vineyards. This is one of the most famous wine areas of Spain and many of the Catalán wines imported to the United Sates come from here. The Via Augusta passed through here, as did the Romans and their love for wine. Bacchus was celebrated here, as throughout Greek and Roman Catalonia, and in 1396 the ambassador Thibaut exclaimed "In Catalonia I have drunk the best wines of Spain." By then wine had made a good comeback after the fields lay fallow under prior Islamic rule. Ironically, earlier and further south, Muslim rulers (and citizens) in Spain had been enjoying drinking copious quantities of good wine as well as writing poetry and songs about the drink and its effects. Nowhere did this exceed the dedication of al-Mu'tamid's Seville of the eleventh century.

BLACK MADONNAS

Enigmatic to most because people ponder the white skin of the inhabitants who worship her, Black Madonnas are found in many places—in Montserrat, Guadalupe, Chartres in France, and Tindari, Sicily—from where do they come? There are many theories. All of the more-plausible and intriguing ones reach back to an ancestral, preceding influence. Some think that the Black Madonna stems from none other than the cult of Isis and Horus, also a story of divine feminine and resurrection, because statues of Isis with her infant son Horus show a striking resemblance to Mary with the Baby Jesus.

Writer Jason Webster posits that given the long contact with Muslims, the color black might come from Islamic symbolism, which for Muslims represents wisdom. Reinforcing this influence is the fact, mentioned in chapter 6, that Mary is the most revered woman in Islam and the only one mentioned by name in the Qur'an, which dedicates a whole *sura*, chapter, to her and is named after her.

Yet a third theory, one reaching into more ancient earth, literally, views the Black Madonna as a manifestation of the Mother Goddess, whose element is deep, rich, dark, fertile earth. Moreover, going into the earth, underground, is like dying and being reborn. Black for the ancient world was the color of fertility and resurrection. While the Lady of Montserrat is a twelfth-century wood-carved polychrome Romanesque work, the ideas that go into her creation are much older. Any one of these theories is plausible, or perhaps it is an amalgam of all these ancient ideas that creates the profundity of the cult, considering that the theories are complementary to one another.

Montserrat to Sant Fruitós de Bages (12 miles/19 km):
Take C-55 N toward Manresa; follow signs to Sant Fruitós de Bages.

SANT FRUITÓS DE BAGES—Catalonia

This region, called Bages, with its municipal capital at Manresa, takes its name from none other than the Roman god of wine, Bacchus (Bages in Catalán), who has given his name to this wine-making region and to several towns in the area, such as Castellnou de Bages, Sant Fruitós de Bages, and Sant Mateo de Bages.

Monasterio de Sant Benet de Bages

A manuscript in the Benedictine monastery of Sant Benet de Bages here indicates that there was once a Roman town in this area, called Bacassis. This speaks well of the blessings conferred by the wine god to this ancient wine land.

Sant Benet de Bages was founded around AD 950. It has a beautiful Romanesque cloister with the familiar style of capital carved characters in human, animal, and plant forms. There are some sixty-four of these capitals, making for a large concentration of surviving carvings in one place. Most are ornamental with images of plants, next are animals, and, finally, three depict scenes from Jesus' life.

Wines of the Pla de Bages

How far back wine making goes here is hard to say, but if it is anything like the neighboring Penedès region, it could date to as early as the fourth century BCE. It certainly dates to the founding of the Sant Benet de Bages monastery in the tenth century.

Today the wine varieties and wine-making procedures are very modern as is the denomination, Denominación de Origin Pla de Bages, officially recognized as a unique area in the mid-1990s. A local grape variety, Picapoll, produces a crisp, bright, and fruity white wine. Some of the best Bacchian explorations can be done in Manresa, Artés, and Sant Fruitós de Bages. A good Web site for more information is: 💻 www.dopladebages.com.

Sant Fruitós de Bages to Ripoll (49 miles/79 km):
Take C-55 to C-25 NE toward Vic; in Vic take C-17 N to Ripoll.

RIPOLL—Catalonia

Ripoll the town gets berated as not being an enticing destination, but I wholeheartedly disagree with these disparaging comments. It is a vital, modern town with an active, industrious heart. It is clean and easy to navigate and the residents are cheerful and helpful. Ripoll's monastery stands at the heart of things.

Monestir de Santa María de Ripoll

Originally a Benedictine monastery founded in AD 589 by the Visigothic king Recaredo, the monastery was rebuilt by Comte Guifré el Pelos in 879 after it was damaged by the Moors. Guifré el Pelos is buried here.

Ripoll became Catalonia's spiritual center in the Middle Ages. In 1885 the monastery was damaged by a fire and thereafter restored so that much of it takes on a late-nineteenth-century feel. But its portal, now protected by an exterior wall and doorway, dates to the early twelfth century. It is referred to as a stone Bible: At its center sits God as Creator and surrounding him are day-to-day scenes or the agrarian cycles of the year carved into the pillars. The cloisters also date to the Middle Ages, spanning building from the twelfth to the sixteenth century (as well as some neo-Gothic nineteenth-century restoration), and are on two levels. They are a delight to wander in, both for the two levels of arched columns and for contemplating the columns themselves—each has a unique capital carving of a persona, an animal, or a plant. The Renaissance-period church feels very Arthurian and Visigothic, as if the interior was inspired by both Celtic and Visigothic aesthetics. Its stones are charcoal gray with natural flecks of gold-color deposits, making for a wondrous space as the sunlight changes throughout the day.

Comte Guifré el Pelos or Count Wilfred the Hairy

A main character in this region is the Comte Guifré el Pelos, best known as the father of Catalonia. He earned this title because in the ninth century he led the building and rebuilding campaign of many sacred sites and the repopulation of many settlements around the area of Vic after the early success of pushing out the Muslim invaders from Catalonia. We know him in English as Wilfred the Hairy, count of Barcelona. Barcelona was a county more attached to France but was becoming largely independent by the time of Guifré el Pelos. (Word has it he was so hairy that even the bottoms of his feet had hair. That might be more foot hair than even a hobbit's! Given that the Catalán interior of mountains, hills, and castles could get quite frigid in winter, this was a useful trait. One could say that Guifré el Pelos rarely got cold feet about anything.)

Guifré el Pelos is buried at Ripoll, one of several monasteries he founded. He died in a battle at Llerida in 897 against the Banu Qasi, a Muslim dynasty that held the area. Curiously, an heir of the Banu Qasi survives to this day and lives in Barcelona.

The Banu Qasi came from an ancient Iberian tribe who were strong men in northeastern Spain and were good at negotiating with new invaders to keep their power. They struck a deal with the Romans, then Visigoths, then Muslims and flowed with the cultural tide of change so as to keep their control and titles. Their name alone holds this history: Once the Iberian-Roman Cassius, when they converted and Arabized they took on the title Banu Qasi, tribe or heirs of Cassius.

Ripoll to Sant Joan de les Abadesses (7 miles/11 km):
Take C-26 NE.

SANT JOAN DE LES ABADESSES—Catalonia

A twelfth-century Romanesque convent and neighbor to Ripoll, this monastery gives a yin-yang balance to the region. It is also set in one of the most gregarious towns anywhere, giving one a sense of optimism to the human condition. Finally, the convent museum houses one of the oddest Virgin Mary statues I have ever seen, a wood-carved fourteenth-century Gothic polychrome statue of a standing Mary with a little glass window covering a niche in her belly that reveals the unborn Baby Jesus inside.

This Benedictine convent was established earlier than the current building, in the ninth century by Count Guifré el Pelos. The first abbess of Sant Joan was Emma de Barcelona, from 898–942 AD. She has a commemorative stone placed in a wall to the side of the nave. She is buried somewhere in the church but no one knows where and so this stone is there to honor the fact.

A solid Romanesque stone church with a cooling somber interior, it has a wonderful alabaster altarpiece to the right of the central nave depicting scenes from the life of Mary. Nearby stands a baptismal font with an interior of blue and green mosaic-tile inlay that looks more like a seascape designed by Gaudí but that works here. Near the entrance a Romanesque capital carving shows a man with one head and two bodies, pulling at his beard in two directions. Perhaps Romanesque humor showing someone being of two minds about something?

The community of nuns existed here until the twelfth century. In the sixteenth century, the convent grounds were turned into a school and by the nineteenth century the church and cloister became the town's parish church. The cloister is especially conducive to meditative space, perhaps all the more so for the presence of everyday life pouring in at the edges, in the form of someone hanging laundry from a second-floor balcony nearby, the bubbly sound of laughing children in the neighboring park, the chat-ter of elders holding down benches on tree-lined streets, or the wafting smell of *cocas* from a nearby bakery (*cocas* are a wonderful Catalán confec-tion that achieves perfection in this town: fresh buttery pastry wrapped around fresh cream or chocolate or fruit fillings and finished with pow-dered sugar).

Sant Joan de les Abadesses to Besalú (29 miles/47 km):
Take C-26 E; follow signs to connect to A-26 near la Canya; take A-26 to Besalú.

BESALÚ—Catalonia

Besalú was its own independent county in the eleventh and twelfth cen-turies until being absorbed into the medieval county of Barcelona. Its Roman bridge was refortified in the Middle Ages and remains the town's sig-nature feature, though it is the Jewish heritage that is currently being recon-structed within, along with some lovely examples of Catalán Romanesque churches, that reveal the town's spirit. Jewish life in Besalú flourished until the late fourteenth and early fifteenth centuries. In 1415, the Jewish quarter, which had in decades before been segregated from the rest of the town, was sealed in with only one gate left open for passage. Jews were persecuted and left so that by 1425 Besalú had no Jewish residents remaining.

Jewish Besalú

Jewish Besalú right now is exciting because the town has dedicated its resources to excavating and preserving its Jewish history. In the town's heart near the river are the twelfth-century *mikvah* (the ritual purification bath), the synagogue, and walls and streets designating the old Jewish quarter. The quarter was not segregated nor sealed off until the late fourteenth century, when the circumstances of Jews in Christian Iberia worsened. Some Jews left and went to Muslim Granada; others held on hoping the circumstances of their home would shift back in more positive directions.

Romanesque Besalú

In the heart of town is the surviving church of the once-Benedictine monastery of Sant Pere. Dating to AD 977, Sant Pere is still the heart of the community. The square on which the church stands was once incorporated into the Benedictine monastery, the remains of which were destroyed in the eighteenth and nineteenth centuries. Sant Pere is testimony to Catalán Romanesque styles as beautiful solid stone with little to no adornment—the stone is enough to convey a powerful sacred space.

Nut Liquor—Ratafia

Though wine is not cultivated here, a land surrounded by hay and sunflower fields, there is a locally made and very sweet but potent liqueur called Ratafia. Its ingredients seem to be inspired by mood and seasonal availability, namely, nuts (chestnuts dominate), herbs, spices, and coffee. It has its own sacred method of being made, wherein the best Ratafia is one made using the powers of the moon and the sun to enhance it. Two weeks' worth of outdoor sun- and moon-ray exposure should do the trick. This recalls other agrarian lore in Spain, wherein farmers and herders, hunters and gatherers, would collect certain plants or plant others during a specific seasonal full moon.

Besalú to Beuda (3 miles/5 km):
Leave Besalú N on a small local road that runs perpendicular to C-26; look for signs for all three chapel sites listed below. There are many signs to them on the roadside.

BEUDA—Catalonia

The area around the town of Beuda possesses a trilogy of chapels, one of which was powerful enough to pardon one's sins upon arrival, as was a journey to the Holy Land. The town is much smaller and more obscure than Jerusalem but is still a sacred oasis for locals who could not make the greater journey to the eastern Mediterranean. The threesome of chapels are interconnected by footpaths in the hills and forests of Beuda, taking the pilgrim through tame wilds, one culminating in a dedicated climb to the top of Mare de Déu del Mont.

Santo Sepulcro de Palera

Coming here is considered as good as going to Jerusalem, earning a person the same indulgences as if they made it to the Holy Sepulcher there. This little Romanesque church dates to AD 1085 and is in the middle of an intimate oak, cypress, and olive forest. On approach up the first set of stairs to the site is a tree trunk that naturally takes the shape of the cross or of Jesus as the Tree of Life. Someone has set a ring of thorns made of barbed wire over the topmost appendage pointing skyward. I visited the church with a friend who by all accounts is quite rational and secular but who claimed that she felt a serene sacred power here.

Sant Feliu de Beuda

Founded in AD 1004, Sant Feliu stands at the foot of the path that takes you the 2.5 kilometers up to Mare de Déu del Mont. Like Santo Sepulcro it is a simple but elegant little stone Romanesque chapel. The closer you get to this chapel, the more vibrant and alive the stone becomes, taking on an interesting multidimensionality. The capital carving at its entry has a fine bull's head surrounded by Romanesque weaving designs, which also look like La Tène Celtic-style designs, right down to the triskelion reflecting a trinity beneath the bull's head. The huge wooden door has a great iron-work handle in the shape of a dragon's head, perhaps a last-ditch effort to remind entering worshipers to tame their ego, that dragon within, or to leave their junk outside.

Sanctuari de la Mare de Déu del Mont

The sanctuary is an important Catalán pilgrimage site both for its sacred association with Mary as well as for its being a place where in 1884 the venerated Catalán poet Jacint Verdaguer (1845–1902) stayed, meditated, and wrote parts of his poem *Canígo*. A poet, farmer, and teacher, he was ordained as a priest in 1870; in 1886 at the monastery at Ripoll he was named Poet of Catalonia. The sanctuary was born out of the tenth-century Benedictine monastery, Sant Llorenç de Sous. The Romanesque church dates to the fourteenth century.

Beuda to Vilabertran
(21 miles/34 km):
Backtrack S toward Besalú and take A-26 E; take N-260 to Figueres; Vilabertran is 1 km NE of Figueres.

VILABERTRAN—Catalonia

This Augustinian church was founded in the eleventh century. Its cloister was added in the twelfth and thirteenth centuries. True to Catalán style, it is solid, beautifully built and kept natural, if austere, and unadorned so that the stone itself shines through.

Vilabertran to Peralada (3 miles/5 km):
Take C-252 N.

PERALADA—Catalonia

The now defunct medieval Carmelite monastery is active in at least one remaining way: its cool, expansive spaces are being used as the aging cellars for a local winemaker, Bodegas y Cavas Castello de Perelada, based in the nearby castle, the Castillo de Peralada (the different spellings reflect actual local usage). If a monastery, a castle, and wine were not a heady enough mix, now the same place offers a wine spa for those wishing to imbibe well-being from spa treatments that apply wine-making extracts as well as good wine. Additionally, the castle holds a vast library of over eighty thousand books, including a good number of wine-relevant manuscripts (Bodegas y Cavas Castello de Perelada, Playa del Carmen, 1, 17491 Peralada, Girona, ☎ 932-23-30-22, perelada@ castilloperelada.com).

Peralada to Monestir de Sant Pere de Rodes (8 miles/13 km):
Leave Peralada S and connect to N-260 NE; exit toward Marzá and follow local road NE to Monestir de Sant Pere de Rodes.

MONESTIR DE SANT PERE DE RODES— Catalonia

Sources are as yet uncertain of this monastery's origins (perhaps the ninth century), but the earliest architectural influences seem to stem from the tenth to the twelfth century. The setting and ruins are ghostly and beautiful. Here in the rocky crags you will find the Iglesia de Santa Helena and the Verdera Castle as well as the familiar and charming Romanesque carved capitals with their mythic and everyday scenes and characters.

This area is rife with ancient and sacred temples. The monastery is very likely over a Roman temple to Venus Pirenaica. The surroundings are rich with scattered Neolithic dolmens.

The site's dedication to St. Peter, Sant Pere, goes back to the story of Pope Boniface IV's effort to hide and preserve certain relics from attack in Rome. He had them sent to the Sierra de Rodes for safekeeping. When the threat was over and the relics were to be returned, they and the cavern in which they had been hidden had disappeared. Instead, this monastery was built on the spot of the disappearances. The high view and beautiful vistas make a perfect place for contemplation. Several footpaths traverse this area.

Monestir de Sant Pere de Rodes to Banyoles (37 miles/60 km):
Backtrack to Figueres; take N-260 W toward Besalú; take C-66 S and follow signs to Banyoles.

BANYOLES—Catalonia

Legend says that even today a beast lives in Banyoles's lake, but that it is a peaceful and vegetarian creature. This was not always so. Apparently during and before the eighth century, a prehistoric and terrible-looking monster terrorized the people of the area. Then in the eighth century a French monk from Charlemagne's army, San Emeterio, got the creature to come out before him and through the use of potent prayers, he converted the monster into a gentle, peace-loving, and plant-eating beast. It still may reside in the deepest, most remote parts of the lake.

If you take a stroll around this lake, where you will find many health-conscious walkers, joggers, and kayakers, you will also come upon the lakeside thirteenth-century Iglesia de Santa María de Porqueres whose interior Romanesque capitals are carved with interesting characters.

Banyoles to Girona (11 miles/18 km):
Take C-66 S to Girona.

GIRONA—Catalonia

One of the major settlements that sat on the Roman Via Augusta (going from Rome across southern France and along Spain's Mediterranean coast), Girona has been an important city for centuries. Muslims controlled Girona briefly, from the early eighth century until AD 797. Thereafter it fell under French and Barcelonan influence. Medieval Girona was also a very important Jewish center and a major place in the exploration of medieval Kabbalistic mysticism. It also houses beautiful twelfth-century Romanesque churches and monasteries. The cathedral stands at the highest part of the city, approached by two hundred steep steps. Destroyed and rebuilt several times, it is cold and unappealing from the outside, feeling largely like a huge rectangular block. But the Gothic interior is transformative, through its nave, which is one of Europe's widest, its high airy ceilings, and the rays of light filtering in through stained-glass windows of jewel-tone emerald, violet, cobalt, and fuchsia.

Romanesque Girona

The Iglesia de Sant Nicolau reflects Lombard Romanesque styles from the twelfth century. It is a small church with an intimate single nave interior. It stands next door to the former Benedictine monastery of Sant Pere de Galligants, which now houses the archeology museum. This twelfth-century building, with its mix of Romanesque and Gothic styles, was vacated by the monks during the 1836 decree to disband monasteries across Spain. Its cloisters are still a delight, a small and refreshing enclosure with hydrangeas growing in the middle. The cloister's column capitals are carved with all sorts of scenes and creatures: medieval personalities, plants, and fantastical beasts. My favorites are the two-legged mermaids that leave very little to a sailor's imagination. Those Benedictines…

Today the Iglesia de Sant Nicolau remains empty except for early Christian tombs brought from the nearby coastal site of Empúries (or

Set today within the Museum of the History of the Jews, this outdoor shrine marks the spot of Girona's fifteenth-century synagogue, Catalonia

Ampurias) where one of the earliest churches (late Roman, early Christian) exists. The tombs are carved with organic images of people and plants. One has a carving of Jesus looking very much like the Buddha in hairstyle and robe/wrap. There are also Roman wine and olive-oil vessels scattered about the church floor. Otherwise, all that is present are the beautiful lines of the building in gray- to charcoal-colored stone. Upstairs, over the cloisters, is where the archaeology museum has its exhibits, from early humans (twenty thousand years ago) through to Bronze and Iron Age Iberian and Celtiberian populations, to the Greek and Roman presence.

Taking the road to the left of Sant Pere will lead you to the Valley of Sant Daniel, an earlier Romanesque monastery founded in the eleventh century. It stands within a natural space that offers a lovely connection with Girona's wild surroundings that is well worth taking the time to walk along.

Jewish Girona

The main artery of the medieval Jewish neighborhood, or *Call* in Catalán, was around the street Força Vella. This also marks the oldest part of medieval Girona. By the thirteenth century, Girona was one of the most influential Jewish centers, for commerce as well as for spirituality. It was a fluid community, mixing easily with the Christians. This began to change in the fourteenth century as policies across Christian Spain as well as other parts of Europe segregated the Jewish community into more and more confined spaces, physically and socially. The Call by then lost its porous spaces and became a walled and separate neighborhood.

Girona contained one of the Mediterranean world's most important Jewish communities, both in antiquity as well as in the Middle Ages. Their neighborhood was an open and flowing place between Jews and Christians from AD 1170 up until the fifteenth century, when the Christian powers that be restricted Jews to living in a certain district and sealed off their entrances to control the area. It went from hundreds of years of being a vital, moving zone of interchange and exchange to one that was like a prison. In 1492 the Jewish population was expelled. Before they left they bequeathed the land where they had their cemetery to a local, who kept it undeveloped. Up to today, that area north of Girona has remained untouched. Because of one influential person who kept his word, the dead have been allowed to rest in peace.

Recent efforts to uncover the prior medieval Jewish section of town have turned this part of the city into the most interesting part. An excellent center, combining the Nahmanides Institute for Jewish Studies and the Museum of the History of the Jews, stands in the heart of the space where the original fifteenth-century synagogue stood and where parts of the synagogue have been revived.

Nahmanides and Kabbalah

When the Almohads invaded Spain in 1171, Jews living in Muslim Spain who had not already left from the prior Almoravid invasions either fled to the north of Spain, into Christian territory, or across the Mediterranean, into other Muslim lands such as Egypt and the Levant. Those who went to Christian Spain entered kingdoms that were stronger than ever before. These were the kingdoms of León-Castile, Aragón-Catalonia, and the newly minted Portugal. The Jews were for the most part welcome, given their knowledge and skill, and many entered into the royal courts as advisors, experts, and physicians.

In Jewish communities across Spain as well as Europe, the thirteenth century marked a time when the rationalist and secular philosophy of Maimonides (born about sixty years earlier than Nahmanides) gained prominence among more liberal members of the communities. Simultaneously and in part in response to this secularizing current, the study of Kabbalah also picked up.

Castilla y León was a major region of Kabbalistic influence, as was Catalonia, especially Girona, a city that was midstream between southern France and the rest of Spain and thus was a great cultural crossroad of ideas, cultural change, and the comings and goings of diverse peoples. In the heart of Castilian Kabbalah we find Moses de León, whose *Zohar* became the definitive text for the study of mystical Judaism known as Kabbalah both for his generation and those that followed. (See chapter 14, under Avila, for more on Moses de León and the *Zohar*.)

In thirteenth-century Catalonia, Rabbi Moses ben Nahman, Nahmanides, was a diplomat in many ways, including in striving to find a balance between the secularists (the Maimunists) and the religious traditionalists. The Kabbalah struck such a balance—it not only was infused with the spirit of faith and religion but also allowed individual expression: each person on this path had to train their senses, feelings, and mind toward gaining greater experience and insight into the divine. But even the Kabbalah could be criticized by the traditionalists because it could also depart from tradition, given its tolerance of individual volition.

Under Nahmanides, a renowned biblical and Talmudic scholar, Girona was a vibrant Jewish center, both for Kabbalistic study as well as for traditional Jewish life. He often served as the representative of the Jewish faith and community before King Jaime I, who included him among trusted advisors and considered him a friend. But it was a time when, while the Jewish community was wrestling with its own interior tensions of faith, certain surrounding Christian orders, particularly the Dominicans and the Franciscans, took an interest in solidifying the Christian faith and took an interest in the Jews, an interest that was not positive.

One of the results was a series of public disputations, the most famous being several days in the summer of 1263 in Barcelona, in Jaime I's court. Nahmanides was called there to engage in debate with the Dominican friar Pablo Christiani concerning Jewish sources about the nature of Jesus and the Messiah. It was a dangerous debate and one where Jaime I guaranteed Nahmanides full freedom of speech, a promise he kept.

The details of this debate and time are too much to enter into here. But this event was an indication of the climate of the thirteenth century and hinted at how the Jewish communities over the next two centuries would become more and more endangered and would have to huddle in on themselves. They would be forced to erect segregating walls around their neighborhoods in the light of a more and more confident Christian society, whose efforts at conquering the Muslim south had been largely successful, with only the Kingdom of Granada holding on.

These trends were already at work in other parts of Europe: Spain was a latecomer in the one-way mentality of faith combined with state because the Iberian experience was still benefiting from the diversity of its people and their richly various skills. The Jews had been the trusted neutral party of medieval Europe when Christians and Muslims vied for power and control. Both sides often would send a Jewish diplomat/interpreter/businessman to the other side because they were trusted by both sides. But when Islamic rule was defeated in Europe and Christianity became the major power of church and state, the critical role of intermediary was also defunct. This alone signaled the new vulnerability of the minority group, which became more insular from within and without. Slowly, some converted to Christianity (only to invite another horror on themselves, being tried on the strength of their faith as new Christians). Some made their way to live as protected citizens of the Book in the Muslim Nasrid Kingdom of Granada, which came into existence in the mid-thirteenth century and ended Almohad rule in Muslim Spain. Some left altogether, going to other parts of the Mediterranean. And yet others held on to their faith, their homes, and their neighborhoods.

Time and mood have cast our ancestors and us in infinite unplanned directions, all temporal and unique. But the power of the *Zohar* and the study of the Kabbalah persist to today, a testimony that the mystical strain, that universal timeless strain of experience, survives temporal struggles.

BENJAMIN OF TUDELA

Benjamin of Tudela was a Spanish rabbi and explorer from the twelfth century. Born in Tudela, Catalonia, he traveled across the Mediterranean world, visiting the Jewish and non-Jewish communities throughout. His books have become an important source for understanding the medieval world, its people, places, and times; his observations and writing style are meticulous and strive for objective accuracy. On his way out of Spain, he stopped in Zaragoza, Tortosa, and Barcelona before continuing through southern France, Italy, the Byzantine Empire, the Levant, the Arabian Peninsula, and Egypt, and returned to Spain via Sicily. He was fluent in Navarrese Romance, Hebrew, Arabic, and most likely Greek and Latin.

Wine, Cheese, and Mushrooms

Daily along Girona's La Rambla de la Llibertat you can find local wine, cheese, and wild-mushroom sellers offering their goods at open-air kiosks along the stretch running parallel with the river. This was also Girona's market street in the Middle Ages.

Girona is a good place to end this tour; it is a city in which to take one's time and relax, taking in several streams of the past and the present. The Rambla reveals the diversity of modern Girona, with Catalans, Latin Americans, and West and North Africans mixing much as diverse peoples might have done on this very spot in the Middle Ages. From here, you can follow in reverse the ancient route outlined in chapter 11, starting in nearby Empúries on the Mediterranean Costa Brava, heading south toward Valencia, and ending farther south in Elche and La Alcudia, the homes of two unique sacred occurrences, the medieval Mystery of Elche and the twenty-five-hundred-year-old grande dame of matriarchal Iberia, La Dama de Elche.

CHAPTER THIRTEEN

························⟨❁⟩························

Zaragoza to Jaca

Growing up in the shadow of Numancia makes people of this region very proud and nonconformist. Numancia has been a symbol of Iberian independence for centuries.
—A woman from Soria living in Barcelona, on a bus in Zaragoza

THIS ROUTE PASSES through Aragón, Navarra, Castilla y León, the southern tip of Basque Country, all through areas that for millennia have been a major melting pot of Iberian peoples. From Celts, Iberians, and Romans, to Jews, Christians, Muslims, Mudéjars, Mozarabes, and French settlers, this route covers their interrelated mélange, in co-creation and in warfare, in a landscape that naturally brought them together at the crossroads of the Pyrenees.

Parts of this route cross into, along, and over, the Camino de Santiago, the pilgrimage road to Santiago, another rich dimension of this territory. There were many detours to monasteries near the Camino, such as Santo Domingo de Silos, San Juan de la Peña, or San Millán de Cogolla. There were also many monasteries, orders, and churches that grew during the time of the Camino but possessed a local following with local folklore independent of the Camino.

Moreover, these lands were a central part of the medieval repopulating policies as the Christian north gained territory (and tribute) from the Muslim south.

From the Bronze and Iron Ages, this part of Spain was like a channel, a great big receiving bowl, of early dolmen-building agriculturalists and Celtic speakers crossing the Pyrenees and mixing with the native Iberians.

Romans made Zaragoza (Caesar Augusta) one of their main inland cities. As was the case throughout large swaths of the medieval period in Spain, the three religious communities of Iberian Jews, Christians, and Muslims often lived together and influenced art, philosophy, medicine, mysticism, and many other aspects of everyday life. Mudéjar structures in the north are a testimony to this medieval reality and leave a unique mark in the building of sacred Christian structures in the northern province of Aragón.

In the Middle Ages, as the French Cluny Benedictine orders gained influence on the Camino, their monies went to hiring artisans from France and from both Christian and Muslim Spain for constructing their sacred buildings. So, it is not unusual to see Mudéjar ceilings over the tombs of Christian saints or to find ancient dolmens or Celtiberian settlements amid the medieval monasteries. These sacred sites are also in prime wine-making lands, with the sacred connections doubtless felt by many who planted the vine and made the wine.

Main Route (409 miles/658 km):

Zaragoza—Veruela—Soria—Numancia—Santo Domingo de Silos—
Yecla—Valvanera—San Millán de la Cogolla—Laguardia—
Leyre—Santa Cruz de la Serós—San Juan de la Peña—Jaca

ZARAGOZA—Aragón

Zaragoza's greatest sacred moment came in AD 40, when on the site of today's Plaza del Pilar where stands the huge basilica of the Virgen del Pilar, the Virgin Mary appeared to St. James atop a pagan pillar.

Zaragoza is a delightful and odd Spanish city. Beyond its historical center, and even including parts of it, like the Plaza del Pilar, it is a city on a grand scale. It feels more like being on Chicago's lake-front boulevards than in Spain. In common with the Windy City, there is also frequently a pretty strong wind, a perennial gift from the plains of Aragón. Avenues are superwide and buildings superbig and modern. Some emulate the Mudéjar style of brickwork and look great next to their older relatives, though they are only about fifty years old.

No Muslim Iberian city felt the brunt of the constant push and pull between the worlds of Christian and Islamic Spain as much as Zaragoza did. Situated in the northern frontier, great crossroads to the Pyrenees, the Mediterranean, and the Castilian interior, and resting on the banks of the Ebro River, Zaragoza has pretty much seen it all. It should come as no surprise that, if indeed St. James came to Iberia to preach, his first miracle took place right here. In this miracle of being visited by Mary, he was still alive, some four years before he would be beheaded after his return to the Holy Land.

Zaragoza's roots go back to Celtiberians and Romans. In spite of St. James's possible visit here, it was Roman and later Muslim Zaragoza—ruled by Berber tribes, not Arabs—that marked the peak of urban and provincial power for the city.

Celtiberian Zaragoza and the Botorrita Bronze Tablets

Zaragoza was at the heart of the late Bronze Age urn-field culture of Iberia, a culture recognized by their urn burials. Some thirty-two hundred years ago people here placed the body of their deceased into a womblike urn—representing a form of rebirth?—and then placed the urn in the earth.

As Celtic-speaking tribes migrated into Iberia and merged with indigenous Iberians, a new Celtiberian culture emerged that centered on this region. The presence of the Celtiberian peoples dates to around twenty-five hundred to nineteen hundred years ago.

The city's museum, **Museo de Zaragoza,** is a wonderful two-part museum of archaeology (first level) and fine arts (second level). It is an absolutely delightful place to spend the afternoon, going from prehistoric and historic displays of the city and onward through Art Nouveau stained-glass doors of beautiful damsels into the fine-art section. In the archaeological displays you will find one of the world's great treasures, the **Botorrita tablets,** which are among the earliest written examples of a Celtic language and considered one of the entire Celtic world's most important textual sources. The tablets were discovered during excavations of the Celtiberian city of Contrebia Belaisca, today near a town called Botorrita twenty-one kilometers south of Zaragoza. The first plaque was uncovered in 1973 and subsequent finds have changed expert ideas about the Celts in Iberia as well as the Celtic languages spoken here.

Dating to around 2,150 years ago, these bronze engraved tablets are the longest Celtiberian texts ever found, largely containing public documents. They offer much material for linguists to analyze to understand better the ancient Celtiberian language, one that principally belongs to the Celtic group of languages. A great deal of the excitement about these texts is that finding any examples of a Celtic language is exceedingly rare, given that it was spoken mostly by people with an oral but not a written tradition. Thus, the Botorrita tablets offer insights not only to Celtiberians but to the pan-Celtic world as well.

Regarding Celtiberian divinity, one of these tablets mentions a god, Neitos, who was a dynamic, warlike god, likely an equivalent to the Roman god Mars. Another god mentioned in the tablet is Tokoitos, a name possibly derived from the Celtiberian word for "oath" and might have been a god who assured solid agreements or pacts. As a people who forged *tessorae*, hospitality agreements with other tribes, often engraved in stone or bronze, this would be an important god indeed.

While little is as yet understood about the Celtiberians' divinities, it does appear that representations of them were more abstract than literal. Some scholars think a particularly powerful divinity might have been the moon. Such a one might have been the Celtic god, Dagda, father of all and deity of the druids who also ruled the lunar cycles.

Feminine divinity was found in place-names and in dedications, such as to the goddess Brigeacis, a name found in Clunia, a Celtiberian settlement south of Santo Domingo de Silos and Burgos. She is likely associated with Brigit, the daughter of Dagda, as well as with the three Mothers, Matres, popularly recognized by us as the Maid, Mother, and Crone.

Given the Celtiberians' proximity to other Mediterranean peoples, it is likely that some of the gods are different names for a shared divinity, as is very likely the case with Neitos, who is so similar to Mars. The overall Celtic and Celtiberian cosmos was likely of a universal divine filled with many forces that had diverse manifestations but that ultimately manifested from the universal. These notions again were abstract and not personified. A spiral or circle, for instance, might represent the unity and the infinite but interconnected nature of things. Similar possibilities occur with sun and moon symbols.

Roman Zaragoza

Throughout town, in the walk toward the **Plaza del Pilar** or the Mudéjar church towers, for example, you will pass by surprisingly huge Roman remains. Though nothing of the Roman sacred survives, except in lore, great stone walls and the well-preserved theater are reminders that this was a powerful Roman city, one that overtook the Celtiberians of outlying areas and absorbed the largely recalcitrant lot into the Roman world.

This sets the stage for the Virgen del Pilar since the pillar was likely a Celtiberian or a Roman one; it was most likely placed over a Celtiberian sacred site. It is also certain that the Plaza del Pilar, where the basilica stands, was once a Roman temple.

In 1934 a statue of the Egyptian god Osiris was found on the left bank of the Ebro River. It is possible that it belonged to a Roman temple dedicated to the cult of Isis. Perhaps it was brought from Egypt by a later, dedicated Roman citizen, as the statue dates to 664–525 BCE. The site's nearness to the Ebro River, water being sacred to the Celts, may also hint at some ancient veneration here wherein the Virgin is the most recent divine player on an established sacred stage. The Ebro River is no doubt a sacred river—in addition to Egyptian idols, it has also produced floating images of the Virgin and some time ago people discovered and pulled out a holy cadaver belonging to one San Dominguito.

La Virgen del Pilar

The legend of the Virgin Mary of the Pillar is the most ancient of the Marian stories in Spain, dating to the time when a still-living St. James was believed to evangelize in Iberia. Around AD 40, the apostle arrived in Zaragoza where an apparition of the deceased Virgin Mary appeared to him at a pagan site marked by a pre-Christian pillar, perhaps a pagan standing stone. Her apparition stood atop this pillar and she spoke to St. James. Since then, that pillar and the Virgen del Pilar have been venerated here.

The current Basílica del Pilar protects the jasper pillar and image of the Virgin, which stand on the spot of St. James's vision. La Virgen del Pilar is Zaragoza's and Aragón's patroness, as well as the patroness of all Spain. Some wonderful legends say that the pillar is supernatural, made of special jasper shaped by the angels and carried down from heaven with the Virgin riding atop.

Today, in spite of the central and mystical shrine of the Virgin and the pillar, as well as the frescoes by spirited Spanish masters such as Velázquez and Goya, I find the interior of the basilica itself to be an ice-cold and overdone Baroque temple. The only thing that warms it are the dedicated devout who come to midday Mass and gather around the temple-within-a-temple, the main chapel where the Virgen del Pilar stands. But given the importance of this Virgin and her seer, the apostle St. James, it is easy to understand the reason for all the over-building and fuss.

But from the outside, this somewhat Eastern Orthodox–looking temple reveals sacred geometry at work. It is a rectangle with each corner held down by a symmetrical tower. Many domes fill the center and work their way to the climactic central dome, a circle holding the center of the universe. That central dome marks where the pillar stands below. The square corners of the basilica ground heaven onto the Earth. The square in sacred geometry is usually associated with the Earth, while the circle is associated with the divine. Catholic-devout and neo-pagan visitors alike have had their share of visions here, so this might truly be a universal power place.

Muslim Zaragoza

When North Africans invaded Spain in the early eighth century, it fell to a few Berber clans to rule Zaragoza. The greatest surviving monument to Islamic rule in Zaragoza is the **Aljafería palace.** The initial foundations of the Aljafería were built in AD 935 under orders from Cordoban Caliph Abd al-Rahman III. It was called al-Jazira, "the island," and was used as a military camp. When the Cordoban Caliphate dissolved in the early eleventh century, the Berber Banu-Hud, or Benihud, family took over the city-state, the *taifa,* of Zaragoza that emerged. The second *taifa* king, Banu-Hud al-Muqtadir, had the palace of Aljafería built within the military camp and it became the Muslim emir's palace. Today you can visit the delightful private royal mosque, which is still largely intact. It reflects a sisterhood to the mosque in Córdoba on a much smaller scale. The mihrab, the prayer niche that faces Mecca, is very similar to the Cordoban mihrab in its ornate inlaid, almost Byzantine, painting and carving.

The Aljafería has mostly maintained its continuity as the seat of power in Zaragoza. In AD 1118 Zaragoza was wrested out of Berber Muslim control by the Christian Aragonese king Alfonso I, popularly called El Batallador, the Warrior. The Aljafería then became the residence of Aragón's Christian kings and later of Isabel and Fernando. Though Christian Spain was enjoying taking over Islamic territories and becoming the kings of the hill, Christian monarchs still valued the artistry of Muslim craftsmen. In the fifteenth century, Mudéjars, Muslims living and working in Christian Spain, were employed to add a throne room in the Aljafería, where their skill is evident today in the walls and ceiling.

The Aljafería, in profound irony, then became a jail for those being tried by the Inquisition. This use lasted until 1706, after which, for the next two centuries, the palace was used as a jail and an arsenal. In 1947 a forward-thinking Zaragozan, Francisco Íñiguez, restored the palace and as of 1985 the Aljafería has been the seat of the provincial Cortes, the parliament of Aragón.

Having in a sense returned to its original purpose as the seat of leadership, the Aljafería has many parts that are off-limits, and security to enter is higher than at most other historic sites. The grand fortified nature of the palace, with its mix of Islamic and medieval Christian fortified walls, towers, and moat, speaks of the place's older security measures.

The Islamic part of the Aljafería is stunning to be in. The carved-stucco latticework, the proportions of the walking spaces and courtyards, the placement of fountains and gardens, the little intimate mosque that feels as if it once were in a forest, are all testimony to a people who built to unify the needs of the body with the desires of the soul. The mosque is octagonal and its doorway is decorated with plants and geometric designs. The interior has carved-stucco detailing and a passage from the Qur'an.

There are lovely medieval Christian additions too, such as the aforementioned fifteenth-century Mudéjar throne room, known as the Sala Baja del Pasos Perdidos, which was once the upper level of the old mosque. Earlier Christian alterations include the Sala Baja del Palacio Mudéjar, commissioned by Pedro IV in the fourteenth century. This room shows the brickwork for which Mudéjar craftsmen were famous, as well as a mix of Islamic and Christian themes; for instance, there are paintings on the wooden beams on the ceiling of plant designs intermixed with human forms, such as a half-human half-eagle blowing a trumpet, animals, sailing vessels, and royal coats of arms.

In the back of the palace is the chapel Capilla de San Martín, a fusion of Mudéjar and Christian art. The doorway is Mudéjar and over the door is a depiction of St. Martin on horseback holding a sword toward a beggar behind him. It represents the most popular image of St. Martin, where he splits his cloak to share half of it with a beggar.

Mudéjar Churches and Bell Towers

After Alfonso I's victory in taking Zaragoza, he and kings after him continued to value the skill of the Zaragozan Muslims in their realm. Aragón today is rich in Mudéjar architecture and decorative arts for this reason. Zaragoza has its share of beautiful Mudéjar structures, including six unique bell towers and the dizzyingly woven brick and tile wall of La Seo Cathedral. The several Mudéjar towers that punctuate the old town make for a nice afternoon walking circuit to locate and ponder each one.

La Seo Cathedral is the Mudéjar sacred site par excellence and Zaragoza's other cathedral after the Basílica del Pilar. It is said the bishop spends six months in one and six in the other. La Seo is short for the cathedral's full title, *Catedral de San Salvador*. It is stunning on the outside with elaborate tile and brick Mudéjar latticework, incorporating esoteric symbols of crescent moons (a sign of Islam and of the goddess and the Virgin Mary), eight-pointed stars, and fleur-de-lis. It is built over a mosque, and beneath the Gothic redo, restorers have found Islamic pillars and Romanesque work that went into the cathedral's makeup before it was overwhelmed by the new Gothic architectural trends of the late Middle Ages. The cathedral dates from the thirteenth to the eighteenth century. The interior now is largely Gothic and also has several fine works of Mudéjar craftsmanship.

When you enter, there will likely be recorded Gregorian chant piped throughout the nave and chapels; it is pleasant and shows off the acoustic beauty of the building. If anything, the chant also keeps less spiritually oriented tourists from talking, allowing for quiet and contemplation for those more inclined.

Regarding the Mudéjar interior, start with the ornate geometric gate to the right of the altar that leads to the Sacristía y Museo Capitular. Next is the inlaid tile work in the floor and walls of the Capilla de la Virgen Blanca to the left of the Baroque altar. In the central nave, where the chorus stands, there are wooden, geometrically carved Mudéjar doors, their dark wood a nice contrast with the white allegorical engravings into which it is set.

The prime Mudéjar bell-tower churches to be sure to visit are the Iglesia de San Juan de los Panetes, Iglesia Parroquial de San Gil, Iglesia de San Pablo, Iglesia de la Magdalena, and the Iglesia de San Miguel de los Navarros. Most of these churches are in the vicinity of the old medieval city. Each one has an interesting quirk. All date to between the fourteenth and eighteenth centuries. San Juan de los Panetes is next door to the Basílica del Pilar and has an octagonal Mudéjar bell tower with arches. San Gil is square, stately, and central, as if it is the anchor of its part of town. San Pablo, farther away from the others to the west of the old city, has a facade representing St. Peter right next to its octagonal Moorish bell tower.

La Magdalena, the church of Mary Magdalene, is considered by some to be one of the most powerful spiritual centers of Zaragoza. It has a sweet, rounded energy. It is so intimately woven into the narrow streets of its neighborhood that you are almost at its side wall before you see its square Moorish bell tower. Then you come upon its rounded Mudéjar apse, which is on a human scale and made of the warm brick the Mudéjars crafted so well. San Miguel has the most open space around it and is surrounded by trees that seem to be in on the sacred effort. It also has an outrageous Baroque entrance of a scallop-shell shape with St. Michael standing overhead right next to his very Islamic-looking bell tower.

Jewish Zaragoza

Though nothing remains of the Jewish quarter, the Jewish population of Zaragoza was a significant one. The first Jews of Zaragoza came here during Roman times. They were severely persecuted under the Visigoths and suffered so much that when the Berbers arrived here in the early eighth century, the only remaining Jews in the city were those who had gone underground as crypto-Jews. Muslim rule over the city elevated the Jews to a secured and higher status and the community thrived and grew, contributing greatly to the public life of Zaragoza and its hinterland. When Christians conquered Zaragoza, and under the kings of Aragón thereafter—

The Mudéjar bell tower of Zaragoza's Iglesia de la Magdalena, Aragón

until Ferdinand, who handed over the fate of his Jewish citizens to his less-than-broad-minded wife—Jews continued to lead rich lives and contribute to the society in significant areas, from high learning to the crafts.

The main Jewish center of activity in medieval Zaragoza revolved around where the Iglesia de la Magdalena stands today. It was in this vicinity that the synagogue of Biqqur Holim stood as well as kosher butcher shops and a Talmudic school.

For modern public esoterica, visit the Plaza Europa near the Aljafería, whose traffic-center art installation is an Egyptian-style obelisk next to a pillar topped with a three-dimensional Star of David/Solomon's Seal. Both symbols represent the joining of heaven and Earth, uniting the two energies. It sits in the center of a high-volume traffic zone.

Zaragoza to Veruela (50 miles/80 km):

Take AP-68 NW to exit 19; take N-122 toward Borja and Tarazona; after passing Borja follow signs to Vera de Moncayo and to the Monasterio de Veruela.

MONASTERIO DE VERUELA—Aragón

To get to the twelfth-century Cistercian Monasterio de Veruela, you arrive in a beautiful river valley at the foot of Aragón's highest mountain, Moncayo. Moncayo was revered by Iberians, Celts, Celtiberians, Romans, and different centuries of Christians, all who built their altars, temples, hermitages, and sanctuaries in the mountain's shadow. Moncayo's folklore is rich in mystical occurrences, power spots, and witchcraft. The stories of witchcraft partake of some of the usual themes: someone was accused of being a witch after a neighbor claimed that he or she saw the accused partying one dark night with the devil, or other misdeeds, like flitting off on brooms, running about naked, rubbing ointments all over oneself and the like. Such folktales almost always end poorly for the accused witch. If she really were a witch, wouldn't you think she'd have the last word and some sweet revenge? I think underneath the tales are some real people who might have been gifted seers or healers and who were valued in their village until someone got jealous or became threatened by the person's special talent.

When you visit Numancia near Soria you will get to see the perfect view of Moncayo mountain from the hilltop of that fortified Celtiberian city, or *oppidum*. Moncayo likely was a source of spiritual support, especially in the last days of Numancia's resistance to the Romans.

The Monastery of Veruela was founded in 1145 by Cistercians who sought such remote and beautiful places in their endeavor to return to traditional monastic virtues. The monastery is enclosed by a one-kilometer-long stone wall. Its church is twelfth century with later Gothic and Renaissance cloisters. The monastery makes good use of its space and cultural appeal by holding art exhibits, concerts, courses, and even a wine museum. Veruela is a mere fifteen kilometers from Borja, one of Aragón's most celebrated wine-making territories. The newer part of the monastery, connected by a baroque stairway, was built in the seventeenth century.

After visiting the monastery, continue west to the **Parque Natural de la Dehesa del Moncayo,** a natural park around Mount Moncayo that is a place of pilgrimage. Ascending through a natural park covered in a lush forest of oak, pine, beech, and juniper, and inhabited by wild boar, deer, and eagles, people travel to the sanctuary of **Our Lady of Moncayo.** Set in a protected natural park, it is a place people seek out for the mix of fresh air and natural magic.

Detour to Tarazona:
Between Veruela and Soria, if you return to N-122, you will pass through Tarazona, with its share of Mudéjar churches. The town was built on a hill and has preserved some of its medieval streets, so be prepared to do a bit of climbing.

Parque Natural de la Dehesa del Moncayo to Soria (38 miles/61 km):
Follow SO-382 NW of Moncayo to Agreda; in Agreda follow signs to Soria and N-122.

SORIA—Castilla y León

Romanesque Soria

In Soria you are in the heart of big-sky farming country, mostly grow-ing grains. The city is sweet and its energy is warm and delightful. People make their small provincial capital a very welcoming place. The immi-grant population from Africa and Latin America also look happier and more at ease here, speaking of the true hospitality of a place. The city also has a remarkable collection of Romanesque churches that are like little jewels throughout town. There are so many of these delightful churches that I can only do justice to a few, what I consider the four most sublime.

In town there are the churches of **San Juan del Rabanera** and of **Santo Domingo.** San Juan del Rabanera is named after the village of Rabanera from whence came its parishioners when they relocated to Soria. It dates to around 1200 and stands on an island in the middle of two streets that lead toward the main square, the Plaza Mayor. It is a very small, and very sweet, Romanesque church that is looked after as if it were a newborn infant by its elderly worshipers. Santo Domingo is larger and slightly older, dating to around 1060. It has a dramatically carved west portal that shows the Virgin Mary on her throne in heaven with the Baby Jesus on her lap contained in the mandorla of the tympanum. They are surrounded by angels and then four layers more of biblical scenes on the Romanesque arches, including more saints and angels, the twenty-seven Elders of the Apocalypse, scenes from Jesus' life, from childhood to crucifixion and death, and the Massacre of the Innocents. The capitals show scenes from Genesis. Usually we see Jesus sitting in the mandorla, so this is yet another case for Mary's importance in Spain.

Just outside of town are two sublime places reached by a riverside, tree-covered walking path along the Duero River. They are the old monastic church of **San Juan de Duero** and the hermitage **Ermita de San Saturio.** The Monasterio de San Juan de Duero is in a green riverbank spot and possesses a lyrical outdoor Romanesque cloister that exhibits several building styles, including a bit of the Islamic, with overlapping arches on one side. Once enclosed, the cloister is enchanting with its green open-air surroundings. You can make a walking meditation along the grass around it; birdsong and wind through the leaves will add to your contemplation.

Next door, San Juan de Duero's church contains carved Romanesque capitals like nowhere else. They are heavily populated with biblical and fantastical beings, with painstaking detail showing emotions, facial features, and hand gestures. Some favorite scenes are Mary and Joseph's flight to Egypt on a donkey, the visitation when Elizabeth, John the Baptist's mother, is greeted by Mary, and Mary having just given birth to Jesus. These carvings are exceedingly well preserved, making you feel as if you have been transported back to the early 1200s when the Knights Templar built this church and you are looking at newly carved works. The chapel overall is also delightful, all of stone, with an apse that feels like a mix of Mozarabic and Romanesque styles. The simplicity enhances the sacred experience. If only the builders of Baroque "architectual noise" had really taken their lesson from earlier church builders. The caretaker of the site is a warm, dedicated man who lives and breathes the life of these stones.

The back wall of the church exhibits medieval materials excavated in Soria. Of special interest are items from Jewish (tombstones) and Islamic times, because there are no other public remains of these peoples who also called Soria home.

San Saturio's hermitage is rarely described for just how surprising it is—it is a hermitage built atop a stone outcropping on a hill near the river, but to arrive there, the entrance is far down at the hill's base where a cave opening takes you in. On entering the cave opening to the shrine, enjoy the craft of the stained-glass window that has been inlaid in a hole of natural stone, something of a natural window frame.

Most of this sanctuary site is cave wall enclosed further by hand-laid stones and plaster. The truly mystical and enchanting part of this journey in is the journey. The chapel at the top, a gaudy neoclassical all human-made room is less enchanting and reminds me of when people used to cover their walls, floors, and furnishings with too much hideously busy fabric. But the views are great, and there is a little chapel to the Blessed Virgin on the way up to San Saturio, set in natural stone niches, that compensates for the lack of sacred good taste at the top. We are here to honor a hermit of old who lived in this cave as an ascetic—I am sure even he would ask that the excesses of the chapel be removed. From the outside riverside view, however, the stone-hugging chapel is truly romantic and beautiful.

Though the hermitage is fairly recent, eighteenth century, the cave of this shrine reaches back in sanctity to before Christianity arrived on this bank. It is an ideal place to meet the threshold world of the divine, be it of the spirits, the ancestors, or the Great Mother, whose abode was believed to be deep in the earth. Early Christians recognized places of power and used them for their own veneration, including taking over others' gods as miracle workers and saints. San Saturio is Soria's patron saint. It is very likely that San Saturio was the name of the previous resident divinity here, Saturn, the farming god of seeds and cultivation. There is another local saint, the obscure San Polo, who some believe is also derived from a pre-Christian power, Apollo, the god of poetry, music, and healing. This is after all the land of the Celtiberians, who were then taken over by the Romans. Scratch the surface of Soria and that's where things go.

Celtiberian Soria

Soria is also near Numancia, the famous last-stand between the Celtiberians and the Romans. To the present day, Numancia is a national symbol for Iberian resistance, and the people of the surrounding area, especially in Soria, are very proud of their vicinity to such an ancestral place. But the region of Soria has many remains of the Celtiberian past. A terrific first stop to get oriented to this rich heritage is the Museo Numantino in the heart of Soria, right on the edge of its medieval town center. There the ages are covered—from the Paleolithic, Neolithic, Bronze, Iron, Roman, Christian, and Muslim eras. The Iron Age, in particular, reveals that this was an area rich in fortified, hilltop castro settlements as early as the sixth to the fourth century BCE.

Like other Celtic speakers, Celtiberians worshiped all the forces and elements of nature, such as the sun, the moon, mountains, rivers, trees, and certain animals. They didn't necessarily build temples but they did have natural sanctuaries, such as a spring, a cave, a tree, a river, a stone, and the like.

Some Celtiberian castros were surrounded by heavily fortified walls. These are called *oppida* (singular, *oppidum*). The most famous of these oppida castro settlements was Numancia, on a hilltop just north of Soria.

Soria to Numancia (4.5 miles/7 km):
Take N-111 N; exit for the village of Garray; follow signs from the village
to the site.

NUMANCIA—Castilla y León

Before you reach the visitors' center at the site, you will pass by two
watchtowers, reconstructed as they might have looked over two thousand
years ago, guarding the wall of the oppidum. Their width gives a good idea
of the protective walls the Celtiberians built.

One of the most important settlements of Spain, this castro site
belonged to Celtiberians known as the Arevaci, who lived here from the
second century BCE to the second century AD. Today Numancia is a holy
spot for all Spaniards as a symbol of the spirit of perseverance, one that has
carried through from antiquity to today's post-Franco era.

Numancia marked one of the last stands between Romans and Celtiberians as Romans sought greater and greater control over the Peninsula's interior, already having secured it along the Mediterranean coast. The Arevaci
were hard to contain, and their town was in a perfect strategic spot, on the
hill with views all around of all the other hills and valleys. Additionally, they
possessed two sources of water, the Duero River and the Tera River. Mount
Moncayo stands steadily on the horizon and was a mountain that contained
sacred meaning for Celtiberians as well as for Romans. The Arevaci were
especially good at surprise attacks. Swift and skilled on their horses and
working in small groups, they plagued the Roman soldiers with sudden well-
orchestrated and unsettling attacks that came as quickly as they vanished
but left a good deal of damage in their wake. For two decades, from 153 to
133 BCE, the Arevaci resisted Roman dominance.

But in 134 BCE, the Romans built a nine-kilometer-long encircling
wall around Numancia's hill. They placed traps to stop water flow on the
Duero. Short on food and water, in eleven months the Arevaci were
finally defeated. Rather than fall under Roman rule, the Arevaci set fire to
their homes and killed themselves en masse. What the Romans got was a
bloody victory and a dead town that they had to rebuild, which they did,
given its ideal position, not to mention the message it sent to others bent
on resistance.

Much of what you will see at the current site is the Roman rebuilding
over the original settlement as well as expansion of the city into new territory. Aerial shots and excavations of the Celtiberian settlement reveal
well-organized urban street plans of the pre-Roman city. There is ongoing

archaeological work here and so each year something new is uncovered. The site management has also had two homesteads rebuilt, a Celtiberian one and a Roman one, to give the visitor a good idea of how the two peoples lived. All tours of Numancia are guided and run by very knowledgeable and inspired presenters.

Consider this whole site a national sacred site, given its powerful hold on the modern Spanish psyche. Spanish friends from all over Spain, including that independent-identity stronghold of Catalonia, have told me that they all learned about Numancia in grade school. Many even came here on organized school field trips. Along with learning history, they were taught to see this as a symbol of Iberian fortitude in the face of adversity.

And for people who live near the site, just one mention of Numancia and they will tell you how instrumental living in the vicinity of its symbolic radiance has been in shaping and forging their personal identity as strong, persevering, and independent.

Every year the village of Garray just below Numancia organizes and puts on a great reenactment of the siege of Numancia. A great outdoor space near the site becomes the staging ground. People dressed as Celtiberians re-create daily life in Numancia, before the Roman victory. Farmers, weavers, basket makers, woodworkers and the like mill about

The reconstructed oppidum watchtowers gazing toward the Sierra del Moncayo from the Celtiberian site of Numancia, Castilla y León

town and show off their skills. People take great pride in the historical accuracy and quality of their attire. Called Keltiberoi, the festivities take place during the first two weeks of August.

Numancia to Santo Domingo de Silos (63.5 miles102 km):
Backtrack to Soria and take N-234 W; in approximately 52 miles/84 km exit W to Santo Domingo de Silos.

SANTO DOMINGO DE SILOS—Castilla y León

This is a beautiful medieval village, whose main economy is farming and the monastery. Though everyone comes here to see the famous monastery and hear the chant of its Benedictine monks, the village is a pretty little Castilian town with warm residents who know they've got a good thing but don't alter their homes' character to exploit it. The little main plaza is filled with life of all ages. Warm, dignified, of golden stone, the village lives its own cycles of prayer and service, as do the monks in their secluded monastery.

The lineage of the land here goes deep, inhabited by prehistoric residents, Celtiberians, Romans, Visigoths, and Muslims. The current monastery was built over a ruined Visigothic monastery that was destroyed during the eighth-century incursion from Muslim invaders. The monastery of Santo Domingo was founded in AD 954 by Benedictines.

The current building dates to the eleventh-century Romanesque, with many alterations in subsequent centuries. The cloisters are the highlight and possess wonderful carved scenes of daily medieval life as well as mythic and allegorical images of people and animals, including witches and fantastic monsters. The ceilings were constructed by Muslim craftsmen and reflect the styles coming from the Muslim south. The columns likewise mix Muslim and Romanesque styles, offering a unique glimpse into the mixing of worlds rather than the idea of their separation. The foot of some pillars have reptiles and birds; it is unusual to find carvings at the foot of pillars in most cloisters in Spain. Each corner in the cloister has large, carved panels depicting the life of Christ.

Santo Domingo, a local monk born in Cañas, Rioja, whose birth name was Domingo Manso, came here in 1041 from the monastery of San Millán de Cogolla. He restored the monastery and infused it with spiritual and cultural vigor. You can find Santo Domingo's tomb here, a tomb held up by stone lions. At the monastery entrance on the other side of the church, you will find a sacred cypress tree towering over the entire court-

The cloisters at the monastery of Santo Domingo de Silos, Castilla y León

yard. It is treated as a sort of *axis mundi*, recalling more ancient shamanic traditions and the World Tree.

The monastery's monks are famous for recordings in what is variously called *cantus planus*, *plainchant*, plainsong, or Gregorian chant. This is a style of sung prayer traced to Jewish and Greek music and defining early Christian music. It was reintroduced to Santo Domingo de Silos during its revival in the late nineteenth century by monks from Solesmes in northwestern France.

The plainchant is actually the form in which the monks pray and is their daily practice. It is such a treat to have this tradition open to the public, six days a week. On Mondays the monastery church remains closed to give the brothers a break from public visits. But on the other six days, their prayers are open to the public, six times a day. I strongly recommend you spend two days here, making it to the whole prayer cycle of each day. The cycle is Matins, Lauds, Eucharist, Sext, Vespers, and Compline. The hours can shift but are generally around 6 a.m., 7:30 a.m., 9 a.m. (12 noon on Sundays and festivals), 1:45 p.m., 7 p.m., and 9:30 p.m. On festival days, including Sundays, these hours are different. It is easy to locate the schedule as any local in the village can tell you, if the hours are not posted on the church. When you engage sung prayer that often throughout the day, allowing it to weave into daily doings, it becomes intoxicating and trancelike. Some people find that each time they go to the church for prayer their state of presence goes deeper and each prayer leads them into mystical realms. And between prayer times they find their experience of the world to be more vibrant and whole. Such experience might help the layperson to understand the appeal of the monastic life. It is really something to have access to this tradition in the modern era.

Next door to the monastery church is the town's parochial church of San Pedro, a Romanesque and Gothic gem in its own right. It houses the Virgen del Mercado, Virgin of the Market, who is the town's patroness.

Because the monastery is near several walking trails, you can take to nature between chants. Either head up the hill toward the lovely Virgin Mary statue that looks over Silos or follow signs to the Yecla Gorge (Desfiladero de la Yecla).

Santo Domingo de Silos to Yecla (2.5 miles/4 km):
Take BU-910 S.

DESFILADERO DE LA YECLA—Castilla y León

If you walk to this gorge, you will be on the road all the way, so be sure to walk on the same side as oncoming traffic and stay on the bank.

The gorge has evidence on its cliff tops of having been occupied by prehistoric peoples, Romans, and Visigoths. Today hundred of *buitres*, elegant grey-black vultures, call it home. Here they nest and rest between hunting. Be sure to look up even though the path will take you through the delightfully narrow, almost subterranean stone passageways below. At the bottom flows a little creek that seems to claim some credit for these formations. This natural zone is held as sacred by locals and visitors today. Villagers repeatedly reminded me that my pilgrimage to the monastery of Silos would be incomplete if I did not also visit the Yecla gorge.

Santo Domingo de Silos to Valvanera (55 miles/89 km):
Backtrack to N-234 and go N; exit onto BU-825, which winds about a lot and becomes LR-113; after 52 miles/84 km turn left and follow signs to the Monasterio de Valvanera.

MONASTERIO DE VALVANERA—La Rioja

This is an enchanting Benedictine monastery set in a remote beech and oak forest. Though founded during the early Romanesque period, the older monastery was destroyed during Napoleon's conquests into Spain and it has been rebuilt in less lyrical style. The mountain setting makes up for this.

La Virgen de Valvanera is a carved oak, twelfth-century statue said to have been carved by a thief doing penance. Jesus sits in a curious twisting position, as if to bless those behind him. Flanking the statue are carved oak trunks. Legend says that Mary's statue was found in an oak tree covered by a swarm of bees (bees we saw at San Juan de Ortega, chapter 7); they represent the unborn souls of children. Bees go back to antiquity as mystical symbols for souls, fertility, and abundance, and Mary is frequently prayed to by people who want to have children.

The Virgin of Valvanera is Rioja's patron saint. The nearby Fuensanta fountain stems from a holy spring said to have healing capabilities. As with so many sacred places, holy springs nearby hint at a pre-Christian sanctity in the same place.

Valvanera to San Millán de la Cogolla (18 miles/29 km):
Backtrack to LR-113 and turn left, going to Bobadilla; at Bobadilla turn left to San Millán de la Cogolla.

SAN MILLÁN DE LA COGOLLA—La Rioja

San Millán was a local boy born in AD 473 in the nearby village of Berceo. He studied under the hermit San Felices in the Riojan town of Haro. He died in AD 574 at the age of 101, and it is said he is interred in his cave in the Suso monastery up on the hill over the village of San Millán, but in truth, people aren't sure where his remains are. It doesn't matter as his tomb in the cave possesses enough mana for all.

San Millán's cult was quite strong in Navarra and Castile and he was often depicted in ways similar to St. James, including as a Moor Slayer on horseback. The way to distinguish him from St. James in this persona is that his slashing sword is wavy, not straight.

San Millán lived as a hermit in a cave deep in the Cárdenas river valley. Word of his miracles spread and he attracted followers, fellow hermits who took to a hermitic existence in neighboring caves. Periodically they would meet to pray together, and their meeting place became the site of the Monasterio de Suso. Eventually, Suso became a community, thus leaving the isolated hermetic ideal for a communal monastic one. As numbers grew, the Suso monastery, perched on a hillside, could no longer house all the brothers. In the sixteenth century, they moved their residence downhill to the new Monasterio de Yuso. Suso and Yuso mean upper and lower in archaic Castilian.

The two monasteries physically represent the allegory of the decline of the hermetic ideal, of a solitary and wild existence dedicated exclusively to God to a group of brothers dedicated to the community and to God.

The sixth- to twelfth-century Monasterio de San Millán de Suso is of pink sandstone built right into the cave wall. This is a unique sacred monument in that it was built over several centuries and contains within its small intimate space Visigothic, Mozarabic, and Romanesque arches and styles, one next to the other in a museumlike logic, though this was their natural execution as a part of each generation extending the monastery to hold the growing numbers of monks. To see the Visigothic horseshoe arch next to the Mozarabic, wider-mouthed horseshoe arch, next to the rounded Romanesque is a treat. Adding to this sweep is a series of caverns enclosed by the sandstone mountain where San Millán, hermits, and later monks meditated. Later these caverns became burial places for royalty. A tomb to San Millán, whose actual remains' whereabouts are uncertain, honors the saint's presence in these sacred spaces.

The Monasterio de San Millán de Yuso was built during the sixteenth and seventeenth centuries with significant eighteenth-century additions. It is a Benedictine Baroque and Neoclassical structure with an attached, but non-monastic, four-star hotel. Briefly abandoned after 1835, it was repopulated by Augustinian brothers in 1878. Today nine Augustinian monks live in Yuso's monastery. The main attraction here is the beauty of the monastery church's steeple against the enchanting river valley. In that church is the alabaster-carved reliquary box of San Millán and of his spiritual teacher, San Felices. These stand next to each other in the church's central nave aisle.

But to truly experience the authentic mystical nature of San Millán, leave the monasteries behind and follow the trail to La Cueva del Santo. Follow the sign to Lugar del Rio and then follow the signposts "Cueva Santa del Santo" with a drawing of a hermit with his staff. These signposts begin at the base of a driveway that leads up to a terrific rural restaurant on the right. The road to its left goes to the cave several kilometers away. The trail mostly follows the little rural road until it nears the mountain of the cave. There it can be climbed only on foot. It leads to one of the original caves deep in the valley where San Millán lived and meditated. It was remote enough as to guarantee his hermitic life.

On this path to the saint's cave you will enter a mythic realm that embodies the original magic of San Millán's life. It is a path where animals and trees look up and remind us that they are our physical and spiritual companions, jolting us out of our arrogance of actually buying into a notion that we are somehow superior to other life on Earth (*this* may really be the great psychic fall from the Garden of Eden).

The forest is filled with vocal, sacred trees, including the Tree of Desires. This beauty throws back her arms and arches her torso with feet rooted firmly in the earth, giving an image of unhindered joy. Her trunk is split open at the middle and people place stones there with their wishes and hopes as they walk by.

Fifth-century hermit San Millán's sacred cave in the Cárdenas river valley

Other companions met on the way are cows, horses, and goats who herd themselves, myriad birds in song and activity, and the occasional mushroom hunter taking a daily ration of fungi home to scramble with eggs for a second breakfast or a late lunch. I recommend the same for you: When you return toward San Millán de Cogolla, take in lunch at the little restaurant up the driveway near where you first found the signpost for this sacred trail. It is connected to a lovely hilltop bed-and-breakfast and is run by a husband and wife whose skill with food, wine, and hospitality equals the saint's with miracles. If you walk the whole way from San Millán de la Cogolla to El Cuevo del Santo, get an early start so that you can be back at the restaurant for a late lunch.

San Millán de la Cogolla to Laguardia (25.5 miles/41 km):
Take LR-205, which joins LR-113, to Nájera; continue on LR-113 through Nájera; follow signs for Laguardia, especially after you pass the town of Cenicero.

LAGUARDIA—Pais Vasco

At one of the medieval stone gates to the town, the Puerta de San Juan, is a tile plaque that reads, *Paz a los que llegan, Salud a los que habitan, Felicidad a los que marchan* (Peace to those who arrive, Health to those who live here, and Happiness to those who depart). This sentiment describes the joy of being in Laguardia, a perfectly preserved medieval wine town whose people are unspoiled by their treasure, preserving it as it was and not allowing artifice and gaudy tourism to overtake it. This is one of Europe's medieval gems, period.

Nowhere else in Spain and perhaps in Europe will you find a stone-carved medieval portal with its polychrome painting still intact. In the church, Iglesia de Santa María de los Reyes, the twelfth- to fifteenth-century Gothic portal was restored and then protected by a seventeenth-century Baroque facade that was built over it, making it an interior space a few meters upon entering the west portal. This protected it from the elements that would have robbed it of its color. It is a unique chance to see what these magnificent portals looked like originally when they had all their color. Unique also are tympanum depictions of the Virgin as pregnant with a bulging natural belly, and another panel of Jesus holding his mother in his left arm as her soul arrived in heaven, reversing the usual depiction of Jesus in Mary's hands or lap. It is a perfect yin-yang, an authentic expression of the sacred energies of mystical Christianity as well as of universal human existence. The mandorla shows Mary in heaven.

Laguardia is an unusual hilltop town with a cavernous, human-made subterranean world below its town streets. These were once underground passageways for escape during times of war. They then were turned into ideal places to make wine. Fragile today, cars, carts, even donkeys, are not allowed in town. There are over 230 caverns. These caverns have the ideal temperature and humidity for wine making, but because the grape harvest must be carried in on people's backs, only two bodegas continue to make wine here today. However, beyond the medieval walls all around the town's hill below are dozens of wineries making traditionally crafted wines in more modern facilities. Laguardia is the heart center of Rioja wine from the Alava region. Rioja has three wine areas: Rioja Alava, Rioja Baja, and Rioja Alta. Each defines a unique soil and climatic area, but all three revolve around the Ebro River. Provincially, Laguardia is in Pais Vasco, but viticulturally it is Riojan.

In this same region there are several stunning dolmen sites to which the excellent tourist office in Laguardia can orient you. Current estimates are that the Alava region has some eighty-five dolmens with seven that are really striking and worth a visit. Dating between four thousand and twenty-five hundred years ago, the dolmens are indications that early agriculturalists in Iberia also saw the potential of Riojan *terroir*. As usual, the dolmens are set in places of exquisite vistas as if to give the deceased buried in them a great eternal view. They are also likely sites of ancient rituals, and so the sacred placement was for the living as well.

The remainder of this route takes you along the stretch of the Camino that crossed the Pyrenees at the Pass of Somport, further east than the more commonly crossed pass at Roncesvalles. Usually people crossing at Somport were coming from roads that passed through, or began at, Arles. All the Pyrenean roads ultimately joined into one at Puente la Reina southwest of Pamplona. For those crossing at Somport, the important places prior to Puente la Reina would have been Jaca, Santa Cruz de la Serós, the Monasterio de San Juan de la Peña, Leyre, and San Miguel de Excelsis. As we are arriving at this road from the western end, we begin at the Monasterio de Leyre and end at Jaca.

Laguardia to Leyre (95 miles/153 km):
Head to Logroño and connect with A-12 toward Pamplona; don't enter Pamplona but skirt SE on the outer highway following signs to A-21; take A-21 to Yesa where you exit; follow signs to the Monasterio de Leyre.

MONASTERIO DE LEYRE—Navarra

In the eleventh century, this was the center of spiritual life in Navarra and like San Juan de la Peña, below, it became the burial place of kings, in this case, Navarrese kings. Its earliest foundations go back to the mid-ninth century. When Navarra and Aragón were briefly united into one kingdom, San Juan de la Peña received more patronage and Leyre's monastery declined. Curiously, in 1954, Benedictine monks from Santo Domingo de Silos came here and repopulated the monastery, reviving not only active monastic life but Gregorian chant, which visitors should be able to hear during certain hours of the day (usually around 7:30 a.m. and 9 a.m., and 7 p.m. and 9 p.m.).

Leyre to Santa Cruz de la Serós (44 miles/71 km):
Return to Yesa and take N-240 E; turn S for Santa Cruz de la Serós.

SANTA CRUZ DE LA SERÓS—Aragón

Both Santa Cruz de la Serós and San Juan de la Peña would have been regular detours for medieval pilgrims passing through Jaca on their way to Santiago. People took their time when going on pilgrimage. The more holy sites visited, the better for one's soul. Today these places are worth visiting for how they uplift the spirit. Shedding their political skin of medieval north-south polemics, they are simply beautiful places to visit, whose lighter spirit remains. Santa Cruz de la Serós preserves two beautiful Romanesque churches, the twelfth-century San Capraiso and the eleventh-century church of Santa María. The latter copied the design of Jaca's Romanesque cathedral but might be even prettier. It has a delicate square tower with layers of double arches that re-create the surrounding mountains' appeal in a human-made medium. This is a place for hiking in good weather, so plan on mixing natural reverence with Romanesque. One way to do so is to walk the four-odd kilometers south to San Juan de la Peña.

MONASTERIO DE SAN JUAN DE LA PEÑA— Aragón

This monastery has two parts, the more recent upper part and the older, Mozarabic lower part. The setting is stunning, in a steep mountain ravine, surrounded by stark, magnificent mountains. It is also important for holding the earliest Aragonese royal consciousness. An isolated chapel in AD 724, here Christian nobles gathered to discuss what they were going to do about the North African invasion south of them. It was a first effort of early Iberian Christians in organizing a resistance to the new invader, and this spot is considered the birthplace of Aragonese "re"-conquest. The event made the beautiful San Juan de la Peña important as well. It was extended into a ninth-century Mozarabic chapel whose frescoes are still visible in the crypt. Ultimately it peaked in the twelfth century as a resting place for Aragón's kings. The twelfth-century Romanesque chapel is one of Spain's medieval masterworks—the apse's chapels are carved out of the rock—and is a delight to visit. Built into and sheltered beneath the overhanging rock shelf, the cloister is semi-outdoors, which adds to its mystique and connectedness to life. The open-air orientation adds to the romantic feel of the natural park that surrounds the monastery.

San Juan de la Peña to Jaca (13 miles/21 km):
Backtrack to N-240; continue E to Jaca.

JACA—Aragón

Originally a Roman fortress built in 195 BC, and briefly occupied by invading Muslims (early eighth to early ninth century), Jaca became an important center for Aragón as it formulated itself into a Christian kingdom. Just thirty kilometers over the border from France, Jaca was also an important stop on the pilgrimage to Santiago de Compostela for those walking the Camino Aragonés. This route crossed the Pyrenees at the Somport Pass, further east than the more popularly known Camino Frances that crosses at Valcarlos Pass to Roncesvalles. In AD 1035 Jaca became the capital of the kingdom of Aragón. Its cathedral was built during this time and is considered Spain's oldest standing cathedral. It is also a splendid example of the early Romanesque style.

CHAPTER FOURTEEN

·················· ❋ ··················

*M*adrid to Guadalupe

The bellota [Holm oak acorn] is very important to Extremadura's economy because the iberico and bellota pigs eat it. And Guadalupe is our Virgin, our Patroness, She looks after us. The nut and the Virgin go together. She assures the abundance and health of the nut and the pig. It all comes from the nut.

—A shopkeeper in Mérida

ALTHOUGH MYSTICS OF SPAIN'S MANY FAITHS exist all across the country, this area captures some of the most famous and influential mystics, such as St. Teresa of Ávila, San Juan de la Cruz, Rabbi Moses de León, and Fray Luis de León, whose spiritual paths forged centuries ago still burn with immediate relevance to the modern seeker.

This is a medieval multifaith and mystics' route. In the heartland of western Castilla y León we first explore the wide expansive landscapes that offered to Spanish mystics what the desert or cave offered their equals in the Middle East. From Madrid, Segovia, and Salamanca we go deeper into western Spain, an area little explored by modern travelers but that heavily influenced the currents of the Middle Ages and the Classical world, traveling from La Alberca's still-persisting sixteenth-century tradition of calling to the souls of the deceased using bell ringers; to the wild and monastic area around Plasencia; to Cáceres, a major stronghold of medieval *convivencia*; to Mérida, one of Spain's two most spectacular Roman settlements with its fabled temple to Diana; and then onward to Guadalupe, the original home of the Virgin who inspired hundreds of sacred shrines throughout the world.

Finally, this western edge of Spain is famous for its high-quality cured hams with their nutty wild flavor, for its Virgins with oak leaves, and for its *bellota* nuts. A most endearing expression of this is a popular keychain for sale at tourist shops in the region, with an acorn that unscrews to reveal the Lady of Guadalupe inside, standing upside down on the nut's cap. It is something of a transportable altar in your pocket for anytime you wish to appeal to the Virgin. When I bought my Virgin nut keychain in Mérida, I asked the shopkeeper why the Virgin was inside the nut. He graciously answered (above) but looked at me as if I were profoundly ignorant, as everyone in Extremadura understood the connection. It made total sense once I got the logic.

Main Route (507.5 miles/817 km):
Madrid—Segovia—Ávila—Salamanca—La Alberca—Plasencia—
Cucao de Yuste—Monasterio de San Jerónimo de Yuste—
Cáceres—Mérida—Guadalupe

MADRID—Castilla y León

Madrid by comparison to many towns is young. Its origins stem to the Muslim invasion and settlement of the Peninsula, when Madrid was made a fortress town to defend the south from incursions from the north. The settlement remained Muslim from the eighth to the late eleventh century. In 1083 King Alfonso VI of Castile and León conquered Madrid and two years later took Toledo.

Called Majerit (also Mayrit, Magrit, and Magerit) by Muslims, very few of Madrid's oldest stones still retain their Moorish character. Those that do are best seen on the Plaza de la Villa just off of Calle Mayor. The building that now houses the library for the Royal Academy of Ethical and Political Sciences possesses a terrific horseshoe-arch entrance door from Islamic Madrid. The library is not open to the public but the door is right there on the plaza for all to see at any time.

In 1561 Phillip II decided to move the Spanish capital from Toledo to Madrid. He wanted a clean canvas on which to put his own distinctive mark. That mark was grandiose but one of a gloomy and pinched spirituality. Phillip II's Madrid comes hard to recommend on spiritual merit. The same holds true for his famous Escorial, which is quite impressive as far as power and wealth go, but as a spiritual center it leaves me chilled to the bone. You will pass by the Escorial on your way to Segovia. If you desire to stop, I can recommend the library, which is rich with allegorical paintings on the walls and ceiling and houses an impressive collection of manuscripts.

Spiritual gems of Madrid in my experience stem largely from the medieval city but also include a few exceptional later temples that are spiritually stunning and that reflect the joyous colorful place Madrid became after Phillip II's gray gloom lifted. He died in 1598. His son, Phillip III, wasn't much better, carrying on his father's policies, including the massively disastrous expulsion of the Conversos and Moriscos. These were originally Jewish and Muslim families who 120 years before had been forced to convert to Catholicism and who now were deemed a threat to the internal stability of Spain (see chapter 1). It was in fact a problem that the Catholic monarchs created for themselves; Phillip's solution was as brutal and immoral as the original forced conversions during and after 1492.

Madrid is considered to be the precise center of Spain. If you stand at the **Puerta del Sol,** Gateway of the Sun, you will be at the geographical center of the Peninsula. (Bear in mind that this statement might annoy the Portuguese who became an independent kingdom by the mid-twelfth century.) The city's as well as the nation's heart center, the Puerta del Sol is the source of many streets that radiate out from it, like the sun's rays. Here we have a not-so-hidden pagan reality: many cities in Spain have been built on a sun pattern, an ancient acknowledgment of the cult of the sun, from Iberian, Celtic, and Roman times. Plasencia in Extremadura also has a Puerta del Sol, a gateway in the heart of the city that leads to the Plaza Mayor. Other cities, whether they have a Puerta del Sol or not, are still designed on this organic, circular plan, something you will see best when you are flying in or out of Spain and passing over the clusters of cities, towns, and villages below.

Madrid possesses many treasures from all over Spain. The greatest, I think, is the original Dama de Elche from the Alicante region (see chapter 11), that famous Iberian matriarch's bust who now holds center stage at Madrid's Museo Arqueológico Nacional.

Madrid is also the center of modern *convivencia.* The city is dramatically diverse with immigrants from all over Latin America, sub-Saharan Africa, North Africa, East Asia, South Asia, and the Middle East, as well as other parts of Europe, including a growing Romanian community. Madrid is home to one of the largest Jewish communities in Spain, with an active outreach and worship center. Europe's largest mosque was inaugurated here in 1992 with King Juan Carlos I and the Saudi Prince Salman ben Abdelaziz attending. A large Buddhist community also worships in this central Castilian city, and the opportunity to find one's own particular expression of spirituality is limited only by one's own imagination or spiritual practice.

Medieval Madrid

This neighborhood is mostly in the area around the Plaza Mayor, especially to the west and south of it. It is worth walking around and wandering into the churches that are open for Mass. Some are open throughout the day, allowing neighbors to come and go for private prayer. The churches of **San Nicolas** and **San Pedro el Viejo** have Islamic-style bell towers that are so pretty that nearby churches of later eras copied them and have neo-Mudéjar towers as well. San Nicolas was built over one of the mosques of Muslim Madrid. Dating to the twelfth century, it is the oldest surviving church in the city. San Pedro is especially inviting as a sacred space. It was also built over a neighborhood mosque. Other churches in the vicinity worth visiting if you have more time are **San Miguel, San Andrés,** and **San Francisco el Grande.**

The cathedral, **Catedral de Nuestra Señora de la Almudena,** is built over one of the city's mosques and is dedicated to the Virgin of the Granary. *Almudín* is an Arabized word for granary. When Alfonso VI entered the conquered Madrid, it is fabled that he found an image of the Virgin by or in one of the city's almudíns. As in other places all across Spain, the Christian conquest is curiously accompanied with dozens of stories of the Virgin's image appearing right before, during, or just after a Christian king conquered Muslim territory, giving sanctity to the act.

Maslama of Madrid

Maslama al-Madjriti was a renowned and celebrated astronomer under the patronage of Cordoban Caliph Hakem II. Hailing from Madrid, where he was born in AD 950, he advanced the science of astronomy, for example, by creating a guide for the construction and use of an astrolabe. In the Middle Ages astronomy was closely allied with astrology, both being viewed as precise sciences, and Maslama the Madrileño was also a gifted astrologer. He was possibly the astrologer for the Caliphate's kings, and some believe he predicted the chaos that broke out in the early 1000s. He died in 1007. By 1010, revolts, looting, and warring clans took a few years to completely destroy the Cordoban Caliphate, ushering in the *taifa* period.

A fun holdover of this cousin-connection between astronomy and astrology is the annually published *Calendario Zaragozano*, something of a

Spanish Farmer's Almanac, which uses astronomical information about the planets and stars to predict the year's weather conditions for planting and harvest guidance. It also lists the markets and festival days of towns across Spain. It is published in Madrid and is for sale in bookstores (*librerías*) all across the country.

Ermita de San Antonio de la Florida

If pressed to pick one place in all of Madrid with the greatest sacred panache, I would say this is it. Fairly modern, the hermitage of San Antonio de la Florida was built in 1798. From foot to ceiling are frescoes painted by Francisco de Goya (1746–1828). The theme on the dome is St. Anthony of Padua's miracle where, before a large crowd, he raised a young man from death so that he could testify to his father's innocence, as his father had been unjustly accused of murdering him. The fresco's crowd is true to Goya's style and is filled with people of Madrid and of the countryside of his time. Angels and mortals alike are dressed in period costume and possess the most animated faces, glances, and body language. I confess, the little boy climbing over the railing, paying no attention to the miraculous unfolding around him—or rather, pursuing his own miracles—is especially endearing. The overall chapel is on a Greek cross plan and more round than square, making for a space that easily invites in and embraces the visitor.

This chapel tends to get fewer visitors than the other temples and museums, but it is well worth the trip to the neighborhood just north of and slightly behind and downhill from the royal palace.

Temple to Isis and Amun

While you are on this side of the royal palace, there is the gift given to Spain by the Egyptian government in 1968. Called the **Templo de Debod,** it stands in the center of the neighborhood park above the Príncipe Pío train station. It was dedicated to Isis, nature and fertility goddess, and Amun, the fertility god of Thebes who became the Egyptian supreme god associated with the sun. Around twenty-four hundred years old, the Debod Temple was a thank-you gift when Spain helped Egypt rescue the temples of Abu Simbel in Nubia at the time of the building of the Aswan Dam. The dam ultimately flooded the area where these antiquities stood. Stone by stone, the temple was delivered from Upper Egypt and rebuilt in Madrid.

The Egyptian Temple of Debod in Madrid, Castilla y León

Museo Arqueológico Nacional

A visit to the national archaeology museum in Madrid is critical in understanding sacred Spain. In one building rests a remarkable collection of sacred art and centuries of diverse belief systems, deities, and ritual objects. The real Dama de Elche is among them, along with many other Iberian sacred works, Roman and Greek objects, some of the most stunning Visigothic and Islamic items, and beautiful examples of the different Christian eras. The Celtic and Celtiberian collection is also remarkable and will surprise people who did not realize the strong Celtic influence in Iberia. Lastly, outside and underground is a small replica of a portion of Altamira. Though not the same as the real thing, it is a nice primer and a fun adventure as other subterranean options in Madrid are pretty much limited to the metro (a highly recommended way to get around efficiently and economically).

Cybele and Neptune

These two pagan gods hold court in Madrid and are beloved by the locals. Each holds its own vortex within a fountain along the Paseo del Prado. Neptune rides on the back of a great horse at the officially named Plaza de Canovas del Castillo, though everyone just calls it Plaza de Neptuno. An ancient Minoan, then Roman, god of the sea, he also ruled the Earth and horses. Sometimes he was the male balance to the Earth Mother. Just north of him, Cybele, the Great Mother goddess, is drawn by two lions in her chariot at the Plaza de la Cibeles. Together Neptune and Cybele seem to create the yin-yang of Madrid.

Madrid to Segovia (60 miles/96 km):
Leave Madrid on A-6 NW; continue on A-6/AP-6; exit onto AP-61 to Segovia.

SEGOVIA—Castilla y León

Passing over the Sierra de Guadarrama north of Madrid, you go through a hikers' and bikers' oasis, not to mention a beautiful mountain range still alive with wild plants and animals. I have seen majestic elk along this stretch, sometimes not far from half-domesticated black bulls with their sharp curved horns.

Segovia is on the other side of this great mountain range. It stands on the ideal spot for Celtic settlers looking for a hilltop near a river. In Segovia's case, it stands at the confluence of two rivers, the Eresma and the Clamores. It was called Segobriga, *briga* coming from the Celtic deity *Briga,* or *Brigit.* In circa 80 BCE Romans took over, as they did in so many Celtic and Celtiberian settlements.

Although most people come to Segovia to see its remarkable Roman aqueduct or its Walt Disney–inspiring castle, the Alcázar, few recognize that Segovia is also a collection of remarkable medieval temples, especially of the Romanesque. Made of warm golden stone, these churches maintain appealing arched porches, lively carved capitals with animated characters, Islamic-style bell towers, and a scale and harmony that later sacred building had a hard time replicating.

Among these treasures are the Romanesque churches of **San Millán, San Clemente, San Martín, San Miguel, San Esteban,** and **San Andrés.** These are all within easy walking distance of one another in the medieval quarter. While I think all are worthy of a visit, San Millán might be the most enchanting, followed by San Martín. In addition to the multiple mythic and biblical characters carved on San Millán's outer capitals, there is magic inside in the saturated colors of stained-glass windows against that deep golden stone, some of the stone still bearing faded medieval frescoes on the walls.

Segovia's Gothic cathedral has a cloister with green spaces and bird-song that makes it the most interesting part of the structure. Therein stands a small shrine to one side dedicated to the Virgin; it pulls the visitor in and offers a peace and contemplation not possible in the grander corridors of the cathedral.

There is a terrific educational center on Jewish Segovia just to the southwest corner of the cathedral. Next to this, the **Corpus Christi** church was once the neighborhood's synagogue.

North of the Alcázar castle at the north tip of medieval Segovia and beyond the great old walls stand two of the city's most mystical places. The river footpath that passes through the minivillage of San Marcos is an enchanting way to get there from the old city. The first mystical spot is the **Iglesia de la Vera Cruz** built in the thirteenth century by the Knights of Malta. It is a wonderful twelve-sided round church with a square Moorish tower. Its structure was plausibly inspired by both the Church of the Holy Sepulcher and the Mosque of the Rock, both near each other in Jerusalem and within the circuit of holy sites for the Knights of Malta and the Knights Templar. *Vera Cruz* means that once the church held a piece of the True Cross. This *lignum crucis* is now held in the church in the nearby village of Zamarramala.

When I arrived at the Vera Cruz church, four young Wiccan women whom I had seen gathering herbs and flowers on my way there were engaged in a ritual in the temple's lower circular level. They stood in the very center of the circle, backs against one another, facing the four directions, arms upheld with herbs and flowers in their hands. The temple caretaker didn't flinch. In the other round prayer niche right above them on the second level, an elderly man sat in deep, trancelike prayer. That second level is where it is said the Knights of Malta vigilantly watched over the *lignum crucis*. All around the round room with benches against the wall, Maltese crosses decorate the space. The temple itself is free of a lot of noisy décor and relies on the stones and the round space to convey the divine, which it aptly does.

The Catholic man and the Wiccans later learned about the others' presence and cheerfully gave one another the utmost respect. Queen Isabel, who in 1474 was crowned queen of Castile up the hill in St. Martin's church, can turn in her grave as much as she likes—this is the new face of Spain, a brighter, more interesting, and broad-minded one at that.

The second mystical place here is the **Convento de San Juan de la Cruz,** the Discalced (reformed) Carmelite convent where St. John of the Cross is entombed. It is just a little further along and down the hill from the Vera Cruz. The convent church is open to visitors and has a very modern altar with terrific cosmic designs of a blue, swirling universe and a great source of light coming down to Earth. The most important chapel here is St. John of the Cross's tomb. It has one of the most spectacular Mudéjar ceilings, sheltering an equally Mudéjar-looking tomb. St. John, whose mysticism was in universal step with that of the Islamic and Jewish mystics, wouldn't have minded one iota. This building was founded in 1586. On December 14, 1591, St. John died in Ubeda, in the south of Spain, and two years later his body was brought here.

St. John of the Cross (1542–1591)

Born into a Toledano family of nobility but no money, Juan de Yepes, St. John of the Cross's birth name, went to school in Medina del Campo and was raised by his widowed mother. When he apprenticed with a silk weaver, they found he had no aptitude for the trade and so he went on to study at a Jesuit college. In 1563 St. John joined the Carmelite order and studied for four years in Salamanca before being ordained a priest in 1567.

It was around this time that through St. Teresa of Ávila's influence he joined her reform movement of the Carmelite order. In 1571 he also became the confessor for the nuns in Ávila at St. Teresa's resident convent. In 1575 St. John was imprisoned by the Calced (unreformed) Carmelite friars who refused his reform and perceived him as a threat. They held him in a substandard prison in Toledo. After nine months, St. John escaped his prison. By then the Calced Carmelites had separated from the Discalced, the reformed branch of which St. John continued to be a member. The rest of his life was a mix of leadership, magnificent poetry, and contending with petty politics from jealous order members. In spite of the persistent narrow-minded religious politics of his time, St. John treated people with dignity and spiritual generosity. He was deeply respected by St. Teresa and beloved and admired by his students. He wrote passionate, feeling poetry that warms the heart and soul. It is the sort of poetry borne of someone who has suffered but risen above his suffering and transmuted it into spiritual gold.

His experience and poetry taught that through faith and deep love for God we are able to overcome and clear the earthly onslaught—karma, if you will—that we accrue while incarnated. Through faith and love, we arrive at union with God, a union so ecstatic that anything inauthentic falls away. Like the mystics of any faith, St. John's veneration has exceeded the boundaries of his order and of the Catholic Church and has given joy and comfort to people of all faiths. Like St. Teresa, he was a great spiritual master, of the universal kind (as they all are).

Among St. John's many works, his best known are *The Spiritual Canticle*, *The Dark Night of the Soul*, *The Living Flame of Love*, and *Ascent to Mount Carmel*. In these we receive a timeless guide, or map, really, of the soul's journey toward the divine. St. John's work uses the strongest human feeling, love and passion, to express longing for God. For St. John, God was El Amante, the Beloved. Indeed, his poetry sometimes sounds like certain Islamic mystical poets, such as Hafez, Sa'adi, and Rumi. They too wrote ecstatic love poetry where God was the Friend, the one longed for like a lover separated from his beloved, the reed cut from the reed bed. Either they could have influenced St. John via Jewish and Islamic arts and scholarship in Spain up until the century before St. John's time, or spiritual truths simply have a way of cycling around again and again.

Segovia to Ávila (53.5 miles/86 km):
Leave Segovia SW on N-110 to Ávila.

ÁVILA—Castilla y León

Approaching the city from a distance is stunning with its solid and complete medieval wall conjuring up all the fairy tales of princes and princesses, dragons and witches, magical helpers and creatures. The great walls were constructed in the eleventh century over Roman foundations. The wall has nine entry gates to the city within. This alone stands as a testimony to the frontier reality of this town, which sat in the middle of medieval north-south skirmishes for power, booty, and divine hegemony.

But Ávila's true heritage lies in the potent magic of the mystics who gained fame here, St. Teresa of Ávila (1515–1582) and St. John of the Cross. Both were of the sixteenth century and of the Carmelite order, and both reformed their order. Both were also inheritors of centuries of mystical lineage in Spain from the three Abrahamic faiths that cross-influenced one another and may have taken the mystical expression deeper in each because of the others' influences. But these two mystics were also among those rare souls who come along every few centuries, true mystics with miraculous gifts and authentically divine visions.

Prior to its Roman or Christian presence, Ávila was in the heartland of the Vettones, the ancient Iron Age, most likely Celtic-speaking, inhabitants of this western reach of today's Spain. Throughout the area you can still glimpse sculptures of boars and bulls, survivors of the Vettones' cosmos, reflecting a strong veneration of both animals. The most dramatic of these called Los Toros de Guisando, the Bulls of Guisando, can be found

The Basilica of San Vicente in Ávila, Castilla y León

near the town of El Tiemblo. These stone animals date from around the fourth to the first century BCE. They tower well above shoulder height.

The Vettones, like so many Iron Age peoples, built on high hilltops for defensive purposes. They also placed altars to the divine there. Today's best-surviving example of this is the shrine at Ulaca (near today's town of Solosancho, twenty-two kilometers southwest of Ávila). It has a double staircase carved out of stone that leads up to a sacrificial platform for making offerings to the gods. It dates from the third to the second century BCE, and the altar looks south to the Paramera mountains, perhaps pointing at some sacred significance in those mountains. When Romans conquered the Vettones, they relocated them from their hilltop defenses to the easier to control flatlands. This is how Ávila came into being. The Vettones of Ulaca were relocated to the plains of Ávila, called Obila in a reference from Ptolemy.

Centuries later, on the frontier between medieval Christian and Muslim Iberia, Ávila oscillated between Muslim and Christian control. In 1085 when Alfonso the VI took Toledo, Ávila's fate as a Christian city was sealed. Saint Teresa's time really marks Ávila's spiritual golden age. That her mysticism is part and parcel to the mystical experiences of all the Abrahamic peoples makes it all the more worth celebrating. What is stunning today is that St. Teresa is still woven into the life and fabric of the town, the very air and earth. It is hard to explain, for there is no blatant touristy commercialism around her and people are low-key about it. It is more an energy field, if you will, that holds sway over the town, as if St. Teresa and St. John are still there. I invite you to record your dreams while you are here, keeping your journal near your bedside, just to see what might happen.

Up until 1492 and the depraved policies executed then, Ávila had a vibrant Jewish community. Upon their expulsion, the city declined significantly, only to be elevated by the grace of St. Teresa and St. John. During its Jewish presence, Ávila was briefly home to the author of the *Zohar*.

Moses de León and the *Zohar*

Rabbi Moses ben Shem Tob de León was influential and active in several Castilian cities and towns, such as Guadalajara and Ávila. Many have posited that Ávila's mystical strands derive from the interwoven influences of Ibn 'Arabi's Sufism (mystical Islam), Moses de León's Kabbalah (mystical Judaism), and St. Teresa's and St. John's Christian mysticism of the sixteenth century. The devotees to their own faith and spirit created a back-and-forth dialogue with other mystics in other times, a dialogue that continues into our own generations.

Between 1280 and 1286, Moses de León is said to have written *Sefer ha-Zohar, The Book of Splendor,* most popularly known as the *Zohar,* the text of Kabbalah as it developed in his times in Spain. Some Jewish scholars and practitioners believe that the *Zohar* originates much earlier in time, right after the second destruction of the Temple in Jerusalem in AD 70, and that Moses de León rediscovered it and interpreted it for his times. Others believe that he is the original author and that he penned an original treatise on mystical Judaism for his generation and those to follow. There is really no contradiction in these two positions. An established formal practice of Jewish, Islamic, and Christian scholarship of the Middle Ages and before was to first study and record all the knowledge and wisdom that had gone before oneself—the "chain of transmission" as it is called in Islamic scholarship—and then to add one's own knowledge and interpretation to that chain. It is very likely that Moses de León did such a thing.

Moses de León was a critic of the moral laxness of his generation, and his writing may in part have been to address this, to offer a more noble path for human conduct and behavior. The *Zohar* is a complex text, more like a manual of study for followers of Kabbalah to systematically attain experience and knowledge through the insightful use of their senses to ascertain the divine.

The Jewish influence in Castilla y León, as well as in other parts of Spain, goes deep; many families had a Jewish ancestry in spite of the Inquisition's effort to eradicate pagan, Jewish, and Islamic lineages. Two of Spain's greatest Catholic mystics, St. John of the Cross and St. Teresa, had Converso ancestors. St. Teresa of Ávila's grandfather on her father's side was a Converso and he had been condemned by the Inquisition for back-sliding to Judaic practices. This may be one good reason why St. Teresa's parents were particularly careful to do everything to assure their Catholic standing. Their aristocratic status was not enough to protect them. Curiously, both St. Teresa and St. John demonstrate a mysticism that would be familiar to any faith's mystical experience. They came upon a universal truth, one beyond the confines of one faith as the path to God. They both showed that it was practice and devotion, not blind belief, that led one to the divine.

Saint Teresa's Ávila

Born here and active here as a mystic, spiritual leader, and reformer, St. Teresa is everywhere you go in Ávila. She was a remarkable woman with remarkable experiences that have expanded our idea of what it is to be a spiritual being. As you explore Ávila's sacred landscape, it is likely that you will feel as if she is still here, weaving her grace into the lives, land, and dreams of all who live here and who visit here.

Saint Teresa was born into a well-to-do Ávileño family in 1515. Her mother died when she was fourteen and her father sent her to the Convento de Gracia to be educated by Augustinian nuns. Shortly thereafter she became very ill and while convalescing she decided to become a nun. At first her father resisted her decision but she eventually entered the Carmelite order at age twenty at the Monasterio de la Encarnación. Shortly after she began her life there, she again fell ill, an experience that deepened her desire to achieve greater union with God and to let her suffering be her pathway to deeper spiritual practice. Over the years of applying dedicated prayer, St. Teresa not only deepened her devotion but also experienced greater mystical experiences. Initially these occasions created a critical reaction, but eventually others realized that something real and divine, not demonic, was taking place in the monastery. It was during this time that St. Teresa became a prolific writer, her mystical works in the form of letters, most particularly to St. John, as well as book-length treatises on the mystical life. She is often depicted with a book and a quill.

Saint Teresa began to promote her ideas for a reform of the Carmelite order, one that would return it to a more austere and dedicated practice of prayer and contemplation. Saint Teresa's reforms concerned returning to earlier monastic ideals, particularly, the vows of poverty and the total devotion to God through prayer. Prayer was the most important service the reformed nuns performed for humankind. Her writings further delved into what the soul gains through dedicated meditation practice. Austere as her reforms were, she had numerous mystical experiences that were testimony to the profundity of her chosen way. She is said to have levitated many times while in prayer as her meditative state went so deep. The other nuns at times had to hold on to her to keep her grounded.

The name *Discalced* comes from *descalzos*, meaning "barefoot" or "destitute." As such, the reformed Carmelites became known as Descalzos as opposed to the older and "softer" order, the Calced or calzado (shod). Barefootedness is a perfect symbol for and a reality of the greater self-discipline and denial of bodily comforts associated with the reformed order. Though some images of St. Teresa show her barefoot, the order did wear simple footwear; the name of the reformed order has more to do with the austerity of its spiritual practices than with actual dress.

In Ávila there are in particular five places to visit to imbibe the Teresan legacy and energy. These are the following, in an order to follow one after the other:

The **Convento de Santa Teresa** was once her birthplace. In 1636 this convent was founded and built on where St. Teresa's childhood home once stood. A side room in the convent church takes you to the room where she was born. Nearby here, a terrific replica of St. Teresa's distinctive handwriting hangs on the wall. Her script looks like a flock of birds about to take flight.

The **Iglesia de San Juan el Bautista** is where St. Teresa was baptized and where the original baptismal font still stands.

The **Monasterio de la Encarnación,** where for three decades she lived, was the epicenter of her reforms. Saint Teresa was the prioress of this convent and it was here that St. John would come to hear the nuns' confessions. In 1630, several decades after her death in 1582, St. Teresa's cell was converted into a chapel. Much of St. Teresa's writing took place here. Her most famous works are *The Interior Castle*, *The Way of Perfection*, and her autobiography. *The Interior Castle* is her most developed work on prayer and the contemplative life.

This is still an active convent. I found it to be a place where St. Teresa's presence was especially palpable. It feels woven into the air, water, and earth of Ávila and is omnipresent. Locals also come here to buy eggs from the nuns. Those have got to be delicious eggs.

Next is the **Convento de San José,** which was St. Teresa's first convent founded under the Discalced Carmelite Order.

Last is the **Convento de Gracia,** where she studied as a girl.

Other delights in the city are the cathedral and the Basilica of San Vicente. Ávila's cathedral dates to the twelfth century and has an interior of wonderful red and white stone pillars and equally uplifting cloisters, in spite of the heavier exterior, which was as much for defense as for prayer. This heavy building of churches as fortresses is something you will find throughout Castilla y León and Extremadura, as well as Navarra and Rioja.

The most beautiful church in Ávila is the **Basilica of San Vicente,** an eleventh-century Romanesque-transition-to-Gothic church dedicated to St. Vincent of Zaragoza and his two sisters, Sabina and Cristeta, who were martyred by Romans in the fourth century. Some believe their remains are here. The garden in front of the basilica is also named after San Vicente and was once a Roman burial ground. To learn more about St. Vincent, see Valencia in chapter 11.

At the church, **Iglesia de Santo Tomé el Viejo,** sacred old and new wed, with a pagan stone bull carved by the Vettones placed in the thirteenth-century Romanesque church's entranceway.

Centro Internacional de Estudios Místicos

If you wonder where Ávileños stand in relation to their illustrious multifaith mystical past, consider the mayor's founding of the International Center for Mystical Studies as an indication of their delight in this heritage. Miguel Ángel García Nieto founded CIEM in 1990 as a part of the city of Ávila's desire to honor its profound mystical history. The center offers rich courses and events that explore mystical Islam, Hinduism, Judaism, Christianity, Buddhism, comparative mysticism, music and spirituality, and women mystics, among other relevant themes (💻 www.info-3.com/ciem/html).

Ávila to Salamanca (60 miles/97 km):
Leave Ávila NW on N-50; connect to N-501 for Salamanca.

SALAMANCA—Castilla y León

In Salamanca, a university town from the early thirteenth century right up to the present and with great pride in this fact, the life of the mind is the most palpable aroma in the air. Before the medieval intellectual golden age, Salamanca's roots went far back to an Iberian settlement that in 220 BCE was raided by the Carthaginian military leader Hannibal. After Romans conquered the Carthaginians and expanded their hold over Iberia, Salamanca was an important post for transporting metal ore from Asturias to the south of the Peninsula. Called the Ruta de la Plata, the Silver Road, this later became the name of the pilgrim's route from Seville via Salamanca to Santiago de Compostela.

Always on a frontier and a crossroads, this lively Castilian town still has a reserved feel that says an invader might arrive on the horizon at any moment. Such frontiers can also allow in a new life for the spirit, as best exemplified by the sixteenth-century mystic Fray Luis de León who lived and taught here.

Fray Luis de León

Fray Luis de León (1527–1591) was a brilliant religious scholar, Augustinian friar, and Christian mystic who lived during the sixteenth century. Like his contemporary, St. John of the Cross, his more mystical lean made him vulnerable to the Inquisition. The Inquisition did imprison him for a number of years. His "crime" was that he had translated the Song of Solomon into vernacular Castilian, and his interpretation of the Vulgate Bible as a Hebrew and biblical scholar was not in keeping with the convention of the church at the time.

De León taught Aramaic, Hebrew, and exegesis at the University of Salamanca, and when he was released from prison he returned to teaching without missing a beat or altering his ways. Like St. Teresa and St. John of the Cross, he was also from a converso family. It seems to be a pattern that people who grew up on the margins of the mainstream—bicultural folks, if you will—tended to see more of the subconscious workings of a society because their mixed background gave them more than one model of reality to work with. These often were the very same folks who made daring contributions to the society at large, often of a positive nature that could uplift the whole society if not devoured by the jealousy of those colleagues less experienced or visionary. De León's lyrical verse is exquisite and he is one of the most celebrated Spanish poets and mystics. Curiously, though de León was fifteen years St. John's senior, they both died in the same year.

Old and New Cathedrals

I find Salamanca's twelfth-century Romanesque old cathedral, the Catedral Vieja, to be warm and welcoming and the adjoining sixteenth-century late-Gothic and Renaissance new cathedral, Catedral Nueva, to be sterile by comparison. The new cathedral is too impressed with itself in all its Baroque and Plateresque efforts. Its scale certainly is impressive and worth experiencing, and there are fun engravings in the new cathedral's facade, a kaleidoscope worth contemplating to see how much you can see. Side by side, these two cathedrals serve as perfect metaphors for the times that created each.

The Catedral Vieja's altar has some fifty-three panels depicting scenes from Jesus and Mary's lives allowing the many nonreaders of the Middle Ages to see the stories they could not read on a daily basis. This altar was only recently uncovered when restorers were cleaning it and found the scenes underneath.

The old cathedral was built during Salamanca's golden age of the twelfth and thirteenth centuries and its grace reflects this. The early modern era to follow was more conservative politically and religiously and the city suffered, its university falling into a backwater after having been one of Europe's finest. Due to this history, medieval works in Salamanca seem more soulful. The most interesting in my opinion is St. Mark's church, the **Iglesia de San Marcos**.

Round churches seem more empowered by their shape (representing celestial spheres and infinite space) than rectangular ones (Earth-bound and finite), and San Marcos is no exception. Polychrome paintings survive on the wall in this Romanesque beauty. Two powerful Virgin Marys hold court, one to the left of the main altar and the other in back, a statue of the Black Madonna. Round Romanesque churches are also rare, so this is a treat to experience.

Salamanca to La Alberca (49 miles/79 km):
Take CL-512 SW, which becomes SA-210; shortly after passing Tamames, take SA-201 S into the Peña de Francia mountains toward El Cabaco and onward to La Alberca.

LA ALBERCA—Castilla y León

While this whole route traverses sacred pig territory, from the great big boars carved in stone by Iron Age peoples to the worship of the Virgin with the *bellota* nut eaten by native pigs destined for slaughter and tabletop delicacies, here in La Alberca we are in sacred-pig central.

In mid-June one pig is selected to become St. Anthony's pig and is released into the streets of La Alberca, where villagers must treat it as a sacred guest, looking after its needs and comfort and giving it endearing words and pats. Half a year later in mid-January a lottery is drawn and the sacred pig goes home with the winner, who is expected to slaughter it and turn it into sublime sausages. In medieval La Alberca when this tradition started, the pig was given to the poorest family in the village. Today the lottery proceeds go toward the church's community works. St. Anthony is often shown with a pig, as he is the miracle worker who gave sight to a blind mother pig and her little blind piglets.

This lovely medieval village, with its unique timber and stone houses, stands in a heart center of old, mostly abandoned hermitages as well as nearby caves and rock carvings. The village has other fascinating and unique traditions including the sacrifice of the sacred pig. The most interesting of all is the bell ringing and prayers for the souls of the deceased.

Several women in the village inherit the role of *moza de animas*, literally, "girl of the souls." Since the middle of the sixteenth century, women in La Alberca have taken on the sacred duty of calling out prayers for the deceased, using their large cast-iron bells to announce themselves at each corner of the village and then to offer a prayer before moving on to the next corner of the village and repeating the grace: three rings of the bell and a prayer to the dead. The bell and prayers are meant for God and the ears of the dead, to help them on their way. This happens every day at nightfall and takes around thirty to forty-five minutes to complete. This tradition has persisted intact, generation after generation, with local women passing on the tradition to daughters and nieces, who since the sixteenth century have not missed a sunset.

Santuario de Nuestra Señora de la Peña de Francia

Just north of La Alberca, perched on La Peña de Francia peak, is a sanctuary that venerates another Black Madonna, this one found in the mid-fifteenth century with images of Jesus, St. James, and St. Andrew. After the images were unearthed, people built a monastery at the discovery site and placed Mary at the center of worship, which you will find at the Capilla de la Blanca. The current statue of the Black Madonna of La Peña de Francia is a replica of the older one, which was damaged in the nineteenth century.

Las Batuecas

Just south of La Alberca on the road toward the village of Las Mestas in a wild, beautiful mountain river valley, sits the Monasterio San José del Monte de las Batuecas. It gets its name from the Batuecas River nearby and was founded in 1599 by an Andalusian monk, Tomas de Jesús, for its inspiring natural setting. Today the monastery offers lodging to male visitors on spiritual retreat. The most famous story of a monk from this monastery reflects its back-to-nature inspiration. His name was José María del Monte and he was a soldier who renounced the world and became a monk here. His chosen meditation retreat was in the hollow of a great old tree in the valley.

Detour to Béjar and Hervás: The journey toward Plasencia from La Alberca takes you into some of Extremadura's prettiest wild landscapes and through villages forgotten by time and by the Inquisition so that old ways could persist under the radar. The road passes through rocky flat hills and gold colors to ancient olive trees as far as the eye can see and then through the rise of the Sierra de Gredos on the left and the Sierra de la Peña de Francia on the right. This channel was the ancient land of the seminomads, some who still take their animals across these mountains from summer to winter pastures and vice versa. Their culture is very much alive and well—Plasencia sometimes feels like a medieval cowboy town where meat is central to the menu and animal husbandry a revered way of life. Hervás is a lovely little village with a well-preserved Jewish quarter set in narrow streets and with snow-capped peaks as backdrop. Béjar likewise retains its medieval character.

La Alberca to Plasencia (61 miles/98 km):
Go E toward Mogarraz; take SA-220 to Béjar; at Béjar head S on N-630/E-803 to Plasencia. Signs for Hérvas appear on this road; follow them if you wish to take the detour.

PLASENCIA—Extremadura

Tuesday morning is market day in Plasencia. It has been so since the Middle Ages and is held in the same place as then, on the Plaza Mayor. Plasencia is an interesting town. It was founded in 1186 by Alfonso VIII of Castile. It is a purely medieval town with heavily built churches that served as fortresses as much as temples.

Plasencia has two cathedrals, built side by side and sharing a wall. As in Salamanca, one is called the old cathedral and the other the new. The old cathedral has very pagan iconography carved in its west portal. Green Men especially dominate. Inside the new cathedral you will find Extremadura's patroness, the Lady of Guadalupe, holding court.

Both cathedrals and the city at large are full of medieval mythic symbols if you are willing to look above, around, below, and at nooks and crannies in passageways, doorways, and window frames. Dragons and other fantastical beasts, Green Men, sun and moon symbols, breast-feeding pigs, and sacred oaks are among the mythic characters that populate Plasencia. And of course, there are the very real and revered storks who nest on the many church towers. Everywhere in Spain storks are revered as symbols of good luck and marital bliss, given their fidelity to each other and their clockwork return to their nests each year in their north-south migrations. But it does seem that in Extremadura the storks are especially prevalent, perhaps because this is the main landing corridor for their migrations. In Cáceres, pay close attention to storks as well.

Throughout the city you will also encounter several Romanesque and Gothic churches that radiate from the roads coming out of Plasencia's solar-plan center, the Plaza Mayor. One particularly appealing place for quiet prayer is the Romanesque-Gothic church of San Nicolás, which dates to the thirteenth and fourteenth centuries. Because Plasencia was also on the Ruta de Plata and had pilgrims going to Santiago de Compostela passing through, you will encounter here a charming little church to Santiago, St. James. It stands outside the walls of the medieval city as you approach the Puerta del Sol, the medieval city's main gateway, through its thick, Ávila-like fortress walls.

Plasencia to Cucao de Yuste (29 miles/47 km):
Take EX-203 E to Cucao de Yuste.

CUCAO DE YUSTE—Extremadura

Just as nuts and pigs are held dear to Extremadurans, so are the red peppers, several varieties as a matter of fact, that go into the famous smoked red pepper pimentón, which comes in three flavors: sweet, bittersweet, and hot. The village of Cucao de Yuste is the heartland of the most famous brand of smoked, ground red peppers. You can't miss it, for the houses are hung with the copious peppers. Every September 30 the town and its peppers are blessed as a part of the festival day dedicated to San Jerónimo, St. Jerome of Antioch. You can find spice cans of the delicious ground pepper everywhere you travel in Extremadura. Often, the can will have a holy persona on the label, the most popular being the Virgin Mary, Our Lady of the Peppers.

Cucao de Yuste to Monasterio de San Jerónimo de Yuste (6 miles/10 km):
Follow signs from Cucao de Yuste to the monastery.

MONASTERIO DE SAN JERÓNIMO DE YUSTE—Extremadura

This monastery was founded and is run to this day by Jerónimos monks. Only one other monastery exists of this order, one in Segovia called Santa María el Parral. San Jerónimo de Yuste monastery is where Carlos I, better known as the Holy Roman Emperor Charles V, lived out the last two years of his life after he handed the throne to his son, Philip II, in 1556. His quarters remain and can be visited. It seems that, after such a busy outward life, all he desired was to retreat from the world in quiet contemplation. This location, so far from the center of anything in Europe, must have been the perfect place. The surrounding countryside is enchanting and worth exploring for spiritual purposes.

Monasterio de Yuste to Cáceres (73.5 miles/118 km):
Backtrack to Plasencia and take N-630 to A-66/E-803 south to Cáceres.

CÁCERES—Extremadura

The first time I came to Cáceres was serendipitously during Carnival, the Tuesday before Lent, and the town was in the height of festival mood, everyone wearing costumes of their choosing. The most common costumes were people dressed up as Muslims and Jews and a few medieval Christians. In the heart of the medieval neighborhood that evening the mayor made a speech, declaring that Cáceres was a city of *convivencia* in the Middle Ages and so it would be in the present.

This launched what have become annual events that celebrate the city's tri-religious historic communities of Jews, Christians, and Muslims, such as tri-faith culinary weekends where celebrity Sephardic, Moroccan Muslim, and Spanish Catholic chefs share their favorite dishes. This is the mood of visiting Cáceres, even though physically the remains of Muslim and Jewish inhabitants are harder to find than the remains of those who came after them, the Conquistadores and the fancy buildings these men built with their New World wealth.

What is sacred in Cáceres is more its medieval city taken as a whole rather than any one place, largely because holy sites were repeatedly built over prior holy sites. Some of this sanctity is diluted by the returning Conquistadores' grand mansions, but these too reflect a shifting spirituality of the time. Wander through the labyrinthine passageways and enjoy the worship of the sun overlaid with the worship of the Abrahamic God of the

Jews, Christians, and Muslims. Note that the Gothic church, San Mateo, is built over the old mosque. Above all, enjoy the beak clapping of those symbols of fidelity and permanence overhead, the storks.

A quirky delight in Cáceres is a museum started by a resident and his son dedicated to Cáceres's Islamic heritage. The **Casa de Yusuf al-Borch,** a Spanish-Arabic name, is a dizzying mix of items from all over the Middle East and North Africa that the owner, José Torres (Yusuf al-Borch/Borj in Arabic, which means "Joseph Tower" in English), collected throughout his life. Since his death, his son has dedicatedly taken over and shares in his father's passion. He explains the place as a part of Cáceres's broad-minded *convivencia.*

Cáceres to Mérida (44 miles/71 km):
Take A-66/E-803 S to Mérida.

MÉRIDA—Extremadura

Mérida feels like a balmy Mediterranean island, even though it is in the river plain of southern Spain. Unlike the rest of Extremadura, it has low buildings of white-, mustard-, and ochre-colored stucco and terra-cotta roofs, a major contrast with the heavy stone of the other cities and towns of the province. Mérida is blessed with a wide river, the Guadiana, a good wine industry that no one seems to know about, and palm trees.

Founded in 25 BCE, Emerita Augusta (Mérida) was the heart and capital of Roman Lusitania. It was the largest Roman city of ancient Iberia and today has the most surviving Roman ruins in Spain, including the Roman Theater and the Amphitheater that stand next to each other. Of sacred interest are four major sites: the purported Temple of Diana, the Temple to Mars, the site reflecting the cult of Mithra, and the fifth-century Basilica of Santa Eulalia.

Mérida was also a central Islamic stronghold, but sacred remains have not survived. The great fortress area, the Alcazaba, holds some remains from Islamic times and later, such as a building belonging to the Knights of Santiago. The Alcazaba is an area that was used by everyone who made this their city. Christian remains are layered on top of Muslim remains, which are layered on top of Roman ones, and so forth.

Sacred Mérida

Current expertise does not support that the **Temple of Diana** really was this great Greco-Roman goddess's veneration spot. But the town won't

*Mérida's popularly named Temple of Diana, a Roman temple that might
more likely have been dedicated to the emperor or to a
sacred water source, Extremadura*

stop calling it Diana's temple and they really feel that she is their goddess; so, if you ask me, when a whole population venerates a goddess at a spot and calls it hers, it's hers. While it might be more accurate to call this a modern temple to Diana, it is well established that the cult of Artemis, AKA Diana, was very strong in ancient Iberia, so much so that Artemisian energy was directed into the Virgin Mary, who represents similar things: virginity and protection of the innocent. Current thinking is that this was a temple to the emperor. Others suggest it was a nymphaeum, a site dedicated to a sacred spring, grotto, or fountain, and consecrated to a water nymph.

The mansion you see behind the temple used to be more extensive. It was built in the sixteenth century by a wealthy man who used the temple as the frame for his mansion. Thankfully, part of the trespassing mansion has been removed to restore the temple.

The **Casa del Mitreo,** Mithra's House, was a private citizen's villa that appears to have been built over an earlier Mithraeum, a place of ritual bull sacrifice. That it also stands next to the later-built bull ring adds to its aura, suggesting a continuity and a modification in rituals.

Mithra was an ancient Persian god associated with the sun and with war. He was often depicted on the back of a bull that he was sacrificing. It was a strong cult in Persia from around the eighth to the sixth century BCE and entered popularity in the Roman world centuries later, much as a mystery cult, around the second and third centuries AD. He was a god especially favored by Roman soldiers, more of a popular people's god than an official state deity.

Mithra was not only a god of war; he was more primarily a god of friendship and contract, one who gave triumph in war and peace beyond it. This is not the first time we have seen a god of contracts as also a god of war. In chapter 13, we saw that the Botorrita Bronze tablet held in Zaragoza refers to a Celtiberian god, Neitos, who was also a guardian of contracts and oaths and a warlike divinity, sometimes even equated with the Roman god Mars.

As for bull sacrifice, the ancient Persian Mithra, connected to the sun, unwillingly sacrificed the moon god, known as Soma, who was often depicted as a bull. He did this unwillingly, perhaps in knowing that it was the only way to keep the cosmos moving along—the moon had to die to be reborn. But bull sacrifice was also the condoned manner in which contracts were sealed and celebrated. The mosaics in the Casa del Mitreo are wonderful, some dedicated to showing the Roman gods and their view of the cosmos.

Santa Eulalia was a Christian martyred by Romans in AD 304. She was a young woman, a native of Augusta Emerita. Not only did she refuse to renounce her monotheistic faith but she refused to pay homage to the pagan gods of Rome when it was demanded; she went as far as to insult them and call them nothing but figures of clay shaped by human hands. For her hardheadedness and slander she was tortured in numerous vile ways, and eventually she caught fire and burned to death. As a result, in Mérida you will see her holding a clay oven. Other depictions of her are with hands clasped in divine joy as flames lick her feet. Her basilica might be over the site where she was buried in the fourth century, as this spot was first a Roman cemetery. The basilica was built in the fifth century and is now beneath the current **Church of Santa Eulalia,** a beautiful thirteenth-century Romanesque structure with a Mudéjar wood ceiling. The city has cleverly excavated the underlying basilica, and it is possible to enjoy a subterranean visit to soak it in. Walls and a few frescoes survive. Openings to the church above give you a good reference point for what part of the church floor you are under at each stage of the visit.

A stone representation of Santa Eulalia at her namesake church in Mérida, Extremadura

At the front of both Eulalian temples, old and new, is a little outdoor shrine to Santa Eulalia on the street that is a hub for local devotion. People shopping, walking their dogs, and going to and from work stop here to utter a prayer. But even this relatively recent shrine stands over the site where the Roman **Temple to Mars** once stood. Santa Eulalia triumphs over the Romans once and for all.

Mérida to Guadalupe (71.5 miles/115 km):
Leave NE on A-5/E-90 toward Trujillo; take exit 294 and get on to EX-102 to Guadalupe.

GUADALUPE—Extremadura

When Christianity was used as a political tool for power over territories and peoples throughout the Americas, the Virgin of Guadalupe became an icon for both sides, perhaps because underlying her pedigree lay a universal and mixed history that could appeal to many people. This cedar-carved, black-faced Mary from Guadalupe is often called the Patron of all Spain. Connected to the land of Extremadura, she is associated with a place that not only produced many of Spain's Conquistadores but also existed for a long time under Islamic and Jewish influences, as well as Christian. At the time when conquerors were going to the Americas, the descendents of Spain's Jews and Muslims were experiencing mass expulsions and forced conversions.

The legend of this famous Mary has many layers: It is fabled that St. Luke carved the image of the Black Madonna during his life in the first century AD and that it was buried with him. Three centuries later, his remains, including this icon, were transferred to Constantinople, where the Black Madonna revealed its first healing miracles. From there, St. Luke's carving went to Rome and then onward to Visigothic Seville, where it continued miraculous healings until it disappeared, or was hidden away, on the eve of the Arab and Berber invasion of the city in 711. Luke's Mary went underground for many centuries. Then, on the eve of Christian conquest, an apparition of Mary came to an Extremaduran shepherd on the spot of the current monastery of Guadalupe, revealing her icon's longtime whereabouts and instructing that a sanctuary should be built there. The monastery was founded in 1340 by Alfonso XI in gratitude for the Virgin's aid in assuring his victory in battle against the Muslims. It is a mix of Gothic, Mudéjar, and later Plateresque styles.

The pilgrimage to and worship of Our Lady of Guadalupe peaked in the fifteenth and sixteenth centuries, coinciding with the time that many Extremadurans, seeking their fortune away from their impoverished land in the hands of a few powerful absentee landlords, went to the New World. They took with them not only their hopes and sense of adventure but also their veneration of the Lady of Guadalupe, whose name and appearance began to emerge across Latin America. One of the most important events was in 1531 when the Lady of Guadalupe appeared to a young native Mexican boy. This was only the beginning of such occurrences.

But there is also a darkness to her history—she is something of a war deity, aggressive and demanding. She brought Alfonso XI victory in battle against the Muslims. She launched many Conquistadores' journeys to a New World that they were about to decimate economically, socially, spiritually, and biologically. It was in the fountain in front of the monastery in Guadalupe that Columbus brought the first Native American peoples to be baptized. Did they come willingly? I would equate this Virgin's energy to a degree with the Hindu Kali, a dark goddess who demands blood and destruction in the cyclical formula of creativity and rebirth. I do not mean to deny the comfort and grace the Lady of Guadalupe has given so many but only to point out how she was used by the conquerors to justify their cause.

The monastery and church of Guadalupe has Mudéjar and Gothic towers and houses the more likely twelfth-century statue of the Virgin, which has an aesthetic more of the Gothic period than of the first century AD. The monastery's cloister is exquisite. A mix of Gothic and Mudéjar work, it possesses that distinctive brickwork and horseshoe arches amid elegant Gothic arches. It is currently occupied and managed by Franciscan monks. They offer guest lodging in the cloisters. This is one of the best places to enjoy monastic hospitality.

$\mathscr{T}$oledo to Xátiva

*The only person who ever successfully unified Spain was Julius Caesar.
No one since has been able to do it; Spain is too diverse and never had a
Richelieu.*

—A man from Córdoba

T HIS CONVIVENCIA ROUTE passes through those areas that
reflect the most extensive coexistence, creative flowering, symbiosis, and
competition and strife between the three medieval Abrahamic faith communities throughout their eight hundred years of side-by-side existence in
Iberia. In it are the sacred highlights of medieval Muslim Spain and the
interwoven faith communities of Jews, Christians, and Muslims. There are
also little side trips that take us through Neolithic, Visigothic, and Roman
sites that were already in place and a part of the medieval person's awareness, often marking a place as an ideal strategic and spiritual settlement.

The route first passes through the most famous places of tri-religious
Spain: Toledo, Córdoba, Sevilla, and Granada. But it continues into lesser
known, by the contemporary person, places that were as crucial to defining
medieval tri-religious Spain. And the route ends in the province of Valencia, known for some of the more enlightened post-Reconquest policies of
once-Muslim Spain under Christian rule. This was the realm of Jaime I of
Aragón, James I, who, though fully spouting Christian language in his
hegemony, never lost sight of the importance of the other faith communities in keeping his region economically bountiful: he accorded important
protections to the Jews and Muslims in his realm and they were able to
continue worshiping and living as they had before, as well as crafting,

plowing, translating, milling, and weaving silk, a rich skill Jaime I's territory inherited with his conquest. Collectively the places on this route give a deep appreciation for the longtime presence of the sacred in central, southern, and southeastern Spain.

Main Route (858 miles/1,380 km):
Toledo—Santa María de Melque—Córdoba—Medina Azahara—Sevilla—Antequera—Granada—Murcia—Santuario de Fuensanta—Caravaca de la Cruz—Bocairent—Xátiva

TOLEDO—Castilla La Mancha

As you approach Toledo from any direction you are left with little doubt as to why Romans, Visigoths, Muslims, Jews, and Christians settled here and built on this hill, with perfect vistas from all sides, a natural wall of sierra protecting it from the north and the deep cut of the Tajo River guarding it as a natural moat on the east, south, and west. Romans saw this strategic spot and settled the area after overtaking several villages in the vicinity in 190 BC. The name they gave their new town was Toletum.

Toledo's Mezquita Cristo de la Luz revealing its Islamic style originally as a mosque, with the add-on of an apse when it was later converted into a church, Castilla La Mancha [This photo was taken by Nahid Bahrami.]

The Visigoths, who took control of formerly Roman Spain in the sixth century and during the rule of King Leovigild in AD 569, made the centrally located Toledo the seat of their throne. As the center of religion and politics, Toledo was where King Recared changed the tide of Visigothic faith and converted from Arianism, a branch of Christianity that negated the Trinity, to Catholicism. It was also under the Visigoths that the Jews fared very poorly, being the subject of bigoted policies toward non-Christians. Such policies helped ease the arrival of new invaders who, aflame with their own new faith, Islam, arrived with a fundamental tenet in the new faith to respect other "Peoples of the Book." This was good news for Jews and Christians but bad for anyone outside the Abrahamic faiths (though the official story is that by the time of the North African invasion in 711, all Iberians were either Christian or Jewish. Unofficially, I am fairly certain there were many people in the hills and along remote coastlines faithfully addressing the gods and goddesses of their pagan ancestors as well, slowly and unconsciously turning them in the fertile soil to come up reincarnated as an old deity with a new saint's name.)

Toledo's central location likewise made it an important town to the invading North Africans and Arabs who took it in 712. They held it until 1085, at which time the northern Christian kingdoms had coordinated enough muster to take it under Alfonso VI's banner, marking a turning of the tide in what was to be called the Christian Reconquest of Spain. It was this taking of Toledo that led the Muslim south to do something it would forever regret: call for aid from a North African sect, the Almoravids, who had taken control of the area today known as Morocco. Fundamentalist and with the zeal of orthodox believers that theirs was the right way to interpret Islam, the Almoravids helped slow the southerly movement of the Reconquista but brought with them less tolerance and more persecution of Iberian Muslims as well as of Jews and Christians living in Muslim territories. They did not succeed, however, in getting Toledo back.

Importantly, Alfonso VI, king of León and of Castile, took Toledo without spilling blood. The three religious communities of the city continued to live together in creative collaboration. It was during this period—from the eleventh to the thirteenth century—that Toledo achieved its fame as a city of translators from all over Europe and Southwest Asia who were rendering classical texts from Greek to Arabic or Hebrew to Latin to vernacular European languages.

As a sacred city, Toledo's history is a mixed blessing. Under Abd al-Rahman III in the tenth century and under Alfonso X in the thirteenth century, people experienced some of the greatest coexistence and creative collaboration, as Jews, Christians, and Muslims worked together on translation, arts, sciences, and trades. It was during these periods that much of Europe's lost heritage was rediscovered via Arab scholars and brought to Europe through Spain, where it was translated before it crossed further north over the Pyrenees Mountains.

The greatest shadow over Toledo came with Queen Isabel and King Fernando and their policy of conversion or exile, first enacted against the Jews and next, a few years later, against the Muslims. Toledo plunged into spiritual darkness at this juncture, being the seat of power of the likes of small-minded and power-hungry, and sadly influential, Grand Inquisitor Juan de Torquemada and Toledo's archbishop, Francisco Ximénex de Cisneros. *Convivencia* in Toledo enjoyed a patchy span of practice from the early eighth century through to the mid-fourteenth century, at which time Jews began being persecuted in earnest. These policies were more supported by Isabel. Fernando refused to allow the policies of forced conversion to spread to his kingdom of Aragón. With Isabel's blessing, the Inquisition was established in 1480 from Toledo. As the Inquisition tried only Christians, testing the strength of their faith, once all people of Jewish and Muslim faith had been forced into conversion, they were vulnerable to being dragged before the Inquisition: it was brutal to anyone deemed a heretic, be they broad-minded bishops, suspected secret Jews and Muslims, or closet Protestants during a time when the Reformation gained strength in other parts of Europe. The Inquisition also tried people accused of being witches, those *curanderos*, healers, who lived in remote rural areas and practiced ancient healing rites and who, though baptized, still retained strong connections to pre-Christian and pagan ways.

From 1085 until 1561 Toledo held sway as the central seat of power for both church and throne. In 1561 King Phillip II, desiring to make his own mark in history on a blank canvas, moved the capital to Madrid, an equally central position.

The beauty of Toledo is its remarkable collection of mixed-faith buildings. No other Spanish town boasts two synagogues in such good shape. Many of the churches stand on what once were mosques. Likewise, many churches incorporate the craftsmanship of Muslim artisans and boast Mudéjar towers, walls, columns, and ceilings (as do the two synagogues).

Toledo also became the final home to one of Spain's great spiritual artists, El Greco, whose obsession with bringing heaven and Earth together in most of his works carried Toledo's sacred history closer to the present. Born in Crete, Domenico Theotocopoulos, El Greco, "The Greek," chose

Toledo as his lifelong home and used the city in background and foreground for many of his paintings, which can be found throughout the city.

Today, walking within the narrow labyrinthine streets of Toledo, you can feel both the dark and the light mingle and dance. Given its physical geographical constraints on a hill, and surrounded by river and sierra, the town has changed little since its medieval shape. It is a pleasure to soak up this lingering past, which easily mixes with the present.

Saint Ildefonsus

Saint Ildefonsus is the patron saint of Toledo. A Visigoth and a student of Isidore of Seville and later the archbishop of Toledo, Ildefonsus died in 667. His life is less known than are his four surviving writings, which contribute to early Spanish literature. His main miracles reflect great devotion to Mary, the Mother of God, who appeared to him. His view of the Jews is more problematic and all too Visigothic; this ambiguity is a part of what one must confront in visiting Toledo, both the "City of Three Cultures" as well as a place of intermittent pogroms, Inquisition, and the grubby human contest for mortal power via religion.

But in speaking with Toledanos, not only are they oblivious to this side of their city's patron saint, but they are far more fascinated and celebratory of their city's three-faith heritage. One Toledano friend told me of the new, revised tours of the city, "There are more Toledanos than tourists on these tours. We are fascinated by what scholars and the tourist board are finding out about the Jewish and Muslim history of our city. Many city residents go on the tours to learn."

El Greco's painting *St. Ildefonsus*, celebrating Toledo's patron saint, is in the Hospital de la Caridad in Illescas, a town northeast of Toledo. The one writing from Ildefonsus that offers a lasting contribution is *De Viris Illustribus*, giving insights into the history of the seventh-century Spanish church.

Alfonso X

Alfonso X, *El Sabio*, "The Learned," was king of Castile from 1252–1284. Though putting into place segregationist policies, such as placing all the Muslims of Murcia in a walled-in suburb of that city, at the same time he cultivated the arts and sciences among the three religious communities. In Toledo especially he patronized the translation of classical and religious texts. He himself leaves an informative, and musically beautiful, body of sung poetry, *cantigas*, dedicated to the Virgin Mary. In them are contained stories of faith as well as of the mixed peoples in his realm, often celebrating those who converted to Christianity when they experienced the Virgin's interceding graces in a crisis.

El Cid

Troublesome he was, for he fought as a mercenary as much for a Muslim ruler as for a Christian. Rodrigo Díaz, his real name, was not unusual; the times were so mixed as to deem his practice fairly logical given that rulers on both sides also sought each other out as allies against another enemy, Christian or Muslim, and then shifted alliances again. His nickname, El Cid, is derived from Arabic, *al-sid*, meaning "sir" or "lord." What is remarkable about El Cid was how successful he was at playing both sides and how he managed to survive the wrath of a once-allied king turned enemy. In the end, he conquered Valencia for himself and reigned there until his death in 1099.

Mezquita de Cristo de la Luz

Dating to 999, the mosque of Cristo de la Luz, then known as the mosque of Bab al-Mardum, was built over the site of a Visigothic church whose stones went right back into building the mosque, which in turn was turned into a twelfth-century Mudéjar church. This structure more than any other gives a good idea of what Toledo's mosques might once have looked like, though you need to imagine away the sealed doorways that once were the mosque's two entrances and that allowed light to pour into this sweet little place.

When worshipers shifted from Muslim to Christian, the old mosque was preserved and the apse was added on to give it the appearance of a church. The horseshoe arches, overlapping arches, foliage-carved capitals, and the striated stone trilobed arches all reflect its sisterhood with the great mosque in Córdoba. Toledo was under the Cordoban Caliphate's rule at the time this mosque was built.

This is a sweet and truly spiritual and quiet space from which to contemplate the many people of Toledo who lived and worked together. Though a light-filled mosque, the name—Christ of the Light—comes from its conversion to a Christian temple. One fable says that El Cid's horse kneeled before the mosque when he entered the city as a part of King Alfonso VI's entourage. At the spot where the horse kneeled, they found a hidden Visigothic lamp within the wall. The story seems to validate the conquerors' agenda, which was to convert the mosque into a church, shedding their own light, as it were, in the sacred space.

Iglesia de San Román

A thirteenth-century Mudéjar church with distinctive Moorish horseshoe arches and colorful and beautiful medieval Christian frescoes painted on the walls between the arches, this site elegantly weaves together Muslim and Christian arts into a space that invites a person to linger and commune with God. Colorful, intimate, and warm, San Román is Toledo's oldest church. It started its life as a Visigothic chapel, later became a mosque, and then was built in 1221 as a Mudéjar church. Today it is a museum of Visigothic culture.

Toledo's Cathedral

This thirteenth- to fifteenth-century Gothic cathedral includes works by El Greco (especially in the sacristy) as well as some hidden signs of its prior existence on the spot as a mosque. Prior to the mosque, this was the site of a Visigothic basilica. Although it is a bright and elegant cathedral with colorful, cheery stained glass throughout, I have some misgivings given Toledo's zealous archbishop Francisco Ximénez de Cisneros's grubby hand in certain chapels. Nevertheless, it is an unusually bright and cheerful structure for a Gothic Spanish cathedral and the energy is largely of this cheer and light.

Iglesia de Santo Tomé

Once the neighborhood's twelfth-century mosque, the seventeenth-century church of Santo Tomé has a fourteenth-century Mudéjar bell tower and the interior contains one of El Greco's most famous pieces, *The Burial of Count Orgay*, dating to 1586 and depicting the count being assisted to heaven by St. Stephen and St. Augustine.

Sinagoga El Tránsito

If ever there were the poster-child building to represent tri-religious Spain, this is it. Built in the mid- to late-fourteenth century, El Tránsito was commissioned by the treasurer of Castile, Samuel ha-Levi, who was in service of the king, Pedro I. Pedro I had used Granadan Muslim craftsmen to rebuild Sevilla's Alcazar and allowed ha-Levi to use the same craftsmen to build El Tránsito. Therefore, you will see similarities in the inlaid work and plaster sculpting of the walls, floors, and ceilings of the two structures. El Tránsito's ceiling reflects Mudéjar craft in its interlocking and ornate wood design, where you can also locate Arabic inscriptions. Additionally, along the upper molding are Hebrew passages along the top and bottom surrounding Arabic passages that run parallel with but are smaller than the Hebrew, with intermittent Castilian coats of arms; the design is completed with the ever-expanding and whimsical branches of the Tree of Life. Today El Tránsito synagogue is also the Sephardic museum, which contains a library and an archive.

Sinagoga de Santa María la Blanca

Toledo's oldest surviving synagogue, it dates to the twelfth century. Under the Muslim *taifa* period (1031–1085) there were at least twelve synagogues in Toledo, though today only two survive. Santa María la Blanca was rebuilt in the 1250s and continued as a synagogue until the fifteenth century, when it was taken over by Christians and converted into a church named after the Virgin Mary. It is a pleasing symbiosis of darkness above, in the wood beams, and light below, in the form of the white arches and pillars. Having visited mosques in Morocco that are based on medieval Andalusian design, this synagogue-turned-church feels very much like the open, quiet, and harmonious places reflected in the cousin mosques of North Africa. It is a space restored to its elegant lines, with whitewashed horseshoe arches, wood and plaster carving, and five aisles with little furnishing.

Iglesia de Cristo de la Vega

This was once a Visigothic chapel dedicated—probably by King Sisebut—to the fourth-century martyr St. Leocadia. Saint Leocadia's spirit appeared to San Ildefonsus on this spot. The chapel has been heavily modified in recent times, showing an eighteenth-century aesthetic. Among its surviving older features is a pleasing Mudéjar apse. This and the chapel's size, and especially its location, speak of a local place of intimate worship. Stories abound of it as a place anyone could come with worries and find peace.

Toledo to Santa María de Melque (31 miles/50 km):

Take CM-4000 W; take CM-4009 S; follow signs to Santa María de Melque.

SANTA MARÍA DE MELQUE—Castilla La Mancha

Santa María de Melque is the remains of what is considered a late-Visigothic church, and hence it offers a glimpse of one of the earliest churches in Spain. Historian Nancy Garen makes a good case for the possibility that this was more likely a church constructed under early Muslim rule. Dated to somewhere between AD 630 and 930, it could be either. Garen notes parallels with other Syrian-Umayyad structures in the eastern Mediterranean that do seem to suggest construction in the mid- to late-eighth century under Abd al-Rahman I's rule from Córdoba. The Church of Santa María de Melque reflects the religious tolerance of this period, indicating that church construction was legislated under new Muslim rule and protected.

Santa María de Melque to Córdoba (216 miles/348 km):
Take CM-4009 S to CM-403 SE to CM-410; take N-401 S to Ciudad Real; take N-420 S then A-4/E-5 W to Córdoba.

CÓRDOBA—Andalucía

Along the bank of the Guadalquivir—"Great River," *wadi kabir,* in Arabic—Córdoba was the capital of Roman Spain, founded in 169 BCE, but the city's truly great age, politically, creatively, and spiritually, was from the mid-eighth century to the first third of the eleventh century. This was the period of the Caliphate of Córdoba, the golden age of al-Andalus, and the co-creative flowering of Iberian Islamic, Jewish, and Christian civilizations under the last surviving Umayyad dynastic branch from the Middle East. It was during this period that Córdoba had lighted streets at night, indoor plumbing, and was one of the world's most populated places. People flocked here for its more open social air (though this was not perfect) and its mixed possibilities. Some of those people brought with them great change. The most influential arrivals had to be Abd al-Rahman I, who founded the dynasty in Córdoba that later, under Abd al-Rahman III in 929 would be proclaimed a caliphate when he proclaimed himself a caliph, the religious political leader of Muslims, a bold and daring move in the Islamic world. And during Abd al-Rahman II's reign, in the early ninth century, the Persian poet Ziryab fled from Baghdad to Córdoba, where he found amnesty and went on flamboyantly to set the tone for so many influential fashions, many of which survive in our own culture. He brought with him trends from the Middle East that made their way into Islamic Iberia.

Abd al-Rahman I

From AD 661, Arab and Islamic authority was in the possession of the Umayyads, who ruled from Damascus and whose power extended from there to ancient Persia, Arabia, Turkey, and North Africa and became the new Islamic presence in Iberia as early as AD 719. But in 750, a rival group, the Abbasids (a dynasty claiming descent from 'Abbas, the prophet Muhammed's uncle), claimed the caliphate and slaughtered as many Umayyads as they could. A formidable dynasty that would go on to rule the Islamic Middle East for another five hundred years, they moved their dynastic center to Baghdad. Spain became more remote to them as the Persian world became closer.

One of the few Umayyad survivors was a young man, Abd al-Rahman, who fled to northwestern Africa, the Maghrib, and took refuge among the Berbers. Then in 756, gathering followers, he went to Spain and set himself up in Córdoba. The newly conquered land was rife with rivalries and squabbles, many born of the manner in which the higher-status Arab minority alienated the Berber majority, the very Berbers who had guaranteed the successful conquest of Iberia. It appears that Abd al-Rahman was able to stabilize the atmosphere, though his hegemony over all of Moorish Spain took years. He first stabilized Córdoba and then set to work on Toledo (761–764), then to Sevilla (770s) and the northeast around the Ebro and Catalonia (around 780).

Cordoban rule gradually extended over the rest of Muslim Spain and an Umayyad dynasty persisted there, whereas the rest of the Muslim Mediterranean was now Abbasid. Córdoba stood alone, and in its isolation flourished a unique civilization of mixed peoples with diverse ideas that infused one another with new ideas and arts, sciences and languages, customs and foods. Though Córdoba was not under Abbasid rule, this does not mean that people did not flock to the city and the region. Word got out that it was a fluid, open, exciting place to be, and people from across Africa, Asia, and Europe came to be a part of it; Córdoba became the place to be, the medieval world's New York City with that same sort of high-voltage creative energy.

Abd al-Rahman III and the Cordoban Caliphate

Córdoba held the seat of power in Islamic Iberia until 1010, when civil strife and revolts could not be suppressed upon the death of Al-Mansur, Córdoba's last unifying ruler, and the empire crumbled into fragments of some three dozen city-states *(taifas)*. Córdoba's apex occurred during the rule of Abd al-Rahman III, from 912–961. He proclaimed himself caliph in 929, something equivalent to proclaiming oneself Holy Roman Emperor *and* pope, the successor to the prophet in earthly matters. He did this more to rally allegiance (or at least respect) from nearby North Africans than to poke a finger in the eye of the Abbasids in Baghdad, who claimed the same status but who by now ignored al-Andalus, for they had enough in the eastern world to keep their attention. This act made Spain completely independent from the rest of the Muslim world. Under his reign, Europe's first university was founded in the city. This was the peak of *convivencia* in Spain, when Jews, Christians, and Muslims studied and worked side by side as equally valued citizens of the same land.

Of all the kings, Abd al-Rahman's son al-Hakam II was the greatest patron of the arts and sciences. His court was one of the most illustriously attended by talented minds from across Europe and the Middle East.

Al-Hakam's son, Hisham II, was a mere puppet upon his father's death; the power of the throne was Al-Mansur, the vizier to the court. Called "The Victorious," Al-Mansur was a great military leader who revitalized the caliphate's lands and coffers through military campaigns—some fifty-two in the span of twenty years—to northern Spain. He sacked Santiago de Compostela in 997 and carried off the cathedral's bells—they stayed in Córdoba until the city's fall into Christian hands in 1236 when the bells were returned to their original perch.

When the Cordoban Caliphate crumbled upon Al-Mansur's death, Córdoba eventually became a part of Sevilla's *taifa* kingdom and then later fell under the control of invading Almoravids, then Almohads. In 1236 Christian forces under Ferdinand III took the city. The Great Mosque became the city's cathedral. The Christian population loved it as it was, wanted none of it altered, and worshiped in it as it was for nearly three hundred years.

Córdoba's Great Mosque

This is perhaps the most sublime sacred building in Spain. Even the most secular and non-spiritually oriented are moved to contemplative awe when they come here. This awe is less toward the great rulers who built it and more toward a divine presence, as the mosque's forest of pillars and quiet spaces create a reverence for creation, for nature, and for humanity.

Perhaps an important part of the great energy of this mosque is how it came into being, a spiritual journey in its own right. In the eighth century, when Córdoba came under the control of the invading Arab and Berber army, the victorious Muslims did something rarely heard of in the human history of conquest, especially of the conquered peoples' holy sites. There stood in Córdoba the main Visigothic church, St. Vincent, on the same spot today's mosque-turned-cathedral stands. Instead of taking it and tearing it down to build a mosque, they bought half of the building and used that half for their prayer, leaving the other half for Christian prayer services. This is the way it went until, in 785, Abd al-Rahman I purchased the other half. He then had the building

Mosaic wall over the mihrab, prayer niche, in Córdoba's mosque, Andalusia

torn down and commenced the building of the mosque. That mosque over the next few centuries was expanded three times, the old part left standing but extended.

In contrast, when the Visigoths first took Córdoba, they tore down the Roman Temple to Janus, most likely without purchasing it from anyone, and built their church. (Janus, curiously, was a uniquely Roman god, the god of thresholds: doorways and arches, exits and entrances.) The Cordoban mosque used both prior sacred-temple materials, those of Janus and those of St. Vincent, as well as materials sent in from all around Spain and the Mediterranean world to create an eclectic but unified forest of pillars, which create a calm, naturalistic space of worship.

Then in the sixteenth century the Cordoban bishop gained long-distance permission from Spain's King Carlos I (1516–1555) to make alterations to the cathedral-mosque. He had the center torn out and plunked in the heart of the old mosque the fashion of the time, a marble main chapel and a mahogany-carved *coro* section (the *coro* is unique in Spain; it is the choir section, set in a walled-off area, often in the center of the cathedral). The shift of mood must have been as when the sun is eclipsed by the moon. The original mosque was built for perfect vision as well as sound. This addition blinded and muted aspects of it.

Incidentally, Carlos I was also King Charles V of the Hapsburg Empire and spent more time in other parts of Hapsburg Europe than in Spain. He had never set foot in Córdoba when he gave the city's bishop permission to alter the cathedral-mosque. When Carlos I finally did visit Córdoba years later, after he saw the mosque-cathedral he said, "You destroyed something unique to build something ordinary."

The Christian citizens of Córdoba were also upset about the alteration of what had been their cathedral for three centuries. The town leaders protested the bishop's plans but to no avail. They loved their place of worship and gained the same peaceful transcendence in their worship as the Muslim worshipers had when it was a mosque. Perhaps, though, the mosque's transcendent beauty is what saved it from the fashion of any century, when one faith is conquered by another, and spared it from being completely torn down during Ferdinand III's conquest of Córdoba in the thirteenth century.

Moreover, there is so much of the old mosque left that you will get a chance to feel this celestial forest for yourself. If you go early in the morning with the intention to meditate or pray, you will find it quiet enough to imagine what it was like in tenth-century Córdoba. Be sure to take in the different sections of the mosque, its eighth-, ninth-, and tenth-century additions, to appreciate the wildly diverse columns (many imported from the Byzantine Empire) and arches that still manage to work together to create a secret garden or primordial forest.

Synagogue and Jewish Neighborhood

This surviving synagogue was built not during Islamic Córdoba but during the Christian period of the city, in the fourteenth century. It nevertheless possesses a strong expression of Iberian Moorish architectural taste, looking as if it popped out of the Alhambra in Nasrid Granada (same time period) and into Córdoba—the main difference being that the inscriptions on the stucco-carved walls are in Hebrew rather than in Arabic. The surrounding whitewashed and narrow streets are typical of Andalusia's white villages, offering respite from the heat and privacy around corners. Though likely altered by modern aesthetics, this section of old Córdoba has preserved its streets, passages, and old protective walls and can give you a feel for what it might have been like to wander these streets as a fourteenth-century resident.

Hasdai Ibn Shaprut

Rising in Abd al-Rahman's court as a physician and then as an administrator, Hasdai Ibn Shaprut was also made the leader of the Jewish community in Córdoba. He lived from 915 to 970. Not only was he learned in Hebraic studies but he studied Latin with Christian clergymen as well as Romance, the predecessor to Castilian that was spoken by both Christians and Muslims in Spain. He caught the caliph's attention through his medical inventions: antidotes for poisons, a useful knowledge given the high rate of court intrigues and mysterious poisonings. Shaprut was quickly welcomed into the court. He remained trusted by the king and rose to other positions, including political head of the Jews in Córdoba and a diplomat for the Cordoban Caliphate to Byzantium.

Córdoba to Medina Azahara (7 mi/11 km):
Go W from Córdoba on A-431.

MEDINA AZAHARA—Andalusia

Shortly after Abd al-Rahman III proclaimed himself caliph, he began the construction of his new administrative center outside Córdoba's city limits. This palace-city was the crown jewel of what the peak of Cordoban rule created. Its life was short, from 936 to 1013, after which time it was looted for its stone, marble, gold, precious gems, and mirrors by rivals, a sign of the swift darkness for the caliphate.

Archaeologists have done a remarkable job of excavating and restoring aspects of Medina Azahara. It once held many mosques, but just one has been found. The city is planned on three levels. The lower level holds the mosque. Above the mosque were the public areas of gardens and receptions. At the very top was the king's residence, the palace. It is a beautiful rural spot today, well worth the drive through pine forests and plains, offering an idea of the peace and tranquility the caliph gained by living here.

Medina Azahara to Sevilla (89.5 miles/144 km):
Return to Córdoba; take A-4/E-5 S toward Éjica and Sevilla.

SEVILLA—Andalusia

Sevilla was founded by Carthaginians around the seventh century BCE and then taken over by Romans by the early third century BCE and called

Hispalis. It was very briefly the Visigoths' main city centuries later until they made the more central Toledo their capital in the sixth century AD. Muslim Arabs and Berbers took over the city in AD 712, and it remained in their hands until 1248 when Ferdinand III of Castile took the city.

The story of the changeover of power in Seville's early days as a Muslim city is illustrative of the manner in which natives merged and mixed with the new invaders. Sara, the granddaughter of the next-to-last Visigothic king, Witiza, sailed to Palestine and went on to the Umayyad court in Damascus to seek the caliph Hisham's intervention in the confiscation of land that prior caliphs had guaranteed her but that her uncle had usurped. Not only did Hisham reinforce her right to inherit the designated lands around Seville, but he arranged for her to marry one of his men, a man by the name of Isa ibn Muzahim, who would accompany her back to Sevilla, where they had two sons. It was one of her great grandsons who wrote her story and preserved it for us. This thread does not end here, however. In 756 Sara traveled to Córdoba to meet Abd al-Rahman I, who had recently arrived and established himself as the ruler of the region and eventually of all of al-Andalus. He reminded her, however, that they had met before, as he was none other than the Umayyad Hisham's grandson and had seen her in Damascus in 730.

Perhaps Sevilla's most illustrious time occurred in the eleventh century, shortly after the fall of the Caliphate of Córdoba. Among the nearly three dozen *taifa* kingdoms that emerged, Sevilla was among the most powerful. In Iberia, from 1023 to 1248, especially during the court of al-Mu'tamid, the city became an epicenter for artists, poets, intellectuals, and scholars. Its famous Giralda tower, the Great Mosque's minaret, was built after this period, commissioned by the Almoravid leader Abu Yacub Yusuf in 1171, a sister tower to the Tour Hassan in Rabat and the Koutoubia in Marrakech, all executed by the same builders influenced by the Iberian-Moroccan connection.

Cathedral, Giralda Tower, and Patio of Oranges

These three must be considered together as the late-Gothic to early-Renaissance cathedral was built over one of the main mosques, leaving no stone unturned except for the tower and mosque courtyard. Christians converted the Giralda from minaret to bell tower and had the additional layer and bell added. The patio of oranges that is the cathedral's main entrance was once the mosque's inviting courtyard that led to its entrance. Here, Muslims washed their faces, hands, and feet before progressing through once-existent gates to the mosque for prayers. That the continuity remains is stunning. The wall and the gate opening to the patio of oranges are the same as they were in the twelfth-century mosque. Soak in the intricate geometric metalwork that gives a sampling of the type of work for which Sevilla was famous, then step into the peace of orange groves, stone walkways, a fountain, dappled light, and fresh air. If you are there in spring, orange blossoms will further enhance this dedication to paradise on Earth.

The later, Gothic cathedral itself is more a feat of "let's build the biggest cathedral possible to show the world our power" than it is a moving spiritual space. It is huge, towering, and grand and reminds us of

The old gate to Sevilla's medieval mosque, with detailed Arabic inscriptions, leads to the patio of oranges, and is now the main gate to the cathedral, built on the same spot over the mosque, Andalusia

our minuteness. It is an act of power, of Christianity triumphing over others, and finally, of Columbus's journey—the fervor to conquer and expand that forged the Castilian character in the Middle Ages onward to new lands, boundaries, and peoples. Columbus's tomb, on the south side, is placed on the shoulders of four men who symbolically represent the kingdoms of Castile, León, Aragón, and Navarra.

On the eastern side of the cathedral is the chapel to Santa Justa and Santa Rufina, showing the two female saints flanking the Giralda tower. Protectresses of the tower as well as of the cathedral, they were third-century natives of Sevilla when it was under Roman rule. Sisters and early Christians, they made and sold pottery in the city, but when they refused to sell their wares for use in a pagan festival, they were put through several physical ordeals until they were martyred. Legend attributes to their watch the preservation of the tower and cathedral from destruction during the 1755 earthquake. That two early Christian saints are protecting what was once the mosque's minaret speaks of the passion Sevillanos have for their heritage. It is an interestingly balanced picture as well, the masculine tower guarded by two strong women.

Ferdinand III's tomb in the royal chapel of the cathedral has multilingual inscriptions. Hebrew here reflects the remaining importance of Jews in Sevilla after the Christian conquest in 1248. Jews were considered an important part of the new Christian society. They were well educated and interconnected in the great web of commerce between Old World economies. Moreover, they were a minority that was not considered a threat the way the Muslim majority, whom Ferdinand III did expel, was. This status, sadly, did not last long. Whereas when Jews lived under Muslim rule in Sevilla there were no designated neighborhoods for them, by the time of the Reconquest under Christian rule, three or four Jewish neighborhoods emerged, indicating a greater degree of separation.

All Holy Week processions leave their respective church and are destined to pass through the cathedral on their way back to their church. This may take half a day to perform and is a form of penitential pilgrimage for all involved.

During Holy Week, many religious brotherhoods proceed through town, with an average of two floats each, one of a stage in the last days of Jesus' life and one dedicated to their particular parish's Mary. There must be dozens of Mary floats, but two are particularly famous, La Macarena and La Esperanza de Triana. These two are the most sought out and people debate which is the more beautiful and the more powerful in interceding in human affairs.

Detail of Islamic mosaic tile work on a wall in Seville's Alcazar palace

Barrio de Santa Cruz and the Alcazar

This thirteenth-century neighborhood is the old Jewish quarter, the *juderia*. The cathedral and the Alcazar are part of its perimeter. Two or three other Jewish neighborhoods like this one emerged under Christian rule and in the thirteenth century.

Such segregation did not exist in Sevilla under Muslim patronage. The Alcazar was first a fortress built in 712 when Muslims first took Sevilla. Different Muslim rulers added to and altered it through the centuries before the city's conquest by Ferdinand III in 1248, who expelled all the Muslims. A century after Sevilla fell to Ferdinand III, the Alcazar was turned into a palace by Pedro I. In 1364 Mudéjar builders brought from Toledo and Granada created what you see today. Arabic script is intermingled with the Castilian coat of arms, and the overall effect is a sister space to the Alhambra in Granada. The extensive gardens offer respite and calm in a sea of green sprinkled with private fountain nooks and pools.

Al-Mu'tamid

If you lived in eleventh-century Sevilla, it is likely you would be well aware of medieval poetry "slams." Poetry reigned supreme in this city and its king Abu al-Qasim Muhammad II ibn 'Abbad al-Mu'tamid (1040–1095) was among the most versed. Poets were expected to compose a poem on the spot at gatherings. Poetry was as much a result of cleverness and education as it was a divine grace. All subjects were fair game but the most popular were love, politics, and satire. Poetry was among a politician's weapons in a world of continually shifting boundaries, loyalties, and factions. Though al-Mu'tamid's reign was criticized by later arriving, more zealous Muslims as being lax in religious observance, the poetry and grace that unfolded here speak of a definite spiritual focus, albeit one that was spontaneous and unorthodox. However, the more common poetic themes for al-Mu'tamid were women and wine.

Ibn Khaldun

Born in 1332 in Tunisia, Ibn Khaldun was from a family of one of the main clans in Sevilla, the Banu Khaldun, but it left in 1248 when Ferdinand III took the city. He lived in Granada in the 1360s and observed firsthand the land of his ancestry. Ibn Khaldun is often referred to as the Father of Sociology, putting onto the page observations about peoples and patterns of the Mediterranean world. One of his greatest contributions was his observation of group feeling among tribal peoples, who were more cohesive and capable of group coordination and invasion. Once people conquered and settled, they lost this group feeling, being softened as it were by city life and therefore easily conquered by the next wave of nomadic peoples.

Sevilla to Antequera (102.5 miles/165 km):
Take A-92 SE; take A-343 to Antequera.

ANTEQUERA—Andalusia

A quintessential Andalusian town with approximately forty thousand residents, Antequera is home to some thirty churches, making the skyline of steeples a lovely site, especially at sunset. Among these churches, a lovely one to step into is Iglesia del Carmen in Plaza del Carmen, near the Islamic fortress that stands atop Antequera's highest hill. Muslim rule lasted in Antequera until fairly late, 1410. The surrounding vista of plains and element-carved hills makes for a landscape of sleeping giants and lurking legends. If you look west you will see a mountain that looks like a sleeping man. It feels as if he is keeping Antequera safe.

Three Neolithic dolmen tombs pull the spirit most here. Perhaps the storyboard landscape drew the dolmen builders, among Iberia's first farmers, to this spot for their tombs some sixty-five hundred years ago. These dolmens may also have been used for rituals, not only burials. Built by early farmers, the connection to the earth and the underworld of the planter and his gods is unmistakable. As with later Bronze and Iron Age peoples, Neolithic farmers likely saw divinity in all things. Perhaps these dolmens were seen as key gateways to the other worlds of the spirits. When you walk into all three of these dolmens' passageways, the feeling of entry into the Earth's womb and into a threshold of another world is profound. Curiously, predating Christian churches and Muslim mosques by several thousand years, most of Spain's dolmen tomb entrances face an eastward direction.

Dolmens Viera and Menga

The dolmen of Viera is the first you will reach and is the smallest of the three. A small narrow corridor of all stone slabs leads into a belly where lies a tomb that once contained a person buried in fetal position with his or her personal effects.

The dolmen of Menga, whose entrance was shown to me by the groundskeeper's gregarious dog, who seemed to know every inch of this mound culture, is the largest Neolithic site in Antequera. Monumental in nature, five huge stone slabs make the roof and are held up by several stone pillars. With a length of 27.5 meters and a width of 6 meters, the five total stone slabs making the roof must be nearly 6 by 5.5 meters each. The height of the roof increases the deeper in you go and in the interior is also a shaft some 19.5 meters deep. Here excavators found the corpse of what some believe to be a chief who was buried in the fetal position. Its entrance curiously faces the sleeping giant of the great distant landscape outside of Antequera, giving possible weight to this landscape's sanctity in the lives of early Iberians.

Around forty-six hundred to four thousand years ago, a village stood around two hundred meters to the east of these two dolmens. It is likely that such settlements were sprinkled throughout the area.

To Dolmen Romeral (2 miles/3 km):

Take the road that passes Dolmens Viera and Menga NE; follow signs to the Dolmen Romeral.

Dolmen Romeral

A rare westerly oriented dolmen tomb, it is also a mound structure currently surrounded by a ring of cypress trees, much like a monk's tonsure. Beyond are Andalusian almond trees. Unlike Viera and Menga, the walls of Romeral's long corridor are built of stacked unmortared stones, which hold eleven large stone slabs on the roof. Leading to the tomb, where the chamber opens into a circle and a dome, two people were once buried here, one in a small chamber beyond the dome's space and one in the larger domed room. Unlike Viera and Menga, each of these two corpses was buried in a different position and neither in the fetal.

No one knows what has become of the bodies buried in these three dolmen tombs. Discovered some four hundred or more years ago, these sites have been hampered by much time and imperfect excavation.

While in Antequera, visit the natural formations of El Torcal, south of the town, which are a cluster of strange nature-carved standing stone landscapes. Neolithic caves exist in this area as well.

Antequera to Granada (63.5 miles/102 km):

Take N-331 N out of Antequera; take A-92 E to Granada.

GRANADA—Andalusia

Granada literally means "pomegranate." It is the fruit of Persephone, goddess of the Underworld, complex, subterranean, and feminine. The pomegranate was introduced to Spain by Muslims. Today it is the symbol of the city. It is a perfect one as it is a beautiful city, alluring and deep in

The Patio of Lions in the Alhambra palace in Granada, Andalusia

history, but it is also a sad city, one that still feels as if half the year it must be separated from its mother and go into the underworld. The sadness of exile has never fully lifted from this place. As a result, it has inspired incredibly beautiful art, poetry, music, and architecture.

An Iberian settlement around the Albaicin area, Granada was mostly a garrison town until the *taifa* period when it became a city-state under the Zirid clan. When the rest of al-Andalus began to fall to Christian conquests in the thirteenth century, Muhammad ibn Yusuf ibn Nasr founded an independent kingdom based in Granada, to which he gave his name. The new independent state Nasrid Granada received Muslims fleeing conquered regions. Granada was never a strong kingdom. From 1246, when Fernando III attacked and took the town of Jaén, Granada became a subordinate of the Castilian king and henceforth paid a tribute to Castile. In this manner, for some two and a half centuries, the Kingdom of Granada survived as the last Muslim kingdom in Spain. In spite of its weakened position, it remained a cultivator of the arts and sciences and acted as a center for trades and craftspeople. The ascension of Isabel and Ferdinand and the desire for a unified Catholic Spain marked the last days of Nasrid Granada.

Though one of the conditions of surrender was the protection of Granada's multifaith communities, the Christian monarchs first set about persecuting Jews with forced conversion and exile as early as the year of conquest, 1492. By 1499 the same edict was pressed upon the Muslims and by the first quarter of the 1500s all citizens in Spain were officially Christian. The Alpujarra mountains south of Granada were populated mostly by Moriscos, converted Muslims, who staged rebellions throughout the sixteenth century. But in the end, all Moriscos, as well as Conversos, converted Jews, were expelled from Spain between 1609 and 1614.

Granada's spiritual gems are the Alhambra and a handful of lovely churches in the neighboring Albaicin neighborhood built in the Mudéjar style, some having once been mosques. I do not cover the cathedral here as one of the sites because by comparison it lacks the spiritual pull of the places listed, but along its outer walls is a daily herb market where you can buy medicinal herbs and tea infusions—a bit of pagan Spain has returned near the royal chapel where the entombed Isabel and Fernando lie, whose religious policies snuffed out so much spiritual strength in the city and in the nation at large. But today, like these herb sellers, many spiritual elements are flowing back in, as witnessed in the New Age bohemian feel of the old Muslim neighborhood, the Albaicin, and the new mosque built primarily by European converts to Islam. But nothing can compete with the singular beauty and uniqueness of the Alhambra.

The Alhambra

The Alhambra was first a fortress and became the royal grounds under the Nasrids when the rest of Spain fell into Christian dominion. The Alhambra palace and fortress city were a separate settlement from the rest of Granada. The walk up the hill following the road, Cuesta de Gomerez, is both beautiful in its tree coverage and a good way to get a feel for the Alhambra's separateness from the rest of Granada.

The Alhambra represents the last peak in Islamic Spain's golden age. Unlike prior centuries when Muslims felt more confident of their place in Spain, Granada was a last stand, but a glorious one at that, having its own gleaming moments of splendor and accomplishment. Part of its original splendor was to create a vision of paradise on Earth for a waning dynasty.

Today the entire Alhambra is a sacred site even though nearly all of its grounds are dedicated to profane and earthly affairs. The site is rife with sacred meaning for all who visit; you will be taken by its mingled human-made and natural beauty.

There are many nooks and crannies in the Alhambra complex, some open to the public and others closed, and some rotating so that each visit is a unique show-and-tell. The whole complex is splendid, with built and natural environments that make the Nasrid palace mime the shapes and moods of nature. Some rooms feel like a forest with dappled light. There are also political statements, such as the current Iglesia de Santa María, dating to the late sixteenth and early seventeenth centuries, that was built on the palace's mosque. A little further north, the Generalife Palace served as an escape for the Nasrid kings when the public life of the Alhambra got to be too much. It was in those days removed enough from the rest of the settle-ment to serve as such a getaway. Try to imagine it surrounded by orchards, farm plots, and pastures as it was in the late Middle Ages rather than the overly sculpted gardens of today. (Both times, however, now and then, do their best to create paradise on Earth, each in its own vision.)

Iglesia de Santa Ana y San Gil

The Iglesia de Santa Ana y San Gil is a small church with a great tile-inlaid Mudéjar tower on the Plaza de Santa Ana, overlooking the Plaza Nueva and lying at the bottom of the Alhambra's hill, next to the Albaicin. Look above you once inside: the entire nave and altar are cov-ered with a wood-carved Mudéjar ceiling. The iconography is dominantly Marian. A favorite is the second chapel on the left upon entering, where Mary reigns from heaven standing on a crescent moon whose tips are each finished with a star and whose shape is closer than most to the original goddess's bull horns. Her hands' gesture of reaching out is particularly warming and comforting.

The Albaicin

Once called *Rabad al-Bayyazin*, the Albaicin was one of many residen-tial quarters to the west and southwest of the Alhambra's hill. Today's Albaicin's location is much the same as the medieval Albaicin and it is the heart of a New Age and multifaith Granada wherein Middle Easterners, Spanish converts to Islam, New Age and alternative-medicine practition-ers, and hippies and young bohemians congregate around the many tea-houses and health-food stores and eateries. It is a tourist scene that engages romantic ideas about medieval Granada and the life of the Albaicin and the Alhambra.

Along the labyrinthine streets of the Albaicin there is one street in particular that is the center of commercial, residential, and tourist activity, Caldereria Nueva. Caldereria Nueva is a mix of traditional homes woven in between and above the teahouses and shops. At the very top of the street is a sweet little church that offers a quiet space for meditation and prayer.

Deeper into the Albaicin the city has set up a Mudéjar Route that allows you to visit several churches with Mudéjar towers: Iglesia de San José, Iglesia de San Miguel Bajo, El Monasterio de Santa Isabel el Real, and Iglesia de San Nicolás. Right next door to San Nicolás church is the new mosque in Granada. A polemic exercise to get it built, polarized between the more conservative converts and the city council, the mosque was finally built in a manner that satisfied everyone, in the style of the other sacred buildings around it, which honors the multifaith heritage of this city while allowing Muslims to return here and build mosques and pray alongside their Christian cousins. All that is needed now is a synagogue for the balance to be struck. (There is already a major Buddhist group here, practicing the Diamond Way, and many nature-based and animistic followers of Earth spirituality who make up a rich mix of alternative faith and practice options in the Albaicin.)

Sacromonte

The Sacromonte, literally "sacred mountain," is a district famous for its Romani residents (many of whom no longer live here) and its well-outfitted cave dwellings. It is also the site of an important local pilgrimage to the Ermita de San Miguel el Alto (on the paseo del Generalife). The hermitage occupies what was once one of the watchtowers of the Moorish defensive wall around the city. It is open only during the time of its pilgrimage, in late September. At the top of the sacred mountain stands a seventeenth- to eighteenth-century Benedictine monastery, the Abadia del Sacromonte, where within its walls rest the ashes of Granada's patron saint, St. Cecilio, the first bishop of the city (Obispo) during Roman times when the city was known as Illíberis. He is believed to have been martyred under Nero's rule (middle of the first century AD) by being burned to death on the Sacromonte, then known as the mountain Illipulitano. His feast day is February 1.

Granada to Murcia (182 miles/293 km):
Take A-92 E toward Guadix; take A-92 N toward Lorca; take A-7/E-15 to Murcia.

MURCIA—Murcia

Very few visitors come to Murcia, and this is a shame, for Murcia was at the center of ancient and medieval Spain's action and today it is a warm, welcoming, and gregarious city surrounded by a part of Spain's agricultural heartland, whose irrigation and terracing legacy can be attributed to the Moorish innovations brought here and kept to the present day. The city is built along the banks of the lovely Segura River, and Mulberry trees with their big fleshy leaves line myriad streets in honor of the once-crucial silk industry that gave this city its main medieval business along with agriculture. Nearly all the vegetables and fruits you buy in the covered or weekly markets of Murcia are local—most produce will be sent to the rest of Spain as well as other parts of Europe.

There are historic medieval buildings in which you can now glimpse earlier foundations of Phoenician and Roman settlements. Muslims founded *Mursiya* in 831 and built the irrigation system that today remains a reason why Murcia is one of Spain's most productive agricultural heartlands. It was a fairly independent Muslim town and region from the early ninth century until 1241 when James I of Aragón took it for his realm.

Murcia is the birthplace of the famous Muslim mystic and philosopher Ibn 'Arabi, known locally as Aben Arabí. Though the city has no physical remains of his presence, the municipal government has set up the *Centro de Estudios Ibn Arabi,* reflecting the persistent pride Murcianos hold in their Muslim son. I have heard but could not confirm that the government of Murcia contributes to the maintenance of his tomb in Damascus.

Ibn 'Arabi

This great Sufi mystic, philosopher, and poet was born in 1165 in Murcia. Ibn 'Arabi left for pilgrimage to Mecca via Fez around the time the Almohads were about to invade the Peninsula in 1200. He traveled widely in the Islamic world. He never returned to Spain, likely because of the rigid Almohad rule or the state of chaos the conquest left in its wake. From Mecca, Ibn 'Arabi traveled throughout southwest Asia and finally made Damascus his home in 1223, where he taught and wrote his mystical treatises, commentaries, and poetry. Today his tomb stands in a mosque and a neighborhood that bear his name. He is considered among the greatest mystics of the world, not only in Islam but in the universal transcendent experience.

Ibn 'Arabi's philosophy and body of literature incite the individual to see beyond the surface and to read the symbolic content of things and occurrences to perceive the message beneath in order to attain a knowing of the divine. For him the divine pervaded everything, and everything was love, lover, and loved. A mystic, he saw God's hand in everything, every leaf, every flower, every bird, every smell and sound, every creature and act, manifesting its glory to the acute observer.

One of his most famous concepts was unity of being, *wahdat al-wujud,* the oneness of all creation. He was concerned with ways of knowing and with experiences of the divine, taking these religious issues out of religious theory and into mystical reality.

The universality and influence of Ibn 'Arabi can be seen in St. John of the Cross's *Dark Night of the Soul* where he evokes similar concepts of God as the Beloved, El Amante. Moreover, Christianity's core message—God is Love—is the central tenet of Sufism. It is with Ibn 'Arabi that this tenet received a lifetime of astute devotion and over three hundred volumes of mystical literature.

Ibn 'Ammar

A Muslim El Cid, Ibn 'Ammar was a talented opportunist, and when he was out of favor with Muslim kings, he fled to the north to serve Alfonso VI. He did, however, return when the dust settled and carried out operations for Muslim rulers, as well as briefly taking Muslim Murcia for his own, that is, before he had to flee again for the Christian north. His oscillating ultimately cost him his head. When he was captured in war in the 1080s he was taken back to Sevilla where al-Mu'tamid cut off his head using a gift ax from Alfonso VI. Both El Cid and Ibn 'Ammar tell us that politics, power, and wealth were the primary motivators of action, not religion. These affairs had very little to do with being Muslim or Christian and it would be erroneous to read cause and effect in that vein.

Cathedral of Santa María

In 1394 Murcia's Great Friday Mosque was flattened and from its dust and stones the current cathedral was constructed. A mix of all the styles, from Romanesque to Baroque, one influence holds from Muslim times: the central area of the cathedral's windows uses the Moorish style of dividing them with colonnettes. Alfonso X literally gave his heart to the city and it is now buried beneath the cathedral's main altar.

The overall feel of this cathedral is very warm, inviting one to participate in Mass or silent prayer. The Capilla de los Velez is a wild masterpiece of carving including a folk-style Jesus on the cross, a plethora of animals such as twined snakes, stags, dragons, as well as pilgrims and scallop shells. The arches are a cross between the Alhambra's scallop-lobed arches and classic Romanesque ones. Behind the main altar looms a stained-glass window depicting boldly the pyramid with the eye of God and God's ever-presence. This nice parallel takes us back to the Alhambra in Granada where a lantern held on four columns once stood in the Palacio de

Comares to represent Allah's ever-present gaze. It is the same God and the same eye represented in two similar manners to manifest abstractly the transcendent in place and time.

Convento de las Claras

Also known as El Real Monasterio de Santa Clara, this convent has Mozarabic grills in its interior, indicating a Moorish influence in its construction. A few years ago archaeologists discovered an Alhambra-style patio garden complex that dated to the thirteenth century, a hundred years older than any of its kind found in Granada. On the current Franciscan convent's grounds had stood a Moorish palace constructed by the descendents of Murcia's Muslim ruler Ibn Hud (Aben Hud, locally, he ruled from 1228–1238). In 1272 Alfonso X (El Sabio, "The Learned") took it over and turned it into a royal home. Then in 1365, Pedro I donated it to the Order of Santa Clara, which constructed the current monastery, which is still active and is the home of several nuns. As the monastery developed and expanded, parts of the palace were built over or remodeled.

Murcia to Santuario de Fuensanta (3 miles/5 km):
On the S edge of the city toward Algezares.

SANTUARIO DE FUENSANTA—Murcia

Dedicated to the precious element of water in the form of a sacred spring as well as of rain, Nuestra Señora de la Fuensanta, Our Lady of the Sacred Spring, is the city of Murcia's patron saint. For an area dependent on irrigation and agriculture, water is truly sacred. Fuensanta is on a spot believed to be an ancient site resonant for many of the peoples who passed through this part of Spain, from indigenous Iberians to Celts, Phoenicians, and Romans.

For Christians, an apparition of the Virgin Mary appeared here in the fifteenth century and sprouted a sacred stream. The church built in her honor on this spot is a Neoclassical and Baroque chapel. The Lady of Fuensanta's distinguishing traits from other Marian apparitions are her miracles as a rainmaker, which began in the late 17th century. People annually made a pilgrimage to the sacred spring during the Middle Ages, but in 1694, during a severe drought, pilgrims petitioned the Virgin's intervention and carried her image into Murcia's town center. Portentously, rain came shortly thereafter, and the Lady who brought water from the earth in the form of a spring was now pulling it down from the sky in the form of rain. The theme of heaven and Earth coming together is nicely reflected here.

The shrine was converted into a church after the rains came. Nuestra Señora de la Fuensanta repeated this miracle many times over the next centuries. Today the practice of carrying her image to Murcia's cathedral and back marks the annual pilgrimage to the church. The sacred shrine still exists and you can visit it at the bottom of the slope on which the church stands.

Murcia to Caravaca de la Cruz (38 miles/61 km):
Go W on C-415.

CARAVACA DE LA CRUZ—Murcia

A visit to Caravaca de la Cruz is well worth it for the medieval feel of the town and for the isolated solidness of its sacred sanctuary and region. Also appealing is its off-the-beaten-path existence. You will likely be the only foreigner outside of the agricultural talent brought in from Africa and Latin America to work in the orchards that surround this otherwise stark, rolling, and dry place. This part of Murcia and of Spain is the least visited and as such holds a special enchantment because of its remoteness and untouched nature.

Legend and Sanctuary of the True Cross of Caravaca de la Cruz

It is said that on May 3, 1232, Abu Zaid, the Almohad ruler, came to Caravaca de la Cruz to look in on the Christian prisoners taken captive and being held in the Moorish castle. Among them was a priest, Ginés Pérez de Chirinos. Abu Zaid was more a mystic than a zealot and believed in universal truths, such as that his god, Allah, was one and the same as the deity that Christians referred to as *Dios*. Curious to learn of the Christian liturgy, he asked Pérez de Chirinos to officiate over the Mass in his presence. The priest thought that he had procured all the items for Mass, but as the Mass began he realized that he was missing the cross. At this moment, with the Muslim ruler witnessing, the sky opened and two angels arrived and placed a cross on the altar right before his eyes. So moved was Abu Zaid by the visit that he converted to Christianity. The sacred cross that appeared to Abu Zaid was a *lignum crucis* in the form of a double-armed cross. It is protected in a jewel-encrusted case that takes the form of the eastern double-armed patriarchal, or Lorraine, cross. In 1998 Pope

John Paul II visited the town and declared Caravaca de la Cruz the fifth holy city in Christendom after Jerusalem, Rome, Santiago de Compostela, and Santo Toribio de Liébana. Every seven years a jubilee is held and pilgrims to the site receive indulgences. The first jubilee year was 2003.

After the decline of Almohad rule, by the middle of the thirteenth century, Caravaca fell under Christian dominion and was overseen by Templar knights. Their highest purpose was to guard the Vera Cruz, held in Caravaca's hilltop castle, which was once the Almohad fortress. Later this duty fell to the Order of Santiago. The sanctuary where the cross is kept dates to the fifteenth century and was built within the confines of the thirteenth-century Moorish castle (the high altar is built into the back of the castle's main tower). Exploring the area you will see walls and towers that hearkened to this fortress structure.

The interior of the sanctuary possesses several enigmatic items, the most important being the cross, which is not on public display and is securely locked away. However, among the other powerful items that *are* on display in the sanctuary is a four-armed wheel carved into the central altar's upper dome side. According to locals and legend, it marks the spot where the True Cross appeared. The symbol is surrounded by what look like Greek letters, but apparently no one has made out what it says and there is a good deal of mystery about it and who placed it there.

Another aspect of the sanctuary is the continuing dedication, as we have seen everywhere in Spain, to the Virgin Mary, who is the main presence on the church's altar. Finally, the chapel at the very top of the sanctuary, called the Capilla de Conjuros, is dedicated to the apostles, who are petitioned here as protectors of the natural world of plants and animals and the land. It is a lovely honoring of our true role as stewards, not masters, of life on Earth, and of earlier, pre-Christian reverence for the natural world.

This is also the annual site of the Moros y Cristianos festival as well as the unique Festival of Wine Horses. The festivals in early May surrounding the Vera Cruz are overseen by the Cofradia de la Vera Cruz, a dedicated, passionate, and gregarious group of town men in whose veins the stories and miracles continue to live.

Festival of Wine Horses and of Moors and Christians

A few decades after Abu Zaid's conversion, after the Almohads had been defeated and the only Muslim kingdom left was that of Granada, it is said that Muslim soldiers from Granada laid siege to Caravaca's castle, where Templar knights guarded the sacred relic of the True Cross. Surrounded on all sides, the knights were trapped in the castle fortress and cut off from their water supply. A few knights managed to sneak past the Muslim watch and procured two horses and wineskins filled with wine. They stormed up the hill with the wine on horseback and into the castle without getting caught. It is said that, when the True Cross was dipped into it, the wine transformed into a miraculous elixir that healed the wounds of the soldiers and strengthened them to conquer the Muslims below.

In the seventeenth century, an annual rite arose with horses carrying wine to the sacred chapel of the Vera Cruz for it to be blessed. Given the importance of wine in Christian worship as well as in the region's economy, this is a perfect ritual reflecting the rhythms of life in this part of Spain.

The Festival of Wine Horses, one of the rites observed in late April and early May to honor the Holy Cross, reenacts this feat with processions and races of beautifully outfitted horses up the hill and ending at the castle. The wine they carry is still blessed with the True Cross.

Another festival celebrated at the same time as the Wine Horses is that of Moros y Cristianos, Moors and Christians. This part of Spain, stretching a bit west and all the way to Valencia and Sagunto, is the heart of this peculiar festival. Each year different groups are designated as either Christian or Muslim and dress up in exquisitely detailed and elaborate costumes reflecting their "religious" affiliation and proceed through the streets. Each town does this differently: either there are diplomatic talks or a mock battle. In the end, the Christians always win, but the general good cheer and democratic feel alerts you to the fact that everyone here is having a great time and is a winner. During these festivities, special Masses and rituals around the Vera Cruz are held at the sanctuary.

Caravaca de la Cruz to Bocairent (94 miles/ 151 km):
Go E on C-330; take C-3314 N to Jumilla; just before Jumilla take N-344 NE to Yecla; in Yecla take CV-81 E to Bocairent.

BOCAIRENT—Valencia

This delightful town off the beaten path is curiously the center of several pilgrimage roads, like a star emitting rays of light all around it. Nearly anywhere you stand in Bocairent is likely to be on one pilgrims' road or another. Here there is a magical concentration of springs, fountains, caves, hermitages, and beautiful mountain vistas where diverse plant life grows, including aromatic and medicinal herbs that local lore states have been gathered for centuries. Try *hebrero*, the local herb liquor, and imbibe the magical medicinal herbs' centuries-old power.

Neolithic as well as Roman remains signal the ancient use of this area, but the Muslims really put the settlement on the map, calling it Bekirén and building it up into the settlement on which you now stand. Perhaps this is why it is also the location of one of the area's most engaging festivals of Moors and Christians, taking place in February and in honor of the town's patron saint, San Blai, or Saint Blas.

The town's parish church, Iglesia de Nuestra Señora de la Asunción, stands atop an eleventh- and twelfth-century Arab castle and was completed in 1516. Its tower is the tower you see upon approaching the town and is like a compass point, offering reference to where you are.

Several pilgrimages radiate out from Bocairent as well. Two outlined here offer a rich exploration of two sides of the town, one into the herb-covered hills north of the village to Ermita del Santo Cristo, and the other south of town, going to the Ermita de San Jaume, into the rolling green forested hills past the River Clariano and the many irrigation ditches that make this place bloom.

Ermita de Santo Cristo

Start from the Plaza de Ayuntamiento and take the road called Baixada al Sant Crist and follow the sign to Ermita de Santo Cristo. It will lead you to a lower road that crosses a stone bridge, which will take you to the beginning of the pilgrim path.

Local popular legend tells of two young men dressed as pilgrims who arrived in Bocairent in 1536 exclaiming that the mountain to the north of the village looked like the perfect place for a representation of Calvary. As they uttered these words to the townspeople, suddenly three glorious lights burst forth on the same spot as where the hermitage of Santo Cristo now stands. In honor of this miracle, not only did the townspeople build a pilgrimage path with stations of the cross leading to the shrine on the hilltop dedicated to Jesus, but each September they celebrate the Festival of the Three Lights (in Valenciano, a language related to Catalán, which is the local language, *Festa de les tres llums*).

The Calvary stations, fourteen in all before you arrive at the hermitage, are spaced to offer a well-paced walking meditation. Each shrine depicts a terra-cotta relief scene from the last days of Christ. At each, offerings from the last pilgrimage remain, such as now-dried twigs of rosemary or other aromatic herbs that grow in great abundance along the hillside, or small stones, neatly stacked on one another. A shrine to Nuestra Señora de Soledad, Our Lady of Grief, stands between stations ten and eleven. By the time you are two-thirds up the hill, if not sooner, you will notice the strong scent of herbs. As soon as the sun's rays hit the hillside, a wild chorus of essential oils from all the plants is released, making you feel like you are walking into an herbalist's medicine cabinet. By the time you arrive at the hermitage at the top, the Sierra Mariola reveals her next layers of hills and scrub.

If you continue along the path that starts behind the pilgrimage, it will take you to a sacred cave dedicated to Baeta Piedad de la Cruz (allow another one to two hours for this stretch and your return, and be sure you have water with you). Along the way you will pass on your left an iron cross dedicated to the fallen victims of the last of the Carlist and Isabeline wars in 1873. Bear in mind that the cave does not announce itself until you are nearly there. It appears suddenly, as if protected by nature spirits who will open the veil only to those who have the patience to arrive with a reverent manner toward the entire natural and untouched world around them.

Ermita de Sant Jaume

The sixteenth-century hermitage to Saint James is set in the forest south of town and stands on the spot of a sacred fountain as well as a celebratory round table made of stone. The table might very well be a millstone for grinding grain or pressing olives. It has fifteen stone seats around it evoking an Arthurian mood. It is likely the place where celebrants on St. James's feast day, May 1, gather with music, food, wine, and communal good cheer.

To arrive here start at the Hotel L'Estacio's parking lot. This was the old station when the train still passed this way. Go uphill from the parking lot, taking the second road from the right, the one that heads down rather than up. Stay on this paved road for approximately 1.5 kilometers until you arrive at a yellow post with a red rectangular marker on top. All along you will notice bubbling irrigation ditches along the roadside, green fertile fields, and rolling orchards. A veritable paradise, continue on this road, which in about half a kilometer snakes around into a hairpin turn to the right. At that point the only sign to Ermita de Sant Jaume appears.

Stay on the paved road and go uphill. You will pass through some wooded residential areas and begin to enter a private gated section. The hermitage is the second-to-last building on your right before this point. (The last building is someone's house and has a doghouse with the name

"Igor" on its entrance. You've gone too far if you see this.) As you quietly take in the wooded grounds, note the tremendous bird activity and bird-song. Woodpeckers with great striped brown, black, and cream wings seem regular inhabitants.

Covetes dels Moros

These "caverns of the Moors" are over fifty human-carved roomlike caverns in a rock cliff wall east of town. Were they Visigothic tombs, living spaces for a community of hermits, or Arab granaries? There are a number of theories, but the caverns seem to have been used for food storage by the ruling Berbers, who settled in this area during the Muslim period, in the tenth and eleventh century. The path approaching the caverns passes through an herb garden showcasing many of the medicinal and sacred herbs of the area, some standard familiars and others unique to the Mariola mountains. Snakes and lizards frequent these areas, as do swallows and raptors overhead.

Bocairent to Xátiva (29 miles/46 km):
Take CV-81 NE to Ontinyent and Albaida; follow signs for Albaida and for N-340; take N-340 N and follow signs to Xátiva.

XÁTIVA (JÁTIVA)—Valencia

Dominated by one of Spain's longest fortress walls, Xátiva's castle is high up on the mountain ridge overshadowing the city, a strategic point since Roman times, if not earlier. It was the seat of the Visigothic See where its church, the Hermitage of Sant Feliu, still stands. Today's Xátiva continues to hug the protective mountain. While in town, wherever you look up, you will see a stretch of the castle fortress wall. A Calvary with stations of the cross appears on the northern side near the mountain. The reaches beyond the mountain are of a vast green fertile plain, making it clear why this location was desired by so many peoples throughout time. The long climb up to the castle on top is worth it for the views and the passing sites.

Ermita de Sant Feliu

On the road to the castle stands a simple thirteenth-century Romanesque church built over the sixth- or seventh-century Visigothic structure, and the feel is a hybrid of both Visigothic and Romanesque worlds. It is a beautiful all-natural space emphasizing wood and stone and unhindered, unadorned space. Polychrome frescoes once covered the walls, and ghosts of their forms remain. The hermitage serves as a mini-museum of Xátiva's many faiths, and inside you will find exhibited relics from the Jews, Muslims, Visigoths, and Romans who once lived here.

Ermita de Sant Josep

Just a little up the hill near the Ermita de Sant Feliu on the road leading up to the castle is the eighteenth-century Hermitage of Saint Joseph. Between the two hermitages stands an old Roman bath currently being excavated. It was taken over by Muslims, another bath-loving culture, and used as their public baths.

Closed and being renovated at the time of writing, the Ermita de Sant Josep has interesting grounds worth exploring. When James I took Xátiva and entered the walled city on June 7, 1244, he passed through a gate called *Aljama*, a word both Jews and Muslims use to designate their community or society. Now sealed in with bricks, it stands next to the Romanesque-style door of the chapel and bears a plaque commemorating this transfer of power right at the threshold where it occurred.

While we could continue this *convivencia* pilgrimage farther north along the Valencian coast or go inland toward Aragón or Castile, we have passed through the heartland of al-Andalus. As much as there was a fruitful living together, there was also turmoil and conflict. So much of what we know about the period of Muslim and medieval Spain is a roster of conquests and of administrative records. But we also have hints and suggestions of Christians, Jews, and Muslims marrying one another, sharing a glass of wine in a local tavern, or attending one another's services, especially in the days when the communities were not as separated, prior to the twelfth and thirteenth centuries. And we have the resonant sacred spaces that have survived, where we can feel our own spirits as well as the echoes of those who worshiped there before us.

$\mathscr{B}$enalmádena to Válor

You are more likely to find spirituality in the more recently arriving religions in Spain than in the Christian religion; because it is so established and mainstream it is more profane than sacred.
—local wisdom in conversation with a resident of Málaga

We Catholics are sick of people—religious authority—telling us what to do and what we want. Now we want to find our own way.
—a Spanish woman on the way to a Tibetan monastery in southern Spain

THIS IS A MODERN MULTIFAITH ROUTE. I have selected a part of Spain rather than a sampling in all regions because this area is a beautiful microcosm of all the many rich new- and old-age spiritualities that have taken root, or been re-rooted, throughout Spain. It is an area that can be tranquilly explored without having to drive to all ends of Spain, while still giving the spiritual traveler a deep taste of the vibrant devotional and spiritual communities of nature-based spiritualists, Hindus, Buddhists, Jews, Christians, and Muslims, whose focus is life-affirming and spirit-deepening practice and philosophy.

It is possible that this most diverse microcosm occurs here in southern Spain because this part in Spain's history was the most crisscrossed and trod upon by Old World peoples, holding the imprints of all the peoples who have come to the Iberian Peninsula, from the Paleolithic to Neolithic, Iberian to Phoenician and Greek, to Roman, Visigothic, Berber, Arab, Sephardic, European, and Castilian. Southern Spain's climate also makes it appealing to diverse people. Today, from Granada to the southern coast are many people from many parts of the world and among them spiritual seekers and practitioners of every ilk. A huge part of the attraction to this region is the juxtaposition of rugged, high mountains with the Mediterranean Sea, especially in the Alpujarra mountains. Sea breezes and alpine air mix in an intoxicating manner. Given this alpine-coastal blend, the light is also unique and draws artists as much as spiritual seekers. Parallels to what they are cultivating here are occurring in all other parts of Spain but not to the same degree of concentration.

As with any spiritual pursuit, old or new, exercising discernment and clarity of thought and intention is always recommended. What is presented here is an honest account of the breadth of expressions of modern spirituality from one of Spain's most multifaith rich areas. But being listed here does not count as an endorsement—that is for the reader to decide.

Main Route (208 miles/335 km):
Benalmádena—Málaga—Granada—Lanjarón—Órgiva—Padre Eterna— O Sel Ling—Pampaneira—Bubión—Capileira—Pitres—Trevélez— Yegén—Válor

BENALMÁDENA—Andalusia

This is an overly built place but a little tour inland gets you away from all the depravity and into some magnificent wild places as well as temples. Before heading away from the coast, visit Benalmádena Costa's Hindu temple. Then head to the next masterpiece spiritual site, the Buddhist temple, or stupa, uphill and inland near Benalmádena Pueblo. Built on a high point on a hillside overlooking the Mediterranean and surrounded by wild Mediterranean scrub plants, it is a world removed from the ugly artifice of destroyed beaches below.

Hindu Temple Benalmádena Costa: *Take N-340 to Benalmádena Costa.* (Avenida Gandhi s/n, near the Parque Paloma, Benalmádena Costa, ☎ 952-57-65-12)

This is an active Hindu temple on the Costa del Sol where most Hindu holidays are celebrated. The spiritual head is Dushyant Sharmaji. The main altar inside holds many gods, including Laxminarayan (goddess of wealth, Laxmi, and her consort Vishnu), Durga (the supreme goddess representing Shakti, creative energy), Sita-Rama Lakshman Hanuman (four deities depicted together: Rama is the seventh incarnation of Vishnu, Sita is his wife, Lakshman is his brother, and Hanuman his disciple), and Radha-Krishna (representing perfect, divine love). All around are images of spiritual leaders as well, including one of the Virgin Mary and another of Jesus.

Benalmádena Costa to International Cemetery and Muslim Cemetery (3 miles/5 km):
Take N-340 E; exit N to Arroyo de la Miel; continue past Arroyo de la Miel; the International Cemetery is on a road on the right before Benalmádena Pueblo.

International Cemetery and Muslim Cemetery

The mood and message of this place is a conscious effort to communicate the value of strength in diversity, and it is as much a mausoleum for the international community and an outlook of this odd retirement haven for world peoples as it is a place to bury loved ones. It is a moving experience to wander through the mixed burial plots, some above ground in the Spanish tradition and others underground as in many other traditions. A Jew is buried next to an Arab, a Protestant, a Catholic, and an Armenian, and so on. This is the reality of the living and so becomes the natural resting place of the dead. Messages on tombstones remind one of another's losses, dedications to a living mother or a gregarious grandfather, to a child who died too early but was surrounded by love, or, in one case, to a prominent leader of the Baha'i faith who found his final work here in southern Spain.

The overall place is built like a Moorish-inspired garden. Even the entrance is like a little piece of the Alhambra, with arched passageways and a fountain. More recently, added to the back of the international cemetery is a Muslim cemetery, fulfilling a desire when possible for Muslims to be buried in a Muslim cemetery. Here it is clear that the devout do not want to be too far away from the benevolence of *convivencia*. Among the many nationalities represented here—all people who came to call this place home at the end of their lives—are Spanish, English, Finnish, Israeli, Lebanese, Egyptian, Iranian, Dutch, Swedish, South African, North American, French, German, and Latin American.

International Cemetery to Benalmádena Pueblo (1 mile/2 km):
Return to the main road and turn right, uphill, and proceed to Benalmádena Pueblo; the Buddhist stupa is further uphill, just after you pass through Benalmádena Pueblo.

Buddhist Group Benalmádena Pueblo

(E-29639 Benalmádena Pueblo, ☎ 952-56-96-62, Benalmádena@ diamondway-center.org, 🖳 www.stupaBenalmádena.org)

Himalayan Buddhist master Lopön Tsechu Rimpoché conceived of the idea in 1995 to build the "biggest Buddhist stupa in Europe." Working with Benalmádena's mayor, Enrique Bolín, he built just that in Benalmádena Pueblo today. Inaugurated in 2005, it is a brilliant, white, heaven-reaching temple capped with a golden steeple that reaches deeper into heaven, channeling good vibes like a radio tower, of prayers going out and blessings coming in. Sealed within the treasure chamber of the building with many other sacred objects are six thousand clay images of the Buddha sculpted by two of Rimpoché's students. Also sealed within the stupa is a seventeen-meter Tree of Life, representing the Axis Mundi, and the Buddha's spine, another heaven-and-Earth synergy with the golden steeple bringing in heavenly energy and the many Buddhas literally grounding it and bringing it deeply into the Earth. What is unusual about this stupa is its interior meditation room. Most stupas are circumambulated and lack this inner space. The meditation area opens up from the entrance stairs facing the sea and offers a terrific space in which to spend as much time as you need in silence. The altar is held down by a large statue of the Buddha, with fruit offerings and lit candles at his feet. The high ceiling connecting you to the heaven needle above is especially exhilarating. The walls are covered with Tibetan scenes of monks, saints, and the Buddha. Tibetan peace flags flutter in the wind outside.

Buddhist Stupa to Fuengirola (5.5 miles/9 km):

Continue on the road uphill and follow it as it loops back toward the coast, returning to N-340; go W on N-340 to Fuengirola.

The Buddhist stupa in Benalmádena, Andalusia

Baha'i Costa del Sol and Multifaith Fuengirola

Again testimony to the sun worship on the Costa del Sol, even if the overdevelopment is not to your taste, it nevertheless attracts a hugely international crowd—this includes world religions and spiritualities.

On your way out of Benalmádena and to Málaga you can contact the Baha'i group in Fuengirola (calle Jaen, 1, 1-J, Los Boliches, ☎ 952-46-64-67). There are also groups in Marbella (☎ 952-78-14-76), Benalmádena (☎ 952-44-24-24), Nerja (☎ 952-52-42-67), and Málaga (☎ 952-21-40-52). Contact information for the community's main organization in Spain is: Comunidad Bahá'í de España, calle Matías Turrión, 32, 28043 Madrid, ☎ 913-88-13-85, informacion@bahai.es, 🖥 www.bahai.es.

Fuengirola also has a high concentration of non-Catholic Christian communities and churches:

Church of England (in Los Boliches nearby): St. Andrews, Avenida Padre Jesús Cautivo, 74, no telephone.

Jehovah's Witnesses: Kingdom Hall, calle Nuñez de Balboa, s/n, ☎ 952-46-90-82.

Evangelical Church: Evangelical Fellowship, Hotel Club Puerta del Sol, Fuengirola/Mijas road, ☎ 952-58-25-18.

Church of Scotland: Lux Mundi, calle Nueva, 7, ☎ 952-58-46-52.

Dutch Evangelical (in Los Boliches, nearby): Skandinaviska Turistkyran, Paseo Marítimo, 77, no telephone.

The Church of Jesus Christ of Latter-Day Saints: Terraza de la Veguilla no. 5, Plaza de la Hispanida, ☎ 952-46-93-92.

Scandinavian (in Tres Coronas, nearby): Svenska Kyrkan Fuengirola, Avenida Alcalde Clemente Diaz, 4, ☎ 952-46-58-87.

Fuengirola to Málaga (18.5 miles/30 km):
Take N-340 E and follow signs to Málaga.

MÁLAGA—Andalusia

From the beginning a successful market town, founded as Malaka by merchant and seafaring Phoenicians, Málaga continued as an important market town under successive occupants. Its development and industry peaked in the Islamic era. Its eleventh- to fourteenth-century Moorish palace-castle-fortress at the top of the city's highest hill overlooks the Mediterranean and stands as a reminder of this era. Today it continues as an important seaport and has a rich international community, which means a rich multifaith life.

Málaga's Sephardic Synagogue

When I lived in Morocco, researching the persistence of the Andalusian identity, that of people descended from medieval Spanish Jewish and Muslim families, I met an older man from Morocco's Sephardic community who was a founding member of a new synagogue in Málaga. Explaining his motive for this effort, he told me that he felt more at home in Spain than anywhere else in the world, including other obvious destinations like Israel, Morocco, and France. He added that he had always been from Spain in the long centuries that separated his family from Iberia.

This was a common sentiment among most of the Moroccan Andalusians I met, but few did more than talk about it or make touristy trips over the Strait of Gibraltar.

Many years later on a visit to Málaga, I found the synagogue and learned that it had a vibrant community of Sephardim from all over the world, mostly from Morocco but also from Latin America. All had felt out of place in their birth countries. The strength of belonging to Sepharad had never diminished and now they were home. For the Latin Americans, the language was the same but the locale made all the difference.

If you wish to attend a service at the synagogue, call ahead to introduce yourself and to learn the time and place for the service (☎ 952-60-40-94). The synagogue is in a modern high-rise building. Nondescript from the outside, the temple space inside has been transformed by the sacred work that goes on here. The service is in a mix of Castilian, Hebrew, and Ladino. Women have a separate section, and everyone should attend modestly dressed.

Convento San Agustín

This monastery and its attached church were built in the fifteenth to the eighteenth century. A piece of a Moorish window stands in the church's rose garden, offering a reminder of the likely foundations of this locale. This is a very active church with locals, and Mass can be packed, particularly on special saints' days. Young and old, healthy and infirm, all are in attendance taking in the words and blessings of the priests.

The Cathedral and Its Gardens

At night a frogs' chorus erupts from the garden fountains. A good sign, being bio-indicators, these earthly messengers riotously alert us to the health of the grounds. The cathedral was begun after 1487 under the patronage of monarchs Isabel and Ferdinand. Built over the Friday or Great Mosque, it is a warm place of worship. The city affectionately calls its cathedral La Manquita, the One Armed, because one of its two front towers was never finished. The asymmetry makes it flow. At night, sit at a café table in the Plaza del Obispo and enjoy a refreshment or meal while facing the One Armed as the sun sets and the swish of swallows is replaced by the flight of bug-eating bats around the one and a half towers.

Iglesia del Sagrario

This church shares the garden grounds with the cathedral and is just north of it, with its brick mosaic outer wall adding to the sanctuary feel of the garden. Built around the same time as the cathedral, it holds daily Mass and has a dedicated following.

Iglesia de Santiago

Built over a medieval mosque in 1490, the church was founded by people who loved aspects of the Muslim edifice enough to keep and incorporate them, such as the outer entrance, which is now sealed and a part of the wall but whose inlaid geometric tiles flow beneath the cross of Saint James, the patron of this church (Santiago). Other Islamic elements are the once-minaret, now bell tower, and the Mudéjar vaulted ceiling. This is the church in which the Málaga-born Pablo Picasso was baptized in 1881, and the original baptismal font for this occasion stands within. St. James appears in

An old mosque door in Málaga that was turned into a window for a church dedicated to St. James, the Iglesia de Santiago, Andalusia

his pilgrim's form on the main altar, but his political image of Matamoros, the Moor Slayer, used by rallying Christians, is also present to the left of the nave, reminding us again and again that people once lived in a world where they contested for the soul of cities over many centuries.

Málaga's Mosque

This is a dramatic and grand structure on the street Calle Ingeniero de la Torre Acosta, a main thoroughfare in town. It was yet to open its doors at the time of writing and the forthcoming policy for visiting and worshiping was unclear. It would be a good idea to inquire in the tourist office first.

Commissioned by the Saudi royal family, it is a monument to Andalusian Muslim architectural styles and is intended as a modern place for prayer, meeting, and worship. The architects who designed the six-thousand-square-meter space are Spanish architects Rafael Medina and Clemente Lara. It will be headed by the Saudi scholar Saleh al-Sonaidi, who studied in Granada and is interested in and attuned to Spanish culture and history.

Iglesia de la Salud

Perhaps because of its name, this is among Málaga's most vibrant churches as far as daily, active visits, prayer, and petitioning are concerned. The Iglesia de la Salud is just off the Plaza de la Constitución on Calle Compañía, and coming here feels like coming to a place fully alive with the spirit of the local people as they weave this sacred spot into their daily lives, stopping in between errands, before or after school, or on the way to work. This sixteenth-century church is completely round, a circle fit within a square. Above are a wonderful fresco-painted dome and stained-glass windows with geometric patterns of turquoise, cobalt blue, deep purple, and emerald green. It was once a Jesuit temple. A shrine to St. Jude stands in the back and all manner of modern offerings hang from its surface, from pictures of family and wedding photos, to little wax models of arms and legs, hearts, notes to the saint, ribbons, and other personal effects understood only by the supplicant.

SOLOMON IBN GABIROL

A Jewish poet and philosopher, credited with being among the great teachers of Neoplatonism in Europe, Gabirol was born in Málaga in 1021. He resided for a time in Zaragoza and then later in Valencia, where he died in 1058. In spite of his short life, he influenced spiritual thinking through his poetry and his Neoplatonic teaching. Neoplatonism was a further development of Plato's teaching, especially as elaborated through the teachings of Plotinus, a third-century AD Roman philosopher. His work influenced the early church fathers, such as Ambrose and Augustine, as well as later Jewish and Muslim thinkers. Its core philosophy is that everything in the world comes from a divine omniscient presence and that individual souls can know this presence inwardly through spiritual discipline such as meditation.

Detour to Córdoba

In addition to the old mosque-cathedral and the synagogue of this city, there are modern currents to follow in Córdoba. The contemporary Muslim community, made up of Spanish converts to Islam and Muslims from all across the Muslim world, has established an Islamic organization, the **Yama'a Islámica de Al-Andalus,** a new mosque, and a university (Universidad Islámica Internacional Averroes de Al-Andalus, Calleja de la Hoguera 3, 14003-Córdoba, ☎ 957-48-32-35, u.averroes@alcavia.net).

Málaga to Granada (90 miles/145 km):
Leave Málaga N on A-45; take A-92M NE to A-92 E; near Granada take A-92G E.

GRANADA—Andalusia

See chapter 15 for greater details on Granada. Highlights of the modern multifaith are iterated here.

The New Age Albaicin

Vegetarian restaurants, Shiatsu, Tai Chi, and yoga sessions, Sufi zhikrs, Hindu meditation sessions, Middle Eastern teahouses, North African and Pakistani groceries, incense, young Bohemians drumming at the foot of a central church, giddy tourists, and green grocers and bar owners doing business as usual in the impeccable Spanish style—these all paint the dynamic New Age picture of Granada's old medieval neighborhood in its modern manifestation.

The Alhambra Complex

Perhaps no place in Spain strikes people as more spiritual than the Alhambra and what it represents. A great complex overlooking Granada and the last residence of the Nasrid kings of Islamic Spain, it has become a symbol of the spirit of the mixing of civilizations for each one's betterment, even though it is at the end of that illustrious experiment of medieval Spain.

Today millions of people from across the world come here to walk through one people's earthly creation of their vision of paradise, and as such it possesses a sacred character. Among these visitors are Muslims from across the world, for whom this is a sacred pilgrimage to one of the places of Islam's golden age. I learned from North Africans that they and their relatives and friends come here as a pilgrimage, something they should do once in their life. Some of these people are making their way to France and make sure that they detour through Granada for this purpose alone. Others come here on vacation and return inspired. I met a man in Rabat, Morocco, who had returned from Granada and commissioned craftsmen to replicate in stucco and wood one of the salons of the Alhambra in his living room. He was not the only person who has done this in North Africa. But I think among the many people who come to the Alhambra, I delight most in the Japanese visitors' exclamations over the balance of gardens with naturalistic architecture. The Alhambra is a place that appeals to the Shinto spirit as much as to the Abrahamic.

See chapter 15 for greater details on the Alhambra.

Granada's New Albaicin Mosque

There was some controversy when this mosque was being built and the town insisted that the minaret be shorter than the surrounding bell towers in the neighborhood. One Sufi in the area remarked that, ironically, most of the bell towers surrounding the new mosque's minaret were once minarets themselves. People seem to have moved beyond these contentions and the mosque is a nice addition to the San Nicolás square area, which now feels more active, populated, and integrated into a multifaith neighborhood. In years past, prior to the mosque's construction, that same plaza was less visited and the church itself felt like a ghost. Today it is a part of a vibrant neighborhood.

While I have learned from some of the more liberal-leaning Muslims that the converts who control the new mosque are rigid, I did not encounter any of them and I found the place to be infused with a peaceful and deeply meditation-inducing energy. It looks across from the Albaicin neighborhood to the Alhambra, maximizing the romantic location to the fullest.

You might be required to set up a time to go through the mosque with a guide so don't be surprised when the caretaker pulls out an appointment sheet and officially sets about scheduling you in.

Medicinal and Culinary Herbs

Look for herbalists with their open-air tables along the cathedral's wall. Each herb has a sign indicating its medicinal properties. The herbalists are always ready to discuss each plant as well as a possible blend for pleasure or for healing purposes. The spiritual aspect of this is the respect for the plant kingdom and the knowledge of plant lore, something associated with the sacred in many traditions.

The Alpujarras

Terraced and well-irrigated mountainsides, snow-capped mountains, sheep and goat herds, olive and lemon trees—all these define the stunning mood of the Alpujarra mountains and valleys. At night, you can reach out your hand and touch the bright stars.

This mountain range south of Granada is famous for many reasons. It is the home of Spain's highest peak, Mulhacén, literally, Mount Hassan. Named by Arabs, it possesses a sacred nostalgia as one of the last bittersweet glimpses that the last Muslim ruler of Spain, the king of Granada Muhammad Abullah (Boabdil), had of his beloved kingdom. It is sacred to Christians as well, as expressed in the annual pilgrimage to Nuestra Señora de las Nieves, Our Lady of the Snows. The Alpujarras is also the last region to carry on its Muslim heritage, even after 1499 when all peoples in Spain were officially baptized and Christianized.

Here in the Alpujarras, the converted Muslims, now called Moriscos, held on to their customs and practices as long as possible and staged a number of troublesome revolts. They also maintained the terraced hillsides and irrigation ditches that their forebears had put in place, making this arid alpine setting fertile and arable. Today their presence is palpable, from the mood of the place as dipped in equal measures in darkness and light, from the form of homes that are still strongly informed by Berber and Arab aesthetics, from each village's church that stands on an old mosque and whose bell towers were once minarets, and from the citrus, olive, and nut trees that bloom and bear fruit on the hillsides.

By 1609 the Moriscos were expelled from Spain. Their villages and fields were left vacant until people from the north were recruited to repopulate the area and take up the slack. These people came from Galicia, León, and Castile.

Today's Alpujarrans are a mix of these peoples along with a growing international expatriate community, from all over Europe as well as a few from North Africa, the Middle East, Asia, and North and South America. Also, there are likely the occasional Morsico descendents whose ancestors successfully blended enough with the other Spanish population as to be overlooked by exile, or, as there are some indications of, sneaked back when no one was looking.

Water has always been a sacred element in these dry, rugged hills. It is an element made more available with the Muslims' introduction of irrigation systems. Moreover, each town and village has several fountains, many with local folkloric color as well as sacred connotations for this life-giving substance.

Granada to Lanjarón (26 miles/42 km):
Take A-44 S; take exit 164 to Lanjarón on A-348 E.

LANJARÓN—Andalusia

The dramatic marker for Lanjarón is its old Islamic castle, which balances precariously on a narrow outcrop of rock. It overlooks myriad terraced hills—another Islamic legacy—with the city immediately to its back, as if it is still casting a protective glance over the valley for its beloved Lanjarón. At the perfect defensive place given this perch, the castle is also a symbol of Lanjarón's Islamic past as well as its fusion of past civilizations, from the healing water spas first installed by Romans to the Islamic occupation and the later Christian settlement. Lanjarón's main church in the heart of town, Nuestra Señora de la Encarnación, has a Mudéjar church tower. Many new buildings going up pull from the Mudéjar style, reflecting a continued pride in this heritage. Medicinal spas operate today following their Roman heritage and offer medicinal mineral treatments.

Heaven & Earth Centre

Just outside of Lanjarón on a hilltop overlooking a vista of valleys, mountains, and the Mediterranean Sea is the enchanting Heaven & Earth Centre. This natural retreat has outdoor spaces for healing, meditation, and

The prayer wheel at O Sel Ling Tibetan Buddhist retreat in the Alpujarra mountains, Andalusia

exploration, which are designed with the centrality of plants and an outdoor connection in mind. A wonderful platform, with a geodesic frame on which plants can grow and offer natural shade and sacred space, acts as both a temple space and a yoga platform. Lodging can be arranged nearby at one of the many rural farmhouses, or *cortijos*, that operate as holiday rentals.

Richard Waterborn, the founder of Heaven & Earth, sets the tone for an authentic spiritual space where he and other instructors offer a variety of sacred work. As he describes it, Heaven & Earth is a center "for healing, and for learning firsthand new-age 'technologies' such as working with natural energies, the earth, the plant and fairy kingdoms, as well as more person-based skills and development." Visit the Web site and write to Heaven & Earth for more information about the programs: www.heavenandearth centre.com.

Lanjarón to Órgiva (6 miles/10 km):
Take A-348 E.

ÓRGIVA—Andalusia

The capital of the Alpujarran region, Órgiva has more bustle and movement than any other Alpujarran town. Surrounded by still-active irrigation plots and orchards from Muslim times, as well as stone ruins, Órgiva today is also the heart and soul of the New Age movement in Spain. Here lives an incredibly international and diverse society where you can find nearly every spiritual expression of known religions, philosophy, practice, and therapy. Here you can go on a Buddhist or yoga retreat, create tailor-made therapeutic vacations that might include Tai Chi, Shiatsu, Qigong, yoga, massage, art therapy, and raw foods. Here there are also some spiritual practices and philosophies that many may not have heard of elsewhere, such as Subud, Santo Dame, and a form of African Shamanism and divination from the Dagara people of Burkina Faso, West Africa.

Subud is a fusion of many spiritualities and is dedicated to authentic, firsthand spiritual practice and outlook. Subud has been described as a fusion of Sufism and Buddhism with a fundamental guidance to feel that one's spirit is guiding one and to honor that guidance. According to locals, Subud began in Indonesia, where the Subud leader is from. He first advised that in practicing Subud, religion was not important, but he later revised this, encouraging his followers to pick one of the three Abrahamic faiths—which one did not matter. The important issue was to follow the flow and guidance of the divine in one's life—to be connected to one's source.

Santo Dame (also Santo Daime), meaning literally "Saint give me," is another form of opening to the flow and benevolence of the universe. It is a syncretic religion born in Brazil of African spirituality, ayahuasqa use, and Portuguese chant, which has found practitioners in southern Spain.

Also, occasionally two practitioners of an African shamanic tradition brought from Burkina Faso hold a Grief Ritual in the Órgiva area. The ritual offers a sacred space through which participants clear negativity of all forms and connect with others in a communal manner. These and many other spiritual activities are posted throughout the many bulletin boards in town.

This area attracts true spiritual seekers of all kinds, most intent on healing, upliftment, and positive community. But there are a few who are also drawn to this area, perhaps because of its open-minded nature, who are more intent on leaving something else behind, or escaping. Sadly this often manifests in being too gullible to the many spiritualities on offer and more often it manifests in excessive drug use. While the town of Órgiva keeps this in check, as do the many surrounding towns and villages and retreat centers that are doing serious and impeccable work, there is a valley nearby made up of these lost souls that affirms what one astute yoga teacher in Órgiva told me: "Places of great [spiritual] light attract darkness, too."

Órgiva is also the center of a critical organic-farming movement that is gaining greater support as people of all backgrounds want to benefit from living in such a historical growing area.

As a progressive, creative, and broad-minded place, Órgiva reminds me of the ideal of *convivencia* that we get from Spain's Middle Ages, as if people are returning to an older pattern of mixing with peoples of other backgrounds and outlooks and faiths toward creating something new and expansive in those in-between spaces. It would be more accurate to describe this place as the heart of the old new age.

While a few other Alpujarran towns partake of this current spiritual energy, Órgiva stands at the center.

Perhaps nothing captures the new mood of post-Franco Órgiva more than the Dragon Festival every mid-March. It is panned by the local press as a hippie festival. It is something of a neo-pagan celebration of spring, with peace songs, a good amount of letting loose, and a desire to enjoy the great outdoors. It began in 1997 in a local expatriate's field and has grown since, not always smoothly, as local authorities have been concerned over its safety and hedonism. To date, however, its main message holds of spring's arrival and the hope for world peace.

Mosque and Mulay Hassan Islamic Center

The Muslim community here is mostly composed of European and North American converts to Islam but is also frequented by Middle Eastern Muslims. There are several groups and most are members of a Sufi order, the mystical branch of Islam. The general mood among the Muslims of Órgiva is very open and welcoming to everyone. The main Muslim center in Órgiva is the mosque and Islamic center in the upper reach of town. Everyone can visit (on Calle Libertad, 21) and there are several groups of Muslims who join to worship, study, and stay here. Some seven Sufi orders alone make up the Muslim mystical following and members hail from as far east as the Caucasus and as far west and south as Mauritania and Senegal. The mosque and center is housed in an old pension or hotel that has a wonderful interior courtyard making it look like an old Islamic caravansary.

To find out about daily prayer schedules as well as weekly or monthly Sufi zhikrs and other gatherings visit the Web site or contact the mosque and center: 🖳 www.al-madrasa.com and 🖳 www.spiritualsonido hotmail.com.

Hindu Órgiva

Hinduism in Órgiva manifests itself in the many yoga practices and retreats, all with a physical-practice component equal to the traditional spiritual and meditation focus of the many schools of yoga taught here. Some of the most established yoga centers and retreats are listed here.

Yoga Under the Sky

A combined effort of several yoga and massage practitioners in the Órgiva area, this is a wonderful center to search for the right yoga and therapeutic retreat for your preferences. The yoga teachers are trained in various modalities: Hatha, Iyengar, Ashtanga, Dynamic, and more. Yoga Under the Sky also offers therapeutic Thai massage and aromatherapy. They offer organized retreats around a select theme or will tailor a retreat to visitors' specific requests. In addition to holding yoga in town, as in the Rio Chico yurt on the riverbank, Yoga Under the Sky also holds retreats at La Cuesta del Almendral (🖥 www.cuestadelalmendral.com), a rural farmhouse in Órgiva with several rooms and a pool. All this information is listed on their Web site: 🖥 www.yogaunderthesky.com.

Sun Food Yoga

Yoga sessions and raw-food retreats are the main focus of Sun Food Yoga and many people use these two together for therapeutic and cleansing retreats. (Your own travel and medical insurance is a must.) Yoga retreats begin the day with meditation and then move into yoga postures. Schedules and more information are on the Web site: 🖥 www.sunfoodyoga.com.

Spanish Awakening Holidays and Personal Growth

"I graduated in Psychology in 1978," writes English-born Alpujarran resident Chris White, "gained an M.A. in Social Work and have been employed in this and related fields. I trained in Psychotherapy between 1988 and 1992, using Transactional Analysis, an open approach where ideas and theories are shared and there is an agreed goal." Through Spanish Awakening Holidays, White offers therapeutic counseling retreats tailored to each person. His motivation is to help people make positive changes in their life and to use the inspirational natural surroundings as a relaxing context from which to manifest change.

In addition, Spanish Awakening offers rural cottage rentals as a part of or independent from any therapeutic program. (Aptdo. 161, Órgiva, Granada 18400, ☎ 958-78-57-12, SpanishAwakening@hotmail.com, 🖥 www.SpanishAwakening.com.)

Plant Walks in the Alpujarras

This is an occasional tour offered in traditional plant lore, including identifying edible, medicinal, as well as poisonous plants. The group meets at designated times, which are posted on bulletins throughout Órgiva. The village of Berechis is their starting point for hiking into the Sierra Nevada. After gathering plants, the group makes an all-wild salad from gathered plants.

Weekly Thursday Market

This Thursday-morning market is a good place to see locals and all the many offerings in this town. Organic farmers, Sufi crafts sellers, Hindu and Buddhist incense sellers, exotic-clothing sellers, esoteric crystal and gem sellers all gather in the upper part of town.

Iglesia Parroquial de Nuestra Señora de la Expectación

This is Órgiva's central church, built in the sixteenth century shortly after the last Muslims were expelled from the town. It stands with its two distinctive Baroque-Neoclassical towers in the heart of town. In addition to being the town's heart for daily and weekly Mass and other religious services and festivals, the residents hold regular classical and folk concerts here, treating their church as a community center. In front of the church, in the tiny Plaza García Moreno, is the church's ancient fountain.

Órgiva to Padre Eterna (5 miles/8 km):

Take A-4132 toward Pampaneira; shortly after passing the village of Soportújar, the hermitage Ermita de Padre Eterna appears on the right. It is a small white chapel overlooking the valley.

ERMITA DE PADRE ETERNA—Andalusia

This hermitage was built in 1991 and is an unremarkable building, but it is still worth a stop for the powerful location and view as well as what this little site represents. It marks the site of one of two related hermitages dedicated to the Eternal Father and replicates an ancestral pastoral nomadic tradition of moving herds from summer to winter pastures and back again as the seasons turn. Across the valley stands the other hermitage, and the icon within this one is carried there to stand for half the year. Then it is returned from there to here for the remaining half of the year. This is not only reminiscent of the shepherd and his flock but also of an equally ancient cycle where Persephone must go to the Underworld for half the year, in winter, and returns above ground for the remainder of the year, in summer. People who live in these hills are still connected to their ancestors and to the ancient ways of the land, of the growing and fallow seasons, of the cycle of life and death and regeneration.

Padre Eterna to O Sel Ling (approx. 4 miles/ 6 km):

The road to O Sel Ling appears on the left when you have just passed the Ermita de Padre Eterna; turn left and slowly wind your way uphill. It will take approximately twenty minutes by car and a few hours on foot, given the steep climb and the rough road.

O SEL LING—Andalusia

The O Sel Ling Tibetan Buddhist retreat center feels like arriving at a remote mountain precipice in Nepal and is for silent meditative retreat. Minimum stays are seven days. Huts built into the mountainside announce themselves only by the ventilation chimney and solar panel that jut out of the ground from the declining slope below. Silence is the rule. From where you can park your car, you will first see a three-sided sacred space with a terrific brass prayer wheel. Prayer flags around the prayer wheel flutter in the wind, and as you ascend the mountain, you will encounter Buddhas of different styles and sizes tucked here and there. As you near the top of the mountain, the Buddhist monastery and retreat announces itself quietly. Honor the signs that demand silence. People are here in a silent retreat and if you walk up to the stupa at the top, do so with quiet and mindful footfall in addition to not speaking. The stupa is at the highest point, offering an incredible view of the mountains and valleys as well as a great sense of transcendence.

This retreat center was founded in 1980 by two Tibetan lamas, the Lama Thubten Yeshe and Lama Zopa Rimpoché, both from the Tibetan Guelugpa tradition. The head of their order is the fourteenth Dalai Lama. He visited the center in 1982 and gave it its name, O Sel Ling, which means "The Place of Clear Light." In 1986, a Spanish couple, Paco and María, discovered by his giving certain answers to specific questions that their infant son, Osel Hita Torres, was the reincarnation of the recently deceased Lama Yeshe. Yeshe had died in California in 1984; Osel was born in Bubión in the Alpujarras in 1985. This event gained a lot of attention in Spain, as it is rare for a Westerner to be discovered to be the reincarnated soul of a deceased lama. Called Tenzin Osel Rimpoché, he is now a young man and has not assumed his position as lama, still wanting to partake of the world. He is considered a reincarnated lama whether or not he assumes that role in the community. And while he wants to help people, he is uncertain about following the path of a lama—one of his hopes is to be a filmmaker. Though this occasion brought O Sel Ling to the public's attention, it is nevertheless a quiet, remote place where silence is the rule and meditative retreat the sole purpose.

There are clear rules about conduct during your stay: your meditation must not be interrupted with visits to the surrounding villages; you must observe the five precepts of respecting life, not stealing, not lying, not having sex, and not drinking alcohol or consuming other mind-altering substances. Moreover, if you smoke they would appreciate it if you can abstain from this habit. And forget about using or charging your mobile phone—that's out of the question and not the point of a retreat!

You can call or write to arrange for a retreat: Aptdo. 99, Órgiva 18400, Granada, ☎ 958-34-31-34 or 958-06-40-53, oficina@oseling.com, 🖥 www.oseling.com.

O Sel Ling to Pampaneira (7.5 miles/12 km):
Return to A-4132; go E to Pampaneira.

PAMPANEIRA—Andalusia

Pampaneira was originally founded by Muslims. Today three sacred fountains in Pampaneira are Fuente de los Poetas, Fuente del Cerrilo, and Fuente de San Antonio. The Fuente de San Antonio is on the side of the Iglesia de la Santa Cruz, which has a Mudéjar bell tower.

Footpaths connect Pampaneira with Bubíon and Capileira but be sure to get a good trail map or local directions from someone who really knows. The road that connects these towns is another excellent option.

Escuela de Vacaciones en la Alpujarra

Run by Angela Martín and Ignacio Molina, this vacation school in Pampaneira, with most courses concentrated in the summer, offers natural therapies in a beautiful natural setting. Courses in various modalities are offered and the annual schedule can be viewed on the Spanish Web site. Courses often combine excursions into the Alpujarras as a part of the package. Martín is a Reiki Master and is trained in acupuncture. Molina is a visual artist with a naturalist and contemplative style. Both also have a background in theater. Among the course offerings are Reiki vacations, craniosacral work, feng shui conferences, therapeutic theatrical work-shops, and I Ching.

Pampaneira to Bubión
(2 miles/3 km):
Briefly take A-4132 E; turn left, N, onto GR-411 to Bubión.

BUBIÓN—Andalusia

A pretty village with Islamic origins, Bubión has a Moorish influence that can be seen in everything: terraced hills, irrigation systems, and houses in what the locals call the Berber style.

The Iglesia Parroquial de Nuestra Señora del Rosaria was a mosque turned into a church, its minaret-turned-bell-tower giving this away.

In the heart of town you will encounter another sacred fountain, the Fuente de los Cuarto Caños.

Bubión to Capileira (1 mile/1.5 km):
Continue N on G-411 to Capileira.

CAPILEIRA—Andalusia

This is another Alpujarran town of Islamic origin, and there is a natu-ral spring on the right of the road when entering town from the south. The townspeople mounted a poem of blue and white tile to the side of this nat-ural water source; the poem's words praise the mountain spirits from whom this spring hails.

In Capileira's pretty town center stands the seventeenth-century Igle-sia de Nuestra Señora de la Cabeza, which was built over the mosque at the Reyes Católicos' order. There is a sacred fountain on the side of this church as well as one in the Plaza Calvario nearby. Like many churches in the area, it was built in the Mudéjar style.

Capileira to Pitres (6 miles/10 km):
Backtrack to A-4132 and take it E to Pitres.

PITRES—Andalusia

Pitres's parochial church, Iglesia Parroquial de Pitres, is built over the town's old mosque. It has a single aisle down the center of the nave, simple white walls and arches, and a warm wood-beam ceiling. Nearby are a gully and medieval footpaths still used today to hike into the surrounding nature.

Pitres to Trevélez (8 miles/13 km):
Continue E then N on A-4132.

TREVÉLEZ—Andalusia

This is the starting point for the higher-elevation pilgrimage, the Romería de la Virgen de las Nieves, on Mulhacén in early August.

Our Lady of the Snows

The pilgrimage to the shrine of La Virgen de las Nieves on Mulhacén has been observed since 1912. Her feast day is August 5, but the pilgrimage, called a *romería*, begins the night before, first on horseback and then on foot. Pilgrims ascend Spain's highest mountain, Mulhacén, so as to arrive at the shrine of Our Lady of the Snows by sunrise. The shrine stands at 3,482 meters above sea level. At dawn, Mass is held and then the pilgrims return to Trevélez and the surrounding areas and celebrate the rest of the day with dancing, food, and drink. Some celebrate by sleeping after their strenuous climb and return.

Trevélez to Yegen (20.5 miles/33 km):
Take A-4132 S to A-4130 E to Yegen.

YEGEN—Andalusia

The English writer Gerald Brenan made this village famous in the English-speaking world. His travel and historical writing from the 1920s brought these hills to life as did his regular walks, which people like to emulate. In addition to this icon's presence in signs and paths, a Japanese Zen retreat is one kilometer before arriving in the village.

Jikô An Comunidad Religiosa Zen Camino Abierto

Coming from Mecina-Bombarón, about one kilometer before arriving in Yegen, take the forest road marked with a sign "Sierra Nevada." This will lead you with little signs and white arrows for another six kilometers to the retreat.

This Zen Buddhist retreat center is intentionally remote so as to place visitors in a deep state of communion with natural, undisturbed surroundings. It was founded by Japanese Zen Master Hôgen Yamahata, who is the founder of Open Way Zen, called Zen Camino Abierto in Spain. Hôgen Yamahata currently lives and runs a Soto temple in a rural community at the foot of Mt. Fuji, Japan, with his wife, children, and a handful of students. An Open Way Zen sister center exists in Brisbane, Australia.

The Alpujarran Zen center offers many courses and retreats in Zen meditation as well as in introduction to Zen and Shiatsu massage, among other offerings throughout the year. The Web site provides a lot of information, partly in English but mostly in Spanish. Call or e-mail to reserve a place: ☎ 958-34-31-85 and 958-85-13-44, info@jikoan.com, 🖥 www.jikoan.com.

Yegen to Válor (4 miles/6 km):
Take A-4130 to Válor.

VÁLOR—Andalusia

This is a good transition point out of the Alpujarras and into Almería, Murcia, Alicante, and Valencia, where myriad villages, towns, and cities hold in common the celebration of the Fiesta de los Moros y Cristianos, the Festival of Moors and Christians. This celebration in Válor is unique in all these because it reenacts the famous 1568–1570 Revolt of the Alpujarras, led by the Morisco of local fame Aben Humeya (Ibn Umayyah, and known by the name Hernando de Válor) in mid-September.

Válor along with the Alpujarras was one of the last places occupied by Iberian Muslims and their immediate descendents, the Moriscos, until 1609 when everyone was expelled en masse. The area was repopulated shortly after the 1609 expulsion with "old Christians" from the Jaén region in the northern part of Andalusia.

Aben Humeya was one of the main leaders of the revolt against the Christian authority that had taken control in 1492. The revolt ultimately failed, in part because the Moriscos were fighting a stronger power, and in part because even the Moriscos could not overcome the centuries-long factionalism that repeatedly tore at al-Andalus—just as for their forebears, tribe and ethnicity overrode religion and nation. Infighting among the Moriscos weakened their revolt, and fighting on both sides, Morisco and Christian, was brutal and nothing to celebrate. Moreover, in the struggle, Aben Humeya was assassinated. The Moriscos lost their cause and widened the gulf of mistrust already directed toward them. But today, the revolt is romanticized, as depicted in mid-September's festival.

Here on the eastern edge of the Alpujarras we end this multifaith route. But throughout Spain you will encounter the mushrooming of many, individualized, and explorative spiritualities, in the spirit of "finding our own way" now that the decades—nay, centuries—of religious membership are no longer enforced. How this will play out depends on your general outlook. Some Spaniards say the country has fallen in its moral standards and others say it is becoming a democracy and a secular nation that allows freedom of religion and all the chaos that comes with such a time and place. Most are delighted with their right to earthly and spiritual self-determination.

ibliography

Alberro, Manuel, and Bettina Arnold, eds. *E-Keltoi*, vol. 6, *The Celts in the Iberian Peninsula*. University of Wisconsin-Milwaukee, online publication: www.uwm.edu/Dept/celtic/ekeltoi/volumes/vol6/index.html. Updated regularly, 2006–present.

Aviva, Elyn. *Following the Milky Way: A Pilgrimage on the Camino de Santiago*, 2nd ed. Boulder, CO: Pilgrim's Process, 2001.

Baer, Yitzhak. *A History of the Jews of Christian Spain*, vol. 1. Translated from the Hebrew by Louis Schoffman. Philadelphia: Jewish Publication Society of America, 1961.

Barish, Eileen. *Lodging in Spain's Monasteries*. Scottsdale, AZ: Anacapa Press, 2002.

Berenguer, Magín. *Prehistoric Cave Art in Northern Spain Asturias*. Mexico City: Frente de Afirmacion Hispanista A.C., n.d.

Campbell, Joseph. *The Masks of God: Occidental Mythology*. New York: Viking, 1964.

Chejne, Anwar G. *Islam and the West: The Moriscos*. Albany: State University of New York Press, 1983.

Collins, Roger. *Oxford Archaeological Guides: Spain*. Oxford: Oxford University Press, 1998.

Crow, John A. *Spain: The Root and the Flower*, 3rd ed. Berkeley: University of California Press, 1985.

d'Arbó, Sebastian. *España Mágica y Misteriosa*. Barcelona: Ediciones del Serbal, 1994.

Dragó, Fernando Sánchez. *Historia Mágica del Camino de Santiago*. Barcelona: Planeta, 2004.

Fletcher, Richard. *Moorish Spain*. Berkeley: University of California Press, 1992.

Fontana, David. *The Secret Language of Symbols*. San Francisco: Chronicle Books, 1993.

Ford, Richard. *Handbook for Travellers in Spain*. London: John Murray, 1855.

Frey, Nancy Louise. *Pilgrim Stories: On and Off the Road to Santiago*. Berkeley: University of California Press, 1998.

Galán, Juan Eslava. *España Insólita y Misteriosa*. Barcelona: Planeta, 2006.

García, María Teresa Costales, and Mónica García Vázquez. *Asturias Consejo a Consejo: Valdés y Cudillero*, Asturias (no city given): Real Instituto de Estudios Asturianos, n.d.

Garen, Sally. "Santa Maria de Melque and Church Construction under Muslim Rule." *Journal of the Society of Architectural Historians* 51 (September 1992): 288–305.

Gerber, Jane S. *The Jews of Spain: A History of Sephardic Experience*. New York: Free Press, 1992.

Gimbutas, Marija. *The Living Goddesses*. Berkeley: University of California Press, 2001.

Goodwin, Godfrey. *Islamic Spain*. New York: Viking Penguin, 1990.

Grunfeld, Fredric V. *Wild Spain*. San Francisco: Sierra Club Books, 1994.

Haywood, John. *Atlas of the Celtic World*. London: Thames & Hudson, 2001.

Jackson, Gabriel. *The Making of Medieval Spain*. Norwich, UK: Harcourt Brace Jovanovich, 1972.

Jacobs, Michael. *Northern Spain: The Road to Santiago de Compostela*. San Francisco: Chronicle Books, 1991.

Kavanagh, William. *Villagers of the Sierra de Gredos: Tanshumant Cattle-raisers in Central Spain*. Oxford: Berg Publishers, 1994.

Kurlansky, Mark. *The Basque History of the World*. New York: Penguin Books, 2001.

Layton, T. A. *The Way of Saint James or The Pilgrims' Road to Santiago de Compostela*. London: George Allen & Unwin, 1976.

Lema, Rafael. *El Camino Secreto de Santiago*. Madrid: EDAF, 2007.

Lunde, Paul. "Ishbiliyah: Islamic Seville." *Aramco World*, 44, no. 1 (1993): 20–31.

MacKay, Angus. *Spain in the Middle Ages: From Frontier to Empire, 1000–1500*. Hampshire, UK: Macmillan Education Ltd, 1989.

Matter, E. Ann. "The Virgin Mary: A Goddess?" In *The Book of the Goddess Past and Present*, edited by Carl Olsen, 80–96. New York: Crossroads Publishing Company, 1983.

McEvoy, Brian, and Martin Richards, Peter Forster, and Daniel Bradley. "The Longue Durée of Genetic Ancestry: Multiple Genetic Marker Systems and Celtic Origins on the Atlantic Façade of Europe." *The American Journal of Human Genetics,* vol. 75, no. 4 (October 2004): 693–702.

Mitchell, Timothy. *Passional Culture: Emotion, Religion, and Society in Southern Spain*. Philadelphia: University of Pennsylvania Press, 1990.

Neila, José Luis Majada. *Morena, Extremadura (Ecología, Historia, Folklore)*. Madrid: ONCE, 1988.

Perera, Victor. *The Cross and the Pear Tree: A Sephardic Journey*. Berkeley: University of California Press, 1995.

Scholem, Gershom G. *Major Trends in Jewish Mysticism*. New York: Schocken Books, 1941.

Sill, Gertrude Grace. *A Handbook of Symbols in Christian Art.* New York: Collier Books, 1975.

Starkie, Walter. *The Road to Santiago.* New York: E. P. Dutton & Company, 1957.

Vega, Teresa de la. *Los Celtas.* Madrid: Ediciones Akal, 1993.

————. *Los Pueblos de la España Prerromana.* Madrid: Ediciones Akal, 2002.

Webster, Jason. *Andalus: Unlocking the Secrets of Moorish Spain.* London: Doubleday, 2004.

Willis, Roy, ed. *World Mythology.* New York: Henry Holt and Company, 1993.

INDEX

223, 227; in Luarca, 146, 147–48; in Madrid, 255; Mary, 54–55, 215; in medieval Spain, 12–14, 15; in modern Spain, 19–20; Moriscos, 15, 18, 39, 182, 256, 300, 324–25, 335, 336; in Murcia, 304–6; in Órgiva, 328; Pamplona conquered by, 73, 75; in Poblet, 208; prayer beads, 76–77; in Roncesvalles, 72–73; in Sahogún, 95; in Sevilla, 294; in Tarragona, 191; in Toledo, 282, 283; in Valencia, 182, 183–84; wine, 205, 214–15; in Zaragoza, 230–31, 234–35, 237
Mu'tamid, Al-, king of Seville, 294, 297
Muxía, 160–61

Nahmanides, 197, 226–27
Nahmanides Institute for Jewish Studies, 225–26
Nájera, 31, 49–50, 68, 84–85
Naranco, 142–43
Nasrid Kingdom of Granada, 10, 15, 227, 300
Navarra, 70, 72–82, 251
Navarro, Enrique, 102
Navia, 148–49
Neitos (god), 232, 277
Neoclassical style, 65
Neptune (god), 259–60
Nicolás de Bari, St., 88
Nigrán, 170
Noah's ark, 162
Noia, 162–63
Nuberu, 140
Nuestra Señora. *See* below by title; *see also* headings beginning with Black Madonna; Mary; Our Lady; Santa María; Virgen; Virgin
Nuestra Señora de la Barquera, 131
Nuestra Señora de la Encarnación, 325
Nuestra Señora de la Fuensanta, 306–7
Nuestra Señora de la Vocación, 185
Nuestra Señora de las Nieves, 324
Nuestra Señora de Miraflores, 92
Nuestra Señora de Roncesvalles, 73
Nuestra Señora de Soledad, 311
Nuestra Señora del Camino, 94

Nuestra Señora del Ebro (statue), 84
Nuestra Señora del Puy, 80
Nuestra Señora del Rosario, 146
Nuestra Señora la Virgen de la Barca, 149
Nuestro Señora de la Peña, 87
Nuestro Señora de la Peña de Francia, 29, 271
Numancia, 7, 43, 238, 241, 242–43

O Cebreiro, 100–101
O Sel Ling, 331–32
Oak, 49
Open Way Zen, 335
Orden de la Merced, 168
Order of Santa Clara, 306
Órgiva, 326–30
Our Lady. *See* below by title; *see also* headings beginning with Black Madonna; Mary; Nuestra Señora; Santa María; Virgen; Virgin
Our Lady of Moncayo, 238
Our Lady of Puig, 29, 55, 185, 187
Our Lady of the Helpless, or Abandoned, 38, 183
Our Lady of the Peppers, 273
Our Lady of the Sacred Spring, 306–7
Our Lady of the Snows (Alpujarras), 324
Our Lady of the Snows (Trevélez), 334
Oviedo, 141–44

Padre Eterna, 331
Padrón, 164–67
Pais Vasco, 108–9, 119–28, 250–51
Palacios, Antonio, 170
Palm Grove, 180–81
Pampaneira, 332–33
Pamplona, 73–76
Parque Natural de la Dehesa del Moncayo, 236, 239
Paul, St., 8, 193
Pedra de Abalar, 160
Pedra dos Cadrís, 160
Pelayo, king of Asturias, 12, 29, 54, 130, 135–37, 146
Peña Tu, 111–12
Peralada, 222
Peregrina, La, 169
Peter, St., 222
Peyra, Asunción, 207
Philip II, king of Spain, 17–18
Phoenicians, 7
Picasso, Pablo, 30, 117, 320

Piercing of the Martyrs, 119
Pig, 45, 99, 270–71
Pilgrimage, 32–33, 61–62, 71; *see also* specific headings, e.g.: Santiago de Compostela
Pitres, 334
Plaça de Catalonia, 199
Plant walks, 330
Plants, 47–51
Plasencia, 272–73
Plateresque style, 65
Poblet, 208–9, 211, 212
Poio, 167–68
Polo, St., 241
Pomegranate, 48
Ponferrada, 99
Pontevedra, 168–69
Portomarín, 102–3
Pre-Romanesque style, 63
Primitius, St., 94
Priscillian, St., 34, 106, 166
Puente la Reina, 78
Puente Viesgo, 117–18
Puerta del Sol, 256
Puig, 29, 55, 185, 187

Rabanal del Camino, 98
Rabbit, 44
Ramirez, Sancho, 81
Ratafia, 220
Recared, 11
Redecilla del Camino, 87, 96
Reina Mora, 175–76
Ribadesella, 109, 110, 139–40
Rimpoché, Lopön Tsechu, 317
Rimpoché, Tenzin Osel, 332
Rimpoché, Zopa, 332
Rioja, La, 70, 82–87, 246–49, 250
Ripoll, 216–18
Roc, St., 188
Roland, 72–73, 75, 80–81
Romanesque Road, 69
Romanesque style, 63, 65
Romans, 7–9, 26, 37
Romeral, 299
Romería, 160
Roncesvalles, 72–73
Rufina, St., 295–96

Sacred animals, 40–47, 50–51
Sacred cities, 32–39
Sacred plants, 47–51
Sacred springs, 26–27
Sacromonte, 303
Sagrada Familia Cathedral, 66, 196, 200–201
Sagunto, 8, 187–89
Sahagún, 94–95
Sahagún, Bernardino de, 94
St. George's Day, 210